WITHDRAWN
NDSU

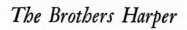

The Brothers Harper

That remarkable brotherhood, which within one generation, built up the great publishing house which has made their name a household word wherever books are read, and became such a power in the land as the land has seldom known.

The Publishers' Weekly, June 2, 1877

THE BROTHERS HARPER

*A unique publishing partnership and
its impact upon the cultural life
of America from 1817 to 1853*

EUGENE EXMAN

HARPER & ROW, PUBLISHERS
New York

167734

Z
473
H29
E9

THE BROTHERS HARPER. Copyright © 1965 by Eugene Exman. Printed in the United States
of America. All rights reserved. No part of this book may be used or reproduced in
any manner whatsoever without written permission except in the case of brief quotations embodied in critical articles and reviews. For information address Harper & Row,
Publishers, Incorporated, 49 East 33rd Street, New York 16, N. Y.

FIRST EDITION

LIBRARY OF CONGRESS CATALOG CARD NUMBER: 65-14651

D–P

In dedicating this book to my wife I can do no better than quote sentiments that Herman Melville expressed in *Moby Dick*.

"And, as for me, if, by any possibility, there be any as yet undiscovered prime thing in me; if I shall ever deserve any real repute in that small but high hushed world which I might not be unreasonably ambitious of; if hereafter I shall do anything that, upon the whole, a man might rather have done than to have left undone . . . then here I prospectively ascribe all the honor and the glory to . . ."

SUNNY

CONTENTS

A section of illustrations will be found following page 160.

FOREWORD

As NINETEENTH-CENTURY book publishers, Harper & Brothers were perhaps as well known for their school and college textbooks as for their periodicals and general books, fiction and nonfiction. In 1890, however, their extensive textbook business was sold to the newly formed American Book Company, liquid assets being required because of the retirement and death of second-generation partners. Increasing financial difficulties in the 1890's necessitated the reorganization of the House in 1900, with the family losing control of the business. Early in the twentieth century, the firm began again to publish textbooks at the college level, having today a leading position in that field. Similar efforts to regain in the schoolbook field what was lost in 1890, however, were unsuccessful until the House merged on April 30, 1962, with Row, Peterson & Co. of Evanston, Illinois, outstanding publishers of elementary and high school books.

One price paid for this merger was the combining of imprints, with the dropping of the word "Brothers" from a name known to five generations of readers of books the world around. I undertook the writing of this book to keep green the memory of the four brothers and their extraordinary partnership. Begun as an exercise in nostalgia, it has ended as a rewarding study of early nineteenth-century book publishing in America. As originally projected, the account would have covered the publishing activities of the brothers through their lifetimes, but it gradually became apparent that such a record was too extensive for the confines of one volume. Hence this story of the life and work of the four brothers ends in 1853, a year that marked the end of publishing on Cliff Street. On December 10, 1853, a fire destroyed nearly all their physical property except printing plates in subterranean vaults. The story of their new beginning, which is a part of the story of Harper & Brothers of Franklin Square, can in this volume only be intimated.

In 1912, J. Henry Harper, grandson of Fletcher Harper, published *The House of Harper* and I originally considered the possibility of writing a shortened version of that 690-page book. However, it gives scant attention to the early decades of the firm's existence, in many respects the most interesting decades, and is written with something less than detachment and critical objectivity. In his foreword, J. Henry Harper wrote that he was beholden to William H. Demarest for records he had left of books published during his forty-five years (1833-1878) with the House. Actually, the Demarest *Catalogue* also covers the years from 1817, and if it had not been constantly at hand the story of the four brothers could hardly have been written. In a thick nine-by-fourteen-inch leather-bound ledger, writing in a laudably legible Spencerian script, Demarest entered 3,176 titles with bibliographical annotations, including items, sometimes amusing and anecdotal, always informative, that comprise an important historical record of American publishing.

The brothers had little sense of their own historical importance. When Demarest began saving bibliographical memoranda in 1847, it was done, he says, "for some time amid ridicule." For the practical-minded brothers, historical records had little to do with the demands of the present and the concerns of the future. What records they did keep were chiefly of a contractual nature, although binders containing correspondence and business memoranda that were destroyed in the fire might otherwise have been retained. None of the brothers wrote memoirs or kept diaries and only one instance is known of their writing for publication; that was a letter that Fletcher Harper wrote in 1862 to the editor of the *Athenaeum* (London) in response to a criticism of Mr. Anthony Trollope. This letter is the proverbial exception to a rule, their policy being not to acknowledge or reply to public criticism. They were said not to have written a line for any of their periodicals, although *Harper's Magazine*, *Harper's Weekly* and, to a lesser extent, *Harper's Bazar* were under Fletcher's editorial supervision. The January, 1854, *Harper's New Monthly Magazine*, the first issue following the fire, carried a brief historical account of the firm written by editor Henry J. Raymond, but it was probably not even read in proof by Fletcher, as it gives the wrong date for his becoming a partner. Therefore, the task of reconstructing the story of the four brothers has necessitated a study of their publications and of the publishing milieu in which they lived and worked, as well as a search for letters saved by those to whom they wrote and accounts of them written by their contemporaries.

This book would not have been possible without the help of many who have read the manuscript in several versions, made source material available, aided in research, and otherwise contributed generously to this story of the early years of the Harpers.

Cass Canfield, chairman of the editorial board of Harper & Row, gave initial encouragement, Margueritte Harmon Bro was responsible for my extending a first study of the brothers into this extensive work, and Allan Nevins and Roger Butterfield read the final draft critically and suggested changes to improve accuracy of statement and facility of style.

For aid in research I am indebted to Erica Szep, Alison Knox, J. A. Henretta, Frances Monson, and Wallace Exman, the latter two also contributing valuable editorial assistance. I am especially grateful to Shirley Barron for deciphering my handwriting and for creating a manuscript out of many versions of copy.

By coincidence the final portion of the manuscript of *The Brothers Harper* was completed on the first anniversary of the death of John Fitzgerald Kennedy. His lively interest in the literary history of our republic was often in my mind as I studied the early Harper contribution to the cultural life of America.

EUGENE EXMAN

Barnstable, Massachusetts
November 22, 1964

INTRODUCTION

IN THIS BOOK a whole literary generation, hitherto mistily vague save for the most eminent authors and enduring books, springs into distinctness with full detail and precise lineaments; as if one of Oliver Wendell Holmes's old-time stereopticon views had suddenly been brought under bright binocular vision. And what a generation it is!—beginning as Washington Irving and William Cullen Bryant gain their first reputations, and closing in that richest of decades, the 1850's, with Melville, Hawthorne, Thoreau and Prescott busy among a body of poets and novelists not matched in the next half-century. Mr. Exman's feat in re-creating the past would have been creditable even had he been able to work from full records. It is remarkable in view of the destruction of nearly all Harper papers in the Cliff Street fire of 1853, so that he had to extricate his multitudinous facts, and draw the hues of his many scenes and portraits, from a thousand diverse sources. This narrative, never lacking interest despite the tremendous industry it embodies, will be one of the basic works for a comprehension of the development of American culture in the first half of the nineteenth century.

Harper's was (and is) a household word among all cultivated Americans. Every reader has known something about the House that published Dana's *Two Years Before the Mast*, Melville's *Moby Dick*, Prescott's *Conquest of Mexico*, and other undying books down to

Mark Twain and later; something about the editors who made *Harper's Weekly* and *Harper's Monthly* so influential; something, perhaps, about its textbooks and its popular series of inexpensive volumes. A firm so important over the generations, literate people knew, must have a solid foundation built for it. Here, for the first time, that foundation and the picturesque brother-architects who constructed it are presented with color and energy.

Four worlds, the world of authors, the world of publishers, the world of businessmen grappling with costs, distribution and profits, and the world of printing technologists, have places in this chronicle. Something has to be said, too, of the world of taste and tastemakers. When the four Harper brothers, led by James (who had read Benjamin Franklin and who rose to be mayor), went into business, the two questions they asked concerning any manuscript were, "Is this book moral as well as interesting and instructive?" and "Is this a plagiarism?" How much this reveals of America of the 1820's! And how gratifying it is, near the end of this chronicle, to find the best Boston bookshop returning copies of *Wuthering Heights* to Harper's because customers could not stand the profanity. Americans of the 1850's tolerated slavery and all its cruelties, but swear words, never!

The world of authors is doubtless the most significant one here rendered plain. Harper & Brothers had to begin with small fry like William Gilmore Simms and James K. Paulding, though both, and especially Simms, who soon garnered $6,000 a year from his verbose romances, were profitable. But the firm moved on to the best American writers and did well by them. It published Washington Irving's potboiler life of Goldsmith. It sought friendly relations with Longfellow, and more effectively with Bryant, whose anthology of poetry it issued. A roster of able historians, from Jared Sparks to John Lothrop Motley, appeared on its lists, and we read here that in 1856-1868 Motley's volumes earned in gold, as he stipulated, more than $60,000. Meanwhile, at an early date Harper was a redoubtable name among British writers. From Walter Scott onward, the firm was accused of regarding their books, which could be had without copyright payments, as a reservoir of genius unusually dependable when American talent ran thin. Bulwer did well in sales, especially *Rienzi* and *The Last Days of Pompeii;* so did the Brontë sisters; but Dickens offered the most inviting pot of money and the firm sold *American Notes* at twelve and a half cents a copy, and the seventeen parts of *Martin Chuzzlewit,* cried by newsboys, at half that much.

The story of Dana's *Two Years Before the Mast,* the most fascinating of a number told here, has to be read to be believed. Dana was one of the authors who regarded dollars as rather degrading even while reaching for them. The tale of his insistence that he preferred a large readership to large returns; of the dickering of his father and his friend Bryant in his behalf; of the objections of a staff reader to the rough language of the book; of Fletcher Harper's sharp bargain, buying it for $250 outright; of Bryant's lusty efforts to puff it in the press; of its bright success in two countries, America devouring copies while the British Admiralty ordered one placed in every naval library; and of the eventual chagrin of both Dana and Harper & Brothers—all this is dramatic. Mr. Exman tells it candidly, with such censure of the firm as is due. Candid, too, is his recital of the almost equally interesting story of Theodore S. Fay's controversy with the House. Like a red thread through the central chapters runs his honest narrative of the battle over international copyright, with Bryant, Irving and other American authors demanding justice to their British brethren, while Harper & Brothers and most other Yankee publishers demanded a free field with no literary tribute to foreigners.

Yet the world of businessmen-publishers is quite as interesting as that of authorship. The firm long emphasized a half-profits policy, sharing gains equally with writers. It also followed a low-price policy, to a great extent forced upon it by the cutthroat competition of those harsh times. We can well believe the statement of Epes Sargent to Longfellow in 1840 that nearly all publishers of books and magazines were "desperately poor." Taking heavy risks for small returns, they carried on a running battle with men like those who in 1842 were accused of setting fire to the Harper building to destroy stock of a new G. P. R. James novel so they could reprint it with a sure sale. It seems clear that superior enterprise alone enabled Harper's to boast to Thoreau in the 1840's that they were making $50,000 a year. They had sufficient acumen to foresee that *The Conquest of Mexico* would sell 5,000 copies the first four months and 7,000 more in the next twelve. The tale of their success with the volumes of Prescott's friend John L. Stephens on Central America, one of the most engrossing here told, is proof of both their shrewdness and their courage.

Their business stability, despite panics, fires and unscrupulous competition, owed much also to their pioneer labors as publishers of sound school textbooks and of cheap uniform series of standard volumes—one such series winning a memorable tribute from John Quincy Adams. Their medical texts, their geographical texts led by Morse's *School Geography*, and their historical texts furnished a backlog of revenue never consumed. It is impressive to find that Anthon's fat *Classical Dictionary* had reached a sale of 30,000 by 1853, and that his classical series was selling each year not less than 50,000 volumes. This was not only good business but good public service; no house did more for the general enlightenment of the reading public, old and young. The time was one of valorous publishers: George Palmer Putnam, coming to New York at sixteen from Maine; Daniel Appleton, who founded New York's most famous bookstore; James T. Fields busy in Boston, and Carey in Philadelphia. But in some respects Harper & Brothers led them all.

In Mr. Exman's rich dish any groping hand can pull out an unexpected plum. Now it is a new fact about Horace Greeley, or the learned Francis Lieber; now it is an amusing anecdote about Sam Ward, who knew how to make himself useful (at a price) to everybody; now it is a glimpse of Evert Duyckinck, telling us that with the Harpers business was carried on as in a four-act drama. The story of Herman Melville's debts and other embarrassments is given new amplitude. He profited satisfactorily from *Typee* as brought out by another publisher, less well from *Omoo*, though little from later works— a proper understanding of *Moby Dick* being left to recent generations. Mr. Exman, mentioning many books deservedly forgotten, sometimes identifies one that ought to be rescued from oblivion. When he assures us that B. B. Thatcher's *Indian Biography*, an account of seventy-four Indian leaders, is still fascinating and instructive, we may hope that scholars will be moved to examine it. Many a glimpse, too, is given us of the city in which the four Harper brothers played such active and varied parts. It is delightful to learn that after Mayor James Harper, who instituted a uniformed police, had decreed and enforced a strictly dry Fourth of July, an evening crowd gathered at his house to give him not the applause he expected, but nine long groans. The book will be a valuable quarry for many purposes. But its distinction lies in the skill with which it achieves its main object of relating just how four brothers, the staff they chose and the House they established became an invaluable center of the cultural life of the young republic.

ALLAN NEVINS

CHAPTER I

Messrs. J. & J. Harper, Printers
1817–1824

In his sixteenth year, his school days over, James Harper had to decide what he wanted to make of his life. He was tall and strong for his age, but too ambitious to stay on his father's farm near Newtown, Long Island. Having recently read Benjamin Franklin's life story, James asked his parents what they would say to his following Franklin's trade as a printer. Since nearly every Sunday Joseph and Elizabeth Harper were hearing of the evangelistic work of the Wesleyans, who relied heavily on the printed word, they gave willing approval. One of their Methodist friends, Abraham Paul, was the senior partner in the printing establishment of Paul & Thomas in New York; they would write to ask if their son James could be given a job and could live with the Paul family, as was the custom of apprenticed workers. Brother Paul replied that he would be delighted to accept James in his shop and in his home.

Cold winds blew desolately around the farmhouse that December day in 1810, the day set for James's departure. Breakfast over, Joseph felt he could not lead family prayers, as was his daily custom, so Elizabeth read from the Bible and asked God's blessing and protection for their eldest son. "Don't forget your home or your religious duties,

James, and always remember that you have good blood in you," Elizabeth said. The three younger boys beside her, she watched James and his father drive away. From Middle Village they took the winding Post Road to the foot of Brooklyn Heights, where they boarded an old scow, propelled by long oars, to be ferried across the East River to James's new home. James had one shilling in his pocket with which to begin his business career.

In 1810 New York was a city of 96,000 which stretched from Battery Park, where the aristocracy still clung to their old houses, northward to Chambers Street. Beyond were farms and swamps and the suburban villages of Greenwich, Bloomingdale, and Yorkville. Thirty-four years later, when James Harper was elected mayor, the city had grown in population to nearly 350,000 and had spread northward beyond Fourteenth Street. In this expanding metropolis, the Astor and Harper families were to figure prominently. John Jacob Astor, who had accumulated an enormous fortune in the fur trade by 1810, was three years older than James Harper's father. His son, William B. Astor, was three years older than James. One young man invested in real estate and became known as the "Landlord of New York." The other invested in culture, and his name on printed pages of paper entered every literate household in America.

Although James lived and worked only a few blocks from the "uptown" Astor mansion at 223 Broadway, he inhabited a different world. His rough boots and homespun clothes set him apart from the city-bred boys who were also learning the trade from Paul & Thomas. James was often subjected to ridicule, most of which he took in good humor. But his patience ran out when one of the boys in sardonic praise of James's trousers asked for the card of his tailor. "That's my card," he replied as he implanted a flat-soled kick on the seat of the other's pants. "Take good care of it! When I am out of my time, and set up for myself, and you need employment, as you will, come to me, bring the card, and I will give you work." Forty-one years later, a man claiming to have received the "card" called at the Harper establishment and asked James to redeem it, which he did.

James had been named for his paternal grandfather, who was born in Suffolk, England, and emigrated to America prior to the Revolutionary War. He made his first home in Newtown, Long Island, where he established a Methodist church; later he moved to Manhattan Island and opened a grocery business in Maiden Lane. Grandfather Harper named his eldest son Joseph, and Joseph returned to Long Island to be a farmer, a house carpenter, and also the proprietor of a small retail store. He married the daughter of a Dutch burgher named Kolyer, who was strongly prejudiced against the new Wesleyan sect. Conflicting loyalties of family ties and religion caused the newly married Elizabeth Kolyer Harper to languish and eventually to fall into a three-day trance resembling death, from which she rose proclaiming a peace that passed understanding. Forthwith she joined the Methodist Church and later named her third son Wesley.

Joseph Harper's home, like his father's, often welcomed visiting Methodist ministers and presiding elders. Indeed, the best bedroom in the house was called the Preacher's Room. In it stood a high four-poster bed with a white stiffly starched counterpane, fragrant with the odor of lavender. Once a visiting Methodist divine (it was probably not Francis Asbury, although he tells in his *Journal* of being in the Harper home) said to Elizabeth, "Sister Harper, you ought to give one of your sons to the Lord to be a preacher."

"That is just what I expect to do," she said, "and I have already selected one—Wesley."

"But why Wesley, rather than James, John, or Fletcher?"

"Wesley seems to be the most feeble and delicate in health," she replied, "and he is rather lazy." Noticing the frown on her visitor's face, she quickly added, "I thought that if I gave Wesley to the Lord, He would take him and make him over again, so that he would be strong and influential." Before Wesley could heed his mother's dedication or the call of the Lord, the Harper family was in the printing business.

In 1812, with James doing well, Joseph agreed that his second boy, John, should leave the farm too, for James had reported that the printers Pray & Bowen could take on an apprentice. And four years later, when Wesley, likewise in his sixteenth year, heeded the call of the printer's devil, Father Joseph decided that he and Elizabeth should rent the farm and move to New York, the better to look after their sons. Their youngest, Fletcher, ten years old, entered the school on Roosevelt Street run by Isaac N. Bragg; here he had a young tutor named Alexander T. Stewart, who was to become New York City's leading dry-goods merchant.

By this time John was in his last year of apprenticeship and James was working as a journeyman printer for Jonathan Seymour at 49 John Street. Another such young printer there was Thurlow Weed, later to become an Albany newspaper publisher, state printer, and the first national boss of the Whig and Republican parties, helping to elect Presidents in 1840 and 1848, but failing in his attempt to block Abraham Lincoln at the 1860 Republican convention. Weed often joined up with James in the two-man job of operating a hand press. Working as partners, one applied the ink to the type form and the other laid the sheet and "pulled" the impression. James was tall, large-boned, and muscular, and always did the pulling, since it required greater strength. Weed recalled those days in his autobiography, saying,

James Harper and I were both emulous to be the first at the office in the morning. Daylight always found us cleaning the balls on which we inked the forms. Often, after a good day's work, he would say to me, "Thurlow, let's break the back of another token [two hundred and fifty impressions]—just break its back." I would generally consent reluctantly, "just to break the back" of the token, but he would beguile me, or laugh at my complaints, and never let me off until the token was completed, fair and square. It was a custom with us in the summer to do a half-day's work before the other boys and men got their breakfasts. James and I would meet by appointment in the gray of the early morning, and go down to John Street. We got the key of the office by tapping on the window, when Mr. Seymour, the proprietor, would take it from under his pillow and hand it to one of us through an opening in the blind. A pressman who could do twenty, or even ten, per cent more work than usual was always sure of a position. James Harper, a man named Kennedy, and I made the largest bills in the city. We often earned as much as fourteen dollars per week—liberal wages when you remember that good board could then be obtained for ten dollars a month.

According to Weed, James had then but one ambition, that of seeing his name on the title page of a book as its publisher. James often remarked, while talking of his future, that he was determined to "make a spoon or spoil a horn." Such clear-cut purpose, coupled with liberal wages and frugal living, enabled James and John together to put aside $500 against the day they could start in business for themselves. Early in 1817—James would soon be twenty-two and John was twenty —they talked things over with their father. They knew where they could buy two old Ramage hand presses and had found a place they could rent. It was small but it would do for a start. Proud of his sons' industry and diligence, Joseph Harper offered to loan them what ready money he had at hand. "I will put a mortgage on the farm," he added, "and sign notes for you to draw upon as your needs require." What he actually supplied in capital—a few hundred dollars—was little; in confidence in their integrity, a great deal. Years later James said, "Yes, sir, the basis on which we commenced was *character*, and not *capital*." Character, including their inheritance of English pluck and Dutch thrift.

In March, 1817, a modest sign "J. & J. Harper, Printers" was hung in front of the second story of a small frame house on the corner of Front and Dover streets. The two older brothers were in business. They took job printing at the beginning, but they were also determined to produce books. They solicited such business from booksellers; in New York, as elsewhere in America, the term "bookseller" was applied both to those selling books at retail and to those publishing books for the trade. "There are enough printers already," one bookseller remarked dourly, and there were many other rebuffs. But with a perseverance which was later called "the mother of their success," they kept on making their round of calls.

Finally James received a word of encouragement from a bookseller who also published an occasional book, a worthy Dutchman named Evert Duyckinck. Even though he had no order to place, Duyckinck said, "My lad, go try what you can do and if you can find nothing, come back again and I'll see if I can't help you." James did return, probably in July, 1817, and wrote up the first order for a Harper book. It was a sizable one: two thousand copies of an English translation of *Seneca's Morals*. Stock was delivered to Mr. Duyckinck on August 5. Although Duyckinck was the actual publisher, this edition of *Seneca's Morals* has long been honored as the first book to carry the Harper name on a title page. (Two anniversary editions have appeared, one in facsimile.) A few copies of the original printing are known to exist, but apparently the copy which the four brothers autographed more than fifty years later is lost. (See illustration 28.) All four of them worked on the book, including eleven-year-old Fletcher, on vacation from school, helping out as copy boy.

Duyckinck was pleased with their work and gave them an order to print and bind 2,500 copies of Mair's *Introduction to Latin*, which was delivered on December 3. In the intervening months they also turned out three books imprinted for Kirk & Mercein, another New York firm engaged in publishing and bookselling. In 1817 the expenditure for books in the United States was only $2,500,000, and five titles printed by the Harpers were a tiny fraction of the whole.

The brothers were to tell a reporter in 1853 that their second book was a Methodist catechism, Thayer's *Religion Recommended to Youth*, printed for Soule & Mason, book agents of the Methodist Episcopal Church, and the third was an edition of the *Prayer Book of the Protestant Episcopal Church*. Both books were no doubt started in 1817, although they were not issued until 1818. The *Prayer Book* kept the brothers busy for eighteen months. Their contract price for the *Prayer Book* was figured on the brothers' setting the type and doing the printing from stereotypes made elsewhere. Learning later that the cost of these stereotypes would cause them to lose money on the book, they decided to make stereotypes and do the work on their own premises.

At this time stereotypes were made by impressing the type into moist clay. The clay was then baked and hot metal was poured into the mold left by the type. The clay was removed and the metal plates were smoothed off and made ready for press use. About 1829 papier-mâché was substituted for clay, making the process cheaper and easier. Stereotyping, one of the most important developments in printing since Gutenberg, was introduced in New York about 1813 by David Bruce, an Englishman. He "found sharp competition at once,"* and the technique soon spread to other publishing centers. The Harper *Prayer Book* stereotypes were called the best ever seen in New York and brought congratulations from fellow printers. With stereotyping equipment and experience, the brothers were now full-fledged book manufacturers.

When J. & J. Harper were beginning to solicit printing orders from the trade, New York City and environs were serviced by thirty-three booksellers. Three of these became important Harper customers and are remembered today because of their associations with famous authors and books: David Longworth, for Washington Irving's and James Kirke Paulding's *Salmagundi;* Charles Wiley, for Cooper's *The Spy* and Irving's *Sketch Book*, the latter printed by C. S. Van Winkle; and James Eastburn, for the early novels of Sir Walter Scott, although Moses Thomas of Philadelphia is credited with the first American edition of a Waverley novel. Many of the books the Harpers printed "for the trade" were small editions of textbooks, including six by Lindley Murray, a New York lawyer who retired to England in 1784 to follow a writing career. Murray's *Grammar of the English Language* was for fifty years a schoolroom favorite in both England and America. "Upon my Soul, he's been studying Murray's Grammar," Melville has a character say in *Moby Dick*. Such books, steadily called for, gave the young Harpers a good idea of the potential of the school and college market, which would always be one of their major concerns.

In the 1820's the Philadelphia Careys towered higher in the publishing world than any New York firm. The same year that J. & J. Harper

---

* Lehmann-Haupt, *The Book in America*, 1939, p. 133. According to R. R. Bowker, in *The Publishers' Trade List Annual*, 1877, the Harpers first undertook stereotyping in the second story of a brick building at 79-81 Cliff Street, about 1829. But this seems to be an error—see the Harper brothers' 1821 letter to Carey & Lea of Philadelphia on p. 8.

began printing books, Mathew Carey made his son, Henry C. Carey, a partner, changing the firm name to M. Carey & Son. Five years later, Mathew having retired, and with his son-in-law Isaac Lea now a partner, the name became Carey & Lea. The Careys were important not only as publishers but also as booksellers, with branches in Richmond and Charleston. Through the New York dealers the Harpers could print editions of books which were distributed east of the Hudson. But if the brothers wanted to tap the southern market, they would have to work through the Careys.

With three years and twenty-one books behind them, the two brothers decided in 1820 to do a selling job on the Careys. On July 25, 1820, they posted a letter, in James's handwriting, which reached Philadelphia two days later. They had put to press Mosheim's *Ecclesiastical History;* set in new pica type, with notes in brevier, it ran to 2,133 pages in four volumes. James wrote, "We have already sold 900 copies to the following persons:

Methodist connexions	400	copies
Mr. E. Duyckinck	250	
Collins & Co.	150	
Collins & Hannay	100	

which leaves but 100 unsold; therefore if you would like to have the 100 yet on hand, we will put them at three dollars 50 cts. per Copy— we are printing it on a handsome $4 paper." Apparently James did not make a sale since neither the Carey account books through 1821 nor their receipt books through 1823 reveal any dealings with J. & J. Harper.

One suspects that for James this letter was a boast of publishing competence—he may not have expected to sell any books. Four weeks earlier the Harpers had rushed *Guy Mannering* by Sir Walter Scott through the press room and bindery, and on March 29 they had issued *Kenilworth* and *The Pirate*. In 1820 the Careys had what they thought was a proprietary American interest in the Waverley novels (which were then being issued without the author's name). Now these young New York upstarts, they complained, were "printing on" them, using a phrase that meant printing a book for which another publisher claimed priority.

For the Harpers all was fair in love of publishing and war with rivals over reprints of English novels. The long dispute over international copyright will be discussed in detail in later chapters of this book. But in the 1820's it was perfectly legal, and in accord with patriotic tradition, for an American publisher-bookseller to produce his own print-ings of books from England (or any other country) without paying anyone except his printer. This situation, in turn, produced keen competition among the printers, for speed was of the essence. It was fun to try to get the latest best seller to the booksellers a day or two—even a few hours—ahead of another printer. It was a race to see who could most quickly snatch a new novel off an incoming packet, involve his compositors and pressmen excitedly in the contest, and, running with bundles of the paper-covered volumes, beat the other fellow to the cheering booksellers. Anyway, one could not lose on a Waverley novel; some bookseller would take the edition at cost even if the other fellow won.

Saying nothing about such enterprises, the Harpers tried again in 1821 to get the Carey imprint on one of their title pages. On February 20, "Jas. & Jno. Harper" started a letter to Messrs. Carey with "Sir," then turned the double sheet over and began again, "Gentlemen: We have been solicited by Messrs. Collins & Co. Mr. E. Duyckinck to print for the trade an edition of 'Gibbon's Rome,' in 6 volumes, 8 vo. on new small Pica Type, and nonpareil marginal notes, and Brevier bottom notes, at 45 cts per 1000 ems and at 45 cts per token, to be printed in a workmanlike manner, on paper at $4 per ream. . . . Our calculation is to reduce the work to about 3104 pages:—that number of pages made out by the above prices, will make the work come to between $5 and 5 dollars and 50 cents per set in Sheets." Even though they pointed out that this edition would undersell the "Philadelphia edition" by $4, Messrs. Carey were not interested. They also ignored another 1821 request; in November "Jas. & Jno." wrote asking for the privilege of printing the quarto *Family Bible* which Carey was planning to sell by agents. "The experience we have had in stereotype printing, in con-junction with the high encomiums passed upon several stereotype works, recently done by us, (viz.) Megary's Book of Common Prayer, royal and medium 8 vo., and Collins & Co.'s Quarto Family Bible,—we are induced to tender our services to Print your Quarto Fam. Bible; with which, if you intrust us, we will not hesitate to say, but that it shall equal, if not exceed, any Printing, on stereotype plates ever before executed." After quoting a likely price for sheet work, they promised, if favored with the order, "to return your plates free from *Bruises,* an evil which inexperience so often meets with."

Again, no order from Messrs. Carey. But this letter reveals what the "experienced" young men were up to after four years in business. They had moved twice to larger quarters, leaving Dover Street in 1818 for Fulton Street, suffering losses by fire at each place, and thence to 230 Pearl Street, which address appears on the letter to Carey. (An old compositor wrote the brothers years later recalling how he "helped to move your office on a cold morning . . . to the southside of Pearl St., over the bookstore of Collins & Hannay," and saying that he had even finished some typesetting before breakfast.) They had also improved their equipment, boasting to Carey that they now had eight presses, six of which "are the approved patents."* This gave them a competitive advantage in issuing their editions of the Waverley novels, two more of which came out in 1822, *The Pirate* and *The Fortunes of Nigel*.

But Carey still had the upper hand because he was buying early proof sheets from a Philadelphia bookseller named Thomas Wardle, who in turn got them from Constable, Scott's Edinburgh publisher. When *Peveril of the Peak* was announced by Constable late in 1822, Carey decided he would make his position doubly secure by dealing directly with Constable and instructed his English agent, John Miller, to purchase proof sheets at £25 per volume (English publishers issued fiction in two or more volumes, a practice generally followed by American houses until the 1840's). Carey did not like paying so high a price for early sheets, ready only two weeks before the English edition went on sale, since the fortunes of winds and waves might get a bound copy by a different packet to a rival publisher before his sheets arrived, the time for an Atlantic crossing varying between thirty-five and sixty days. Carey wrote Miller, ". . . if a complete copy arrived in New York with ours, they [Harper's] could print it in the time it requires our copy to come here and [our edition] go back . . . the only advantage we derive from the purchase is the sale of three or four days until another Edit. can be printed in New York, Boston, and here."

By late January, 1823, Carey had printed Volume I and II of *Peveril* and impatiently awaited early proofs of the last section, as he was sure the Harpers had also printed the first two volumes. At the end of February, he received the proofs and rushed Volume III through the press. On Saturday, March 1, he shipped Volume III to Daniel Arden, his New York agent, with instructions not to open the parcels until Monday. If they were opened earlier, "Harpers will print it on Sunday and be in the market on Monday." He misjudged one characteristic of his competitors; as devout churchmen they would not work on Sunday —that was to break one of the Commandments. (Indeed, John had

---

* These hand presses may have been Columbian presses invented by the American George Clymer. A massive lever lowered the platten (plate) over the inked type form and was then pressed down on the sheet of paper to make the impression.

risked being fired by Seymour a few years earlier by refusing to finish setting an auction sale catalogue; he had laid down his composing stick at midnight Saturday and walked out on his boss. Virtue was its own reward, though, and Seymour, admiring the young man's moral courage, made him foreman of a department.) Carey, however, correctly judged the production speed of the brothers. They procured a copy of *Peveril* on Tuesday, the 4th, and had their edition set up, printed, and bound twenty-one hours later.

Such battles of wits, printers, and machines were not infrequent. Once, in order to get out a complete Waverley novel, additional typesetters were hired to work around the clock and the seventeen-year-old Fletcher did not leave the composing room for three consecutive days and nights. His meals were brought in to him and he got snatches of sleep under the "stone"* on a rug. George W. Curtis was to write years later in *Harper's Weekly* that he frequently heard Fletcher "refer to these early times with great enthusiasm and say, with a tinge of regret in his voice, that there was no longer the excitement and 'fun' in the book business that once spurred the publishers on to enterprise and competition."

Long hours of diligent labor, plus a keen competitive spirit, set the tone of the Harpers' establishment. Neither fires nor pestilence could stop their progress. When in the summer of 1822 a yellow fever epidemic swept over New York with a general suspension of business from August through October, the brothers moved presses and type to the Harper barn on Long Island so the flow of work might not be impeded. In the following winter, Wesley found the long days in the composing room injurious to his health and sought less confining work (probably with the merchant Philip J. Arcularius). However, after a few months, when his health had improved, he wanted to go back to work with his brothers on Pearl Street. He talked the matter over with his father. "I think it is time that you set up in the printing business for yourself," Joseph Harper said. Wesley was surprised at that suggestion and pointed out that his savings were not large enough for any such venture; moreover, he would not want to be in competition with his brothers. "You do not need to be," his father replied. "Talk with them about buying into the partnership. I have put aside what you have been paying me every month for board and room. This, with your savings, may be enough." So Wesley had his talk with James and John and

---

* A table topped with a flat stone on which to impose type, i.e., to arrange type pages in a form, say, of eight pages, so that the sheet printed from this form, when folded, would order the pages in proper sequence and with correct margins.

arrangements were made for his purchase of a partnership, and he was advanced to foreman of the composing room.

James, also, made a new partnership agreement in 1823, when alderman-merchant Philip J. Arcularius gave the hand of his youngest daughter, Maria, to the twenty-eight-year-old James. This was the second Harper-Arcularius wedding. In 1799, the eldest Arcularius daughter, Christina, had married Samuel B. Harper, the son of Grandfather James Harper by a second marriage. Thus Samuel Harper, uncle of James, became also his brother-in-law.

James was not the first of the brothers to start his own home. In 1820 John had married Tammisin, daughter of Abner Higgins, another well-to-do New Yorker. With James and John no longer under the parental roof, Joseph and Elizabeth Kolyer Harper were able to furnish board and room for their sons' apprentices, one of whom was a handsome Irish Catholic immigrant boy named Nicholas Murray. Partly because of Elizabeth's piety, young Murray stopped setting type to study for the Protestant ministry; he was to come back to the brothers thirty years later as an author.

CHAPTER II

From Printers to Publishers

1825–1829

THE YEAR 1825 was a turning point in the Harper brothers' business career. For one reason, it marked their move, the third in eight years, from Pearl Street, where they were burned out, to a narrow, four-story building at 82 Cliff Street, which was soon to become the best-known publishing address in America. Here they put up a sign, nearly the width of the building, lettered in gold on a black background. It read J. & J. HARPER'S PRINTING OFFICE. (This sign is remembered by Amelia Myra Harper of Rockport, Massachusetts, who as a child often saw it in the Sands Point, Long Island, barn of her grandfather, John W. Harper.) They also purchased a two-story building across the street, No. 81 Cliff Street. Having extra space, they rented a few rooms to the recently organized Mercantile Library Association of New York, a connection that lasted till 1830, when the library needed larger quarters and the expanding firm required all their own space. By then they had purchased 79 Cliff Street and soon they were to buy two more buildings, one adjacent to No. 82 and the other back of it on Pearl Street. Among these acquisitions was the old Isaac Roosevelt mansion, built by President Franklin Roosevelt's great-great-grandfather and occupied by DeWitt Clinton when he was mayor of

New York. In this complex of buildings, connected by passageways and additions, the brothers employed fifty persons and operated ten presses, their payroll and book output making them in 1825 the largest printing establishment in New York.

Partially responsible for their rapid growth was the energetic Fletcher, now nineteen years old. That same year he was rewarded for his enterprise by being made a partner; he paid $500 for his partnership, which in 1869 was to be valued at $312,500. Now all four brothers had equal stakes in the business. A card was engraved bearing each partner's name, as well as the firm name. Equal stakes in the business meant that each partner could draw from the cash drawer whatever money he needed for his living expenses; it was 1861 before partnership accounts were kept. (See illustration 3.)

For Fletcher this open account meant that he could now afford to get married, and the romantic story of his engagement became a family legend, romantic because it was part of the city's grandest celebration to date, the opening of the Erie Canal. On November 4, 1825, the *Seneca Chief* arrived from Buffalo, bringing two elegantly painted kegs of Lake Erie water, and Mayor Philip Hone with other celebrities reviewed a parade in which Fletcher had a part, being foreman of a volunteer fire company which marched with their engine, *Lafayette*. Previously Fletcher had written a proposal of marriage to a Miss Jane Lyon, asking that she appear in the window of a certain building on the parade route if her answer was "yes." When she waved from the window, the *Lafayette* stopped the parade while Fletcher's men gave three rousing cheers, much to the embarrassment of Miss Lyon.

While the year 1825 was important because it saw the firm established on Cliff Street and enlarged to include Fletcher as a partner, its chief significance for the Harpers lies in the fact that the brothers were now thinking of themselves as publishers as well as printers. To be sure, they had functioned somewhat as publishers when they brought out seven Waverley novels in the early 1820's. For these novels, however, James did not solicit trade orders in advance but took an early copy to booksellers and sold the Harper edition before the competing edition was ready. According to a later account, "The House then purchased the opposition edition upon advantageous terms and sold it with surprising rapidity and success." There is no evidence that the Harpers followed normal publishing procedures by reprinting these early novels or keeping them in stock.

Cataloguer Demarest considered 1825 the year that the brothers began to give serious attention to their publishing vocation. He lists ten novels by John Galt, English reprints issued between 1822 and 1830; following the entry for *Rothelan*, published March 16, 1825, he appends a historical note: "After some few years [following 1818] their imprint appeared on their publications, with the suffix 'Publishers to the Trade.'" Demarest then says that *Rothelan* was thus published. Furthermore, in a brief history of the House in the January, 1854, issue of *Harper's New Monthly Magazine*, it is stated, "In 1825 the house removed to Cliff Street . . . and entered more largely upon the publication of books on their own account."

To publish for the trade is, in part, to announce new books as ready or forthcoming. *The United States Literary Gazette* for June 15, 1824, carried a listing of five titles "By J. & J. Harper—New York," four of which came out that year and one in 1825. This, the first known Harper advertisement, was followed by one from Collins & Hannay listing the ten-volume Shakespeare printed and bound for them by the brothers.

THE UNITED STATES LITERARY GAZETTE.

eing a portion of the Vordsworth.

:ationes Quædam Se-ites.

aken with the approbation ,Principal of Exeter Acad-r .the work was originally)e improved by alterations |y respectable instructers, 'ed to avoid errors of the

;ral Philosophy, The-
| By William Enfield, an edition, with improve-

;ment and Digest of |:asional Notes and Com-|e, LL. D. In Eight vol-|

a Minora. Sixth Cam-.h the Latin of the Notes .ated into English.

[aro;—Bucolica, Geor-£nglish Notes, for the use

By J. & J. Harper—New York.

Elements of the Etiology and Philosophy of Epidemics. In two Parts. By Joseph Mather Smith, M. D.

Mosheim's Ecclesiastical History. 4 vols. 8vo.

Blair's Lectures. 1 vol. 8vo.

Gibbon's Decline and Fall of the Roman Empire. 6 vols. 8vo.

Goslington Shadow. A Romance of the 19th Century. By Mungo Caultershoggle Esq.

By Collins & Hannay—New York.

Scott's Life. 12mo.

Leusden's Greek and Latin Testament. Corrected edition. Stereotyped.

Shakspeare. 10 vols. 12mo. With elegant Plates. Stereotyped.

Ryan's Algebra. By the author of "Key to Bonnycastle."

Prideaux's Connections.

Ruddimens Rudiments. Stereotyped.

April 22, 1824. By Pete Provost of the Academy.

History of the Co. English, on the Continen their Settlement, to the. War which terminated ii

A Treatise on the in Civil Actions; compri the whole Proceedings in ry John Stephen Esq.

A Compendium of By Thomas Peake, Serje with the addition of No the American Authorities Esq.

A Treatise on the By Neil Gow Esq. Wi can Notes and Reference ham Esq.

Transactions of th ical Society. Vol. XI: With several Plates.

Conversations on 12mo. With the Notes ' Keating.

Another leading literary publication, *The Port Folio*, did not mention J. & J. Harper as publishers until 1826, when it reviewed their reprint of the English novel *Granby* by Lister. "We may swagger as we please about ourselves," the reviewer wrote, "but . . . there is very little national feeling in favour of domestic literature. We reward our booksellers for republishing English books, but if they venture to print an American book, they must look for indemnity to—*the consumer of waste paper.*" Not till 1827 did the *Virginia Evangelical & Literary Magazine* notice a Harper book, the honor going to Sismondi's *Historical View of the Literature of the South of Europe.* However, the imprint was not well known; the second book reviewed in this publication, *The Living and the Dead,* by "A country curate," was credited to J. & S. Harper.

The Harpers were still in a stage of transition between printing for others and publishing in their own name. In 1825, for example, they manufactured Cooper's *The Pioneers* for two New York bookseller-publishers, Charles Wiley and Collins & Hannay. (Four years earlier they had printed Cooper's anonymous *Precaution* for A. T. Goodrich.) One title is of special interest in tracing this evolution. The *Works* of John Wesley, begun in 1826 and completed the following year, contained ten volumes. The first three volumes were imprinted for D. & S. Neal & W. Stockton of Philadelphia, but the remaining seven carried only the Harper imprint. Whether a disagreement arose between the brothers and the Philadelphia concern or whether the brothers decided to go it alone is not known. Since their "Methodist connexions" were planning to publish their own edition of Wesley's *Journals* and *Sermons,* they obviously did not participate in the Harper project. Volumes V-VII (*Sermons*) and Volumes VIII-X (*Miscellaneous Works*) are listed in the earliest extant Harper catalogue, that of 1833, so it is fair to assume that at least by 1826 the brothers were planning to keep some titles regularly in stock to fill reorders from the trade—an important publishing function. The discounts they were allowing booksellers at this time is not a matter of record; probably it was around 20 percent, which was the usual discount allowed by Boston publishers.

Outside of Boston, New York, and Philadelphia, booksellers were scarce and difficult to reach. In 1829, Isaac N. Whiting opened a bookstore in Columbus, Ohio, and was the only bookseller of note in the state at that time. Cummings, Hilliard & Co., of Boston, advertised the names of eighteen dealers from Portland, Maine, to New Orleans who in 1825 were selling their edition of Wordsworth's *Poetical Works.* That same year Cooper became convinced that his own system of publication was inadequate; he discontinued paying the printing costs and dictating distribution policies through Charles Wiley, and turned his novels over to Carey & Lea. He realized that Carey's wholesaling operation was the surest means of getting books into stores along the Eastern Seaboard and that theirs was the leading name among American book publishers at the time.

During this decade Carey was also aggressively selling through agents, who received a commission of 25 percent for selling and delivering a book to the buyer's door. An early and picturesque Carey agent was the Rev. Mason Locke Weems, who traversed southern roads and forded streams to hawk Bibles and copies of his own *Life of Washington*, with its famous hatchet and cherry tree anecdote. Once Weems complained to Mathew Carey, "You may compare my business to water running down hill, but let me tell you it would be more just if you compared it to a shad climbing a pine tree."

In fact, selling subscription books was made more difficult by unscrupulous Yankee peddlers who were unloading wooden "nutmegs" and oak-leaf "cigars" in the southern states. In his autobiography, Samuel G. Goodrich, author of the "Peter Parley" books, tells of a peddler from Berlin, Connecticut, who attended an auction of a New York bookseller named Riley and was the successful bidder for one thousand copies of a cheap edition of Young's *Night Thoughts*. These he sold at $5 a copy in the South and West, not as an inspirational book but as a naughty book. Like Weems, most of the peddlers operated from wagons which were fitted with portable bookcases. "Among the curiosities of American Literature," wrote the editor of the *Virginia Evangelical & Literary Magazine* in 1825, "may be mentioned the itinerant book trade. There are more than 200 wagons which travel through the country laden with books."

In 1826 the Harper brothers began using agents when they started the *National Preacher*, a monthly issue of one or two sermons in paper covers, saddle stitched. These were collected in annual volumes issued biennially through 1831. By that time two hundred agents were selling advance subscriptions at $1 per year, postage extra, in all twenty-five states, the District of Columbia, Arkansaw (*sic*) Territory, Choctaw (Indian) Nation, Canada, and South America. Some agents were established booksellers but the majority were clergymen and students who took to the road during their vacations. The Rev. Austin Dickinson of New York, editor of this homiletical monthly, was partial to eminent New York and Philadelphia divines, to professors in the Yale, Princeton, and Andover seminaries, and to eastern college presidents, most of whom were clergymen. Volume III contained several "big name" preachers: Leonard Bacon, Sr., Lyman Beecher, John H. Rice, Archibald Alexander, and Ebenezer Porter. In his preface the editor claimed

200,000 circulation for the year, ranging from 14,000 to 25,000 per month. How long the *National Preacher* was published is not clear. Demarest could not locate any volume after VI (1831), but he knew that it was still being issued in 1833 when he began working for the brothers. This publication was important for two reasons: it helped the brothers build up a list of agents, and it demonstrated the value of a series, or library, of books.

In the early days at Cliff Street, at least by 1828, horsepower was added to manpower through the purchase of one of the new presses invented and manufactured by Daniel Treadwell of Boston. However, hand presses were not discarded. As late as 1837 twenty-four hand presses were still in use. The Treadwell press was connected by a system of gears to a vertical shaft which extended to the basement. A horizontal beam was then connected to the bottom of this shaft and at the far end of the beam a white draft horse was harnessed. As the horse walked steadily in a circular path, the shaft turned the gears upstairs and the presses flapped away as fast as the sheets could be fed to them. In 1833 the new Adams steam press was installed, and the horse was retired to Father Harper's farm on Long Island. For a while he frolicked around the pasture enjoying his new freedom; then old habits asserted themselves. When a seven-o'clock whistle blew, he emerged from the barn, went to a solitary tree in the pasture and walked steadily around it till the twelve-o'clock whistle told him he might rest till one, when again he took up his solitary and circular tramp till the six-o'clock whistle released him for the night.

Another innovation with which the brothers are credited had more lasting results. In 1827 they issued *Rome in the Nineteenth Century* by Charlotte A. Eaton (Miss Waldie), a two-volume work that has the honor of being the first book in America known to be bound with cloth over boards. The brothers chose a purple muslin for half binding —cloth over the spine and a portion of the front and back boards. For years, "bound in muslin" was used to describe what today is called "cloth binding."

Miss Waldie's muslin-bound book was an English reprint, as were nearly all of the J. & J. Harper issues. Some of these reprints were the sort of standard works they had printed for other publishers. In 1826 *Crabb's Synonyms*, a 719-page volume, was issued, followed a year later by *English Synonyms* in 535 pages. The latter was to be a staple item in the Harper catalogue for decades. Other reprints were fiction, and before the decade ended they began publishing a young English novelist, E. L. Bulwer (later Sir Edward Bulwer-Lytton), who showed great promise. Bulwer's second novel, *Pelham*, was a study of dandyism and was widely read even though panned by a new weekly review, *The Critic*. William Leggett, *The Critic*'s twenty-seven-year-old editor, called at Cliff Street for an early copy of Volume I, which he pronounced immoral, and eagerly came back three weeks later for Volume II, which he pronounced pernicious. Mr. Leggett did not care for another 1828 novel, *Life in the West* by Crockford; its style was "loose, hard and ungrammatical," but he felt the Harpers performed a service in exposing the villainous practices of (London) gaming houses. Perhaps readers of *The Critic* were not interested in such outspoken criticism, for the magazine lasted only ten months. But Leggett had attracted the attention of William Cullen Bryant, who made him associate editor of the New York *Evening Post*.

As the *Port Folio* had pointed out, American publishers made their profits on English books. But the sounds of a different drummer were also being heard. Cooper's novels were selling. Irving, Bryant, and Paulding were names to be reckoned with. Every time Americans heard Sydney Smith's query, "In the four quarters of the globe who reads an American book?" they became more self-conscious and annoyed.* They also became more critical. Even English books often needed editing to make them more palatable, and an American editor's name, the Harpers found, would discourage publishers in Boston or Philadelphia from "printing on" them. In 1829 they brought out Hooper's *Lexicon Medicum*, with additions from American authors by Samuel Akerly, M.D. They knew this dictionary well, having printed it for other publishers in 1822 and 1824. The sales of this "Americanized" edition encouraged them to sign up Dr. David M. Reese to go through *A Dictionary of Practical Surgery* and add notes, "embracing all the Principal Improvements and Greater Operations introduced and performed by American Surgeons." The brothers did not attempt to improve another dictionary which they also published in 1829. But they claimed that Brown's *Dictionary of the Holy Bible* was the "only *perfect* edition of this work published in the United States." Both the Hooper and Brown dictionaries were still in print when the 1874 Harper catalogue was printed.

As the decade ended, the brothers could survey their achievements with considerable satisfaction. They were now generally credited with

---

* This witticism, which appeared in the *Edinburgh Review* in January, 1820, was quoted for years at nearly every literary function in America and in 1859 was to inspire the title of a famous series of articles on books and publishers carried by the Boston *Post*.

owning the largest book-printing establishment in America. At first with diffidence and then with growing confidence, they had entered the greener pastures of publishing, learning early how to compete in the piratical war over English reprints. Recognizing their own editorial limitatons, they were searching out authorities in all fields, including fiction, to give them guidance and to edit outstanding reprints from England. As "Publishers to the Trade" they had from the beginning nurtured the good will of booksellers; they knew how and where to get orders that kept their presses busy. Most importantly they did not compete with their own customers by a wholesaling or retailing operation, ambitious only to become the leading publishers of books.

Each of the brothers had found where his best job could be done. Each had worked in composing room, pressroom, and bindery, assuming supervisory work; now that work was done by others and the general oversight of manufacturing had come to be James's responsibility. He knew all of the firm's employees by name and enjoyed being among them; he was "boss." John's liking was for figures, and almost from the beginning he was purchasing agent, bookkeeper, and paymaster. John was the quiet, square-shouldered partner. Handsome, blue-eyed Wesley was the most avid reader of the four; by 1829 he had read enough of the books they had printed to give him the equivalent of a college education. He also had an easy hand for composition, and his brothers soon learned that he was the best of them at writing a clear, concise, and correct letter. He was the one who each day wrote the dozens of letters that went out over the signature of J. & J. Harper. He also wrote prefaces to Harper editions of English reprints and probably prepared copy for catalogues. Curly-headed Fletcher had the best sense of what books to take on and how to get them merchandised. If James could be said to head the printing division, then Fletcher was the head of the publishing division.

Even though they gradually found that each had special gifts and interests, they functioned as a unit, no major decision ever being made without consultation and unanimous agreement. Each day they met in the Cliff Street counting room, a good deal as members of a string quartet might gather for practice in a concert hall. The score called for an occasional solo part, but it was composed for four instruments playing simultaneously. Together they were creating something greater than the sum of the four parts, and soon they would need to change their corporate name to signify this fraternal unity.

CHAPTER III

Stereotypes and Series

1830–1832

THE BROTHERS were the first American publishers to adopt stereotyping as a regular procedure. In 1830 they were advertising the superiority of the stereotyped editions of their works; they took a page in
the back matter of Russell's *History of Modern Europe*, published by
them that year, and listed thirty-one new titles, of which all but twelve
were printed from stereotypes. Their edition of *Waverley* was thus
mysteriously better, and it contained twelve thousand more words
than any former edition. Wesley's *Works* were not stereotyped, and
all but the last three volumes were soon out of print; neither were the
Works of Samuel Johnson, of which only two volumes were issued,
and they also were out of print by 1833. Hence the brothers were
obviously stereotyping books that they believed would be in continuous demand over a period of years. By this means they saved either the
expense of holding type for a possible reprint, or the cost of resetting
the same book, if the type was not kept standing. These factors, commonplace considerations in modern-day publishing, were exciting discoveries for the young Harpers.

Furthermore, they were simultaneously pioneering on another publishing frontier, the related one of marketing. How could they make

doubly sure that these books with a good life expectancy were properly exploited? Their answer was to group some of them into series of worthwhile books. As the names of these "libraries" became known, new titles so published would get special notice, and the list of older titles would often be checked by readers, with resultant orders—cheap advertising. This discovery was not an inspiration of the pondering gentlemen on Cliff Street for, as early as 1825, Constable in Edinburgh had started a *Miscellany*, at 3s. 6d. per volume, each printed on whitish-brown paper and bound in paper-labeled boards. While the Harpers were thinking up their libraries, so were four English publishers: Longmans launched a *Cabinet Cyclopedia*; Charles Knight, a *Library of Useful Knowledge*; Valpy, a *Family Classical Library*; and John Murray, a *Family Library*, started in April, 1829, with books selling at five shillings.

Thus Murray gave the brothers the title of their most famous non-fiction series, *Harper's Family Library*. This handy and expandable set became known wherever books in English were read, growing in fifteen years to 187 titles. For years the brothers advertised the *Family Library* as the cheapest series of popular works ever published. Single copies were sold at 45 cents, and annually, as the series expanded, the volumes were grouped and sold as a set. Thus in 1844, 171 volumes were priced at $75.70, and after 1845 the complete lot was catalogued for $80. The most famous American book to be issued in the series was Dana's *Two Years Before the Mast*, and the most famous American author to be attracted to the House because of the series was Herman Melville. A study of the selection of titles for the *Family Library*, their distribution and cultural impact, might well be a challenging thesis for an aspiring Ph.D. candidate.

Less successful was the *Library of Select Novels*, also launched in 1830. This grew to thirty-six volumes but was discontinued in 1834 because, according to Demarest, the style of binding was unpopular. In 1831 the brothers began the *Boy's and Girl's Library* and *Harper's Classical Library*. By 1840 the juvenile series had run up to a total of thirty-two titles, at which time it ended, and the series of classics to thirty-seven by 1847, when it too was discontinued. Two even shorter-lived libraries were launched in the fervor of stereotyping standard works: the *Theological Library* (1830-1834) with nine volumes and the *Dramatic Library* (1831) with five volumes.

While such ventures helped to keep their stereotyped works in continuous demand, the brothers knew their main dependency was on the booksellers. Their 1830 edition of Russell's *History of Modern*

Europe, Volume III, illustrates how they and other publishers flattered their customers by title-page mention:

𝕹𝖊𝖜-𝖄𝖔𝖗𝖐:

PUBLISHED BY J. & J. HARPER, 82 CLIFF-STREET.

Sold by Collins & Hannay, Collins & Co., O. A. Roorbach, G. & C. & H. Carvill, William B. Gilley, White Gallaher, & White, E. Bliss, A. T. Goodrich, W. Burgess, N. B. Holmes, S. Wood & Sons, D. Felt, E. B Clayton, G. C. Morgan, M'Elrath & Bangs, C. S. Francis, M. Bancroft, and J. Leavitt;—*Albany*, O. Steele, and Little & Cummings;—*Philadelphia*, J. Grigg, Towar & Hogan, Carey & Hart, J. G Auner, U. Hunt, T. Desilver, Jr.; S. W. Toby, J. Crissy, and M'Carty & Davis;—*Boston*, Richardson, Lord, & Holbrook, Carter & Hendee, Hilliard, Gray, & Co., Crocker & Brewster, R. P. & C. Williams, and W. Felt;—*Hartford*, H. & F. J. Huntington, and Cooke & Co.;—*Baltimore*, W. & Neal, J. Jewett, Cushing & Sons, and F. Lucas.

1830.

This good-will device was soon dropped—perhaps because booksellers were increasing in numbers. "And for sale by the principal booksellers throughout the United States" then followed the Harper imprint.

By 1830 the brothers had also clarified their editorial policy. Basic to this policy was outside "reading" of likely English reprints and original American works by authorities in the fields covered. No doubt they had been consulting "learned authorities" by 1825 when they began to take their publishing function seriously. Certainly they were claiming no editorial omniscience on their own part when they advertised in 1830: "J. & J. Harper are publishing, weekly, new and standard works by the best authors, English and American. Several gentlemen, of high literary acquirements and correct taste, having been engaged to examine all new works as they emanate from the English press, and also such original works as may be presented in manuscript, the public may rest assured that no works will be published by J. & J. H. but such as are interesting, instructive, and moral."

Soon they employed a full-time reader. That a publisher should go to such trouble and expense was noteworthy to Asa Greene, M.D., who published a book in 1837 entitled *A Glance at New York*. Dr. Greene had been a bookseller himself, hence he knew something about publishing practices. "As certain kings and great men, of whom we read, used, in former times, to keep a taster, whose business it was to see that the food was not poisoned," Dr. Greene wrote, so the Harpers "employ a *reader* to whose critical judgment and moral taste are subjected all new works . . . and without whose sanction none of these works are ever permitted to see the light."

The Harper boast of a new book each week was made late in 1830. At the end of that year fifty titles had been issued, which was pretty close to the mark. In 1831 exactly fifty-two books were published, and thereafter this figure was always exceeded, except for the depression years of 1837-1839, and 1842. However, the gentlemen with "literary acquirements" were reading very few original manuscripts; more than 90 percent of approximately 234 titles in the 1833 catalogue were English reprints. It is doubtful if the Harpers were then directly soliciting manuscripts from many American authors. While they were becoming more confident of their own editorial acumen, they also were men proud of their position. If American authors wanted a good publisher, they could easily locate No. 82 Cliff Street. George W. Curtis later wrote that authors found there "a small and very plain office, in which there was little room for idlers, and a brisk and incessant industry was everywhere apparent. They met a frank courtesy, clearness of statement, and decision. It was strictly a place of business."

For twenty-five years the trumpets were to blare out the cause of American authorship; when these sounds were heard above the clatter of the presses, the brothers listened and took note. In these years they signed up American books with great enthusiasm, sometimes without due caution. However, English reprints remained their staple in trade, not only because they were free of royalty and thus could be issued at low prices, but also because by far the best books being written in the thirties and forties were by English authors—books of scholarship, travel, and adventure, and books of fiction.

American publishers who reprinted English books were called "pirates," even though the best and leading houses paid the English author or publisher for "rights" of a book and procured early proofs from which to manufacture an American edition. The real pirating was done after an English book reached this side of the Atlantic, as was illustrated by Thomas Moore's *Letters and Journals of Lord Byron*. In his diary Moore wrote, "Left some of the printed sheets with [Washington] Irving to be sent off to America, he having undertaken to make a bargain for me with the publishers there." The brothers were honored to have Irving invite them to make an offer and they responded by sending £300 (in terms of today's monetary values, better than $7,500). The real pirating began before the Harper two-volume edition was fairly marketed, the work being reproduced in several forms in 1830 by several American publishers, including Munroe & Francis of Boston. This unhappy experience, early in their publishing career, taught them a lesson about English reprints that they never forgot.

An obvious retaliation was to "print on" a competitor and underprice him. Thus it is not surprising to find the brothers striking back at

Munroe & Francis. Between 1831 and 1833 they in turn pirated twenty fiction titles by Maria Edgeworth, the most widely read novelist of the time. The Boston firm had been selling her complete works for $19.50, boasting that prior to their enterprise American readers had to pay $37, and their British cousins, for their edition, over $67. The brothers were even more sympathetic toward those who wanted to read Miss Edgeworth's tales and novels, and brought out the lot of them in ten volumes at 75 cents each. And along with Edgeworth they could boast of seven fiction titles by the promising Bulwer and six by another Englishman, G. P. R. James, whose Harper output was to reach more than fifty novels, a fecundity exceeded only by a later Zane Grey.

Thus, by the beginning of the 1830's, the four gentlemen on Cliff Street had learned something else about book publishing. To their enthusiastic acceptance of stereotyping, merchandising in "libraries," and editorial guidance can be added another exciting discovery—the stimulating effect of low retail prices on the volume of sales. Fortunately they had the equipment and personnel to turn out one million volumes a year, and they had the courage to be satisfied with large sales and small profits on individual items. A publisher's record of large sales is always a tempting turkey to carve before hungry authors.

In 1830 the market value of books published by Carey & Lea was $150,000. While no comparable Cliff Street figures are known, it is likely that the brothers, because of their dual role of printers and publishers, were netting more than their Philadelphia competitors. Profits were being put into stereotyping and other ventures to consolidate and expand their business to support their growing families. The cords of affection and mutual respect which tied the brothers together so closely bound in their families as well. The cousins grew up almost as brothers and sisters in one large Harper family. Their homes and that of Father and Mother Harper were the centers of most of their social life.

In the early thirties two young New Englanders began careers which were to importantly influence American publishers in seeking out American authors. George Palmer Putnam came to New York from Maine and was apprenticed at the age of sixteen to George A. Leavitt, who had dissolved his partnership with his brother-in-law, Daniel Appleton, to start in the book business for himself. While Appleton was developing New York's leading bookstore, young Putnam moved into publishing. In the late thirties, he was to leave Leavitt to team up with John Wiley, the firm name becoming Wiley & Putnam in 1840. The other embryonic publisher, James T. Fields, stayed in New England. In 1831, at the age of fourteen, he left the Portsmouth home of his widowed mother to take a job in Boston's Old Corner Book Store, which was purchased a year later by William D. Ticknor. In 1843 Fields was to become Ticknor's partner, and to establish a flourishing business in publishing such writers as Hawthorne and Whittier.

In the meantime the Harpers themselves had "discovered" a native prospect—a youthful journalist and poet from South Carolina named William Gilmore Simms. In 1832 Simms arrived in New York with a manuscript in search of a publisher. His friend James Lawson, editor of the *Mercantile Advertiser*, introduced him to the brothers, and their reader reported that Simms's sea fairy story, written in verse, was sufficiently interesting, instructive, and moral to justify publication. Entitled *Atalantis*, the work sold well enough to encourage Simms and the brothers to venture another book, a collection of eleven tales in two volumes, entitled *Martin Faber*. According to Simms's biographer, William P. Treat, Simms received $100 from the Harpers on the first edition, which sold out in four days. Unhappily Simms later was accused by some reviewers of plagiarism, and this upset the brothers considerably. For his part, Simms was not a little annoyed with the Harper reader who had written critically of the manuscript in the first place.

Another author who considered it an outrage to have a "reader" criticize his manuscripts was James Kirke Paulding, whose first Harper novel on the manners of the early settlers, entitled *The Dutchman's Fireside*, was published in 1831. But, unlike Simms, Paulding was an established writer. His first work, *Salmagundi*, was written in collaboration with the brothers William and Washington Irving while James Harper was still a Long Island schoolboy. Thus for this new book Paulding could demand $1,500, a large sum for those days.

A review copy of *The Dutchman's Fireside* was sent to Thurlow Weed in Albany—for years the brothers sent him nearly every book they published—and his review in the *Evening Journal* accused Paulding of a small plagiarism. A few days later Weed was in New York and went around to call on his friend James, who greeted him by saying, "You are just in time to give an account of yourself. Here is Mr. Paulding, against whom you have brought the charge of plagiarism." Considerably embarrassed, Weed asked for a copy of Moore's *Letters and Journals of Lord Byron*, published the year before, and showed

Paulding the passage in which Byron had used the figure of a jungle tiger. Paulding admitted that he had used Byron's simile and language but insisted that he was unaware of doing so at the time. After Paulding left, Weed protested that strangers should not be placed in so difficult a situation at their first meeting. James laughed at Weed's discomfiture and said he supposed he had put Weed in a tight place but knew he could get out of it somehow. However, he expressed regret that Paulding had been touched on the raw.

The Dutchman's Fireside was issued as part of the Library of Select Novels. It has bibliographical interest because it is one of the first Harper books to appear in full cloth binding. Front and back boards and spine were printed in black on a smooth, light green muslin to display on the front cover the series title, series number in Roman numerals, title, author, and publisher's imprint. The printing was difficult to read then—almost undecipherable after 130 years—and may have been the reason for the unpopularity of the binding to which Demarest referred. However, the brothers were then considering the muslin binding as their descendants today consider a book jacket—a means of calling attention to the book itself by use of display type for the name of the author and title on front cover, with listings of other titles on the back. These books also seem to mark the transition from half-cloth to full-cloth binding on all titles. (According to Joseph Rogers in Bookbinding in America, the Harper 1831 stereotype edition of The Young Duke, by Disraeli, was "bound in the full red cloth typical of the time.") Cases were made by cutting the boards and cloth to size. The cloth was then glued to the boards and edges turned over. A paper label was used on the spine, as in the 1820's, to give author and title, with an occasional stamping in gold. By the mid-thirties the brothers were using beautifully embossed cloth which, with the chaste label, made a more handsome book for the library table, when new, than popular-priced items which are being issued today. In the forties bindings became more ornate, with elaborate use of gold stamping on the spine, where, also for the first time, the publisher's name began to appear.

Encouraged by the success of The Dutchman's Fireside—six editions in twelve months—both Paulding and the brothers were eager in '32 to launch Westward Ho!, a novel with a Kentucky locale. Again, $1,500 was the agreed-on price, but the first printing of 5,000 copies got off to a slow start and another author then frequently on Cliff Street, William Dunlap, wrote in his diary, "I find from Harper's & from Paulding that there is dissatisfaction between them. 'Westward Ho' don't [sic] sell well. It has not been republished in England owing (Paulding says) to its being sent through the Post Office & Bulwer refusing to pay £5 postage. P. says he will have nothing more to do with them." However, an English edition, as well as a French translation, came out the following year.

Simms and Paulding were the leading American authors to sign up with the Harpers during this period, although James and Mary E. Brooks, popular versifiers, brought in *The Rivals and Other Poems*, which was kept in print for several decades. William Leggett called again at Cliff Street, this time to leave his manuscript *Tales and Sketches by a Country Schoolmaster*. The New York *Mirror*, a literary periodical noted for its elegant appearance and taste, said Leggett was "superior to Cooper" in delineating female character—faint praise perhaps. In terms of Americana, the Harper author who contributed most was Paulding's friend William Dunlap, whose *History of the American Theatre* (1832) was a pioneer work and a milestone in the literature of the theatre.

There is no extant contract for *American Theatre* (as it was called) so we do not know whether the book was published on a half-profits arrangement or purchased outright (which seems likely). From Dunlap's diary it seems evident that the brothers had accepted the book on Dunlap's agreement to obtain quantity orders from friends. Thus Gouverneur Kemble agreed to take a hundred copies in two equal shipments and his fellow Knickerbocker, Paulding, took some of the second lot of fifty. Judging from entries that Dunlap made in his diary, he was buying copies from the brothers for $1.33 a copy and selling them for about $1.93, thus netting 60 cents a copy.

American Theatre was published on October 26, a little more than four months after Dunlap left the manuscript at Cliff Street. On November 12 he copied a letter he had just received from the Harpers: "About a week ago we sent to all the persons on the list you first gave us. . . . We have sent to Washington, Baltimore &c. Collins & Hannay have sent to New Orleans. They have it by this time all over the country. The Editors in all the principal cities have been supplied."

The book would have been issued earlier but the brothers stopped work on it for a week in order "to supply the demand" (Dunlap's phrase) for Mrs. Trollope's *Domestic Manners of the Americans*. This juxtaposition of titles did not bother Dunlap so much then as it did later on learning that a set of advance sheets sent to publisher Richard Bentley in London contained a signature of Mrs. Trollope's book. Dunlap had asked James Fenimore Cooper, to whom he had dedicated *American Theatre*, to act for him in negotiating an English edition with Bentley. Cooper was then in Paris. In September Dunlap posted a set of sheets to Cooper and a few weeks later sent the "book complete." On November 15 Cooper wrote from Paris to say that he had asked for £100, but Bentley would agree only to paying £50 with a note for six months, duplicating these terms after 450 copies had been sold. "All the book has arrived, with the duplicate copy & all has been forwarded to London," Cooper wrote. "By an oversight of the printers Sig: H of the duplicate copy is signature H of Mrs. Trollope! This mistake might have been serious, but being a duplicate is no great matter."

Another printer's error got into the book itself. Mathew Carey wrote Dunlap in early December to say that he had written the Harpers for an imperfect copy but had been told that they "had no imperfections." Dunlap noted this exchange and then wrote in his diary, with a customary disregard for punctuation marks, "He therefore requests me to send him a complete copy. I must write to him that I have not a complete copy, as everyone has not only my imperfections but those of Messers. Harper, for mine let him find them out but for the printers p. 236 makes me say that my countrymen the new Jersey-men had retired before their [British] enemies 'to await the time of resurrection.' . . . I beg of him to substitute retribution for resurrection. . . ."

During the ensuing months Dunlap went often to Cliff Steet, hoping that he could get the brothers to publish his novel, *Zeb Spiff* (*Zebediah Spifford, Hero of Thirty Years Ago; or the Memoirs of a Water Drinker*). Henry Carey had rejected it earlier, recommending Harper's. On April 9, 1833, Dunlap wrote the following in his diary: "The Harpers. They agree to print Zeb Spiff: it is to be submitted to John Inman who is their hired reader & who saw part of it before. I showed them Carey's letter. They are to take their time as to publishing. Dekay asked them 1500 for his Constantinople & they offered him 750—he took it to Carey & brought it back to them for that sum. Verplanck is editing Sands' work & publishing a vol: of discources."

Thus Dunlap, bless him, gives us the name of the first Harper reader. John Inman was a brother of Henry Inman, the portrait painter. In addition to his editorial work on Cliff Street Inman helped George P. Morris on the New York *Mirror*. Later he gave his whole time to the *Commercial Advertiser*, the newspaper mostly used for publishers' announcements. On July 10, 1833, Dunlap wrote, "Call at the Harpers. John Inman has married Clara Fisher's Sister [Caroline, sister of the actress]. Harper thinks he has injured himself by theat^R connection."

Dunlap failed to get James to publish *Zeb Spiff*, even though he agreed to Dunlap's terms and promised once "to slide it in," when the manuscript was satisfactorily revised. Dunlap's temperance novel finally got published in 1836 by Bancroft & Holley (New York) under the title *Thirty Years Ago.*

The increasing prestige of their imprint and the avowed interest of the brothers in building up the American side of their list brought other authors representing many fields. Professor Charles Davies of the United States Military Academy gave them *Elements of Surveying* in 1830, followed two years later by three textbooks in mathematics. Another Davies had been published posthumously in 1828, of possible interest today to collectors of Princetoniana. The title page of his book reads, "Sermons on Important Subjects by the late Rev. and pious Samuel Davies, A.M., sometime President of the College of New-Jersey, etc."

The 1832 author that the brothers were probably most excited about was Captain Benjamin Morrell, Jr., who had recently returned from his fourth voyage to the South Seas. They knew that sure-fire sales would result from the publication of a book of travel and adventure in strange, colorful, and distant lands. Born in 1795, Morrell ran off to sea at the age of sixteen, was imprisoned twice—once taken by the British from an American privateer. He was taught navigation by Captain Josiah Macy, himself a famous salt. When he was twenty-seven, Morrell became master of his own ship and commenced a series of sealing voyages to the South Seas, his largest schooner being 175 tons. He was the first man to penetrate beyond the Antarctic Circle and also the first white man to be seen by natives of many South Sea islands. On March 7, 1832, he contracted with J. & J. Harper for *A Narrative of Four Voyages, etc.*, a book that would depict his adventures. But could an expert navigator and explorer also be an accomplished writer? In Morrell's case, no. Whether he or the brothers suggested editorial help is not known, but help he received from Samuel Woodworth, who the preceding year had "Americanized" *Festivals, Games, and Amusements*, a book that was No. 25 in the *Family Library*. Woodworth thus became the first known ghost writer of a Harper book, although his more lasting claims to literary fame are his having established the New York *Mirror* in 1823, in collaboration with General George P. Morris, and having written a few verses which he entitled simply *The Bucket*—"The old oaken bucket, the iron-bound bucket, etc."

The contract stipulated that Woodworth was to take Morrell's notes and memoranda and his memorial to Congress and "to rewrite and make a valuable book of four or five hundred octavo pages [it went to 492] printed on Long Primer type." The brothers agreed to compensate Woodworth and to cover stereotyping and printing costs out of the first 3,000 copies, afterward paying Morrell $250 for every 1,000 copies printed. Similar terms were made with Mrs. Morrell, who also had literary inclinations. Her book, *Narrative of a Voyage to the South Seas,* was ghosted by a Colonel Samuel L. Knapp and published the same year. The Morrell books were the lead items in the four-page, twenty-four-title section, "Voyages, Travels, &c." in the 1833 Harper catalogue, although more descriptive space was given to *Polynesian Researches* by William Ellis, and nearly equal billing to *A Description of Pitcairn's Island and Its Inhabitants* by John Barrow, which first told American readers of the mutiny of the ship *Bounty.*

From the islands to which he gave his name Captain Morrell had brought the young Prince Darco to New York even as Captain John Smith had taken Princess Pocahontas from Virginia to London. On March 9, 1834, Morrell again set sail for the South Seas in the brig *Margaret Oakley.* With him he took Darco and Thomas Jefferson Jacobs, a young man just out of college and eager for adventure. Darco was reunited with his people, and Jacobs eventually returned to his home in suburban Harlem. In 1844 he was to give the brothers *Scenes, Incidents, and Aventures in the Pacific Ocean,* based on a journal he kept. Morrell never returned to America.

In 1832 the brothers began having authors' contracts copied into a leather-bound volume, one of the few record books that escaped the fire of 1853, protected then and now by a sturdy old iron chest. The first contract so copied was made with Theodore Sedgwick, Jr., for his biography (it was called a memoir) of his great-grandfather, Governor William Livingstone of New Jersey. Young Sedgwick, just old enough to vote, was part of another Harper "first"—the first family to provide four authors to write for the hungry presses at Cliff Street. His aunt, Catherine Sedgwick, was already famous for her novel *Hope Leslie*—a book that earned her the title "Miss Edgeworth of America" —and for her frequent pieces in magazines and "annuals." It may be that the brothers were plotting to get her when they signed up Theodore, Jr. If so, they edged closer in 1834 by publishing his mother's novel, *Allen Prescott.* Catherine did come in 1835 with her next novel, and Theodore Sedgwick, Sr., arrived the following year with the first part of a long treatise on economics. The prolific Sedgwicks were descended from one of Cromwell's generals, and Theodore, Sr.'s, father, Judge Sedgwick, had been a member both of the Continental Congress and the Federal Congress.

The Harper contract with Theodore, Jr., was drawn on a "half-profits" basis, the type of author's agreement most generally used by the brothers in the thirties and forties. It did not specify a royalty rate, but stipulated that net publishing profits should be accounted for regularly and this amount equally divided. To ascertain this figure, they first added up the out-of-pocket expenditures in running off an edition: the cost of labor, rent, fuel, light, and materials. To this was added one-third of the total as overhead, and the result was the cost of the manufactured edition, ready to be marketed by the publisher.* Thus, if John Harper's cost card on an edition worked out at 30 cents a copy, he would add 10 cents to cover overhead and charge 40 cents to the publishing division. As publishers, the brothers might decide that they could market the book to the trade at 80 cents or 20 percent off the retail price of $1. If so, they would divide the "profit," 40 cents, equally with the author, who could hopefully reimburse himself at the rate of 20 cents a book for the time and expense of writing. The brothers out of their 20 cents a copy would hopefully be able to pay for sales, advertising, promotion, bookkeeping, salaries, and other publishing expenses. However, as advertising expenditures became more extensive in the latter days of half-profits contracts, they were probably deducted before profits were figured, as was another charge called "guarantee." This item, at first figured at 2½ percent of the wholesale price, was apparently a sort of insurance allowance to cover losses of stock in shipment, bad debts, and other liabilities.

In his book, *Literary Publishing in America, 1790-1850,* William Charvat has nothing good to say for half-profits contracts, with special mention of the Harpers' fondness for them. However, authors then knew more about publishing profits than do most of their present-day descendants. They also knew more about printing. Many authors had worked as printers and had figured costs. They, too, could speak glibly of "ems," "picas," "octavos," and "signatures." Furthermore, some had ventured to publish their own works and knew what a risky business it was. To be sure, a half-profits contract negotiated by a dishonest publisher was not worth the time of the clerk who drew it, but no one can study the publishing record of the four brothers without being convinced of their honesty. They had many faults; overscrupulosity was

---

* This method of figuring is known because it was made explicit in the 1845 contract for Morse's *School Geography*. (See p. 235.)

one of them, and they would follow a big penny rolling from the counting room onto the street. But, by the same token, John would as soon have jumped into the East River as have made a false entry in a ledger. In 1863 William H. Appleton was to be asked to referee a disagreement between the Messrs. Harper and Mr. Thomas Ewbank, there being a misunderstanding between them as to whether a 10 percent royalty was to be paid for the sale of all copies of Ewbank's *Brazil*, or only after the sale of one thousand copies. Appleton, who was then president of the Publishers Association, arbitrated the dispute on a half-profits basis, saying that he knew "no more equitable arrangement, between author and publisher, than a fair division of profits."

Another 1832 half-profits author, along with the youthful Theodore Sedgwick, was his grandfather's namesake, Theodore Sedgwick Fay. Fay's work was a two-volume collection of articles, written for the New York *Mirror*, entitled *Dreams and Reveries of a Quiet Man*. The following year, aged twenty-six, Fay married Laura Gardenier and took her abroad, and for over two years they traveled in Europe, Fay sending back articles to his friend and colleague on the *Mirror*, George P. Morris. The short, ruddy-faced, curly-haired, and convivial Morris was often called "General" because of his association with the state militia. A strong bond of friendship developed between him and Fay, perhaps because each saw in the other qualities that they themselves lacked. Fay was less convivial and more retiring in temperament. He was also introspective, intellectually inclined, and stubborn as a mule. Fay's first book, *Dreams and Reveries,* had only a modest sale and for long years afterward the brothers were to regret the day they became his publisher, for no author was to give them so much trouble as Theodore Sedgwick Fay.

Much more to the brothers' liking was a young Bostonian and Bowdoin College friend of Longfellow and Hawthorne, Benjamin Bussey Thatcher, who contributed a two-volume *Indian Biography* (1832) to the *Family Library* and *Indian Traits* (1833) to the *Boy's and Girl's Library*. Thatcher's biographies of seventy-four Indian orators, warriors, statesmen, and "remarkable characters" were based on solid research. Indeed, his was perhaps the first scholarly effort to penetrate the myths of barbarism and sentimentality and to give the Indians "the poor restitution of historical justice." In his preface, Thatcher wrote that he was seeking not only justice for the Indians but also "collateral light on the history and biography of our own nation." Fascinating and instructive reading today, *Indian Biography* deserves a paperback reprint with a critical introduction and scholarly annotations. Likewise, his *Traits of the Boston Tea Party*, issued three years later, is still interesting reading and was selling at the rate of two thousand copies a year twenty years after publication.

Apparently Thatcher's *Indian Traits* and his later juvenile, *Tales of the American Revolution*, were written especially for the *Boy's and Girl's Library*, which also included the first American publication of the juvenile classic *The Swiss Family Robinson* by Johann Rudolf Wyss. American authors in addition to Thatcher were Almira Phelps with *Caroline Westerley, or, the Young Traveller from Ohio*, Eliza Robins with *Tales from American History*, an anonymous lady with *Distinguished Females*, and the Rev. Francis L. Hawks, who eventually produced nine titles under his pseudonym "Uncle Philip." Then rector of St. Thomas Episcopal Church in New York and a popular preacher, he was also a man of quick wit and great personal charm. Hawks was nothing if not versatile. The nine books he wrote for Harper's between 1833 and 1840 ranged over diverse topics: the trees of America, whale fishing, the Lost Colonies of Greenland, the truths of Christianity, and the states of Virginia, New York, Massachusetts, and New Hampshire. It may be that the Rev. Mr. Hawks sank the juvenile boat, for his nine titles ended the *Boy's and Girl's Library*.

In the *Family Library*, running to thirty-five titles and fifty-two volumes at the end of 1832, the only American writers with complete books of their own were Thatcher and George Bush, whose *Life of Mohammed*, No. 10 in the *Library*, helped to get him named Professor of Hebrew Language and Literature at the newly founded New York University.* American representation in the *Library* would later increase markedly. But in the 1830's both readers and reviewers seemed to be happy with what the Harpers served up to them in the form of English reprints. Critics acclaimed the brothers for their selection of *Family Library* titles, the Albany *Daily Advertiser* saying, "The publishers fully deserved their daily increasing reputation by the good taste and judgment which have influenced the selection of works. . . ." They were also praised as economic benefactors. They were making books available at a price so low that persons of the most moderate income might purchase, according to the Boston *Constellation*, while the *U.S. Gazette* of Philadelphia called the *Family Library* "one of the cheapest means of affording pleasing instruction, and imparting a proper pride in books, with which we are acquainted."

* Although founded as "The University of the City of New York," this institution, frequently mentioned hereafter, will be indicated as it is now known.

After three years of issuing books in five different series, the brothers had clearly established themselves as publishers well known to the reading public. Not the least of their accomplishments was their reputation for bringing out inexpensive books in all fields. Their dramatic price cutting on Mrs. Edgeworth's novels was characteristic of their 1831 attack on that perennial favorite, Gibbon's *The History of the Decline and Fall of the Roman Empire;* they reset their 1821 six-volume edition, bringing it down to four octavo volumes totaling 1,924 pages, an edition they claimed to be letter-perfect. These four volumes marked the decline and fall of competing editions if their further claim was heeded: "The London editions now offered for sale in this country are without the necessary maps, etc., and are printed in a type so small that it is injurious to the eyes to read . . . [yet] they are sold at a higher price than this *American* edition" ($5 the set in sheep binding).

The word "American" was in their own italics. Fortified by their experience with stereotypes, in which they had invested $75,000, the brothers were obviously eager to edit reprints for American readers, and to cultivate American authors. Original works could be issued after the critical, bifocal scrutiny of their readers, who were instructed to recommend only what was of both literary and moral worth. With such editorial assistance, the brothers knew now how to manufacture and how to merchandise what Americans wanted to read and could afford to buy. They were also seeking to improve the physical appearance of their output. "The press of the Harpers," the *American Monthly* commented in December, 1833, "improves daily, and bids fair to rival in typography that of any other press in the Union."

CHAPTER IV

The Beginning of Harper & Brothers
1833

In 1817, THE YEAR that the J. & J. Harper imprint first appeared, the first scheduled line of packet ships, the Black Ball Line, began operating between New York and Liverpool. Within a few years there were sixteen packets arriving regularly in New York from England. The importance to American publishers of these frequent and dependable sailings can hardly be overestimated. Each packet brought new English books that a few weeks later had multiplied by thousands, to go by stagecoach, wagon, and side-wheel steamer to cities and towns along the Eastern Seaboard; to Albany and then by canal boat to Buffalo, by lake boats to Cleveland and Detroit, by river to Cincinnati and Louisville and St. Louis, and down the Mississippi to Memphis and New Orleans. To newly founded academies, colleges, and seminaries that were buying books for their classrooms and libraries. To old James Madison on his five-thousand-acre Virginia plantation and to young Abe Lincoln in his new log cabin beside the Sangamon River in Illinois.

Routes of communication were important to the brothers in selling books to faraway places. And there were books to be published about the routes themselves. In 1830, the Harpers republished *The Northern*

Traveller in a fourth and enlarged edition, a book they had earlier printed for A. T. Goodrich. This 444-page work described trips to be taken to Niagara, Quebec, and springs such as Saratoga, and tours through New England and to the Pennsylvania coal mines. There was a good market for travel books in general, such as Henry Schoolcraft's *Travels in the Central Portion of the Mississippi Valley*, which the Harpers had printed for Collins & Hannay in 1825. Schoolcraft was an author to keep in mind.

But books of travel did a publisher no good collecting dust in a bin. They had to travel too. By 1833 the brothers were debating, as were Americans everywhere, what the future held for the steam locomotive. Three years earlier Peter Cooper had built the first American locomotive, and rails had been laid in South Carolina, Maryland, and Massachusetts. It might not be long before a publisher could get books across New York State or Pennsylvania faster than the four- or five-mile-an-hour speed of a canal boat. DeWitt Clinton's "Big Ditch" had cut travel time between Albany and Buffalo by one-third and freight rates by one-seventh. The rails might do even better. And now plans were being made in London to operate fast steamships across the Atlantic Ocean on regular schedules. One thing was certain, the speed and power of steam were here to stay.

In 1833, a steam-powered press was installed at Cliff Street, possibly the first such press to be used by an American book manufacturer. It is not known whether this press was the type invented by Isaac Adams of Boston, or the more recent, improved Napier press. In either case it reversed the hand-press method by pressing the flat form of type or stereotype plate in an up-and-down motion against the stationary platten. Actually, the Adams press may have been used earlier on Cliff Street, with the 1833 installation being a Napier press. A historical article on book publishing appearing in the New York *Tribune* in March, 1854, commented in part, "When James Harper and Thurlow Weed worked together in the office of Jonathan Seymour . . . only two hundred and fifty impressions from a single form could be produced in an hour, but the Adams press, in a few years, made it possible to reach a thousand; and the double cylinder Napier, in 1830, three thousand, and the splendid invention of Mr. Hoe, in 1847, full twelve thousand in the same time—each four times the size of those worked off by the chrysalis Mayor and the State Printer in the first quarter of the Century."

The honor of being the first steam pressman went to William K. Colyer. Chosen for first runs on the new press were two popular reprints, the *Penny Cyclopedia* and the *Penny Magazine*. The employee given the job of selling these and other reprints was William Jackson. We know about this new press, the name of the man who operated it, and the name of the first man hired as a Harper salesman because of an observant fifteen-year-old boy who started working for the brothers as a printer's devil on the first Monday of February, 1833. He was William Demarest, future cataloguer. After a year, Demarest was promoted to apprentice printer.

William's elder brother, Gerherdus, was then working in the literary department, presumably as a clerk, and his name begins appearing in 1833 as a witness to the brothers' signature on contracts. Later he assisted with the correspondence, his flourishing "G. L. Demarest" signature appearing on several letters to Longfellow in the late 1840's.

One of the first extant contracts that G. L. Demarest witnessed was drawn up for republishing James K. Paulding's earlier *Works*, seventeen titles in all, several of them revised. This is one of the most important documents in the Harper archives, since it is the earliest contract to carry the new name of Harper & Brothers. The contract, dated November 19, 1833, carries the name of each of the brothers in the first paragraph, "doing business under the name of 'Harper & Brothers.' " It is the only known contract that so lists each name and one of the few known which each of them signed. Unhappily, the document was later desecrated when James Thorne Harper, witnessed by J. Henry Harper and Frederick A. Nast, an employee, cut the brothers' signatures from the last page. Apparently they had decided in 1889 to place engraved portraits of the brothers in a framed picture and wanted signatures to place under each. Where could they find signatures? Someone, alas, remembered the old Paulding contract.

Judging by this 1833 contract, Paulding and the brothers had made up again after the little quarrel that Dunlap had noted. Paulding was offered $10,000 (equivalent to $50,000 today) for all of his copyrights. He refused, unfortunately for him, and signed a contract specifying ten cents a copy on each copy sold after two thousand. Paulding had contributed two stories to *Tales of the Glauber Spa*, published the year before, as had William Cullen Bryant, who edited the volume. Other stories were contributed by Robert Sands, William Leggett, and Catherine M. Sedgwick. The humorous story that gave the book its title told of an ill-fated venture of making a watering place out of the farm of a Dutchman whose wife and daughters forced him to live in a distant shack because he was not fit company for authors and other famous people who came to partake of the healing waters discovered on the farm. When a Negro servant developed cholera, the guests fled precipitately, and the Dutchman found a manuscript left behind. This he took to Cliff Street, having heard that the Harper brothers knew how to print books.

Robert Sands was a promising young writer and editor, associated with Bryant for two years on the *New York Review* and with Bryant and Gulian C. Verplanck in publishing an annual called *The Talisman* (1828-30). But Sands's literary career was cut short by death. His posthumous *Writings*, both prose and verse, came out in 1834 and 1835 in a two-volume Harper edition, edited by Verplanck. Of his poems, *Yamoyden* was the best known. Written in the style of Scott's poetical narratives, it related the story of the celebrated Sachem of Pequot* Indians King Philip, and its popularity even before book publication had started a rash of poems on Indian characters and plays on Indian themes.

Tales of the Glauber Spa is of special bibliographical interest because the brothers sold sheets to England with the imprint: "New York: Printed by J. & J. Harper . . . sold at the Depot for American Publications, 12, Red Lion Square, London, 1833." This was the address of Obadiah Rich.† In the early decades of the nineteenth century few Americans made a greater background contribution to literature than Rich did. An American diplomat and librarian in Spain from 1816 to 1829, he amassed an enormous collection of Hispano-American works, disposing of some to Bostonians George Ticknor and William H. Prescott, basic to their later scholarly writings. When Washington Irving went to Madrid in 1826, he lived in Rich's book- and manuscript-strewn home and wrote his *History and Voyages of Christopher Columbus* at Rich's suggestion. Born in 1783 at Truro, Massachusetts, of a long line of Cape Cod seafaring folk, Obadiah Rich was graduated from Harvard, became an early member of the Massachusetts Historical Society, and was a charter member of the Boston Athenaeum. His love of books and knack for picking up rare volumes at low prices led him to establish a bookstore in London in 1829; here he could better act as an agent for American libraries and collectors. In 1835 Rich issued 250 copies of *Bibliotheca Americana Nova*, imprinted Harper's name with his own on the title page, and shipped 150 sets of sheets to Cliff Street for United States distribution.

This joint imprint implies a close relationship in the 1830's between

---

* According to Thatcher, "this ill-fated" word should be spelt "Paukamakett." *Indian Biography*, Vol. 1, p. 151.

† The building no longer stands but nearby is the house in which Dante Gabriel Rossetti lived twenty years later.

the brothers and Obadiah Rich. Did he also act for them in negotiating deals for early sheets from English publishers and vice versa? Such an association is implied in a letter Longfellow wrote Harper's on February 28, 1835, in which he enclosed a letter for Rich. However, the association is confirmed by the discovery—as this book goes to press—of letters that the brothers wrote Bulwer from 1830 to 1867. (See page 393.) This correspondence definitely states that Rich was Harper's London agent.

Government posts for literary men such as Rich and Paulding helped them to subsidize their avocational interest and to add a prestigious luster to their names. However, in the case of two other Harper

LONDON:

O. RICH, 12, RED LION SQUARE.

NEW YORK:

HARPER AND BROTHERS, 82, CLIFF STREET.

1835.

authors with Washington connections, William Jay and Gulian C. Verplanck, authorship itself was the primary concern. William Jay signed a contract on March 23, 1833, authorizing the brothers to publish a two-thousand-copy edition of a biography of his father, the late John Jay, first Chief Justice of the Supreme Court. Jay may have brought his manuscript to the brothers because his maternal grandfather, Governor Livingstone, had been the subject of Sedgwick's biography the year previous. According to the contract the two-volume, thousand-page work was to be completed in sixty days, and the brothers were to pay their Bedford, New York, author $1,700 on November 1. (Priced at $5, the biography thus earned Jay the equivalent of a 17 percent royalty.) Jay also received thirty copies free, three times the number his descendants today would be favored with in a new book contract. While the brothers were given publication rights for only two years, the biography was still catalogued thirty years later, with the retail price reduced to $3. Possibly the royalty terms had been reduced in the interest of a wider sale at a lower price.

Certainly Jay's copyright had not expired, for thanks to the Hon. Gulian C. Verplanck, Congress in 1831 had extended the life of American copyright from fourteen to twenty-eight years. Verplanck was a descendant of early Dutch settlers in New Amsterdam. He had inherited wealth and the family estate at Fishkill, and was one of the best-known New Yorkers of his time. During the six years that he was a Congressman, he got a copyright bill enacted that not only extended the life of copyright but also enabled a next of kin to renew it for fourteen years in case of the author's prior death; heretofore only an author himself could renew copyright. On the eve of Verplanck's retirement from Congress, the brothers published his 1833 volume of addresses, including a speech on "The Law of Literary Property," given at a dinner in his honor by the New York literati.

During Verplanck's last term, in the twenty-second Congress, while he was chairman of the Ways and Means Committee of the House, his most responsible task was to find ways and means of getting a proper tariff bill passed. Increasingly high protective duties had been enacted in 1824, 1828, and 1832, advantageous to the industrial North but unfavorable to the agricultural South. John C. Calhoun, exponent of States' rights, had brought about the famous "nullification" of the tariff acts by South Carolina which led to a historic debate in the Senate chamber. The Compromise Tariff Act of March, 1833, was called a master stroke of policymaking, satisfying both the North and the South. This bill, which gradually reduced duties till they reached a revenue basis of 20 percent, is generally credited to Henry Clay, but except for Verplanck's leadership it would not have passed the House.

In the midst of this tariff tussle Verplanck wrote to the brothers for their thoughts on protective tariff and received a reply dated January 11, 1832. "Any reduction of the present duties on foreign books," said the brothers, "would operate very seriously not only against the Printers, Publishers, Bookbinders, Paper makers, etc. of the United States, but also against the interests of the country in general, so far as literature is concerned." Fortunately Verplanck preserved the letter. Addressed to "Hon. Gulian Verplanck, Washington City, D.C.," it is one of the last letters carrying the signature "J. & J. Harper." It also carries the signatures of nine other printers including that of Jonathan Seymour, the printer and paper wholesaler who gave James and John early employment.

This "high tariff" letter spoke for book manufacturers then and for generations to come. Two years after their firm name was changed, the brothers were still using the title page imprint "New York: J. & J. Harper, Printers, 82 Cliff Street." In hurrying reprints through the press they would change dates without correcting the imprint. They still thought of themselves as printers long after the reading public knew them only as publishers, and their printing concerns often conflicted with their publishing interests and accounted for their ambivalent attitude toward an international copyright law that would protect the interests of English authors. As book manufacturers, they had employee responsibilities and plant investments jealously to be guarded, on the theory that the flow of production would be impeded unless there was a reservoir of English works to draw upon when the American streams ran dry. This mind set of the graphic arts industry delayed enactment of an international copyright law till 1891, when the Chance Act incorporated the "manufacturing clause," making American manufacture of a foreign book a prerequisite to copyright protection. Even as late as 1955, when America's copyright isolationism finally ended, with membership in the Universal Copyright Convention ratified, the book manufacturers' lobby in Washington got a proviso in the implementation bill limiting to fifteen hundred the number of copies of an original work of a United States citizen that could be imported from abroad without loss of copyright. J. & J. Harper, printers, would have approved.

Another distinguished New Yorker, the naturalist Dr. James E. DeKay, became a Harper author—as Dunlap noted in his diary—with the publication of his *Sketches of Turkey*. DeKay and the brilliant young poet Joseph Rodman Drake married sisters, daughters of the wealthy shipbuilder and naval architect Henry Eckford. (Eckford was famous for building the steamboat *Robert Fulton* and also the ships-of-war that helped Perry win his Lake Erie victories in 1813.) DeKay accompanied Eckford to Turkey in 1831, where Eckford organized a navy yard and where he died in November, 1832. Returning to New York, DeKay wrote his detailed and comprehensive book on the Turks and their country. His book was followed a year later by Commander David Porter's *Constantinople and Its Environment*, published at Paulding's urging. The two-volume work contained letters that Porter wrote Paulding, although neither gentleman was identified by name. Porter was then chargé d'affaires to Turkey following his stormy career as an American naval officer.

During this time the brothers published two further books that have interest today to collectors of Americana. One was *Sketches and Eccentricities of Colonel David Crockett of Tennessee*, also published anonymously, although the J. & J. Harper contract, dated September 8, 1833, acknowledged James S. French of Mississippi as owner of the copyright and the one to whom a royalty of six cents a copy should be paid. Apparently Crockett did not know who had written the Harper book and hurried to correct certain impressions it gave by publishing his *Autobiography*. Carey, Lea & Blanchard issued it in 1834, and according to Mott's *Golden Multitudes* it was a best seller. With "Davy" achieving great notoriety in Congress, the brothers made money on their venture too.

Equally flavorsome was a book of *Letters*, purportedly written by Major J. Downing and obviously patterned after the successful "Jack Downing" letters by Seba Smith of Maine, which were widely read in the newspapers. The Harper book was also political satire, written in the vernacular, and had been published first in the New York *Daily Advertiser*. The real, but then unknown, author, Charles Augustus Davis, wrote, "Zekel Bigelow [Wall Street banker and mackeral packer] says that Mr. Harper & Brothers in New-York are master hands at printin books and they can turn 'em out there nigh upon as fast as Peleg Bissel can wooden clocks." Typical of his approach to national problems was this sentence: "If it warnt for Congress meetin, we cou'd jest go about pretty much where we pleas'd, and keep things strait too; and I begin to think now, with the Gineral [Jackson], that arter all there is no great shakes in managin the affairs of the nation." So great was the demand for the book that at least ten editions were issued from Cliff Street that year. According to Jacob Blanck, writing in *Bibliography of American Literature*, "the binders were unable to keep up with Davis or the printers [as letters were added] and spine labels marked with the number of the edition are frequently misleading."

In 1833 the brothers were also busy with new fiction titles and additions to their "libraries." They launched books by Bulwer, Edgeworth, and James, and two novels by Mrs. Trollope, *The Abbess* and *Refugee in America*. Her controversial *Domestic Manners of the Americans*, on their 1832 list, had created a ready market for her new books of fiction. They added ten titles to the *Family Library*, the most important of which was *Inquiries Concerning the Intellectual Powers* by John Abercrombie, an English reprint destined to be their best-selling book of the decade; by 1839 they had disposed of twenty thousand copies. The *Boy's and Girl's Library* was being advanced cautiously. "We have lately engaged works that will carry the Library up to 20 volumes," Wesley wrote John O. Sargent of Boston. Whether more would be added would depend on the success of the series. Apparently Sargent, just three years out of Harvard, wanted to do a book of tales of the American Revolution. Unfortunately for him, the brothers had received "several offers" for books in this field and had pledged "to take the work from the pen of one of your literary friends in Boston [Thatcher]." Wesley hoped Sargent would "employ his pen" to their mutual advantage on some other subject. While John Sargent did not so employ his pen, his brother, Epes Sargent, was to write books for them later and, as a newspaper editor, was to have many dealings with them.

Such editorial activity over English reprints and budding American writers was giving James and John both delight and concern. In sixteen years their business had prospered beyond the most extravagant dreams they had shared as young men. Their concern was that their younger brothers were not getting the recognition they deserved. Of themselves, James and John could not procure and merchandise the flood of new books that kept their pressroom and bindery operating at peak load. Increasingly they spoke of their pride and satisfaction with the diligence of the two "boys." By October, 1833, they had decided to change the wording of their imprint to indicate that the partnership was not in name or in fact that of James and John only. So they expressed themselves to Wesley and Fletcher.

To be sure, they all agreed, something would be lost in a change of name. Booksellers, authors, English publishers, and the public at large had become familiar with "J. & J. Harper." The name had prestige value. On the other hand, publishers were constantly changing their imprints to recognize new partners. In Boston William Hilliard had changed to Cummings & Hilliard, then to Hilliard, Gray & Co. In Philadelphia, Mathew Carey had changed to M. Carey & Son, later to Carey & Lea, and now it was Carey, Lea & Blanchard. Yes, changes had to be made to indicate new partners. Why not add "and Brothers" to "J. & J. Harper"? J. & J. Harper & Brothers would bring Wesley and Fletcher into the firm name, yet keep the old familiar designation. At that point John would probably have been the one to speak up: they were all Harper and they were all brothers. Why not drop J. & J. and call themselves simply Harper & Brothers?

Having agreed on the new name, they sent a card giving the change of firm name to the New York *Commercial Advertiser*. It appeared on October 29, along with two routine announcements of new publications. Thus on the last Tuesday of October, 1833, there appeared modestly and for the first time in print the words Harper & Brothers. (See illustration 4.) And with characteristic dispatch they put their new imprint on a new catalogue then being printed, the cover of which is printed below (trim size 5½ × 8½).

Curious about "Harper & Brothers," people began to ask, "Which is the Mr. Harper, and who are the brothers?" For years they received the same pat answer, "Any one of us is Mr. Harper, and all the rest are the brothers."

In a real sense, however, James was *the* Mr. Harper. He was spokesman for the brothers on public occasions and the popular "Mr. Har-

☞ The business of J. & J. Harper, Printers and Publishers, will in future be transacted under the firm of

James Harper,
John Harper,
J. W. Harper,
F. Harper.

HARPER & BROTHERS,
82 *Cliff-street.*

CATALOGUE

OF

VALUABLE WORKS,

EMBRACING

HISTORY,	MATHEMATICS,	NATURAL HISTORY,
THEOLOGY,	MEDICINE,	POETRY AND FICTION,
BIOGRAPHY,	PHILOSOPHY,	VOYAGES AND TRAVELS,
	&c. &c. &c.	

(WITH THE WHOLESALE PRICES TO THE TRADE,)

PRINTED AND PUBLISHED

BY

HARPER & BROTHERS, 82 CLIFF-ST.

NEW-YORK.

Oct. 1833.

per" at the semiannual Book Trade Sales. Fletcher often called him "Boss," and to employees of the firm he was that in fact. His was a physique to command attention. Tall and robust, he towered head and shoulders above most men about him. His high color showed his health and his twinkling blue eyes testified to his humor, a characteristic which impressed all his contemporaries. In fact, his humor was incorrigible at times, often offending persons who took themselves seriously or expected only sedate formalities from the senior partner of a great publishing house. Like Lincoln, whom he resembled somewhat in profile, James loved to poke at pretentiousness and spiced his conversation with colloquialisms. He was not a scholarly man with pocketfuls of literary allusions and historical anecdotes; he found himself ill at ease with the poets and savants who not infrequently called at Cliff Street. Perhaps his humor was also his protective coating. "I am only a humble maker of books," he said on many occasions. And he spoke the truth.

The exuberant James played counterpoint to the taciturn John, who rarely took part in general conversation. Although shorter than James, John was also sturdily built and his massive head was set closely on his shoulders. He had the stolidity and firmness of a bulldog, and also its persistence. It had early fallen his lot to handle business details, order supplies, and manage the finances of the firm. His scrawling "Harper & Brothers" appears on many of the old contracts, and some authors seemed to gravitate to him. When the Rev. "Uncle Philip" Hawks, after a year of research and study in England, had finished reading proofs of the book embodying his work, he posted them to John. The 1836 letter accompanying the proof sheets of *A Narrative of Events Connected with the Rise of the Protestant Episcopal Church in Virginia* was addressed to Colonel John Harper. How he earned the sobriquet of "Colonel" is not known, but it was commonly used. John also found time to advise the head of the composing room on book format and to proofread title pages as a matter of course; his early experience as a compositor had trained him to spot typos. But chiefly the books he read were ledgers and his pen was more facile with figures than with words. Whatever makes publishing glamorous and exciting is mainly focused in the editorial and sales-promotion departments, where the indirect lighting of famous authors blends with the fluorescence of best sellers. But there would be no bright lights for authors or for the people they talk to in the front offices if it were not for the practical men of business who study balance sheets and work over figures showing profit and loss. Such a practical man of business was the Colonel. In modern terms, he was management.

Wesley's nickname was "Captain," a title he earned as a young captain of an artillery company. Yet of all the brothers he was the one with the least military bearing. Conciliation, not combativeness, was his temperament and the quality of his physique. Unlike his two elder brothers, he was slight and of a delicate, almost feminine, appearance. An early portrait gives a Byronic cast to his features. (See illustration 7.) He had brown hair, and his eyes, like those of James, were blue. His high forehead bespoke the scholar, but he would have protested such a designation although he did acquire a considerable knowledge of Latin and Greek and was among the best-read publishers known by J. C.

Derby. In his book, *Fifty Years Among Authors, Books, and Publishers*, Derby wrote of Wesley, "His manner was invariably courteous and affable, and no one could be long in his presence without feeling at home. The most sensitive author found in him a sympathetic friend and advisor." His editorial advice was freely given in person and by letter, and his editorial solicitude forced him to spend many hours of every week reading proofs before they went to the composing room for final corrections. Wesley was also the most spiritually minded of the four. Once James told a Methodist gentleman who had come soliciting funds, "You will have to see Wesley. He attends to God's business."

Fletcher was twenty-seven years old when the firm's name was changed. By now the publishing responsibilities were increasingly in his hands. Readers' reports were read and discussed by him and Wesley. If they were of a mind to undertake a new book, they asked approval of the elder brothers, prepared for James's usual question, "Is this a proper book to do?" If it was acceptable, terms were agreed upon after John had worked out preliminary estimates, and Wesley's letter to the author was composed and posted. Often approval of editorial changes was recommended. Often, too, such suggested revisions were protested. Who was this reader whose authority might challenge an author's inspiration? For men like Paulding and Emerson, publishers were mainly printers, inhabiting a necessary middle world of ink and enterprise, who should respect genius and not prattle about public taste or sales potential. Furthermore, to question an author on matters of style or content was to put the wrong party on the defensive. Authors should raise the questions, not provide the answers. What William H. Prescott, the Boston historian, called "the slippery 'trade' " should be on the defensive. Publishers, not authors, needed to be checked and questioned.

It was the sagacious Fletcher who, beginning in the thirties, answered the questions and suggested compromises. He was already sensitive to what the public wanted to read, a characteristic that was later to make him successful in launching the *New Monthly Magazine* and later the pictorial *Weekly*. There was also the task of interesting this public, whose taste he knew, in buying a book. This presented Fletcher with a threefold assignment. The first, best, and easiest means of promotion was a liberal distribution of review copies, aided and abetted by the authors themselves, who frequently wrote to each other to get "puffs" for their new books. The second was to get advance proofs of forthcoming books into the hands of the editors of the leading review media and to flood them with releases about books in press and about their authors. The third was to get support from agents and booksellers. To obtain bookseller cooperation, Fletcher sent out letters and catalogues, supervised the work of his one or more salesmen, made some calls on dealers himself, and twice a year coached James on the new books he was to present at the Book Trade Sales.

With his strong, open face and florid complexion, Fletcher resembled James more than the others, although he had closer ties with Wesley, partly because they were nearer of an age and worked side by side in all editorial enterprises. The New York *Tribune* said that in Fletcher "was centered more of the vigor, dash, enterprise and speculative spirit of the house than in any of the others, or perhaps all combined," a characteristic more tersely put by R. R. Bowker when he observed that Fletcher was the "steam engine of the house." These comments were made at the close of Fletcher's publishing career, but the quality of the man was recognized by his two elder brothers when they decided to drop the prefix "J. & J." from their firm name and add the suffix "and Brothers."

The new name, Harper & Brothers, symbolized what had been increasingly a fact since Wesley and Fletcher had been made partners, an equality within which a diversity of talent could freely operate. Now the responsibilities of each had been fixed, and save for the business depressions looming ahead, "cheery James, indomitable John, gracious Wesley, and vigorous Fletcher" were headed for two decades of unchecked progress.

CHAPTER V

Competition for English Reprints
1834–1835

WHEN HENRY C. CAREY organized America's first Book Trade Sales in Philadelphia, in 1824, he had been inspired by a book fair which his father, Mathew Carey, had organized in New York in 1802. (The senior Carey had in turn been inspired by the celebrated and historic German book fairs held in Frankfurt and Leipzig.) Lemuel Bangs became the leading auctioneer at these American trade sales. He was the son of the Rev. Dr. Nathan Bangs, for years the principal manager of the Methodist Book Concern, "the ablest and most successful manager it ever had," the New York *Tribune* said in 1854. Lemuel Bangs worked as a young lad with the Book Concern, along with Thomas McElrath, but they left it after a few years and in 1829 formed a partnership to publish books on their own. This partnership soon came to an end, however, with Bangs seizing the opportunity to run the new Trade Sales and become New York's leading book auctioneer. McElrath turned to banking, and was made president of the Nassau Bank, but, with printer's ink still on his hands, he bought a partnership in the New York *Tribune* with Horace Greeley in 1841.

Lemuel Bangs may have been encouraged to undertake book auctions by Fletcher Harper. They had known each other ever since 1825, when the nineteen-year-old Fletcher proudly sent in to Dr. Bangs the newly engraved Harper card, showing his name as a partner. Then their discussion was about the Bible the brothers had printed for the Methodists, and Dr. Bangs might well have said to his sixteen-year-old son, "There is a young man you should emulate." Emulate him Lemuel did, and later even named his son Fletcher Harper Bangs. The son grew up to succeed to his father's famous book auction business, and kept the firm of Bangs and Co. going until it dissolved at his death in 1903. Lemuel Bangs chose James C. Cooley as his partner in 1837, about the time of the twenty-sixth Book Trade Sale. Mr. Cooley was married to Daniel Appleton's daughter so the partners were cozily connected with the two best-known names in the New York book world at that time.

Even though Henry Carey was to retire from publishing in 1838, at the age of forty-five, to make another career for himself as a political economist, he seemed to take great pride in being known as the father of Trade Sales. What he did was to organize what had heretofore been casual and impromptu meetings of Eastern publishers, most of whom also sold books at retail, to buy or sell stereotypes, and to "trade" stock. Retail booksellers were also invited to attend the sales, and, as a convenience to dealers, the sales were held, at first annually and then semiannually in March-April and August-September, in Philadelphia, New York, and Boston. To these publishing centers, booksellers would come first by steamboat and stagecoach and later "by the rails" to bid in their stock of new books. After a few years, however, Trade Sales ceased in Boston, with booksellers and publishers in New England doing their buying and selling in New York. Beginning in 1838, as Cincinnati developed as a publishing and distribution center in the Midwest, Trade Sales were also held in the Queen City, with some Eastern publishers meeting booksellers there.

This means of funneling books from publishers to booksellers and to the public, long before the advent of the trade salesman, was so taken for granted that, while several descriptions of book auctions are extant, only two accounts are known that describe *how* new books were auctioned in order to establish a wholesale price. One account was written by a Philadelphia bookseller named Theodore Bliss. "Bids were offered for books presented in this form of auction, and, when the bid was accepted, the figure at which such a bid was sold became, for that sale, its standard price. . . . All books sent to the auctioneer were catalogued." These quarto-size catalogues were furnished by the firm of auctioneers and each title listed (according to publisher) carried a figure indicating the lots, generally three, five, or ten, which were the basis for bidding. After the highest bid determined the wholesale price, a bookseller could duplicate as many lots as he wished. Each bookseller was billed for his total purchases by the auctioneer, who in turn charged publishers for their total sales.*

At these Trade Sales, publishers were now offering slightly more original American works than English reprints. In 1834, of the 114 novels and tales published in the United States, 19 were by American authors and 95 were reprints; however, of the total of 454 books published, 253 were original works and 201 were reprints. Another estimate of the 1834 output gave the ratio of original works to reprints as 252 to 198. It is not known how new issues of classical works (Greek and Latin) were classified. That year four such titles were published in *Harper's Classical Library*. They were a part of the fifty-nine Harper issues that year, 13 percent of the total output of all publishers.

Henry Carey published forty books in 1834, less than half the number that comprised his list the previous year. And the brothers too had cut back by nineteen titles. The brake on publishing expansion resulted from the worsening of economic conditions following the Treasury Department's order of September 26, 1833, that public funds should be removed from the Bank of the United States and deposited in certain state banks. This action grew out of President Jackson's antagonism to the Bank of the United States, a crucial issue in his re-election in 1832. When the Bank began to contract its loans in the summer and autumn of 1833, the business community was headed for trouble. The first blow to the book trade came in February, 1834, when Collins & Hannay, J. & J. Harper's best friend in the twenties, went bankrupt. Other failures of booksellers followed, with publishers bearing the brunt of their losses. Blame for this sad plight was generally directed to Jackson, and Carey wrote to his London agent in September, 1834, "The monster at the head of our government ought to have a mad shirt put upon him. . . . If he were not deranged he ought to be hanged. His mad experiment has cost us $20 or $30,000."

Quite obviously Carey did not care to issue an English reprint, a life of Andrew Jackson, even though the author, William ("Peter Porcu-

---

* Cf. *Theodore Bliss, Publisher and Bookseller* (privately printed in 1911). The second known description of the bidding procedure is given in a Harper book published in 1841, *Popular Technology; or, Professions and Trades*, by Edward Hazen, a work first issued five years earlier by Uriah Hunt of Philadelphia. Hazen said that the auction houses were allowed 4 and 5 percent for their services. Extensive collections of Trade Sales catalogues are held by the American Antiquarian Society, Worcester, Massachusetts.

pine") Cobbett, had been a friend of his father, Mathew, years earlier. James Harper may have known Cobbett during his second sojourn in America from May, 1817, to October, 1819, for Cobbett was then publishing his *Register* in Wall Street, commuting from his Long Island farm and combining political writing with his avocation of gardening and farming. An ultra-conservative during his first stay in America, during the 1790's, Cobbett became an ardent democrat, and when he returned to England to stay he took with him for reverent burial the bones of Thomas Paine, a man he had once professed to hate.

Whether there was disagreement among the brothers about publishing Cobbett's pro-Jackson biography can only be surmised. James, who became a whig, would have supported Verplanck, who ran for mayor in 1834; Verplanck, having broken with Jackson, was defeated by the Democratic candidate in this, the city's first mayoralty contest. John's sympathies, too, would have been with the conservative banking community. But Fletcher was a member of the Jacksonian Democratic party, and Wesley would join him to argue that the Jackson book should have a wide sale because the President was still a hero to the majority of Americans. Furthermore there were an increasing number of Irish immigrants who would buy the book since it was dedicated to "the working people of Ireland" and showed how Jackson had been inspired to greatness by his recollection of the ill treatment his parents received before they emigrated from Ireland. (Similar ill treatment had driven Mathew Carey out of Ireland when, disguised as a woman, he sailed for Philadelphia in 1784.)

The Harpers would not have shared all of Henry Carey's hard feelings since they were not so badly pressed economically. In May, 1834, the Buffalo *Literary Inquirer* began its review of Abercrombie's *Intellectual Powers* by saying:

The editor of a New York newspaper, in noticing a more recent publication of the Messrs Harper than the one we have just named, observes with equal force and propriety, that these everlasting Harpers seem absolutely beyond the influence of all ordinary courses. The iron pressure that crushes the community, has no perceptible effect upon the presses of Cliff Street. Banks may stop—merchants break—commerce turn upside down— yet they still remain undaunted and unannoyed at their post, as caterers general to the literary world, pouring forth from their capacious shelves edition after edition "quickly treading on the heels of another" of every kind of books [*sic*] in which literature rejoices, or by which the idler may be amused. The novel—the Romance Philosophy and Travels—fiction and fact, "in quick succession before our eyes."

(Another encomium had appeared in the January issue of *Booksellers'*
Advertiser. Apparently the editor had been studying the recently issued 1833 catalogue, finding 234 titles in 413 volumes. "Ten years
ago," he wrote, "these brothers worked the presses with their own
hands, and it is within that time that they have commenced publishing;
now they are employing 200 persons, and diffusing knowledge to millions, while their names are familiar wherever the English language is
spoken.")

In January, 1835, Henry Carey wrote a long letter to the brothers
urging their cooperation in Trade Sales. When Blanchard, Carey's partner, had called on them, they expressed indifference but said they
would do nothing "in opposition to the interests of those who had
signed the paper containing the sales." Now they were apparently
supporting a Mr. Gurly who was appealing to the pride of New York
publishers to set up their own rules and not follow Philadelphia's lead.

This letter is one of at least fifteen, most of them controversial,
written from Fourth and Chestnut streets, Philadelphia, to 82 Cliff
Street, New York, between August, 1834, and September, 1835. The
Harper letters were not kept; thus reading this one-sided correspondence in the Carey *Letter Books*, save for direct quotations from Harper
letters, is like listening to half of a telephone conversation—what the
other party is saying can sometimes, but only sometimes, be guessed.
Most of these letters, along with others which Carey wrote to John
Miller, his London agent, pertain to English reprints being pirated in
Philadelphia and New York. They are significant as a case history of
the making of ground rules whereby American publishers were to
respect and to a certain extent safeguard each other's interests. Later
Fletcher wrote, "We have no protection against 'piracy' except the
courtesy of the trade, which is enforced by reprisals against trespassers."

This "courtesy of the trade" was achieved only after much cajoling,
bluffing, and punishing, as this correspondence reveals. Since Carey,
Lea & Blanchard and Harper & Brothers were the leading publishers of
English reprints in the mid-thirties, it was their necessity that established the ground rules covering reprints. By the summer of 1834,
when the correspondence opens, one rule had been agreed upon: first
announcement of a forthcoming reprint established a prior claim. The
recognized medium, so far as the Harpers were concerned, was the
New York *Commercial Advertiser*, although Carey seemed to consider
announcement in a Philadelphia newspaper equally valid. *Who* first

announced *what*, therefore, was an important and often disputed point. This rule also led to an obvious ruse, that of announcing likely titles even before they were read and often failing to print what was announced. Knowledge of forthcoming titles was obtained from *Blackwood's*, the *Metropolitan*, the *Athenaeum*, and similar periodicals. In one letter to Miller in London Carey complained that the English gazettes and magazines were not reaching him promptly, the Harpers often learning of new books before he did.

After spotting a likely author or title, it was equally important to be the first to reach an agreement with the London publisher for the purchase of early proof sheets. It did little good, at the beginning at least, to announce your title if the other fellow could get proofs or the book itself before you did, divide the pages among a dozen compositors, and soon have the presses running off an edition. Printing on each other was profitless, however, and both Carey and Harper were determined to stop the practice, except as a punitive measure. Carey wrote once to New York that there was an ample supply of English books to go around, although he was also writing Miller that the country was flooded with reprints by Harper, himself, and Carey & Hart, the firm his younger brother, Edward, had started in 1829 with bookseller Abraham Hart, taking quarters in Henry's building in Philadelphia.

The correspondence reveals that the brothers were determined to establish two further rules, in addition to "first announcement." One was the right to publish an author exclusively, and the second was "reprisal against trespassers." Carey was unwilling to accept the first and mystified and angered by the second. Carey was attempting to establish a trading position: if a dispute arose concerning two or more titles, no matter who the author was, he saw no reason why hunters could not divide the game between them. He was willing to be generous, sometimes allowing New York to have the larger share. "We are easy people," he said once. But the brothers were impatient with the method. It was not sufficiently clear-cut, especially with authors such as Bulwer and G. P. R. James, in whom by 1833 they felt they had a proprietary interest, having published seven and six titles, respectively, of each. Bulwer's *The Last Days of Pompeii* was obviously to be a test case.

By the autumn of 1834 they had arranged with Bulwer for the purchase of advance sheets of what looked like his best novel to date. On September 13, 1834, Bulwer wrote to the brothers in care of Obadiah Rich, "I trust you have received safely the previous sheets. You must not believe the Papers that advertise my Book for the 15th Inst.

—judge for yourselves—these are *proofs* not even clean sheets that I send you. But about the 1st of October—I expect it to appear—& by next week I shall send *all* the Proofs."* (See illustration 11.) The brothers had announced *The Last Days of Pompeii* as forthcoming, only to be nonplused on learning, no doubt from Rich, who was obviously their agent,† that Carey had ordered a copy from Richard Bentley, the British publisher. Jumping to the conclusion that Carey was planning to print on them, they looked about for a proper means of reprisal. One was easily at hand: William Beckford's *Italy: With Sketches of Spain and Portugal.* In August, Carey had reminded them that he had announced this book before their purchase of sheets. Whereupon they had replied, "Beckford we assign to you." But they cannily held on to the sheets. Now they posted them to Adam Waldie in Philadelphia, suggesting that he might like to reprint the book in his *Select Circulating Library.* (Waldie had been Carey's source of supply for early sheets of the Waverley novels a decade previously.) "From [Waldie's] pages it was made into a Book form," Carey wrote angrily to Cliff Street in November, apparently knowing the source of Waldie's supply but refusing to see that he was being punished for trying to get *The Last Days of Pompeii.* However, he did say that they need not hurry with "Bulwer's last novel"; he had it but he would not injure them. He sought to interpret the Waldie incident not as a reprisal but as a Harper failure to keep their word, reminding them that as recently as August they had written, "If you dispose of any work that we are publishing to Waldie in the editions of the New Mag. it is more than we would do under any circumstances of the kind." He reminded them also that they had ignored his request for their proofs of Beckford's *Italy* when he failed to get his own copy because it was "stolen" from an incoming packet. Carey did not accuse the Harpers outright of having a hand in that mishap. Did he suspect them? If not, he should have known that in order to spank him with the Waldie paddle they had to delay his publication by intercepting his copy. "We heard,"

* The Bentley edition of three volumes (a "three-decker") was published on September 29 and retailed for 31s. 6d. ($7.50). However, a "reprint" was published in December, 1838, in Bentley's *Standard Novels* at six shillings.

† On September 30, 1834, Carey wrote to Miller saying in part, "We have several other works at press of which early sheets will be sent you. these may be of service to you with Bently—who is the agent of Harpers & Brs. we suspect they have some direct communication with Bentley, as they have rec^d some of the first of Bulwers New novels." In his book *Messrs. Carey & Lea of Philadelphia,* David Kaser interpreted the sentence, as copied in the firm's letter book, to mean that Bentley was the Harpers' agent in London. However, in view of Rich's name in the Bulwer letter of September 14 (and later evidence), Dr. Kaser now thinks that the original of the Carey & Lea letter should have carried a question mark after "Brs."

they replied to his protesting letter, "that your copy was accidentally dropped between the ship and the wharf." There is more than a suggestion of tongue in cheek in these innocent words.

At any rate, *The Last Days of Pompeii* was worth a good scrap. A year after publication, the brothers had sold eight thousand copies, four times the sale achieved in England.

In the following June, Carey recognized the Harper right to Bulwer's next book, *The Student*. But he was writing to Miller two months later that Bulwer was writing a historical work; Miller should "send it on as soon as you can put your fingers on it." Carey likewise stepped aside from publishing *The Gipsy* by James when the brothers pressed their claims for that book. However, he was apparently not assenting to the rule of author proprietorship but holding to a trading principle; he got the brothers to agree not to issue the new novels by Mrs. M. W. Shelby, "his author," using their argument.

Even so, by 1836 both new Harper rules had been accepted with the Harper principle of reprisal ricocheting on them. In one of the last issues of the short-lived *Booksellers' Advertiser* (1834-36), reference is made to the first-announcement rule, which "is sometimes excepted by courtesy in the case of a work by an author whose previous ones have been published by any house. For instance Bulwer seems to be identified with Harper; Marryat, with Carey and Hart. But the Rubicon has been passed. Harper printed Marryat's *Stones of the Sea. . . .*" Perhaps Captain Marryat (widely read because, with Mrs. Trollope, he was critical of Americans) was being printed on Carey & Hart by the brothers for some real or suspected wrongdoing. At any rate Abraham Hart determined to retaliate by printing Bulwer's *Rienzi* and got his advance copy the same January day the brothers received theirs. By nine o'clock the next morning, the Carey & Hart edition had been completely set and printed. Sheets were sent to several binders, who had cases already made, and by late afternoon five hundred copies were ready to be packed into the overnight mail stage from Philadelphia, Hart's having found space for them by purchasing all but one of the passengers' seats. By dawn the following morning, Hart was in New York, beginning the distribution of his edition to waiting booksellers, a full day ahead of the Harper issue. One wonders whether James Harper had this *Rienzi* frenzy in mind when eighteen years later at the New York Spring Trade Sale he delivered on behalf of the New York publishers a fulsome tribute to Hart on Hart's retirement, saying he had never known "one more honorable and generous, or more prompt, courteous and intelligent." Hart was surely prompt with *Rienzi*.

The recently established *Knickerbocker*, however, gave the publishing laurels to their New York neighbor, ignoring Carey & Hart in a three-page review of *Rienzi* in the February issue. And as Lewis Gaylord Clark, the young, handsome, and well-dressed editor was writing his monthly book reviews, he had before him a freshly printed circular from Cliff Street. It inspired him "warmly to commend the new enterprise of the Messrs Harper to the literary public, of whom they have long been bountiful benefactors. They have recently commenced publishing a cheap and handsome series of novels, to embrace only the best and most popular works. . . . The series commenced with *Rienzi*. . . . All the works are neatly and accurately printed, and substantially bound in muslin for FIFTY CENTS per volume—each volume containing an entire work."* What Clark did not say was what really inspired the brothers to be so enterprising. His praise of them was akin to that of the poet Petrarch for Cola di Rienzi. And Rienzi could not have been more jealous to restore fourteenth-century Rome to its place of power than the brothers were to establish New York's leadership in publishing. They had manufacturing resources behind them which the Careys lacked; figuring costs closely—even allowing for possible losses —they could underprice and undersell their competitors. Rienzi rationalized his conquest as "the redemption of Rome"; the brothers, as a boon to book buyers. Rienzi's life inspired Byron to write verse; Miss Mitford, a play; and Wagner, an opera; but it was the publication of Bulwer's novel in America that reflected Rienzi's spirit of conquest.

Henry Carey's *Letter Books* do not cover the *Rienzi* affair since the letters did not continue into 1836. But they hint at similar incidents; often they bristle with reprimands and as often seek conciliation. Only reading between the lines with a knowledge of the Harper "eye for an eye" principle of justice can give a sense of *their* letters bristling over *their* announcement, not seen or ignored, *their* accusations of bad faith and *their* admonitions to good behavior. Carey's respect for the brothers is evidenced in several letters to Miller; they had "nearly printed" *Vistas and Sketches* by Mrs. Jameson ("she is very popular here") before his copy arrived. "Our New York people are *very, very* sharp,

---

* According to *The Knickerbocker*, the Harper circular stated, "It is scarcely necessary to point out the great and numerous advantages afforded to the purchaser by this mode of publication over that of being obliged to receive whatever the publisher may choose to give him—the care and risk of loss, attendant upon the necessity of preserving the numbers as they come out, will be avoided—the expense of binding will be saved— the form in which they will be published, duodecimo, will be found much more convenient, as well as beautiful than the lumbering quarto or octavo—and finally, the purchaser will escape the vexation of having to wait from week to week for the continuation of a story in which he has become interested."

indeed," he wrote once; again, "Harpers are making great exertions to get early copies in sheets," and "Harpers are driving on again with vigor." Judging from the Hart-Harper-*Rienzi* incident (which was inspired by Henry Carey, according to David Kaser's *Messrs. Carey & Lea of Philadelphia*), Henry had finally accepted the brothers' twin principles of proprietary interest in authors and of reprisals against trespassers.

Dr. Kaser suggests that only Henry's retirement in 1838 prevented a total war between the houses since each was determined to be the leader and there was room for only one. It seems more likely that the war had been fought and the victor acknowledged. Years later a Philadelphia bookseller commented, "It is a pleasure to know that when the seat of empire in publishing passed away from Philadelphia (Mathew Carey retiring like Charles V, and H. C. Carey and I. Lea abdicating gracefully), the sceptre passed to these hard-handed men [the Harpers] . . . whence was scattered the seed which has filled the land with living leaves of knowledge."

In 1836 both Carey and the brothers were challenged on English reprints by an English publisher, Saunders & Otley. Saunders sent his twenty-nine-year-old son, Frederick, to New York to set up a branch office. He came with great expectations of establishing in America the firm's "property rights" in English books and with little awareness of publishing realities when neither country respected the other's copyrights. Saunders arrived in New York on May 14, 1836, after a thirty-nine-day crossing on the packet ship *Montreal*. He brought with him a letter of introduction to Washington Irving, whose aid he solicited after establishing an office in a building near the corner of Ann and William streets. One of the first books Saunders undertook to publish was *Memoirs of Prince Lucien Bonaparte*, for which Harper's had what they considered "rights" in America. They may have rationalized this concept from their 1831 publication of the *Court and Camp of Napoleon Bonaparte*, which contained memoirs of the Bonaparte family, including Napoleon's brother Lucien. Fifty years later Saunders dictated his memories of his early days in New York to his grandson, Walter Bobbette, in which he said, "A good start was made with the agency, but soon trouble began . . . for Harper & Brothers got hold of proof sheets of our books, one of our pressmen having been tampered with, and published [it] . . . several days sooner than we could. . . . This action of the New York firm was announced with placards proclaiming 'great American Enterprise.' Being helpless, with no copyright to aid me . . . our enterprise had to be abandoned."

Saunders scolded the brothers in the *Evening Post* for pirating Bonaparte's *Memoirs* and they answered in an advertisement, attempting humor and ridicule. It was a fictitious proclamation signed by "J. Pope, Prince Cunningo, and Lady Dawdling," saying that Americans were a ridiculous people for "excluding foreigners from the advantage of copy-right in books," and a pertinacious people "in availing themselves of the benefits . . . of getting books at *fifty cents* a copy, for which, but for these laws, they would have to pay *two dollars and fifty cents.* . . . The American publishers are ridiculous, too, in preferring the system of large sales and small prices, to that of small sales and high prices, so wisely and properly followed in Europe, and especially in London. . . . These barbarians of the Western World are getting knowledge at too little cost, and the system must be amended."

However, the brothers were properly spanked in an editorial in the *Evening Post*, undoubtedly written by William Cullen Bryant: "We regret extremely that it becomes our duty to animadvert on an act of the Messrs. Harper, the well-known publishers, which seriously affects their reputation for honour and integrity. . . . We have hitherto often alluded to the indefatigable industry of the Harpers, and in common with our contemporaries, eulogized their exertions in aiding to gratify, while they improved, the literary tastes of the community. In doing so, we merely did what justice demanded, and in now censuring them for an act very far beneath them, we obey the same impulse. . . ." Bryant gave Saunders access to his columns for rebuttals that Saunders himself wrote, dictating to the compositor, "who set up in type . . . my replies to adverse criticism of my efforts, and people used to wonder how it was possible that I was heard from so soon, for at times criticism and reply were printed on the same day." Saunders continued in publishing, issuing *The Authors' Printing and Publishing Assistant* in 1839. By 1838 he had made his peace with the brothers, no doubt on their terms, since *Retrospect of Western Travel,* by Harriet Martineau, carried a joint imprint of Harper & Brothers in New York, and Saunders & Otley, London. Sometime in the mid-forties, finding that "his cake was all dough," to use Demarest's phrase, he took an editorial job at 82 Cliff Street. If he could not lick the brothers, he would join them.

A more important English reprint of 1836 went unchallenged by the brothers, for apparently Henry Carey had established his right to issue in November the first four numbers of *Pickwick Papers.* "The author was unknown and the enterprise a doubtful one," Henry C. Lea wrote later (*American Literary Gazette,* May 15, 1867). "The edition, printed from type, was only 1500 copies, and the numbers were issued at the price of 45 cents, in one volume, in the thin, duodecimo shape, bound in boards, with which all readers of old novels are doubtless familiar." Two years later the Carey firm sent "Boz," as Charles Dickens was then widely known, £50 in acknowledgment of their success with the work.

The brothers were not gambling on unknown authors that year; they were satisfied with two works each from Bulwer, James, and Marryat.

CHAPTER VI

Launching American Authors

1834–1836

THE NEW YORK EDITOR who in 1834 sang the praises of "these everlasting Harpers" (page 51) may have been either General Morris of the *Mirror* or Colonel William L. Stone of the *Commercial Advertiser*, for both men were often at Cliff Street picking up new books to review and seeing their own books through the press. The brothers no doubt asked Morris to edit a selection of articles from his paper, similar to their successful English reprint of November, 1831, the *Club Book*, an anthology in which the popular John Galt figured most prominently. Morris's *Atlantic Club Book* was a two-volume potpourri of sixty-four selections written by himself; by the poets William Cullen Bryant, Nathaniel Parker Willis, and Fitz-Greene Halleck; by Harper authors Fay, Leggett, Paulding, and Simms; and by Fanny Kemble, then playing Shakespearean roles in the United States, who later married the wealthy Pierce Butler and wrote a scathing exposé of slavery on her husband's Georgia plantation. Morris had no difficulty in getting good writers for the *Mirror*, for he was himself a poet (later "Poe"tized "our best writer of songs") and remembered now for "Woodman, Spare That Tree." About this time, Morris was bragging that "our annual disbursements for literary contributions alone exceed *five thousand* dollars!—a sum that has never been paid . . . by any periodical in this country, whether daily, weekly, monthly, or quarterly, for a similar supply."

Colonel Stone had contributed "Uncle Tim and Deacon Pettibone" to his rival's anthology. His own book of essays he entitled simply *Tales and Sketches*. A great newspaper editor and a great public citizen, Stone later became a distinguished historian of colonial and Revolutionary times in New York. His *Border Wars of the American Revolution* (1843) is still referred to today. Colonel Stone was often to praise the Harpers for their publishing enterprise, and no doubt to criticize them severely for their somewhat mysterious role in printing (but not publishing) *The Awful Disclosures of Maria Monk* (1836), a tissue of anti-Catholic prejudice and fiction, which was certainly the most disgraceful book the brothers ever had any connection with. Stone himself went to Montreal and inspected a nunnery to expose the book as a vicious hoax (see page 186).

Another 1834 caller at Cliff Street was a young Maine poet with fame and fortune still ahead of him, Henry Wadsworth Longfellow. He came in August. Longfellow had tired of his teaching post in Bowdoin College and was seeking an appointment to the faculty of New York University. While in town he called on the brothers to ask if they would publish the third volume of his travel sketches, *Outre-Mer: A Pilgrimage Beyond the Sea*. He was dissatisfied with his Boston publishers, Lilly, Wait and Company, who had brought out No. 2, and were now in financial difficulties. Knowing that Longfellow, inspired by Irving's success, was doing a kind of "sketchbook" of France, Spain, Germany, and Italy, Wesley and Fletcher said "yes," but added that they should certainly take over the rights to the earlier volumes of *Outre-Mer*, and should publish the whole series as one book on a division-of-profits basis. On his return trip Longfellow stopped in Boston to reach an agreement with Lilly & Wait but, finding them stubborn, he wrote the brothers asking if they could better their offer. They replied that, even though they could not do so, Longfellow would "never realize either fame or money" by staying with the Boston firm. In early September, Lewis Gaylord Clark, of *The Knickerbocker*, wrote Longfellow offering to help him make terms with the Harpers, and again, on November 2, he urged, "half of the profits of an edition from Harpers would be worth $400 perhaps 600 to you. They tell me they can lose on *no* book, now—even the worst. Get off Lilly & Wait if you can." Clark's letter prompted Longfellow to write to the brothers asking when they could publish and whether they would give him an advance payment. Aware of the difficulties of shipping books till after the spring thaws opened up water navigation, they replied suggesting publication in March or April and promised to send an advance when required. So Longfellow gave them the manuscript of No. 3 of *Outre-Mer*, apparently on another visit to New York, and waited impatiently for proofs. He asked Clark in February to jog them, and Clark replied on a cold day in early March ("The wind bites shrewdly") that they were "*despert slow*," finishing off several books arranged for earlier, "together with another voluminous and profitable job, 'The Laws of Georgia'. . . . Since writing the above, I have been down to the Harpers' and they tell me that they are coming on bravely with your book."

Clark's call, along with a further letter from Longfellow, prompted them to write on March 6, apologizing for the delay caused by "old contracts [that] are now completed, however—and we are again proceeding with *Outre-Mer*, the second volume of which is already in type. But we shall not be able to publish it *before* the time you propose visiting New York." (Presumably in early April, before Longfellow's departure for a second period of study abroad to prepare for his new professorship at Harvard.) The book finally was printed and copyrighted on May 26, 1835, with Clark getting early sheets that enabled him to publish a review in the May issue of *The Knickerbocker*. In 1859, Longfellow was to write the brothers in a nostalgic vein, speaking of "pleasant recollections of the times that are past, when I began my literary career with you."

Other publishers besides Lilly & Wait were having difficulties early in 1834. The editors of the new literary magazine, the *American Monthly*, had no literary news for their readers in February, complaining, "There is no annunciation of works in press, no list of new publications—no matter whereon to found literary notices. . . . That times will look up, we sincerely hope. . . ." But soon they could write about Dunlap and Schoolcraft. William Dunlap and Henry R. Schoolcraft are less well known now than Longfellow, but first editions of their books bring higher prices at book auctions than does *Outre-Mer*. Dunlap's new book was entitled *History of the Rise and Progress of the Arts of Design in the United States.** Based on a diary that he had

---

* Despite the fact that Harper was listed in Roorbach's *Bibliotheca Americana* as the publisher of this work and that Demarest catalogued it, the first edition was printed by George P. Scott & Co. of New York, with Dunlap acting as his own publisher. "I wish to have control of the work," he wrote in the preface. Another Dunlap book,

kept for decades, he wrote not only a criticism of art but also gossipy, anecdotal stories of artists he had known: Stuart, Peale, Trumbull, Copley, S. F. B. Morse, and others who, like Dunlap himself, had studied painting under Benjamin West, the expatriate American Quaker who was long lionized in London. Because of his prominence as a playwright, translator, and producer, evidenced in his *History of the American Theatre*, published by the Harpers two years earlier, Dunlap had many artistic associations outside this coterie of painters. Few American men of arts and letters were unknown to him or his diary. "He was a slovenly writer, discursive, untidy, and garrulous," Van Wyck Brooks wrote, "but a modest, honest and tireless collector of facts."

Schoolcraft's book was entitled *Narrative of an Expedition through the Upper Mississippi to Itasca Lake, the Actual Source . . .* , and was based on an exploration he headed in 1832. This remarkable scientist and frontiersman, who was married to a half-breed Chippewa girl and had lived among Indians in northern Michigan, was well known to the American public because of his earlier book, *Travels in the Central Portion of the Mississippi Valley*. This work described a seven-week canoe trip Schoolcraft made with Governor Lewis Cass of Michigan from Detroit to Chicago, where Cass bought Michigan land from the Indians, and then on to the Mississippi via the Illinois River.* When the brothers published *Narrative of an Expedition* in 1834, they knew that it would sell more widely than the earlier *Travels*. Schoolcraft was a famous man and books of travel were doing better every year. The earlier book had treated only of the central portions of the great river; the new one carried armchair travelers to its source, entertaining them with descriptions of virgin lands, instructing them in geography and geology, and informing them about Indian life. Schoolcraft wanted Americans to know Indian history and Indian lore and to share his concern and affection for the tribes still inhabiting the regions to the northwest. This concern was to lead to his 1839 book on the mental characteristics of the North American Indians. In calling this book *Algic Researches*, he coined a word, "Algic" (from "Allegheny" and "Atlantic"), his name for the Indian nations inhabiting the country east of the Mississippi. This two-volume work of nearly five hundred

---

History of New York, with maps and engravings, was published by the brothers in 1832, and an abridged edition (two volumes) was placed in the first series of the *School District Library*.

  * Schoolcraft dedicated his book to Governor Cass, the great-grandfather of Cass Canfield, the present editorial chairman and head of the House of Harper & Row.

pages contained forty-six tales and legends, "mythologic and alle-
goric," of many tribes including the Chippewa, whose language was
the lingua franca of most of the Algonquins. While serving as agent
for Indian affairs on the northwest frontier—in fact during the year he
read proofs of *Narrative of an Expedition*—he negotiated a treaty with
the Chippewas, whereby the United States obtained title to the northern third of the lower peninsula and the eastern half of the upper
peninsula of Michigan, where a county is named for him.

One of the "old contracts" that Wesley referred to in his letter to
Longfellow concerned the James K. Paulding titles that were contracted for in November, 1833. No doubt Paulding had been even
more impatient than Longfellow in prodding the brothers toward publication. A plate in the back matter of Coleridge's *Table Talk*, published in the spring of 1835, advertised that a "new edition of Mr.
Paulding's Works" was in press and listed *Koningsmarke*, in two
volumes (remembered now for the jingle it contained, "Peter Piper
picked a peck of pickled peppers"), and *Salmagundi*, in four volumes,
the latter "Revised and corrected by the authors" (Irving had returned
to New York in 1832 after seventeen years in Europe). This same
plate was used in the back matter of Paulding's *Letters from the South*
(two volumes), which was also ready in 1835 but was apparently
printed after the Coleridge book, because in the interim someone discovered that the plate carried two lines with the caption "Published by
Harper & Brothers," and routed out the duplicate line.

The 1836 catalogue was to announce other Paulding reprints
"nearly ready for publication." Published in a uniform series, they
were *Three Wise Men*, *The Book of St. Nicholas*, *Slavery in the
United States*, *John Bull and Brother Jonathan*, and *Tales of a Good
Woman*.

In giving priority to *Letters from the South*, the brothers recognized
as do present-day critics that it was Paulding's best book of nonfiction.
The *Letters* told of his 1816 travels in Virginia (but were revised and
updated), where he met plantation farmers in the Shenandoah Valley,
rough woodsmen in the Blue Ridge Mountains, and the socially elite at
the famous springs, "hot and cold, bitter and sweet." His descriptions
of scenery are often superb, as that of the valley of the Caphon River
and the view from Jefferson's Rock, near Harpers Ferry. Jefferson
himself had also described such a view in *Notes on Virginia*, in which
book he had portrayed the Natural Bridge; this account, wrote Paulding, was "so provokingly happy and inexcusably correct" that the less

he said about the bridge the better. What Paulding experienced led him into long detours of political and social philosophy; he reaffirmed his belief in America, finding in Virginia "a deep and noble and universal attachment to the Union"; he ridiculed Americans who toadied to Europeans, and showed, as in other books, his "defensive" hostility to England. He had a great zest for life, a wide interest in people and events, and a deep concern for human values. Physically he was above medium height and strongly built. His son William said that in profile he resembled an ancient philosopher.

The production of the complete *Works* of Hannah More was begun in the winter of 1835-36, since the brothers knew that Carey had hopes for an American edition. An enormous amount of time had to be scheduled in composing room, pressroom, and bindery to make possible spring publication of two octavo volumes of 1,148 pages and of seven "well-printed and elegantly-bound" 12mo volumes, containing 2,978 pages of tales, ballads, hymns, sacred drama, allegories, essays, and poems. Another English author also had top priority in 1835-36, because he was writing two books bound to be popular with American readers. He was C. J. Latrobe, nephew of Benjamin H. Latrobe, who helped to rebuild the Capitol in Washington and, with Jefferson's patronage, established Greek Revival architecture in America. The younger Latrobe was favorably known as the friend and companion of Washington Irving on Irving's trip to the Far West. His books for Harper's were *Rambler in North America*, which the *American Monthly* called "beyond comparison" the best book ever written on the country, and *Rambler in Mexico*, which the Boston historian William H. Prescott praised highly. The Latrobe-Irving-Prescott interest in Mexico had interesting repercussions on Cliff Street. By 1837 Prescott had completed his first major work, *Ferdinand and Isabella*, and was thinking of following it up with a book dealing with the conquest of Mexico. Irving returned from his trip with Latrobe fired with the same idea, but on learning of Prescott's plans he gracefully disqualified himself. Had Irving written the book on Mexico, it would probably have been published by Lea & Blanchard; the brothers were to publish Prescott's *Conquest of Mexico* in 1843.

As the Harper editorial program expanded, the Harper composing room needed more type to keep in step. Not having a type foundry of their own, the brothers arranged with George B. Lothian, who owned one, to have Fletcher go into partnership with him. Lothian could thus obtain additional capital and an assured customer; the brothers could get priority on deliveries and a 20 percent discount off trade prices. But, by the summer of 1835, Fletcher was running into difficulties with Lothian and brought suit against him for $1,250, an action that caused Lothian to hurry over to Cliff Street. A document was drawn up which they both signed, dissolving the partnership. On his part,

INTERESTING WORKS

PUBLISHED BY

HARPER & BROTHERS,

In 3 vols. 18mo, with Engravings, Maps, &c.,
THE HISTORY OF THE JEWS.
From the earliest Period to the Present Time.
By the Rev. H. H. MILMAN.

In 2 vols. 18mo., with Portraits,
THE LIFE OF NAPOLEON BONAPARTE.
By J. G. LOCKHART, Esq.

In one vol. 18mo., with a Portrait,
THE LIFE OF NELSON.
By ROBERT SOUTHEY, LL.D.

In one vol. 18mo., with a Map,
THE LIFE AND ACTIONS OF
ALEXANDER THE GREAT.
By Rev. J. WILLIAMS.

In 2 vols. 18mo., with numerous Engravings,
THE NATURAL HISTORY OF INSECTS.

In one vol. 18mo.,
THE LIFE OF LORD BYRON.
By JOHN GALT.

In one vol. 18mo., with Engravings,
THE LIFE OF MOHAMMED.
Founder of the Religion of Islam, and of the Empire of the Saracens
By Rev. GEORGE BUSH.

Fletcher agreed to pay all "costs and charges" of the suit and any claims against the partnership excepting three; Lothian, in turn, promised to supply over a period of four months $2,000 worth of type of "as good a quality as [he] usually manufactures," and to turn over to Fletcher all claims "due or coming due" to the erstwhile partnership for him "to collect, receive, and retain." On January 31, 1837, Fletcher was to endorse Lothian's copy of the agreement, acknowledging that he had received his $2,000 worth of type. Some of these fonts of type were so fancy that it is likely they did not get used for book composition, but young William Demarest, then an apprentice, had a lot of fun showing them off when he set up the 1836 catalogue, creating pages as elegant and difficult to read as could be found anywhere around town. (The trim size of the catalogue was 5½ × 8½. See preceding page.)

Composing and pressroom time also had to be scheduled for important technical books being readied for 1835 publication. Medical books, especially. Having done well with Dr. Reese's Americanized edition of Cooper's *Dictionary of Practical Surgery*, the brothers now had that old staple Good's *Study of Medicine* doctored up for reissue. The treatment was administered by Dr. Sidney Doane, soon to be one of the organizers of the Medical Department of New York University. Originally a four-volume work, Good's study came out in the Doane edition in two octavo volumes of more than fifteen hundred pages, presumably a more convenient and less expensive edition for medical students. Dr. Doane must have done little else for months on end than write books for the brothers and read proof. In 1835 he saw through the press Maygrier's *Midwifery Illustrated*, which he had translated from the French and annotated, and was working on his *Surgery Illustrated*, based on the work of four European surgeons, an 1836 publication. These works, with Cooper's *Dictionary* and Hooper's *Lexicon Medicum*, gave a strong foundation to the growing list of Harper medical books. Of a more ephemeral nature were two books on cholera, one written by Dr. Lloyd Ferris, who had worked in the Duane Street Cholera Hospital in the summer of 1834, and the other by Dr. Reese following the epidemic in 1832. Calling his book a *Plain and Practical Treatise* on the subject, Dr. Reese could not forgo adding an appendix on the medical use of ardent spirits; he was convinced that the use of alcohol was as unnecessary as it was mischievous, either in sickness or in health. Later, when James Harper was president of the Washingtonian Total Abstinence Society, he liked to quote from this essay by his friend Dr. Reese. However, the best-selling physician-author in 1835 was not Doane, Ferris, or Reese, but Caleb Ticknor, whose *Philosophy of Living, or the Way to Enjoy Life and its Comforts* came out that spring. With such words on the title page, the book was bound to succeed, and its happy title was backed by generous reviews, *The Knickerbocker* calling it a "sensible and truly valuable book on a vitally interesting subject." It was put in the *Family Library*, and ten years later a niche was to be found for it in the *School District Library*.

What Doane was paid for his work on Good's *Study* is not known, but a record was left concerning a financial arrangement made about the same time with George Bush of New York University for his preface and notes to a much smaller work, Dymond's *Essays on the Principles of Morality, etc.* Wesley's letter offered $200 outright or a royalty of 8 cents a copy up to fifteen hundred copies, presumably the size of the first printing, and 4 cents thereafter.

Wesley was doubtful if the book would sell well, despite Bush's apparent enthusiasm, or be profitable to either party. But the book was still in print in 1869, having varied in price from $1 to $1.50 in the interim. The mortality of a book, however, seemingly had no relation to sales. A steady demand, even though small, was kept alive by the brothers with printings of 250 or 500 copies. Such a policy would be extremely popular with many authors today. Now slow-selling titles go quickly out of print, for large printings and quick turnovers of inventory are the price that publishers must pay to the gods of the machine age. Bush was a true scholar and his knowledge was encyclopedic. From his book-filled study on the third floor of a Nassau Street building, the tall, lean, and amiable professor brought to Cliff Street not only the Dymond book and his own earlier volumes but one on the prophecies of Daniel as well. His eschatological and metaphysical bent led him in 1845 to join the Swedenborgian church.

Another scholar, this time from Columbia University, also came to Cliff Street in 1835. His name was Charles Anthon, and he did not have far to walk, since Columbia, where he was Jay Professor of Greek and Latin Languages, was nearby—at the head of Park Place. On October 3, he signed a sixty-four-word agreement which was one of the shortest and most profitable contracts that any author ever signed with the brothers. He agreed to edit a series of "Classical and Auxiliary Works" for use in schools and colleges, all books to be stereotyped and printed at Harper's expense. On the thirty-five books, averaging about one a year, that were thus to be published and to be accounted for on the half-profits basis from 1836 to 1867, Charles Anthon was to earn $100,-000, a cool half-million dollars in terms of today's currency. He was nicknamed "Bull" Anthon by his students because of his massive build. His large head was supported by a square jaw and topped by a high forehead. He spoke with a sonorous voice and was feared by the boys in the Grammar School of Columbia College, of which he was principal for several years. He liked to wear pearl-colored, tight-fitting trousers and carried a light cane. The manuscripts he turned in were models of neatness, as was his dress.

The Harper half-profits contracts earned for Anthon, John N. Reynolds, and many others the equivalent of royalties of at least 15 percent of the retail price, since overhead charges were minimal and discounts to dealers were on the short side. The 1835 contract for Reynolds's *Voyage of the Potomac* is a case in point. Specifying half ownership of copyright and plates and a half interest in profits, the contract stated that a retail price of $3 and a wholesale price of $2.50 should be established. With 80 cents estimated for manufacturing cost for the 560-page octavo work, $1.70 was thus left for division, or 85 cents to each party. The brothers, however, were first to reimburse themselves for the cost of plates and engravings. Having paid Reynolds $1,000 on signing the contract for joint interest in the copyright, it seems likely that they also desired to earn this amount back from sales as well as their half investment in plates; they also had to set up a sum to cover credit losses since the contract made losses their responsibility. At any rate they agreed that Reynolds should never be paid less than 66 cents a copy, an amount equivalent to a royalty of 22 percent of the retail price. Incidentally, this contract, like most drawn in those days, ran for only a short term of years; after seven years Reynolds could obtain the copyright in full and his share of the cost of plates for $550.

The Voyage of the Potomac was based on a journal that Reynolds kept while on the United States Frigate *Potomac*, under the command of Commodore John Downes, during its circumnavigation of the globe in the years 1831-34. Published early in 1836, the book quickly sold out its first printing of three thousand copies and two more were rushed through the presses. Reynolds helped the sale of his book by lecturing widely. He was an impassioned speaker with a platform manner that was graceful and impressive. The book was also given a tremendous boost by reviewers who linked literary criticism with flag waving. At the end of its June issue (and seventh volume), *The Knickerbocker* printed twenty-four pages of "testimonials" to *The Voyage of the Potomac*, clipped from newspapers from Boston to Charleston, S.C. The New York *Courier and Express* hoisted a banner both to Reynolds, "an honour to his country," and to Harper's for the book's "elegant dress . . . typographical accuracy and neatness." The Boston *Galaxy* said that in "England, France, or Russia the book would have been published at the expense of the government. It is got up here by individual enterprise. Nevertheless we shall persist in calling it a *national* work." The *American Beacon* solemnly declared, "The Messers Harper have succeeded in erecting the most beautiful as well as the most durable monument that has hitherto commemorated any military or naval expedition of America." And the Boston *Courier* reviewed the book three different times.

Professor Anthon's first Harper book was his 1836 translation of Sallust's *Jugurthian War*, with four further works ready by 1838. Among Anthon's students at Columbia one of the brightest at this time was George Templeton Strong, son of a wealthy New York attorney. On Sunday, October 4, the day after Anthon signed his Harper contract, fifteen-year-old Strong decided to keep a diary. Begun the next day and continued till late June, 1875, a month before he died, Strong wrote more than four million words, a literate and illuminating forty-year record of men and events.* Strong often refers to "Bull" Anthon, who was recognized both by students and faculty as the best-known representative of the college. Strong was to be graduated three years later as second in his class, with Anthon devoting many hours to him as he was "manufacturing hexameters" for his Latin Salutatory.

Textbooks for academies and colleges, as the brothers well knew, made a substantial publishing backlog, less subject to fads and fancies than fiction. But books for common schools were equally important, books such as Webster's *Speller* and McGuffey's *Readers* (1836 on) enjoying extraordinary sales, but not to the benefit of Cliff Street. Two books issued from these presses in 1834 gave encouragement in this field, J. Orville Taylor's *The District School* and Lyman Cobb's *Miniature Lexicon of the English Language*. Taylor had spent several years visiting schools, and his book, according to the New York *Commercial Advertiser*, would be of lasting value to the cause of elementary education. In the autumn of 1837, eighteen-year-old Herman Melville was reading *The District School* while teaching about thirty pupils in a one-room schoolhouse near Pittsfield, Massachusetts; he wrote his uncle who had given him the book that he faced precisely the obstacles and difficulties that Taylor described. The district schools were needing both new textbooks and libraries. These needs could be supplied from Cliff Street, textbooks right away. So Cobb set about preparing two, his *North American Reader* coming out in 1835 and his *Explanatory Arithmetic* the next year.

Although subject to the public's fancy, fiction and its authors could not be disregarded, particularly when there was a writer on leash like the handsome young Simms. His Harper best seller, *Martin Faber*, was followed in July, 1834, by *Guy Rivers*, a novel that went through three printings in a little more than a year, despite the fact that Simms

---

* In his introduction to the condensed, four-volume edition of the *Diary* (1952), editor Allan Nevins describes George Templeton Strong as "one of the most cultivated, sincere, intelligent, high-minded, and delightful gentlemen that New York ever produced."

would not permit the Harper reader to correct careless grammar, a stilted style, and obvious crudities. In the spring of '35 his new novel, *The Yemassee*, was ready for publication. All at Cliff Street who read the manuscript agreed that it was better than the two earlier novels, so a first printing of twenty-five hundred copies, twice the usual size, was run off. It sold out in three days, for here was a Southern Cooper, perhaps a superior Cooper, as Poe believed, who could describe the Georgia Border country at the close of the eighteenth century and bring to life the warfaring Indians who roamed the South Carolina forests before the Revolution. *The Yemassee*, the best of his books and the only Simms work in the new American library at the White House, was the story of a young Indian chieftain who gave aid to the English against his own tribe when it was all-powerful about 1715. To his ethnological knowledge of Indian sagas, war dances, and battle rites, Simms added his great gift of storytelling. The public loved it. A dramatization of the novel opened on August 17 at the Bowery Theatre.

James considered Simms to have the most remarkable talent for writing of anyone he had ever known and believed that Simms should have considerable popularity in England as well as in America. Planning a trip abroad in the autumn of 1835, he talked with the other brothers about business he might transact in London. They agreed Simms would strengthen his hand in trading for first proofs of important English books. They also agreed that it would be right for James to take Maria and eleven-year-old Philip along for sightseeing on the continent and in England. From Paris, where they went without disembarking at Liverpool, Maria wrote on November 27 to "Dear Sister Jane" (Fletcher's wife). She confessed her fear of the ocean, "that element so much dreaded," extolled the services of her stewardess, Sarah, and described the excellence of the ship's cuisine. Luncheon was served at twelve o'clock, gentlemen only eating at the "public table," ladies being served elsewhere at their pleasure; a three-course dinner was served at four o'clock, with high tea following at eight; twice a week plum pudding and champagne were served. Presumably James abstained, as would "two female ministers of the Friends order." One of the Friends, Anne Thorne, was Maria's favorite shipboard companion. In pious words that would have done credit to Mrs. Lydia Huntley Sigourney, who was at this time revising for Harper's her *Letters to Young Ladies*, Maria spoke of "much mingling of the spirit while conversing with this lovely Saint," and of the outpouring of Grace that enabled her to surmount her fears.

Another reason for James's trip abroad was to collect fairy tales for what was to be one of the most beautiful books issued from Cliff Street in the thirties. One suspects that the brothers were sold on this unusual editorial venture by Verplanck, who later wrote a fulsome introduction to the book: "Our meritorious publishers perceiving the lamentable neglect into which this choice part of our literature has fallen amongst us . . . determined to supply the deficiency. At great expense, for in addition to the cost of foreign correspondence, one of the partners of the house has travelled over the greatest part of Europe with no other object. They collected the most approved and earliest editions of the ancient English story-books and a large selection of those best-attested in France, Holland, and Germany." Twenty-five stories were thus selected of which twelve were new translations. Verplanck also disclosed an ambitious Cliff Street project: the *Fairy Book* was to be the introductory volume of the "Harper's proposed splendid cabinet edition of all the works of true fiction [*sic*] ever written." But so laudable an editorial venture could not withstand the economic storms looming ahead. Verplanck signed the introduction "John Smith" and reviewers had fun trying to identify the authorship. The New York *Spectator* defended the claim of John Smith himself, claiming that he was one of their columnists. The brothers engaged Joseph A. Adams, a rising young engraver, to illustrate the book with eighty-one wood engravings. Some were made from his own sketches and others from drawings by the artist John G. Chapman. The borders of the chapter-head engravings pictured five naked fairies, something a contemporary artist could hardly get away with. Adams did fifty engravings for two other issues that year, Defoe's *Robinson Crusoe* and Bunyan's *Pilgrim's Progress*, the latter containing a life of Bunyan by Robert Southey.

When James returned to New York with his family is not known, presumably not until after May, 1836 (see page 216). He was proud to announce on his return that Bentley was to bring out British editions of *Guy Rivers* and *The Yemassee*. No doubt James had told Bentley his favorite Simms anecdote, illustrating his author's remarkable talent for composition. During the summer of '35 while writing *The Partisan*, a tale of South Carolina during the Revolution, Simms decided he wanted to take a week's holiday. "But we are out of copy," James protested. "Unless you can furnish more we shall have to suspend work on your novel until you return." Simms replied immediately, "That will never do. Give me pen, ink, and paper, and I'll go upstairs and find a place to write." In less than half an hour he returned with more copy than would be required during his absence.

In a letter to Rufus Wilmot Griswold, Simms later recalled that *The Partisan* "was better liked by readers than by critics. Though distinguished by delineations and scenes that satisfy me, the design was feeble, the parts clumsily put together. In truth the printing of the book was begun before the first fifty pages were written."

Joseph Holt Ingraham was a contemporary of Simms and his equal in turning out fiction at break-pen speed. His first Harper novel was called *The South-West* and described life in Jefferson College, Washington, Mississippi, where he had taught. Now, in 1836, the "Professor," as he was called, was back in Cliff Street seeing *Lafitte* through the press. *Lafitte*, a yarn about the Gulf of Mexico pirate, came out in July, with a second printing called for in September. On each of these novels Ingraham was earning 50 cents a copy, and *Lafitte* soon netted him $1,250, enough to inspire him to make his living by writing. Soon he was to negotiate for further books, badgering Fletcher to buy them outright for $1,500.

Another outlaw, a "land pirate," figured in a Harper book that year —the true story of Virgil Stewart's exciting adventures in capturing the notorious John A. Murrel and his gang, who had terrorized residents in northern Mississippi by robberies, rapings, and murders. This book helped Robert M. Coates nearly a century later to write a best seller, *The Outlaw Years*.

The Simms contracts were on the half-profit basis, as were those of Catherine M. Sedgwick, who signed up in 1835 for her novel on the home, entitled *The Linwoods*, the first of nine titles she was to have published from Cliff Street. Miss Sedgwick looked the part of the novelist of the home and of homely virtues. She was a little over medium height and her open face was characterized by dark, piercing eyes, a slightly Roman nose, and a well-formed mouth and chin. Now in her late forties, she was soon to wear a lace cap, which made her look decidedly matronly. As a writer Miss Sedgwick was admired in her own day as the only woman who had gained a literary reputation when an American author was still something of a phenomenon. Prior to Harriet Beecher Stowe, Miss Sedgwick was the most widely read novelist in America and was captioned by Hawthorne as "our most truthful novelist." When Edgar Allan Poe reviewed *The Linwoods* in the December, 1835, issue of the *Southern Literary Messenger*, he wrote, "By those who are most fastidious in matters of literary criticism, the author of *Hope Leslie* is the most ardently admired, and we are acquainted with few persons of sound and accurate discrimination who would hesitate in placing her upon a level with the best of our creative novelists. Of American *female* writers we must consider her the first."

In the *American Monthly* for November, 1835, Charles Fenno Hoffman counted off three American novels in addition to *The Linwoods* that were being published, with two more soon to come from Harper's, making "six works of fiction by native authors, upon native subjects, within as many weeks." Two of the six books he mentioned were published by the Careys, *Clinton Bradshaw* by F. W. Thomas, and *Hawks of Hawk Hollow* (a tale with its setting around the Delaware Water Gap) by Robert Montgomery Bird. However, Bird published *Sheppard Lee* from Cliff Street in August, 1836. "Of all the native productions of the season," Clark wrote in *The Knickerbocker*, this novel was "*American* in everything." *Sheppard Lee* was published anonymously.

Anonymous authorship was characteristic of this period. What accounts for this vogue of writing under an assumed name or no name at all? Were writers a bit ashamed of putting their names to fictional works, as Scott had been in his Waverley novels? Perhaps they enjoyed hearing what their friends said about their books, frank opinions that might later prove embarrassing. Once G. P. R. James was suspected of publishing anonymously in order to obtain American copyright and royalties by thus disguising his authorship. Anyway, it was a game that everyone enjoyed playing. Readers and reviewers had fun guessing the identity of authors, and publishers found that it often increased sales. Sometimes no one ever guessed. The identity of the author of *Herbert Wendall, A Tale of the Revolution*, written in 1835 by a Harper author apparently living in Newark, New Jersey, is as yet unknown; the publishing brothers left no clue. The following year they published *Gifaral Barmeki*, an oriental tale, whose author was unknown to editor Horace Greeley of the *New Yorker*, himself somewhat unknown—a young journalist on the make. The author turned out to be Gardiner Spring, Jr., whose father was the popular minister of Brick Church in New York. Earlier in 1836, *The Doctor** was published and Clark wrote in the July *Knickerbocker*, "The London world are agog to find out the author. *Blackwood*—good authority in such matters—indicates [Robert] Southey. But we question the assumption." But *Blackwood's Magazine* was correct, as Clark

---

* *The Doctor* contains the famous story of the Three Bears.

admitted five months later; he took eight pages to establish that Southey was indeed the author and deciphered the eleven oddly spelled names on the penultimate page as the first syllables in the names of Southey and ten of his friends. In the meantime, the Harper edition was in its second printing, priced, like *Rienzi*, at fifty cents. English readers had to pay a guinea, or ten times as much as Americans, to participate in this game of "Who's the author?"

In that same December issue of the *Southern Literary Messenger* in which Poe puffed Miss Sedgwick, he reviewed what must stand as the quaintest book the brothers ever published, a life of George Washington in Latin. This *Georgii Washingtonii . . . Praesidis prima Vita* was written by Francis Glass, an itinerant teacher in southwestern Ohio, who likened his log-cabin schoolrooms to temples of the Delphian God and chanted the multiplication table along with *Musarum Sacerdos*. John N. Reynolds, unable in 1824 to complete his studies at Ohio University, sought Glass out and was tutored in Latin and Greek. Reynolds was so impressed by the literary ambition of this rustic genius that he established Glass in Dayton, where he could complete his *Vita*. But Glass did not live to see the book printed. By the time Reynolds, himself a successful author, could obtain Anthon's imprimatur and guarantee the brothers against possible loss, the picturesque author had died, the exact time and place unknown. When Poe reviewed the Glass book, he wrote, "We confess that we regarded the first announcement of this *rara avis* with an evil and suspicious eye. . . . Mr. Reynolds was quizzing us—the brothers Harper were hoaxed— and Messieurs Anthon & Co. were mistaken. . . . We now solemnly make a recantation of our preconceived opinions."

Poe used up all his kind words on Sedgwick of Massachusetts and Glass of Ohio. By the time he was finished reading another Harper novel, *Norman Leslie*, by Theodore Sedgwick Fay of New York, he was ready to dip his pen into the caustic ink that was already making him famous as a critic. "Well!—here we have it! This is *the* book bepuffed, beplastered and be-mirrored: the book 'attributed to' Mr. Blank, and 'said to be from the pen of' Mr. Asterisk: the book which has been 'about to appear'—'in press'—'in progress'—'in preparation' —and 'forthcoming' [apparently the brothers kept reviewers well posted]: the book 'graphic' in anticipation—'talented' *a priori*—and God knows what *in prospectu*, for the sake of everything puffed, puffing, and puffable, let us take a look at its contents." Fay had said in his preface that, while the story was founded on fact, he had taken certain licenses and had transformed the character of a young lady.

Whereupon Poe exclaimed, "Oh, fi! Mr. Fay—oh, Mr. Fay, fi!" He detailed the plot, which involved a handsome Italian rogue and the American girl with the transformed character, and then let go with his critical opinion, "the most inestimable piece of balderdash with which the common sense of the good people of America was ever so openly or villainously insulted. . . . As regards Mr. Fay's *style* it is unworthy of a school boy."

On November 2, 1835, Theodore S. Fay returned to New York for seven months' stay. *Norman Leslie* had been published two weeks earlier and there was scarcely a copy of the first edition left unsold at Cliff Street. The only sour note in Fay's homecoming song was rendered by Poe in December, but the literati of New York were angered by Poe's outburst and flattered their New York author with good reviews, good dinners, and good wine. A dramatized version of the novel, written by Louisa H. Medina and produced by her husband, Thomas S. Hamblin, enjoyed a two-month run at the American Theatre on the Bowery; on February 18, 1836, a benefit performance was given, netting Fay $750.* For several months during the winter and spring, Fay earned $20 a week editing the *Mirror* for General Morris, and also received $478.50 from Harper's as his share of profits on the first edition of *Norman Leslie.* Paying only $70 a month for board and room, he was able to liquidate some of his more than $2,000 of indebtedness, but needed more money before he and his wife could sail in June for London.

Believing in the way of all authors—a laudable trait—that publishers should be an ever-present help in times of financial strain, Fay went to Cliff Street several times that spring to ask the brothers for advances and loans. They advanced him $1,000 on the second and stereotyped edition of *Norman Leslie* and on a further novel, advances that, unhappily, Fay was to forget about. In making these advances, the brothers were taking little risk, for everybody seemed to be buying new books that spring without much attention to price; money was plentiful and the currency inflated. The brothers also agreed to loan Fay $1,500. But, because hazards of travel and residence abroad introduced a considerable element of risk, they asked him to obtain two endorsers for the note, which they then discounted to cover interest for one year at 7 percent. Fay also had to pay for a year's insurance on his life in the amount of the note at the request of General Morris, who endorsed it along with another friend, E. A. Jones. Going abroad and not knowing

* This is Fay's figure, given in his *Statement* (1845). According to *The Knickerbocker*, February, 1836, Mr. Hamblin presented Fay a check for $1,044.

when he would return, Fay himself was not too sure about his future and asked Wesley whether the firm would buy all rights to *Norman Leslie.* "You ought not to sell it for $500," Wesley replied, and Fay was reassured. He and Mrs. Fay bought passage on the packet ship *Montreal,* which had brought Frederick Saunders to New York on the incoming voyage. It was scheduled to depart for London on June 1, but, being wind-bound, the vessel tarried in the New York harbor till June 8. Busy months at the American Embassy in London and later in Berlin gave Fay little time for writing anything except articles mailed back to the *Mirror.* The year was to pass quickly without his having even begun the promised Harper novel.

Somewhere on the Atlantic the *Montreal* met another vessel, also with an editor of the *Mirror* on its passenger list. Nathaniel Parker Willis was returning to New York, with his English bride, after several years abroad, during which time he sent articles to Morris, some of them so indiscreet that when portions were reissued in book form in England Willis was subjected to criticism—one attack published by Captain Marryat being considered by Willis so personal that he demanded satisfaction, and shots were exchanged between them. Willis had a longer editorial association with Morris than Fay had, but unlike Fay Willis did not add slender earnings as a writer to income as a foreign service officer—that welcome avocation of American authors in the nineteenth century.

In 1831 before going "a-Willising in foreign countries" (Poe's phrase) for the *Mirror,* Willis had contracted with the brothers for the publication of a book of poetry, the first poem of which, *Poem Delivered Before the Society of United Brothers at Brown University,* gave a long, cumbersome title to a small 76-page book. It sold for 62½ cents a copy. The brothers were not the first publisher to appreciate the literary genius of young Willis, nor the last for that matter, but they published only the one book for Willis, who was one of the most widely read authors of mid-nineteenth-century America.

Having published his work in anthologies, the brothers hoped that William Cullen Bryant might come to 82 Cliff Street with a work of his own. And so he did—on June 8, 1836—to contract for a third edition of his *Poems.* Did he take the initiative? Probably so. In April, shortly after his return from nearly two years in Europe, he went to see the brothers about their taking over his collected poems from the Boston firm of Russell, Odiorne, and Metcalf, with whom he had made a short-term agreement two years earlier. (The first edition had been published in New York by Elam Bliss in 1832.) After talking with the brothers, Bryant wrote his wife, "If I had been at home I might have done this earlier and touched the proceeds."

Bryant's Harper contract called for a royalty of 25 cents a copy, the amount he had received from the Boston firm, and he was paid $625 for a first printing of 2,500 copies. For this third edition he added 12 new poems, making 105 altogether. Bryant thought that it was better printed than the second edition had been. He helped with the book's design, asking the artist, R. W. Weir, to draw a vignette title page. Weir's title page was exquisitely done, showing that he could produce a work of art in miniature as well as on the vast scale of "The Embarkation of the Pilgrims," which he was then engaged in painting for the rotunda of the United States Capitol. Bryant's 274-page book contained poems for which he was famous even then—"Thanatopsis," which he had written at the age of twenty, and other oft-memorized poems such as "Forest Hymn," beginning "The Groves were God's First Temples." Reviewing the Harper edition, Poe wrote in the *Messenger*, "In regard to his [Bryant's] proper rank among American poets there should be no question whatever: Few—*at least few who are fairly before the American public* [Poe's italics are a revelation of his ego] have more than very shallow claims to a rivalry with the author of Thanatopsis."

Most pictures we now see of Bryant show him as an elderly man with flowing beard. But at the time he was dealing with Harper's he was a far-from-patriarchal forty-two, only a few months older than James. Bryant was highly esteemed by the literati of New York. In the spring of 1836, on returning from his European trip, twenty-five of them signed an invitation to a public dinner in honor of his contributions to American literature, an invitation which out of modesty he declined to accept. How did the poetic, sensitive Bryant get along with the busy and practical-minded brothers? What was the attitude of each to the other? Their meetings were probably concerned only with business matters at hand, with a minimum of literary shop talk. For them, he was America's leading poet, whose book they would know how to produce well and market widely. For him, they were merchants who could solidly establish him as a poet; according to William Charvat in *Literary Publishing in America, 1790-1850*, "His [Bryant's] professional poetic career did not begin until the Harpers, with their tremendous market in the West, brought out a series [of printings] at their own risk." A further revision of his *Poems* came out in 1839, and in 1840 he was to give them an anthology of American poetry. During these two years, also, he was to be the go-between when arrangements by the gifted young son of Bryant's Boston friend, Richard Henry Dana, Sr., were being made to publish *Two Years Before the Mast*. Thus he was often on Cliff Street. Perhaps he had the Harpers in mind when in 1855 at the Crystal Palace banquet of authors and publishers, he said, to the accompaniment of laughter and applause: "I have often wondered that among the subjects which have attracted the pens of authors, no one has ever thought of writing the Lives of Eminent Booksellers. What a study it would be to portray the rise, the progress, the characters of the Publishers—to describe the generous bearing of the Bookseller who takes the author's manuscript, and, with scarcely a glance, consigns it to the Press, pays the author a handsome compensation, and only retains a trifling fee, scarcely worth mentioning, for himself."

But Bryant of the *Evening Post* was never as close to the brothers as his rival, Colonel Stone of the *Commercial Advertiser*, whose recent books, *Tales and Sketches* and *Matthias and His Impostures*, a study of a fanatical free-lance preacher and murderer, were more to their interest than poetry. The rivalry between the two editors had come to blows several years earlier. In April, 1831, the *Commercial Advertiser* printed an article slandering Bryant by name. Bryant was egged on by William Leggett to attack Stone. They met on Broadway early one morning (Philip Hone, the ex-mayor, was shaving and observed the fracas from his window). Bryant attempted to use a horse whip, but Stone, who was the stronger of the two, snatched the whip and became the aggressor till by-standers separated them. The following day Leggett challenged Stone to a duel, naming his friend Prosper Wetmore as his second. Stone accepted the challenge and asked Robert Sands to represent him. After the two seconds had corresponded for two weeks, the affair was dropped by mutual consent, everyone's honor somehow satisfied.

Early in 1836 Edgar Allan Poe put together a collection of his short stories, wrote "Tales of the Folio Club" on the title page, and asked Thomas W. White, his "boss" on the *Southern Literary Messenger*, who might best influence the Harpers to publish them. Perhaps Paulding. White posted the manuscript with a note to his friend Paulding, who replied on March 3 that he had no influence with the brothers, and indeed should have none for his taste did not conform to that of the public; anyway, they had a reader, he noted sourly, "by whose judgment they are guided in their publications, and like other traders are governed by their anticipations of profit and loss, rather than [by] any intrinsic merit of a work or its author." Two weeks later Paulding wrote Poe that the reader could from long experience tell almost to a certainty what would succeed. Presumably this oracle of editorial wisdom was still John Inman, but Paulding did not care for the *censor librorum* whose pen was so respected at 82 Cliff Street. He was to say later that he wanted his publisher to say "yes" or "no" to his book without consulting any *reader*. Perhaps he had got his way at the time he was writing to Poe, for his best seller *Life of George Washington* had been accepted and was off for an eventual run of nine printings.

The Harper reader advised against publication of Poe's *Tales* and it was Paulding's unhappy task to pass the bad news along to Richmond. But Poe too was a critic, accustomed to pass on the merits of what men wrote; he was curious to know why his manuscript was rejected and wrote to the brothers on June 30 to ask. Wesley's reply is so skillful and sympathetic that it deserves to be quoted:

We have the honour to acknowledge the receipt of yours dated the 30 inst. Since it was written, the mss. to which you refer have reached you safely, as we learn from Mr. Paulding, who has been so informed we presume by Mr. White.

The reasons why we declined publishing them were threefold: First, because the greater portion of them had already appeared in print. Secondly, because they consisted of detached tales and pieces; and our long experience has taught us that both these are very serious objections to the success of any publication. Readers in this country have a decided and strong preference for works (especially fiction) in which a single and connected story occupies the whole volume, or number of volumes, as the case may be; and we have always found that republication of magazine articles, known to be such, are the most unsaleable of all literary performances. The third objection was equally cogent. The papers are too learned and mystical. They would be understood and relished only by a very few—not by the multitude. The number of readers in this country capable of appreciating and enjoying such writings as those you submitted to us is very small indeed. We were therefore inclined to believe that it was for your own interest not to publish them. It is all important to an author that his *first* work should be popular. Nothing is more difficult, in regard to literary reputation, than to overcome the injurious effect of a first failure.

We are pleased with your criticisms [in the *Messenger*] generally—although we do not always agree with you in particular, we like the bold, decided, energetic tone of your animadversions, and shall take pleasure in forwarding to you all the works we publish—or at least such of them as are worthy of your notice. We are obliged to publish works, occasionally, which it would scarcely be expected of the Messenger to make the subject of comment.

The last number of the Messenger came to hand last evening, and in our opinion fully sustains the high character which it has acquired for itself. The notices of the Life of Washington, and Sallust we presume will prove highly pleasing to Mr. Paulding and Professor Anthon.

The closing paragraphs of Wesley's letter not only took the sting out of the rejection but were also a sincere recognition of Poe's critical gifts. Later that year Wesley forwarded to Richmond a review copy of the newly published *Letters, Conversations, and Recollections of S. T. Coleridge,* a book that undoubtedly influenced Poe considerably; he gave it an enthusiastic review. Before Poe received Wesley's letter, he had asked his friend Edward W. Johnson, of the College of South Carolina, to send his manuscript *Tales* to Frederick Saunders. But, convinced by Wesley's argument, he recalled it and began working on a book-length story. Today's quick judgment might be that Wesley gave Poe bad advice and that his *Folio Club* would have sold. But this reflects later reader interest and a high rating of Poe as a literary figure, neither of which conditions existed in the 1830's. Even as late as 1849, James T. Fields of Boston was urging his author Nathaniel Hawthorne to expand a novelette called *The Scarlet Letter* into a full-length novel —again this was good contemporary advice based on a knowledge of what readers of fiction wanted when they went into bookstores.

Having done so well with Catherine Sedgwick's *The Linwoods* the year before, it is perhaps surprising that the brothers were dragging their feet early in 1836 on purchasing the plates of her earlier books. The author wrote to her brother, Charles, on February 4 saying that the Harpers had promised to make her an offer "as soon as the French question was settled. . . . I suppose our President-king's offer [Jackson's proposed settlement of American claims for injuries to shipping during the Napoleonic Wars] to his brother sovereign must first be known to be accepted. I trust Harper will choose to repurchase the copyrights that have been sold, and then, for better or worse, we shall have it in our hands." On July 22 she wrote again to Charles, urging him to conclude the arrangements. With commendable concern for sales, she asked him to tell the brothers that their correspondents in New England country towns should be reminded that the new book was written for popular consumption. But the brothers were too busy reissuing Paulding's earlier works to take on Miss Sedgwick's quite yet—maybe *Hope Leslie* later. However, *The Poor Rich Man and the Rich Poor Man* came out in November. "I think I understand the secret of its success," Miss Sedgwick wrote on March 8, 1837, to Miss K. M. Sedgwick, her favorite niece. "It is like bread stuff . . . suited to the market, the thing wanted."

On November 22, 1835, Wesley wrote to John P. Kennedy, leading littérateur of Baltimore, "we usually share profits . . . equally. We publish for Miss Sedgwick, for Messers Paulding, Simms, Slidell, etc. upon these terms." Lieutenant Alexander Slidell was already a famous young writer before he signed a half-profits contract in 1835 for *The American in England*. Ten years before he had taken a year's leave of absence from the Navy for reasons of health, during which time he toured Spain, meeting Washington Irving and Obadiah Rich, and in 1829 published his immediately popular *A Year in Spain*. It was issued by Hilliard, Gray, Little & Wilkins in Boston and in 1830 by C. & H. Carvill in New York. In London it was issued first by John Murray and later by Bentley. The Murray edition prompted Irving, then in England, to write home, "It is quite the fashionable book of the day, and spoken of in the highest terms in the highest circles. If the Lieutenant were in London at present he would be quite a lion." Irving had reason for pride in his friend's literary success for he had been indebted to Slidell for help on nautical matters when he was writing his life of Columbus.

The American in England, despite rhetorical flourishes so popular at the time, is interesting reading even today, with its colorful pen pictures of midshipmen scurrying over decks and up masts and descriptions of diners in a London restaurant. ("Having completed my observations under cover of the sirloin, I deposed my knife and fork, and the watchful waiter hastened to bear away the formidable bulwark by whose aid I had been enabled to reconnoitre the inmates of the coffee-room.") While reading proofs of this book, Slidell was also writing *Spain Revisited* in two volumes, and revising *A Year in Spain*, both of which works were published with gusto by the brothers in 1836 and read avidly by his growing public. In his revision of *A Year in Spain*, Slidell added a third volume which the publisher of the first edition had urged him to omit for reasons of economy. "It may be an inducement to the purchasers," Clark wrote in *The Knickerbocker*, "though the reputation of the publishers renders this praise supererogatory—to mention that the work is well executed, and clad in a garb 'neat but not gaudy.'" Slidell also took time out in his two years as a literary land-lubber to marry Catherine A. Robinson of New York and, in the following year, at the request of a maternal uncle and by special act of the State Legislature, to add his mother's name to his own. Thereafter, as an author and Navy officer, he was known by the name of Mackenzie.

Evert Duyckinck, the bookseller whose name was joined with "J. & J. Harper" on the title page of the first Harper book, had two sons who were to follow the pursuit of literature in New York. The elder, Evert, Jr., was one year old when *Seneca's Morals* was published and had often heard his father and others tell how the Duyckinck name had helped the brothers start their famous business. After young Evert graduated from Columbia in 1835, he and his bosom friend, Cornelius Mathews, decided that literature and not law (which both were studying) was their true calling. They would articulate the nascent voice of young literary America. Obviously the thing to do was to start a magazine and obviously the publishers for it were the Harpers, who might want to return a favor to a Duyckinck. So in 1836, fired with youthful zeal, they went to Cliff Street to call on James to do a selling job. They reminded James that he was doing very well with Paulding's *Works*, some of which had originally been issued as fugitive pieces. What would he think of a series of satirical articles on New York that would do for these days what those written by the youthful Paulding, Irving, *et al.*, had done for an earlier period?

The hearty and sentimental James agreed at once, and if any of the other three brothers had any qualms, they remembered that they had done extremely well with publishing sermons serially and it might be a good idea to try a literary series. In fact *Literary* would be a good name for the magazine. Messrs. Duyckinck and Mathews proudly brought in the manuscript for the first number and a format was agreed to. It would fall smartly into even forms of forty-eight pages. None of the brothers took time to read proofs until stereotypes were made and a publication date of November 15 was agreed to. Then one of them, probably Wesley, took the proofs home. He was shocked by what he read.

It fell to James to break the bad news to young Evert. They could not go on with the magazine. One of the pieces they considered libelous, and as much as they hated to do so they would have to decline to publish. If Evert could interest someone else in venturing this first number, they would gladly turn over the stereotypes. Duyckinck did get the Henderson Green imprint, without being sued, apparently, but according to cataloguer Demarest this first and only issue of *Literary* "failed to secure popularity."*

Anyway, Gaylord Clark's *Knickerbocker* was serving the cause of the literati very well and it already had one New York rival to deal with. This was the *American Monthly Magazine*, whose two editors

---

* Demarest says that Duyckinck not only verified this bibliographical statement shortly before his death (1878) but also gave Demarest a copy of the number, which in turn was passed on to James Harper, Jr.

also had ambitions in 1835 to publish books with the Harper imprint. They were Charles Fenno Hoffman and Henry William Herbert. Hoffman had in fact established *The Knickerbocker* in 1832, but after a few numbers he left New York to go West for reasons of health. Letters he wrote (a popular literary device) were brought out in book form in 1835. The brothers had, of course, known Hoffman because of his editorial connections and also as the son of a famous judge and the nephew of their author Gulian Verplanck. They also knew that Hoffman's half-sister, Matilda, had been engaged to Washington Irving and that her untimely death was one of the reasons that Irving had left America in 1815 and had never married. But Hoffman's manuscript deserved publication on its own merits; it was entitled *A Winter in the West*. A two-volume work of nearly seven hundred pages, it was to stay in print for many years.

Herbert, later better known as "Frank Forester," also had good family connections. Born of aristocratic English parents and graduated from Caius College, Cambridge, he had come to the United States apparently at the urging of his family, who were displeased with his predilections for sports and gambling. In New York he made his living by teaching Greek and Latin to schoolboys until the *American Monthly* was launched. He was a tall, muscular man and wore a heavy mustache, the ends of which often needed to be twirled as he talked. Always well dressed, he was popular with the young bucks around town, and his English accent and mannerisms helped him socially. He brought the manuscript of his novel to Cliff Street after a few chapters had been printed in the *Monthly*. The Harper reader recommended publication but apparently urged that no further portions be serialized. Herbert could agree to this proposal more easily than he could to another: that the novel be published anonymously. The brothers finally convinced him that public interest would be aroused by an anonymous book, and as such *The Brothers, A Tale of the Fronde* came out in July, 1835.* This novel makes interesting reading today, when historical romances are more sophisticated; and Herbert's background knowledge of mid-seventeenth century France was equal to his gifts as a storyteller. The surprise ending to *The Brothers*, when the father of the noble-born Isabel de Coucy is disclosed, would do credit to any denouement that O. Henry ever wrote.

---

* In *Henry William Herbert: The American Publishing Scene*, Luke White says, "Results vindicated the publishers' judgment. . . . The edition of 2500 was exhausted within a few months. Despite Herbert's urging the Harpers did not see fit to undertake another printing and there is no record that the book was ever reissued in America."

Still another young man with literary ambitions, Rufus Wilmot Griswold, stopped in at 82 Cliff Street one March day in 1836. He knew the place well since he had been on the Harper payroll in the winter of 1833-34, during his first stay in New York.* This time he came not to ask for a job or to leave a manuscript but to look up his old friend Marcus Butler. Butler's work over for the day, the two young men started out for an evening together. Walking along Clinton Street, they had to look for shelter as a sudden rainstorm burst upon them. They dashed for the nearby house of Mrs. John Angell, a friend of Butler's. Here the dripping Griswold was introduced to Caroline, the nineteen-year-old daughter of Mrs. Angell. It was love at first sight and the only genuine attachment of Griswold's life, although he was to form both sentimental and marital ties with ladies in later years. He married Caroline the next year, but his happiness ended five years later when his young wife died in childbirth. Griswold was inconsolable; his behavior over the body of his beloved was as macabre as any described in the tales of his friend Poe.

The years of 1835 and 1836 were noteworthy ones for the gentlemen at 82 Cliff Street as they developed a strong list of original American books. Noteworthy because of Stone and Morris and Dunlap and Schoolcraft and Bryant and Sedgwick and Paulding, names of recognition and repute. Noteworthy because of Dr. Doane and Professor Anthon, leaders in special fields to be worked. But most of all these were noteworthy years because of Longfellow and Stephens and Fay and Simms and Ingraham and Slidell (Mackenzie) and Poe and Duyckinck and Hoffman and Herbert, young literary talents just coming into their own. Excepting Duyckinck, the youngest, their average age in 1835 was between twenty-eight and twenty-nine.

For those who study the American publishing scene in the nineteenth century, an obvious fact to consider is the absence of international copyright until 1891. Other facts are that Putnam in New York was a leading supporter of the cause of international copyright and that Fields in Boston often paid royalties to English authors even though under no legal obligations to do so. Also that the Harpers became the leaders in publishing English reprints and were enabled

* Demarest's note under Griswold's name in his *Catalogue* reads in part: "Dr. Griswold began his career in New York as a compositor in the office of H. & B., and worked in the same 'alley' as the compiler at 79 and 81 Cliff Street." Since Demarest's employment began in 1833 and the two Cliff Street buildings were torn down in 1834, the time of Griswold's first residence in New York was probably the winter of 1833-34. Furthermore, neither Griswold's son nor his biographer was able to account for Griswold's activities during that winter. For a period Griswold did some preaching, which led to his being addressed both as "Reverend" and "Doctor."

because of unparalleled manufacturing facilities to turn out vast quantities of them at low prices. From these facts easy generalizations have been drawn, one that American literature, with the possible exception of Mathew and Henry Carey, had to await publishers Putnam and Fields to bring it to profitable flower. Another generalization is that most publishers were so busy pocketing profits on cheap reprints that American authors were discouraged from writing or found their books unable to meet the reprint competition. The record of Harper & Brothers as they fostered, promoted, and sold American authors in the 1830's seems to question such easy generalizations.

CHAPTER VII

Depression Years

1837–1838

ONE OF NEW YORK's best-known and most-interesting citizens in the nineteenth century (surprisingly overlooked by biographers) was Dr. John Wakefield Francis. In his book of reminiscences, published in 1866, "Harper's Book Entertainment" appears at the head of a page discussing literature and the arts. "About thirty years after [Mathew Carey's 1802 gathering of publishers] I was one of a large assembly brought together by the Brothers Harper's great entertainment," Dr. Francis recalled. "I still see in 'my mind's eye' the prominent group of American authors who participated." The "great entertainment" that Dr. Francis remembered was no doubt the Booksellers' Association dinner for authors held at the City Hotel on Thursday, March 30, 1837, with 277 authors, publishers, and booksellers attending. Although James and Fletcher Harper figured prominently, the dinner was sponsored by the New York book trade as a whole. Dr. Francis remembered Chancellor James Kent, widely respected for his *Commentaries on American Law,* as one of the prominent authors attending. Other writers who spoke or proposed toasts included Washington Irving, James K. Paulding, L. Gaylord Clark, General George P. Morris, Edgar Allan Poe, and ex-mayor Philip Hone, who noted in his diary that it "was the greatest dinner I was ever at," with the possible exception of the one given to Washington Irving on his return from Europe. In his speech Hone chided the publishers for using bad paper and ink (books printed in London or Paris were much superior) and urged them to "discountenance all works calculated to infringe the laws of propriety and good manners, to bring into discredit the wise institutions of our country, or to subvert the principles of religion and morality."

Before Hone spoke, letters were read from distinguished men who were unable to attend the dinner, including J. Fenimore Cooper, Daniel and Noah Webster, Mathew Carey, Gulian Verplanck, and Lieutenant Governor Samuel T. Armstrong, at that time the oldest bookseller in Boston. Armstrong had written a toast to "The Booksellers of New York: Liberal, enterprising and prosperous. May prosperity still wait on their enterprize [*sic*] and enterprize follow prosperity." According to the New York *American,*

Mr. James Harper being here long and loudly called for, finally arose, and observed that he was at a loss to know why he should be singled out to respond to the compliment of Governor A., as there were many of the trade present greatly his seniors. Besides, it was well known to his brethren, that he was no orator—that it was entirely out of his line to make *speeches* —that he was simply an humble maker of *books*—and that this alone was his profession. Therefore, although the subject and the occasion were of a highly prolific character—still he should not attempt a speech on the occasion—for if he should, he would assuredly find himself in the dilemma of a certain Massachusetts orator, who, while addressing a public assembly, unfortunately lost the thread of his discourse, and, hesitating to recover his lost ideas, was addressed from the gallery by a raw country lad,—"I say, Mister, I guess you're stuck!" And, Mr. President (added Mr. H., after a pause) so am I!—(Laughter and applause).

His modesty, however, did not keep James from proposing a toast later on, one of the few that the assemblage drank standing, "The memory of Walter Scott and other illustrious authors who, in our own time, have built up intellectual temples for the admiration of future ages, and rested from their labors." Messrs. Putnam, Dearborn, Collins, and Carvill were among other New York publishers who gave toasts, as was thirty-one-year-old Fletcher, who as first vice-president of the association was called on to take the chair before the banquet was over.

The outstanding address of the evening was made by Colonel William L. Stone. His speech not only credited publishers with encouraging American writers ("It is but a few years since we began to think of having native authors") but also gave statistics to show that original works were gradually outnumbering English reprints. He thought American authors were doing well financially; "The house of Carey, Lea & Blanchard paid $30,000 last year [1836] to American authors, and our own firm of Harper & Brothers has 'transferred the deposits' to about the same amount for several years." In fact, the American people were fortunate because in "no country are books more read, or furnished to the people at lower prices."

These were exciting words. The gentlemen who listened to them forgot about their starched shirts and swallowtail coats and applauded vigorously. Their faces, lighted by flaring gas lamps, beamed their approval. They were bookmen, American bookmen, making an important contribution to the cultural life of the nation.

Newspaper publishers other than Stone also spoke at the banquet, including Charles King, a man of wealth, who along with Verplanck had founded the New York *American*, of which he was still editor and publisher. King sounded an intellectual note, saying that everyone looked to the authors, publishers, and booksellers for the education of the rising generation. "Education is the greatest aim which writers and publishers can propose to themselves—education wide-spread, popular, and founded on religion." King often spoke on educational themes and twelve years later he was to be installed as the ninth president of Columbia. One newspaper editor was not invited, James Gordon Bennett, who had founded the New York *Herald* two years earlier. He was infuriated, although he well knew that his critical and often flippant attacks on authors, editors, and public citizens made him unpopular. He wrote in the *Herald*, "They [the committee] debated half a day on the important question,—'*Shall James Gordon Bennett be invited to our festival?*' and decided in the negative, thus gaining one of the greatest triumphs that literature ever won." But he did attend, invited or not, and, refusing to be ignored, got to his feet during the evening to propose a toast "to the American newspaper press."

Hoffman attended the dinner, although he was not mentioned in the eight-column story in the *American*. Other Harper authors or soon-to-be authors present were Bryant, Leggett, Fitz-Greene Halleck, Herbert, Dr. Caleb Ticknor, and Matthew L. Davis. Also John G. Chapman, the artist whose illustrations for the new Harper editions of the *Fairy Book* and *Pilgrim's Progress* were currently being admired. Chapman may have sat with two other famous artists who attended, Henry Inman and eighty-one-year-old Colonel John Trumbull. But the most famous man there was America's best-loved author, Washington Irving, who proposed a toast to his friend the English poet Samuel Rogers. It was probably Irving's longest public address, though it occupied less than five column inches in the *American*.

The 1837 banquet was so significant to J. C. Derby that in his *Fifty Years Among Authors, Books and Publishers* (1884) he devoted a chapter to it even though he did not attend, being at that time only a neophyte bookseller in Auburn, New York. He believed that the only man who had attended that dinner still living when his book came out was Charles Francis, who had published *Birds of America* from his place on Broadway. But when Francis had proposed a toast, it was not to Audubon but to "The author of the 'Linwoods'—in the midst of the bright lights around us, let us not forget those at *Home*"—a pun on an earlier Sedgwick title and a reminder of the fact that even successful lady authors did not attend public dinners with their male counterparts. Derby made his first call at 82 Cliff Street the following year when he came to New York for Henry Ivison, his Auburn employer. "I recall now, as though it were but yesterday," Derby was to write in his autobiography, "the pleasant smile and courteous manner with which I was greeted by each of the four brothers."

One New York bookseller who would have attended the dinner gladly was William Gowans, who had started his forty-year career about 1830. Years later he was to write to the firm about his frequent visits to 82 Cliff Street:

I always paid cash for my small purchases, and soon became intimate with James Harper. One day he asked me if I ever bought on credit. I answered that I never did, adding that I had once or twice made the attempt, and had always been refused, and had come to the conclusion that nobody would trust me to the amount of five dollars. He jumped up from his arm-chair, and clapped his great hand on my shoulder, with the words, "You look like a brave, honest young man; I'll trust you for anything you want." This was, with one exception, the first expression of kindness and confidence that had greeted me in my new home; the other was from a kind-hearted Quaker, a true gentleman, like James Harper. In both cases the kindness was proffered, not solicited. An offer of credit for half a million of dollars would not now produce upon me a tenth part of the effect produced by this offer from James Harper. That incident is stamped upon my memory. While I live I can never forget it or the man who made it.

If Gowans did attend the dinner, he would have returned home with Poe, who was living in the same house. Poe had toasted the "Monthlies of Gotham, their distinguished editors, and their vigorous *collabora-*

teurs," a nice compliment to Gaylord Clark, who in turn ingratiated himself with the Harpers by proposing the "protection of the Home Manufacturers, whether of the hands or the intellect."

Another likely member of the feast was Dr. Asa Greene, whose book, *A Glance at New York,* was privately published that spring. In this work, Dr. Greene took a long look at "The City Government, Theatres, Hotels, Churches, Mobs, Monopolies, Learned Professions, Newspapers, Rogues, Dandies, Fires and Firemen, Water and Other Liquids, etc. etc." Dr. Greene enjoyed a small reputation as a satirical novelist and wrote with a degree of humor, as indicated in this counsel to pedestrians on how to cross a street: "To perform the feat with any degree of safety, you must button your coat tight about you, see that your shoes are secure at the heels, settle your hat firmly on your head, look up street and down street, at the self-same moment, to see what carts and carriages are upon you and then run for your life."

Ignoring or perhaps reveling in such risks, Dr. Greene explored all parts of town, and devoted a full chapter to New York's literary progress. He was especially impressed with the growth of libraries. The New York Society Library, founded in 1754 with seven hundred volumes, now boasted twenty-five thousand, a number greater than either of the other two general subscription libraries—the Mercantile Library Association and the Apprentices' Library. (The year 1837 had been a special one for the Mercantile Library Association, as their former Cliff Street landlords printed their *Systematic Catalogue,* a 324-page book, replete with indexes and appendices.) A library catering to a restricted clientele, that of The New-York Historical Society, had an estimated ten thousand volumes.

On his precarious pedestrian tours, Dr. Greene counted about sixty booksellers (he had for a while been one of them), ten of whom sold only in outdoor stalls. "Several booksellers who are doing a large indoor business in this city, first began by doing a small one in the open street," he wrote. "The book trade, at the best, is one of little profit and great hazard"—an unhappy complaint booksellers still make in our modern day of increased costs and discount houses. Being something of a bibliophile, Greene found better typography in books being printed in Boston, binding on the whole deplorable, although the increasing use of cloth was "a decided improvement over the binding in boards, which was a common use, for novels and other light works, ten years ago." But the worst feature in modern publishing, he concluded, was the "vile paper" on which most of the books were being printed "and in this respect the Philadelphia publishers beat ours."

According to his census there were six firms publishing books for the general trade. "But it is believed that the amount of books, published by Harper & Brothers, equals, if it does not exceed, that of all other publishers in this city. We are informed that the number of volumes of all sorts, issued by them in a single year is not less than *one million*. Last year they published about 20,000 volumes of original American works."* Pearl Street was described by Greene as "that great mart of business and the principal scene of wholesale operations."

In 1837 the brothers purchased the plates of a multivolume set of classical works from George Dearborn, when he went out of business. He was known for his fine editions and for publishing the *American Monthly*.† The Harper purchase included works of Addison, Boswell, Burke, Dryden, Samuel Johnson, Plutarch, and Shakespeare (eight volumes). It was not the first time the brothers had handled Shakespeare's works. In February, 1821, they had set up and printed a ten-volume *Dramatic Works*, including engravings taken from the famous Boydell plates. They apparently made stereotypes, for they reissued this edition again in 1824 and 1826. The standard literary works from Dearborn's list fitted nicely into a growing category of books for schools and colleges, and as sturdy, back-list titles helped offset their loss, the following year, of the textbooks of Professor Charles Davies. Teaming up as a partner with young A. S. Barnes of Hartford in 1838 and taking his four Harper titles with him, Davies began earning publishing profits as well as royalties. By 1845, A. S. Barnes was established in New York and Davies was turning out even more textbooks, soon to sell at the rate of 200,000 copies a year. Derby says they were the most celebrated series of mathematics books ever published in America.

Sometime after the booksellers' dinner, James went abroad again. It seems likely that he would have sailed before May 10, 1837, when the New York banks suspended specie payments, precipitating one of the country's worst financial panics. By late July and in early August the Harper brothers who remained at Cliff Street were experiencing difficulties. But on July 8 they still had enough cash on hand to help

---

* At the booksellers' dinner Colonel Stone credited half a million volumes a year to Harper's, and something more than that to Carey, Lea & Blanchard in Philadelphia. Dr. Greene also made a survey of periodical publishing in New York, but his statistics do not tally with others published soon after by a more authoritative source, Horace Greeley's *New Yorker*. According to the issue of July 8, 1837, New York produced ninety-three periodicals: eight quarterlies, twenty monthlies, seven semimonthlies, thirty-three weeklies, nine semiweeklies, and sixteen dailies.

† "Our city is fortunate in the possession of two such publishers as Harper and Dearborn," said the *American Monthly* in January, 1835, "the one supplying us with novelty after novelty, in a constant and luxurious flow, the other sending forth at intervals his beautiful and correct editions of the standards of literature."

Simms get out of a financial hole—and to do a good stroke of business for themselves. On that day Simms wrote out a memorandum of agreement conveying all his rights to five titles, one still to be published, "for certain sums of money [not stated]—which though not enough —I am yet satisfied (perforce) to receive full compensation thereof, and which by this instrument I acknowledge myself to have received. . . ." Although hard-pressed, Simms was always the gentleman. His parenthetical "perforce" was a humorous and gallant fillip against necessity.

Paying cash for Simms's copyrights could not have been easy, however. Booksellers were asking for extended credit; some were going into bankruptcy. Payrolls had to be met and accounts receivable were falling off. The *New Yorker* noted on August 5 that "the Harpers . . . do not now announce a single work as in press," and on August 26, "In the height of and throughout the revulsion derisively styled the Panic of '34, the Harpers alone issued on an average of two new works per week or an aggregate of 20,000 volumes in the same time; now one work a month, and that a work of necessity or mercy—in fulfillment of some long-standing contract, or in reference to some present emergency—drags its slow length from the press."

The three brothers wondered whether they could keep going. An employee was later to describe what happened. "In 1837 I was an apprentice in their house. We boys used to think James Harper was of no more use to the firm than an ornamental fringe to the moon. He would sit and chat for hours when a friend came in, and apparently pay no attention to business. That year, when merchants were failing all over the country, he was in Europe. His brothers thought they would be compelled to stop payment, and go down with the rest. They held a long consultation; but could arrive at nothing satisfactory. Finally one of them suggested sending for James. They did so, and he arrived in the next boat. He had not been in the office an hour, before everything appeared changed as by magic. He said 'the House of Harper shall not go to the wall'—and it did not."

This catalytic quality of James endeared him to those who knew him well. Yet his hearty, extroverted, and earthy qualities were likely to offend more sensitive persons. Saunders considered him coarse, disliking particularly his habit of sitting with his feet on his desk. Neither James nor John had had as good a schooling as Wesley and Fletcher and they undoubtedly made mistakes in pronunciation and grammar, using words such as "ain't," even as Lincoln did. It was difficult for James to write a letter or compose a speech, as shown in some of his extant mayoralty papers. Even so, he was good at aphorisms, and one of his favorites was, "Observe carefully three rules and happiness will attend you: trust in God, pay your bills, and keep your bowels open."

Yes, they must pay their bills to keep solvent, James would have said. They could also trust God, but how about mere mortals? Had they collected from everyone possible to whom they had loaned money? Someone remembered the note of author Theodore Sedgwick Fay for $1,500 that had fallen due April 20. How about that? However, to call on endorsers for payment was out of the question, for such action would embarrass Fay, and his novel should be arriving at any time; in fact, it was overdue. Furthermore Van Buren had just named Fay secretary of the American legation in Berlin, and the brothers had great respect for embassy officials. John said he would ask his father-in-law, Abner Higgins, if he could take over the note. Higgins agreed to pay them the principal, as the note had good endorsers and would earn him interest. And he knew that his daughter would be pleased if he relieved some of her husband's worries. So the Fay note stayed in the family and the Higgins check for $1,500 added a cupful to the dwindling store of liquid assets at Cliff Street.

One brand-new author around to boost everyone's morale was John L. Stephens. He had been graduated from Columbia College in 1822 at seventeen and after studying law in Litchfield, Connecticut, had practiced for eight years in New York. Because of a throat ailment, brought on possibly by his vociferous activity as a Tammany Hall speaker, his physician advised that he travel abroad. He returned to New York in the autumn of 1836 after spending nearly two years in Egypt, Arabia, and the Holy Land. Some letters he wrote from abroad were handed to Hoffman, who printed them in the *American Monthly*. Copied widely in other papers, these letters had made him known to the brothers when he called on them shortly after his return. He may have brought with him a letter of introduction from "Uncle Philip," the Rev. Mr. Hawks, who had seen Stephens in London and urged him to write a book. According to one account, Stephens asked James Harper what books sold best.

"Travels sell about the best of anything we get ahold of," James replied. "They don't always go with a rush, like a novel by a celebrated author, but they sell longer, and in the end, pay better." He urged Stephens to write up his experiences, but Stephens replied that he had gone to out-of-the-way places, had traveled very fast, and made no notes that could now be useful.

"That's no matter," James retorted. "You went through and saw the signs. We have got plenty of books about those countries. You just pick out as many as you want, and I will send them home for you; you can dish up something."

Stephens did dish up something. By May, 1837, his book, *Incidents of Travel in Egypt, Arabia Petraea, and the Holy Land*, was being set in type. Early proofs were sent to Clark for selections to be used in *The Knickerbocker*. Clark was delighted, for here was an American who could write about travel and exploration as well as John Barrow, Hugh Murray, or any other Englishman. And he was as courageous and ingenious as a later T. E. Lawrence, dressing as Arabs dressed, speaking their language, and conforming to their customs. His book came out in late summer and by September Stephens was correcting and enlarging it. He signed an agreement for a second stereotyped edition, the first edition having been printed from type. He put up a welcome $400 "as a part of the amount necessary for getting up publication," and stipulated that after seven years he could purchase copyright and plates at the cost of the latter. The *New York Review* gave fifteen pages in its October issue to a criticism of the book written by Poe, who was intrigued by evidence brought forward by Stephens of the fulfillment of Biblical prophecy, a subject Poe was then concerned about. In his autobiographical novel, *Redburn*, Herman Melville tells of reading Stephens's "arid-looking book in a pale yellow cover," of having Stephens pointed out to him by his aunt one Sunday in church, and of being so fascinated by "this wonderful Arabian traveler" that he wanted to follow him home.

What financial writers called "the pressure" curtailed publication of other works and definitely ruled out Miss Sedgwick's earlier titles. Books on the 1837 list were those which were well advanced by early May or which received special preference because of their authors or sales potential. Among them were an abridged version of William Dunlap's *History of the State of New York* and Dr. Francis Hawks's *Contributions to the Ecclesiastical History of . . . Virginia*. Volume II of *Memoirs of Aaron Burr*, by Matthew L. Davis, got priority as did a rather moving miscellany of sermons, letters, and biographical sketch of the Negro preacher Samuel Haynes.* Miss Sedgwick's latest books

---

* The book was edited by the preacher's son, Lemuel, who wrote to the brothers two years later asking to purchase their interest in the plates, as he wanted an edition printed by "another establishment" which owed him money. When in return he received a Cliff Street statement of his account, he found that he had not been credited with a $100 payment he had made. He wrote, "Perhaps Messers John and Wesley Harper will recollect my paying them a $100 bill, Phoenix Bank, Hartford (yellow paper or reddish) last fall, for which the receipt was given. I have it by me and find it was overlooked in both Bills of your account rendered."

obviously could not be put off; anyway her *Live and Let Live* was well along and was issued in early summer. Her preface suggests that she wrote the book to help prepare young brides for an important responsibility, that of superintending domestic help. Having a fondness for capital *L*'s Miss Sedgwick gave the name Lucy Lee to the heroine of *Live and Let Live*, the story of a fourteen-year-old girl who left the home of a drunken father and God-fearing mother to enter domestic service. Lucy's trials and triumphs with a series of mistresses gave Miss Sedgwick an opportunity to take her readers inside wealthy homes in New York City while entertaining them with a success story of a virtuous girl who overcame all vicissitudes. Horatio Alger, Jr., was three years old when *Live and Let Live* was published; the book was probably in the library of the manse in which he grew up.

Miss Sedgwick's juvenile, *A Love Token for Children*, was published just in time for Christmas sales. The *New York Review* took this occasion to say that Miss Sedgwick was "the most agreeable living writer of fiction," and her romances, as compared to those of Cooper *et al.*, were "a pure spring among brackish water." Clark wrote in *The Knickerbocker*, "Miss Sedgwick is pursuing a literary path of usefulness and honour. Possessing a heart softened with the love of human kind, she delights to seize upon scenes and events of common life [which serve] to rob adversity of its sting." It was doubtless this quality of her writing that Wesley found so moving as he read proofs of her books for final corrections before they went to press. "In performing that office," Bryant once wrote, "he [Wesley] once remarked to me that he was fairly carried away by his emotions, and could not restrain himself from weeping profusely. I can assure the reader that it is no easy feat to draw tears from the eyes of a veteran proof-reader."

One book that obviously had to be postponed was *The Narrative of Arthur Gordon Pym, of Nantucket*. To be sure its author, Edgar Allan Poe, was a clever fellow and had followed Wesley's advice, writing a full-length novel. When he had brought the manuscript around to 82 Cliff Street personally in the spring of 1837, the Harpers had expected to publish it promptly. Announcements were soon sent to literary editors that it was "nearly ready." It was copyrighted on June 10 and the date of registry duly copied in the copyright book, but the brothers were under no legal obligation to offer it as a sop to bad times. In fact, a year's delay might be a good thing, since Poe's stinging review of Fay's *Norman Leslie* was still remembered by his rivals among the New York critics; the salve of time which soothes all bruises would heal that one too and give the *Narrative* a chance for better reviews later on.

But work was needed in the plant to cover salaries, etc. What could they undertake? As an answer to prayer, a fat, bulky manuscript came in from Alphonso Wetmore, Surveyor General for the State of Missouri. Entitled *Gazetteer of Missouri,* it had no knotty royalty or credit strings attached. It would keep everyone, including engravers, busy for several weeks, since it would make an octavo book of nearly four hundred pages of text, maps, surveys, sketches, and other illustrations. Such a work did not add literary treasures to the Harper hold, but it was a nice breeze from the West to keep the boat sailing along. It may have been this *Gazetteer* that prompted Professor Bradsher to say in his chapter "Book Publishers and Publishing," in the *Cambridge History of American Literature,* that as late as 1837 the House of Harper did printing for anyone who would bring it to them. Perhaps Bradsher was more knowledgeable of American literary history than he was of the economic facts of publishing.*

A few English reprints, including books by Bulwer, James, and Harrison Ainsworth, were also published during the summer and autumn. But two large volumes of Mrs. Sherwood's works, announced in May as "nearly ready," were postponed to 1838 and 1839. (Her earlier thirteen volumes had been issued in 1833.) That summer Frederick Saunders succeeded in publishing an English reprint, Harriet Martineau's *Travels in the United States,* without being challenged by Cliff Street, or by Philadelphia, for that matter. "Rumor adds," Horace Greeley wrote in the October 29th *New Yorker,* "that neither of our great publishing houses, who would otherwise have been eager to obtain it, have thought proper to make proposals for the American edition." It was not good business—especially during such hard times—to rush into print a book that was written by a lady who identified herself while in America with the extreme Abolitionists and wrote so severely of Southern slavery. This timidity of American publishers was strikingly in contrast to the zeal of their English brethren, who had be-

---

* How much outside book printing was undertaken is not known since no records were preserved. However, such printing was probably extensive, and references to it are occasionally found, as in *Rochester, the Water-Power City 1812-1854* by Blake F. McKelvey. Writing of Henry O'Reilly, editor of the *Advertiser,* Rochester's first daily newspaper, McKelvey tells of O'Reilly's efforts in 1836 to publish his 480-page book, *Sketches of Rochester.* "When the local publisher, William Alling, hesitated at the last moment to print the book in Rochester, the manuscript was rushed to New York by sleigh in five days and nights in order to secure the assistance of Harper Brothers." The book appeared with the Alling imprint.

sieged Miss Martineau as soon as the London press announced her return from America. Bentley, Colburn, and Saunders, Sr., waited upon her with offers up to £2,000 for a travel book if she would write one; Saunders's bid of £900 was accepted, apparently because she found him the least offensive of the "booksellers." The Harpers noted, however, that Miss Martineau's book sold well, and teamed up with young Saunders to issue her next book, *Retrospect of Western Travel,* in 1838.

The shadows of the 1837 panic lingered on Cliff Street for several years. On June 17, 1838, Longfellow wrote asking if the Harpers were interested in publishing a further work. (Probably *Hyperion,* which was published in New York in 1839 by Samuel Colman, who went bankrupt shortly after issuing the book.) They replied on June 25, "When the 'reaction' came on, it found us with extensive engagements on hand—and the state of the times have been so unfavorable that we have not been able to do much for the last year. Consequently we have still remaining on hand, and engaged, a large number of unpublished works—enough probably to last us until next spring. We are therefore compelled to decline negotiating for additional works at present. We have still on hand some of *Outre-Mer,* about 400 copies. It will take, we fear, a long time for the book business to recover—being generally the first to suffer and the last to recover."

Early in 1838, under constant pressure from his friend General Morris to do something about the Harper note, Fay wrote to Colonel Morgan L. Smith, who advised him on stock purchases, to ask if he would pay off the brothers. Fay promised to repay him in cash or through the proceeds of his new book. Smith replied that he did not have the funds, as he had suffered great losses in the panic. However, he went to see the brothers and wrote Fay that he found them ready to carry out their contract for his next novel. Their understanding was that should the novel (*The Countess Ida*) not be forthcoming, the endorsers would make good on the note. "The impress of truth," he wrote, "is all with the Harpers. . . . *I have heard the stories of all parties,* and as a friend, I would advise you to write a kind letter to the Harpers. Give them the whole cause of delay, etc., etc., and in as good time as you can, produce them *the* book. They feel hurt that you have neglected writing them."

Fay had also neglected to complete his novel. Having waited for it nearly two years, the brothers notified Morris in the latter part of 1838 that if the manuscript was not forthcoming, Higgins's (or Harper's) attorney would have to bring suit to recapture the principal and accrued interest on the note. Morris asked Fay to hurry up with his book, and Fay promised to mail it shortly after the first of the year. On January 7, 1839, Higgins's attorney obtained a judgment, which Morris resisted. Whereupon the attorney obtained a writ of seizure on the contents of Morris's office at the *Mirror*, but agreed to stay proceedings till the Fay manuscript should arrive. By June it had not come, and on the 27th Morris paid part of the principal of the note and the costs of the suit. In July of '39 the manuscript for *The Countess Ida* finally reached 82 Cliff Street with Fay's request that it be "a satisfaction as far as it would go of the judgment." Perhaps because their reader was less than enthusiastic over the manuscript or because business conditions were so depressed, the brothers told Morris that they were extremely reluctant to publish it. On their recommendation, but fruitlessly, Morris sent the manuscript to Lea & Blanchard in Philadelphia. On October 24, Morris wrote Fay, "The Harpers have your book in the press after a great deal of trouble to get them to print it on any terms. Blanchard & Lea [*sic*] would not touch it." However, the brothers contiued to procrastinate and did not publish *The Countess Ida* until July, 1840, a few months after Bentley issued it in London under the title *The Countess*.

Ingraham was proving to be a more dependable and profitable novelist than Fay. His *Burton, or, the Sieges* came out in the early summer of 1838. It was a sensational defamation of the early career of Aaron Burr, and according to the July *Knickerbocker* the first edition sold out in a week, with a second and larger one hurried to press before Ingraham could correct a few errors. Ingraham thus had no difficulty in negotiating the sale of the copyright of his next novel for $1,200; it was published under the title *Captain Kyd or, Wizard of the Sea*. The March, 1839, *Knickerbocker* commented that its sale equaled "the anticipation of the publishers." Whereupon Ingraham immediately raised the ante to $1,500 for *The Quadroone, or St. Michael's Day*.

On May 29, 1839, Ingraham wrote:

The merchant the planter the publisher and [others] . . . are accustomed to anticipate the fruits of their labours & negotiations, through the facilities offered by the banks. Why then should not an author have the same privilege? He cannot live on air better than his neighbor. I have hired (?) a house in N. Brunswick where I shall reside until I can build and remove to West Point. To enable me to furnish this house at once I want to anticipate the profits of my next work after the Quadroon. My brother B. T. Ingraham says if you will promise to pay me $750 towards it within *30 days after you receive* the ms he will himself give me a check for the money. This . . . places you under no obligation whatever, while it will be doing me a great favor. It will also secure to you the rights of publishing the novel when I have completed it which will be by September or first part of October. For the Quadroon you have already paid me $600.

The news of *The Quadroone's* pending publication was given to readers of the *Southern Literary Messenger* in September, along with another bit of literary gossip, that after spending the summer enjoying the health-restoring breezes of Schooley's Mountain, Ingraham was to make an autumn voyage to England, along with George D. Prentice, the brilliant editor of the Louisville *Journal*. Ingraham's letters to Fletcher Harper reveal with what difficulty he balanced himself on his financial tightrope. That he ventured to make his living from his books during depression years indicates his confidence in his ability to turn out salable fiction fast ("two a year for the next two years for $1,500 each"). But economic conditions were applying brakes to publishing, and *The Quadroone*, the last of his five Harper books, was not published till April, 1841. Ingraham's letters refer to three other manuscripts, one of which, *The Revolt of the Mexitile*, was "in the possession of the Messers Harper" in 1841. Perhaps even more were rejected because of adverse reviews of *Quadroone* (Poe was ashamed of it). Ingraham was to tell Longfellow in 1846 that he had written eighty novels, twenty of which had appeared in newspapers and some in book form. Longfellow noted in his *Journal* that this "young, dark man with soft voice" claimed to earn $3,000 a year from his writing. In 1849, Ingraham was confirmed in the Episcopal church, studied theology in Nashville (where he also established a school for young ladies), and was ordained a priest in 1851, all of which helped him win the hand of the daughter of a wealthy Mississippi planter. Although he no longer depended on his pen for a living, he was to write some immensely popular religious novels in the fifties. In 1860 he was killed by an accidental discharge from his own gun.

CHAPTER VIII

The End of the Decade

1838–1839

THE YEAR 1838 was filled with excitement for loyal Englishmen everywhere, for the nineteen-year-old Victoria was crowned Queen on June 28 in impressive ceremonies at Westminster Abbey. No Englishman is more loyal than the expatriate, and whenever the aristocratic Henry William Herbert was around Cliff Street that spring, to check on the progress of his new novel, *Cromwell*, the brothers, James especially, were resigned to discussing the latest news of the coming coronation.

Another visitor at Cliff Street was considerably less enthusiastic than Herbert about the royal goings-on in London. He was William Lyon Mackenzie (grandfather of Mackenzie King), then in the United States with a price on his head because he had led an unsuccessful revolt in Canada the previous December in an attempt to establish a republican government. Why he called on the Harpers is not known—perhaps he was there to ask if his enforced leisure might be profitably spent in writing a book.

Herbert himself could not have imagined a better scene for one of his novels than the Harper counting room during Mackenzie's visit. On that afternoon, Herbert walked in with the latest news from Buckingham Palace. Immediately James, the practical jokester, sensed that this was a fecund moment. With a wink to Mackenzie, he introduced the royalist Herbert, giving Mackenzie the name of a loyalist Canadian legislator. Mackenzie, to James's immense satisfaction, entered into the subterfuge and talked at length about the mendacity of the Canadian rebels and the best means of capturing and punishing them.

After Mackenzie left, James told Herbert he had a confession to make. The man with whom they had been conversing so earnestly was none other than the revolutionist Mackenzie himself. Herbert was nonplused. "Do you mean . . . ?" But he could not finish his sentence. He twirled his heavy mustache, his sharp gray eyes snapping fire. He had been taken in. This was too much. His biographer, David W. Judd, describes what happened next: ". . . finally after the employment of the most vituperative invectives known to the cosmopolitan lexicon, he consigned the humourous offender to eternal perdition, with a firm assurance that neither he or any of his several brothers should ever again see the light of his countenance nor a line of his manuscripts. Vainly the publisher endeavored to placate his jocular offense, but every proffer of apology augmented Herbert's ire until with gnashing teeth and scathing words, he left the office vowing never to set foot within that which he vindictively designated to be a 'palace of authors' skulls.' "

James was in turn infuriated that his offer of an apology was spurned and ordered that not another copy of Herbert's two novels should be shipped. He cooled off later, but Herbert did not forget or forgive and, assuming the nom de plume of Frank Forester, turned to Stringer & Townsend with the series of sporting books by which he is now remembered. One wonders whether James learned a lesson of tact in handling authors, knowing that he had lost one so profitable. Did his brothers remind him that he had almost lost Paulding by his bluntness? What was in James's mind when he read in the papers on May 18, 1858, that on the previous day the author he had lost because of a practical joke was now lost to the world? Depressed by the failure of his second marriage, Herbert had committed suicide.

A more welcome visitor than Herbert that spring was the indefatigable Professor Anthon. He was seeing four textbooks through the presses that year, with three more to come in 1839. *Latin Lessons* and that old favorite Caesar's *Commentaries on the Gallic Wars* were followed by editions of Cicero and Horace, prompting Horace Greeley to sing out, "Those indefatigable, excellent and most deserving publishers, 'The Harpers,' as they are called (and melodious *harpers* they are sometimes) have commenced a series of the Latin classics." *A Grammar of the Greek Language* appeared in the summer ready for fall adoptions and by the same time in 1839 *First Greek Lessons* was ready. Each was given a laurel wreath by *The Knickerbocker*, "the best ever published," and neither author nor publisher could ask for more than the *New York Review*'s hope that the *Grammar* would be "universally adopted in every school and college in America." For upperclassmen Anthon supplied *Greek Prosody* (the title and subtitle ran to forty-two words) and, in successive years, *Greek Lessons* and a *Greek Reader*. His series of classics was being vigorously publicized in the journals and promoted to schools and colleges, and was also getting serious attention in England. An English correspondent of *The Knickerbocker* had noted, "The Americans are acknowledged to excel in making school-books, and not a few are extensively adopted here; such as Anthon's editions of Sallust, Cicero and Caesar." Always pleased by praise from England for themselves and their books, the brothers knew that such kudos went a long way with American readers.

In 1838 Charles Sumner, a young Boston lawyer of much promise, wrote from Paris to Judge Story, " . . . I start for England, and how my soul leaps at the thought! Lord of my studies, my thoughts, and my dreams!" Sumner's enthusiasm was not unusual, even shared to a degree by other young men who were to speak up in the forties for a national literature. The year that Sumner wrote to Story was a banner year for European travel. The seven-hundred-ton S.S. *Sirius* arrived in New York Harbor on April 23, the first crossing of a steamship especially constructed for overseas voyaging. The *Sirius*, sailing from London, beat the *Great Western*, sailing from Bristol, by a few hours only. Soon steamships were replacing the packet ships on regular sailings and bringing early proofs of English books with greater dispatch.

Travel within the country was also speeding up, with railroad lines stretching out from the leading seaboard cities. In 1836 diarist Strong, going to Boston for a school holiday, took a train at Providence. "I was soon, for the first time in my life, traveling at the rate of a mile in 2 min. 35 sec. In spite of 'great danger,' 'terrible accidents,' 'upsettings,' and so on, as Mr. Caphagus hath it, we stopped at the depot in Boston at a quarter-past ten in perfect preservation, except that we were copiously sprinkled with dust." Travel in the hinterlands was still at tortoise speed in comparison. That same year D. B. Cooke left New York for Columbus, Ohio, to begin his career as a midwestern bookseller. His "long and tedious journey by canal" took about three weeks. Chicago, a village of four thousand inhabitants, would wait another decade for the railroad boom to arouse her to the possibility of becoming the railroad center of the nation.

Whether Americans traveled or stayed at home, they loved to read about the trips others made. Along with textbooks and biographies, books in the "Voyages and Travels" section of the Harper catalogue would go like burning leaves before an October wind. Two such books helped see the brothers through the depression year of 1838. *Notes of Travel in Europe* was written by Dr. Wilbur Fisk, president of the recently founded Wesleyan University, Middletown, Connecticut. Dr. Fisk's 692-page book, replete with engravings, told of experiences in eight countries and contained a few sermons and addresses for the further edification of his readers. Four editions sold out in less than four weeks. More distinguished as literature was John L. Stephens's second book of *Incidents of Travel*. This time he provided an armchair tour of Greece, Turkey, Russia, and Poland. Two weeks after publication, a third large edition was in press and *The Knickerbocker* was predicting that it would go to six printings in as many months. However, *The Knickerbocker* was wrong, and other reviewers were not so enthusiastic. The *New York Review* thought the engravings of the new book were "shabby" and found some "vulgarisms" that needed correction before reprinting. Of all boosters for Stephens and his books, few could outdo Clark; for several years he printed excerpts from them in *The Knickerbocker* and applauded author and publisher. But what helped most was the unqualified praise given the two Stephens works by the popular English lecturer James Silk Buckingham; many from his audiences in New York and in other parts of the country bought copies immediately.

Two American ladies added a bit of elegance to the Harper output in 1838. Mrs. Caroline Gilman wrote *Recollections of a Southern Matron* as a companion volume to her *Recollections of a Housekeeper*. Mrs. Gilman had a built-in market to offer to the brothers, since her magazine, the *Rose Bud* (later to blossom into the *Southern Rosebud*), had thousands of feminine readers ready to buy and carry home any book she might write. Evert Duyckinck thought her books were admired for their simplicity, quiet humor, and amiable spirit. They pointed up practical lessons for life and a reviewer worried about the competition that Miss Sedgwick would now have, since she had a counterpart in the wife of a Unitarian minister of Miss Sedgwick's own state. For herself, Miss Sedgwick was satisfied to hear that both *Live and Let Live* and *Love Token for Children* were being published in England. Stephens could do no better.

Miss Sedgwick's real rival was Mrs. Lydia Huntley Sigourney of Hartford, whose 1838 Harper book was a revised edition of *Letters to Mothers*. It was, in fact, virtually a new work. As in the case of Mrs. Gilman's *Recollections*, this was a companion book to an earlier one, entitled *Letters to Young Ladies*. In adding Mrs. Sigourney to their list the Harpers acquired a seasoned and professional author. Her output eventually extended to a total of sixty-seven books, of which the brothers published five. Magazines and "Annuals" were consuming reams of Sigourney poetry and prose and for a while Louis Godey listed her as one of the editors of his *Lady's Book*. Her Harper contracts were based on the half-profits formula. The one for *Mothers* was among the first to designate semiannual payments to a writer, August being named as well as February, heretofore the only month of the year during which checks went out to authors. The ten-year contract for *Young Ladies* was to expire two years before someone realized that profits were being divided without proper authority, so a new contract was quickly and agreeably drawn up between the two parties.

Just as the year 1838 drew to a close, the last William Gilmore Simms novel with a Harper imprint appeared, a historical romance, entitled *Pelayo*, with a Spanish setting. Even as *Pelayo* was being issued, two more Simms works were on press carrying the name of publisher George Adlard. Both Carey firms in Philadelphia were also to undertake Simms's books, and other publishers brought out collected editions of his novels, which eventually made a seventeen-volume set.

Another year-end project was a dramatic poem by young Epes Sargent, a Bostonian who followed a well-beaten path to New York in search of a literary career. It seems surprising that a play should get published in times of economic stress when more salable books could be had. Yet *Velasco* had literary merit, as most reviewers* chorused, and Sargent was a writer of promise. Word got around that Ellen Tree, famous English actress then touring America, would play the feminine lead in this story of the tenth-century Spanish captain El Cid. However, Miss Tree went off to spend the winter in New Orleans where it was warmer, and the play, a disappointing performance, was produced at the Park Theatre without her.

It is not likely that any of the Harpers saw its première, since they did not often go to the theatre. Playgoing was frowned upon by the best Methodist families, and Henry Ward Beecher spoke for many

---

* Among them was Horace Greeley, who wrote in the *New Yorker*, "The most finished drama that has yet been published this side of the Atlantic."

churchmen when he said the theatre was "the gate to Hell, the road to ruin, the nursery of all abominable crime, and the Seminary of infidelity and moral death." Wesley never forgot the time he had gone to a theatrical performance, persuaded by some other boys. He could not enter into their spirit of fun and anticipation as they sat in the pit waiting for the curtain to rise. Suddenly he remembered that it was nearly time for his father to gather the family for evening prayers. He made it home just in time.

The most important publishing project that the brothers developed in 1838-39 was *Harper's School District Library*. It had been under way at least since 1836, for "The Common School Library" appears as an enigmatic line in that year's catalogue. By 1838 they had assembled a boxed set of fifty volumes, with plans under way for a forty-five-volume set the following year. On July 13, 1838, J. Orville Taylor agreed to rewrite his book *The District School*, "adapting it to the second series of [the] Common School Library . . . provided it shall be recommended . . . to advance the reputation of this series." Taylor had to get an imprimatur from three of a panel of five gentlemen, including King, Hawks, and Verplanck, and had to promote sales of the Harper libraries in his travels and lectures to school districts. All very candid and clear-cut. Taylor, for his part, was to be compensated for his work by a royalty of 12½ cents on each copy of his own book he disposed of and by a commission of $4 on each set of the books placed in a district school. (The boxed set sold for $20, while single copies were priced at 38 cents each.)

After a long second thought, the brothers decided that this agreement was not sufficiently binding. Competitors would be after so influential a schoolman, and they asked Taylor on August 21 to agree to sell no other library. He agreed and a few weeks later advertised that he was taking orders for the fifty-volume library under the auspices of "The Society for the Diffusion of Knowledge," and that the library was recommended by the superintendent of common schools, the governor of the state, and the Hon. Gulian C. Verplanck. (Verplanck was a member of the Board of Regents of the University of the State of New York from 1826-70.)

In 1839 the State Legislature took cognizance of the importance of school district libraries and passed a law requiring each district with a population of more than ten thousand to set up a library. The law further provided that the state would distribute $55,000 a year for five years as matching funds, the various districts putting up amounts based upon school populations of children between the ages of five and sixteen. "Within the five years limited by the Law," Governor Seward said in his message to the Legislature, "there will have been expended in the purchase of books more than half a million dollars." The superintendent of common schools was to recommend to the district such books as he considered useful and instructive. This gentleman, who was also Secretary of State, was the Hon. John C. Spencer.

Now Mr. Spencer was obviously a more important factor in getting libraries sold to district schools than even the well-known Mr. Taylor. Fletcher showed a newspaper account of the new legislation to James. "Boss," he said, "give me a letter to your friend Thurlow Weed, and ask him to introduce me to Mr. Spencer." James fell in with the plan, and a day or two later Fletcher presented the letter to Weed in his editorial office of the Albany *Evening Journal.*

After reading the letter, Weed thought for a moment and then said with a smile, "Well, Fletcher, I shall be glad to do what I can for you for your own sake, as well as on account of my dear friend your brother. Now, Spencer is a very difficult man to approach. He is sensitive and always suspicious of possible jobs; he requires to be approached with some delicacy and caution." He then added, suddenly, "Why! he is coming to my house tonight. The governor will be there and the lieutenant-governor and Spencer and some senators and assemblymen."

Fletcher replied, impulsively, "That is the very time I can meet him."

Mr. Weed shook his head. "Now, don't be in such a hurry, my boy; don't be in such a hurry. I will manage that. I don't think it would answer for you to meet him at my house. Let me arrange it for you."

Accordingly, during the evening and in the presence of a number of friends, but not directly to Secretary Spencer, Weed casually remarked that he had had a pleasant interview that day with a young man from New York, a hardworking, intelligent, industrious, straightforward young printer, and that he was the youngest brother of his old friend and fellow-pressman, James Harper. Spencer, overhearing Weed's remarks—as he intended he should—turned to Weed and said:

"Who is this wonderful young man, this young printer? Where is he, and why didn't you ask him here tonight?"

"Why, Spencer, he is very sensitive," remarked Weed. "He has come to Albany expressly to see you on business."

"Then why not have him here tonight?" repeated Spencer.

"Because," said Weed, "he is not that kind of a man, and he is too proud to avail himself of a social occasion for business purposes."

The Secretary immediately replied: "Well, you make me very desirous of knowing him. I should like to see him early tomorrow morning. Where is he?"

"He is down at the Eagle Tavern," said Weed. "I will bring him up tomorrow, but, mind, he is very proud and sensitive."

Accordingly, the next day Weed presented Fletcher to Secretary Spencer. He said, "I understand, my young friend, that you want to furnish the state with the School District Library books."

Fletcher replied, "Yes, that is what I have come for, Mr. Secretary."

"How do you propose to do it?" asked Spencer.

"I propose to do it under your direction," said Fletcher.

"You haven't all the books," observed Spencer.

"We will buy them, then," replied Fletcher.

"But suppose you cannot buy them?" said Spencer.

"We will make arrangements of some kind," Fletcher assured Spencer.

"How about the price?" asked Spencer.

"That," said Fletcher, looking the Secretary squarely in the eyes, "You shall decide. Whatever arrangements you may make will be satisfactory to my brothers and to me. We shall put ourselves in your hands."

In recalling this incident years later, Weed wrote that Spencer told him that Fletcher Harper was the most charming young man he had ever met. One of a book salesman's greatest assets is a charming manner but even that helps little unless he can deliver the goods. In Fletcher's proposal, Secretary Spencer saw at once that the problems confronting him as he sought to implement legislative action could easily be solved. These problems, as Clark was to point out later in *The Knickerbocker*, were threefold. One, special means had to be found to get recommended books to the libraries, as the ordinary supply of books would be insufficient. Two, many editions of desired titles would be too expensive and some of an inconvenient size. Three, some books, otherwise suitable, would have to be revised in order to delete or rewrite material otherwise unobjectionable to the adult reader. Clark wrote,

Now we cannot but regard the enterprise of the Messers. Harpers as being the thing that was required to obviate all these difficulties by securing to the school districts an ample supply of books, selected and prepared with distinct reference to this simple object, of a suitable and uniform size, at the lowest possible cost, and, with a view to their more convenient purchase, distributed at a great number of different points throughout the state. . . . Nothing is admitted into the "School District Library" without the approval of the superintendent of common schools. The public, there-fore, have the most satisfactory assurance that the works introduced into this library will be the very best that can be selected, and that the undertaking, generally, will be so prosecuted, as to entitle the enterprising and highly respectable publishers who have engaged in it to the most liberal and extensive patronage.

Clark's two-and-a-half-page review was based on the first two *Harper's School District* series, which he said had been commended by the governor of the state and his immediate predecessor. He went on to say

It is likewise due to the publishers, that we should acknowledge the unprecedented cheapness of the two series, consisting together of ninety-five volumes, handsomely printed on good paper, substantially bound, copi-ously illustrated with engravings, averaging over three hundred pages, and still afforded to the public at the surprisingly low price of thirty-eight dollars.

In one of the school districts—there were nearly eleven hundred of them—a central New York boy named Peter Carter avidly read the books that came in the Harper *S.D.L.* boxes. His boyhood love of reading led him eventually to become a New York publisher; later he wrote with nostalgia of the anticipation with which he and other farm boys saw the Harper boxes of books arrive. Here they could choose books of travel, of science, of biography, of fiction, books to take home to read after the winter evening chores were done: Thatcher's *Indians Traits*, "Uncle Philip" Hawks's *Whale Fishery*, Paulding's *Life of Washington* and ten volumes of Sparks's *American Biography*, Miss Sedgwick's moral tales and *Swiss Family Robinson*, and an eye-brightening pile of other books.

In eight years the *School District Library* grew into six series total-ing 212 titles bound in 295 single volumes. It soon spread beyond the Empire State to become known in all parts of the country, a school superintendent in Maryland saying, "A plan as well devised cannot be too highly commended to the favor of the rising and spreading popu-lation of our great Republic."

When Fletcher promised Secretary Spencer that "arrangements of some kind could be made to procure important books not published by the House, he perhaps had in mind Harper's recent coup in procuring from Hilliard, Gray & Co. of Boston the Jared Sparks series of *Ameri-can Biography*. The first volume had appeared in 1834, with the tenth coming out just before the brothers took them over and just before Dr. Sparks was named professor of ancient and modern history at Harvard, the first professor of history, other than ecclesiastical, in any American university. The Boston firm may have sold rights on these books because they were under financial strain and eager for cash or negotiable notes. However, even solvent publishers seemed to hold loose reins on books and authors the Harpers wanted. Lea & Blanchard sold or leased them plates of Sir Walter Scott's *History of Scotland* and four other works, all histories of European countries, in 1840 and 1842. The purchases may have been made at the request of Albany.

Two other gentlemen from New England figured in the output of nonfiction from Cliff Street in 1839. One was Theodore Sedgwick, Sr., who published the third and concluding part of *Public and Private Economy*. The second and third parts were written after a tour through England and France, where Sedgwick found substantiation for his thesis that a sound economy is based on thrift, economy, and industry, as well as a safe system of currency and credit. Sedgwick's work was appropriate for 1839 because the stagnation of business was much on people's minds; Hone noted in his diary in March that trade was at a standstill, with the city in "commercial gloom." While addressing a political meeting in Pittsfield, Massachusetts, on November 6, 1839, just prior to a state election, Sedgwick suffered a stroke from which he did not recover. Mrs. Sedgwick was to survive both her husband and her son. She published her second Harper novel, *Walter Thornley*, in 1859, the year of the death of Theodore, Jr. The son was one of Fletcher's leading contributors to the early issues of *Harper's New Monthly Magazine* (1850) and was Fletcher's choice for managing editor of *Harper's Weekly* when it was established (1857), a position he filled for more than a year.

The other New Englander was the Rev. Dr. James Murdock of New Haven, who made a new translation from the Latin of that old J. & J. Harper favorite Mosheim's *Ecclesiastical History*, which James had tried unsuccessfully to sell to the Careys in 1820. The title was one of five named in 1824 in the earliest-known periodical listing of new Harper books. Demarest had also seen it listed among works announced in 1830 as "lately published." Now, nine years later, they came out proudly with a new translation printed from new stereotypes. It made a three-volume work, totaling 1,461 pages, and retailed for $7.50, an amount that included $1 for Murdock. Little is known of Murdock. He was a classmate of Lyman Beecher in the Yale class of 1797. After teaching theology at Andover for nine years, he moved to New Haven in 1829, where he indulged his literary and scholarly

interests for a quarter of a century, apparently without having to
depend either on teaching or preaching for income. Next to the works
of Jonathan Edwards, Murdock's translation of Mosheim was in the
mid-century the most frequently withdrawn book from the Yale
library. According to Demarest, in 1844 the brothers bought the
plates of still another two-volume set of Mosheim's *Ecclesiastical History*, edited by Charles Coote. In fact, the Harper involvement in
Mosheim was so complicated that Demarest noted with pleasure one
fact he could be sure of: the Murdock-Mosheim plates were sold eventually to Murdock for $1,243.13. However, he did not know the date
of the sale; apparently it occurred sometime between 1847, when the
catalogue listed both editions, and 1853, when only Coote remained.

Another scholarly work that Murdock brought to Cliff Street was
his annotated edition of Milman's *History of Christianity*—annotated
sufficiently to obtain American copyright in 1841. This was the second
book by Canon H. H. Milman on the Harper list. The first and more
important, *History of the Jews*, was published in 1830 and was given
the honor of making Volumes I, II, and III of the *Family Library*.
Murdock was interested in Milman because of a concern both had
with historical writing and German theological scholarship. Milman
was still at Oxford when he published *History of the Jews*, one of the
first books to show the influence of the German historical criticism of
the Bible. It created such a storm of protest that John Murray took the
book out of his catalogue; the brothers, however, were far removed
from this personal controversy and decided that this scholarly work
should be allowed to find its own public. In 1849, Milman was named
Dean of St. Paul's Cathedral, his unpopularity at home having been
replaced by respect, even reverence.

An edition of Paley's *Natural Theology* also made its appearance in
1839, with copyright protection made possible because of "Observations and Notes" added by the Rev. Dr. Alonzo Potter, of Union
College, Schenectady. Paley's book, an argument from design to prove
the existence of a benevolent Creator, had first been published in 1802
and could stand some updating from the up-and-coming Dr. Potter,
who was to do several chores for the brothers, even after he was made
Episcopal Bishop of Pennsylvania in 1845. One of his chores was to
edit six volumes for the *Family Library*, including two of his own.
Perhaps Potter urged the brothers to issue two of Paley's earlier books,
The Principles of Moral and Political Philosophy and *A View of the
Evidences of Christianity;* at least the latter volume was put in the
School District Library in 1842, and Potter was in on the councils of

the state superintendent in nearby Albany. It is perhaps significant that Paley was being read widely a half century after his books had been published; a more tolerant theology was stirring within Protestantism and Paley's latitudinarian views were more palatable after his death.

The nonfiction output from Cliff Street in 1839 included a mid-summer issue of *Fanny*, the poems of Fitz-Greene Halleck that had been the talk of the town when first published by Charles Wiley twenty years earlier, but which had been long out of print. The Harper edition contained additional poems, and reviewers were reminding their readers that Halleck's light verse still ranked him among the best of American poets. "Halleck has been persuaded at last by the Harpers (they must have *harped* on one string for a long time) to publish 'Fanny' and his Croaker pieces," one reviewer noted, hoping there would be more to come. And there was more. The brothers harped on two other strings, in fact, one for an anthology and the other for a further volume of Halleck's own verse. Poe ranked Halleck third in his listing of American poets, giving Longfellow and Bryant first and second places; he considered Halleck "a man to be admired, respected, but more especially beloved."

Halleck's friend, the veritable old Knickerbocker, James K. Paulding, now saw at last a Harper edition of *The Three Wise Men of Gotham*, the latest to appear of his collected *Works*, for which he had signed that first Harper & Brothers contract back in 1833. The delay was not to Paulding's advantage, for bright young men who trafficked in words were placing Paulding on the back shelves. "We sincerely trust," Horace Greeley wrote, "that the speculation of republishing the Honorable Secretary's literary commissions is his own and not the Harpers." But Nathaniel Parker Willis went much further. Taking the cue that there were two Pauldings, one who had just become Secretary of the Navy and the other the writer, he wrote a long piece for *The Corsair* on "Paulding the author Disinterred." Pretending that Paulding, the author, was now dead, Willis proceeded to write a vicious, though often humorous, attack on Paulding's early works; they had best be forgotten. Willis's piece was reprinted by the *Southern Literary Messenger* and was answered there and in the New York *Courier & Enquirer* by Paulding's supporters. One explanation of the attack was that Willis had been hurt by a fancied social slight. While he had been a guest of General Morris, at the latter's country estate near Cold Spring in the Hudson River highlands, Paulding was visiting his relative and Morris's neighbor, Gouverneur Kemble, who entertained widely for Paulding. Willis was not invited to any of these festivities and blamed Paulding. Willis had also been hurt by unfavorable comments on his own work, published in the *Courier & Enqurirer*, which he wrongly attributed to Paulding. Hence the diatribe.

Thus harm had been done to Paulding, even though the Harpers were quoted in the *Messenger* that September as saying that among their American authors Paulding was the best seller. Of course they may have been misquoted, for they were apparently deciding not to reprint the last three of his older works. That they failed to carry out their commitment is a mark against their record. Despite adverse criticism and bad times they should have completed the job. The lack of a complete edition of his *Works* brought much sadness to the old Knickerbocker in the closing years of his life. While he probably earned as much as $50,000 for writing books and articles, he was to complain in 1855 of his minuscule royalties ("from the Harpers I earn nothing"). However, his books must have continued to sell, for the 1859 catalogue, issued a year before his death, devoted nearly a page to listing and describing all his titles. Paulding's biographers, Amos L. Herold and Ralph M. Aderman, note a growing interest in Paulding and believe that he deserves a place in American literature more nearly that of his friends Irving and Cooper.

During the years of 1838 and 1839, publishing new books of fiction for writers, most of them young and all of them anonymous, called for a different type of promotion. The vogue for anonymity was at its height. In addition to its being a literary game in which all could participate, anonymity is explained by Perry Miller, literary historian of this period, as an "aristocratic pretense that he [the author] did not scribble for pay, that he gave out his trifles as the amusement of his leisure." What posterity now regards as the most important of these anonymously published Harper novels probably had the poorest sale. It was Poe's *The Narrative of Arthur Gordon Pym, of Nantucket*. Actually Poe's authorship was known, at least to readers of the *Southern Literary Messenger*, which had carried two installments under his name early in 1837. Wesley did his best to attract attention to the book by crowding upon the title page those glowing adjectives to which publishers are always addicted and which now can be used even more liberally on wide jacket flaps. His sentence (or was it Poe's?) included the phrases, "mutiny and atrocious butchery . . . horrible sufferings from famine . . . incredible adventures and discoveries . . . distressing calamity."

Not only was the *Narrative* published anonymously, but the literary game was also given a new twist. Was the book fiction or fact? Gaylord Clark, with tongue in cheek, wrote, "We would not be so un-courteous as to insinuate a doubt of Mr. Pym's veracity now that he *lies* 'under the sod,' but we should very much question that gentle-man's word . . . that he *believed* the various adventures. . . ." And the *New Yorker* commented that "Mr. Edgar A. Poe is understood to have assisted in preparing the work for the press," after calling it "of extraordinary, freezing interest, beyond anything we ever read." The *New York Review* was not taken in, saying, "The work is all a fiction. . . . It is not destitute of interest for the imagination, but the interest is painful. There are too many atrocities, too many strange horrors, and finally there is no conclusion to it; it breaks off suddenly in a mysteri-ous way which is not only destitute of all *vraisemblance*, but is purely perplexing and vexatious. We cannot but consider the author unfor-tunate in his plan." Such a review did not help sales and Wesley wrote an apologetic letter to Poe seven months after publication saying ". . . 'Pym' has not succeeded or been received as well in this country as it has in England. When we published the work, we sent 100 copies of it to London—and we presume they have been sold. In addition to which we understand that an English edition has been printed. . . ." Actually *Pym* did do better in England, partly because of Dickens's enthusiasm for it, and was reissued in 1838, 1841, and 1861. (Neither did Poe's other 1839 book, *Tales of the Grotesque and Arabesque*, published by Lea & Blanchard, succeed. Favorably reviewed, it sold less than 750 copies in three years.)

Experts on Poe have spent pleasant hours in detecting sources of *Pym* in other writings, and agree that he borrowed from such Harper authors as Benjamin Morrell and J. N. Reynolds; in his last ravings, Poe is said to have cried out, "Reynolds." The inscriptions that Stephens found on the rocks in Sinai's wilderness were the inspiration for the strange oriental inscriptions (Arabic, Ethiopic and Coptic) Poe's hero Pym found in the rocks of his island of Tsalal.

Three further anonymous novels came out in the late summer and autumn of 1839, and one of them, entitled *Sydney Clifton*, has stalked mysteriously down the years wrongly attributed to Theodore S. Fay. Demarest so credits it, though he should have known better, for more than one Harper catalogue he handled listed it as written by "Strong," but in type so small that an oversight is excusable. Demarest looked for authority to Allibone, who in turn may have depended upon Duyc-kinck's *Cyclopedia of American Literature* (1855). Even modern bibli-ographers such as Lyle H. Wright, Alexander Cowie, and Jacob Blanck have put Fay down as the author, as does the Library of Congress. Evidence that Fay did not write it is contained in his 1845 *Statement* concerning his business relations with the brothers; that title is not mentioned. However, Clark knew who wrote it and told readers of *The Knickerbocker* in August, 1839. The author was George D. Strong, a West Indian merchant and president of the Commercial Bank. Strong had written poetry for various periodicals but this was his first prose work. Clark was impressed by Strong's talent and thought that *Sydney Clifton* was a very clever novel deserving public favor.

Another Harper novel that came out for late summer reading, *Charles Vincent,* was also written by a businessman. Here, too, Clark was the detective, possibly tipped off by his friends on Cliff Street. He identified the author as William H. Willis, "a highly respectable hardware merchant in Pearl Street," and puffed the book as "fairly entitled to a respectable rank among American novels." In his valiant attempt to credit anonymous novels, Demarest got the surname correct, but after the entry "Willis" he added "Nathaniel Parker"!

And, finally, there was *Morton's Hope,* ready in the bookshops for any returning vacationer who might inquire for the latest anonymous American novels. Proofs of the book had been ready in the summer, but American publication was delayed till the book could be issued by John Colburn in London and possibly obtain English copyright. Of course the book was copyrighted in America, a fact that Clark apparently overlooked when he guessed that the work was an English import. The two-volume novel, however, was soon linked up with its proper author, John Lothrop Motley of Boston, who had recently returned from Europe, where he had topped off his Harvard studies with a year each at the universities of Berlin and Göttingen, where he met and made a lifetime friend of Bismarck.

Motley was introduced to the Cliff Street publishers by his brother-in-law, Park Benjamin, a magazine editor and poet, who came to see them not only to introduce Motley but also to attempt to talk them into publishing a volume of his own poems. Benjamin had taken early proofs of *Morton's Hope* to his friend Greeley, who was glad to do a favor for his former colleague. He drew a deep breath and blew a maximum puff, prophesying in the *New Yorker* that the book would elicit "higher praise from higher sources than any work of its kind ever before given to the public in this country." However, Motley's story of an American who left Morton's Hope, his country place near Boston, for study in Germany, received scant praise, and modern commentators have assumed that it was a publishing failure. Yet it must have enjoyed some continuing sale for in 1853 it was still in print. Fifteen hundred copies were printed with Motley sharing profits after 1,250 copies were sold. While no Harper records indicate profits, if any, there are ample records showing Motley's earnings on *The Rise of the Dutch Republic* and *History of the United Netherlands,* to be published between 1856 and 1868. The contracts for these two works were to call for payments in gold as a safeguard against changes in the value of money taking place during that time. Motley's gold-standard Harper royalties were to amount to more than $60,000.

The last year of the 1830's had brought the usual lot of English reprints plus some that had been postponed from previous years. There were five Bulwer titles and six of James, enough to kill off an author's popularity in modern times. Everyone knew that Bulwer was now Sir Edward, having been created a baronet in 1838; they also knew that he and his wife had been legally separated. Therefore there were eager buyers for Lady Bulwer's 1839 novel, *Cheveley, or the Man of Honour,* a bitter caricature of her husband and an insight into their matrimonial difficulties. In fact, two printings were called for at once, with one reviewer complaining that the public's "maw is still capacious." The verdict of history is that, even though her spouse was not a model husband, Lady Bulwer greatly exaggerated the wrongs she claimed to have suffered.

The Harper-Bulwer correspondence that has recently come to light shows that the brothers contracted in 1835 to pay Bulwer for early proofs at the rate of £50 per volume of a new English novel, or £150 for the usual "three decker." This was more than the £125 that Henry Carey proposed a year later that his English agent offer Bulwer, and more than "about $500" that the *Democratic Review* said three years later Harper's gave. Bentley, who was Bulwer's early publisher in England, paid an average of slightly more than £250 ($1,250) for the copyrights of English novels between 1830-50, according to Bentley's biographer, Royal A. Gettmann. However, Bentley may have paid Bulwer more. In an undated letter, Bulwer asked £1,200 for an "unborn novel," which may have been *The Last Days of Pompeii,* and in 1848, in order to lure Bulwer back to his nest, Bentley was to offer him £1,000 each for two novels. Also Bentley frequently made bonus payments for books that went well. But there is no record of the Harpers paying anything extra for *Rienzi* even though it sold fifteen thousand copies by 1839, nor for the highly successful *Last Days of Pompeii.* The initial payment for first proofs, or early corrected sheets, apparently completed the transaction, for them as for other American publishers. Another popular English writer, Captain Marryat, may have received up to $750 for first proofs from Harper's. Ingraham, in bargaining with Fletcher in May, 1839, for more money, said he had to date been paid $4,100 for five novels, "which [average] is less than Marryat gets for one of his novels."

But payments for first proofs were not adequate compensation to English authors for the popularity and sales of their books in America. Criticisms of the practice were beginning to crystallize on both sides of the Atlantic. The first of many efforts to persuade the Congress to pass legislation permitting foreign authors to obtain copyright in the United States was begun in 1837. This action was in the form of two memorials submitted in February to Henry Clay, chairman of the Select Committee of the Senate, one signed by fifty-six English authors and the other by thirty American authors. As a result, Clay prepared and offered a bill, but through popular indifference it did not come to a vote. When the new session of Congress convened in mid-December, Clay reintroduced his bill. Immediately the graphic arts industry busied itself to combat it. Before the year ended, a meeting of booksellers, papermakers, type founders, printers, and binders in Philadelphia protested; signatures were affixed to a memorial to Congress claiming that passage of the bill would jeopardize an industry employing an estimated 200,000 persons with a capital investment of between $30 and $40 million. Similar groups in Washington, New York, and Boston sent in protesting petitions. Memorials favoring the legislation arrived in Washington from groups of authors in these and other cities, the document from New York carrying 136 signatures. On June 25, 1838, Senator Ruggles of Maine summarized the arguments that had been presented for and against the legislation, concluding that "the committee have been unable to find sufficient reason for recommending the passage of the bill."

That same year England accepted a proposal from the German Confederation that reciprocal privileges of copyright be granted Prussian and British citizens. The refusal of Congress to pass the Clay bill was an early frost on this budding growth of international copyright and a deplorable failure to recognize the property rights of authors in what they published. To be sure, authors themselves were partly to blame because so many of them professed to be ashamed of the commercialism that tainted their profession; such leading authors as Irving and Cooper did not lend their support in 1837 and 1838. Editors of literary periodicals were also divided in their attitude toward international copyright; Dr. Henry of the *New York Review* was for it, while O'Sullivan of the *Democratic Review* and Greeley of the *New Yorker* (for a while) were against it. But what really squelched the Clay bill was the confusion of copyrights for foreigners with protective tariff, and Americans were frightened of any change that might hurt native industry or throw people out of work.

Thus English books continued to flow into the American market without copyright privilege, and likewise American books had no protection in England save a London "courtesy of the trade." To be sure, it was believed for several years by some that prior publication of an American work in Britain would give a kind of *ipso facto* protection there. But the uncooperative and rather unscrupulous publisher Thomas Tegg, of London, soon showed how tenuous any such claims were. Putnam, who represented Wiley & Putnam in England during the forties, was to observe that the "appropriation" of books by "pirates" was as active in London as in Boston, New York, and Philadelphia. With a difference. In America, an English author's name gave prestige to his work. In Britain, with few exceptions, the contrary was true. Putnam found that vast numbers of American books were freely revised or rewritten and often issued with different names designated as authors.

The lack of an international copyright was thus for authors in both countries unfair and often onerous. Even so, claims to that effect made then, and often repeated today, may easily be overstated. Particularly exaggerated is the charge that English reprints stifled the growth of American literature. Writing of American authors of the 1830's, the late Van Wyck Brooks generalized, "They could not compete with the popularity of the leading writers of England and Scotland, who were printed in cheap editions by half a dozen houses, editions that were all the cheaper because the writers were not paid and fared as badly, in fact, as the American authors. The trade was a chaos in which only a few pirates throve, and scarcely a handful of authors could survive at all. . . ." Mr. Brooks was obviously more interested in authors than in the businessmen who marketed their wares, and more knowledgeable of the hardships of authors than of the problems of a large-scale publisher. A contemporary generalization made by a man who was both a writer and a publisher is more accurate historically. Horace Greeley knew that "scarcely a handful" of publishers "could survive at all" during the two depression periods of the thirties. In the *New Yorker* of November 10, 1838, he wrote: "The Harpers have probably done more for the advancement of literary taste and the advantage of native authorship than all the other publishers. Their treatment of authors has always been liberal and generous, and we have never heard a complaint uttered against them. On the contrary, we hear them highly commended by all men of letters who have had any dealings with them. This is great praise, for the warfare of authors against publishers is proverbial."

O'Sullivan of the *Democratic Review* claimed that the flood of English imports did not drown American authors but invigorated them. The same sentiment had been expressed by Charles Fenno Hoffman several years earlier when, in 1835, in the *American Monthly* he claimed that Americans were already the most imaginative people in the world or soon to become so since they bought four times as many copies of a Bulwer novel as the English did. "The pioneering and settling of this vast country," he wrote, "is abundant material for novelists, as Charles Brockden Brown discovered a few years ago. His great success was matched by the authors of *The Spy* and *Hope Leslie*, and the excitement over these authors is now shared by at least a dozen new competitors." A few months later Hoffman was claiming that ten works of native talent were being published for one that came from the presses five years earlier.

In his biography of Charles Fenno Hoffman, H. F. Barnes uses the well-worn argument of cheap English reprints, as well as adverse economic conditions, as probable reasons for the Harpers' rejection of Hoffman's *Wild Scenes in the Forest and in the Prairie* in 1839. But if such were true, they would not have published his *Greyslaer* in 1840, when both conditions still prevailed. A more likely reason was the advance serialization of *Wild Scenes*, the brothers being convinced that prior publication in a periodical siphoned off potential book sales for American authors. "The Harpers were specially noted for declining American authors, and were stubborn in their opposition to the idea of an international copyright," said Barnes, citing as his authority Earl Bradsher's chapter, "Book Publishers and Publishing," in the *Cambridge History of American Literature*. Both Barnes and Bradsher wrote, apparently, without attempting to study what the Harper record really disclosed about American authors published and promoted by them.*

---

* Bradsher gives wrong dates for the publication of the *Illuminated Bible* and Verplanck's *Shakespeare*. Noting that 615 volumes had been published in the *Library of Se-*

Hoffman himself waxed enthusiastic over the demonstrable increase in the output of native works, saying further, ". . . this change has been brought about mainly by the instrumentality of a single house in this city, we are proud to believe. That the Messers Harper are, by their liberality towards young writers of their own country, and by their publication of whatever works they may consider worthy of attention without regard to names or persons, bringing about a revolution in our literature, we are bold to assert." Such a comment, and others from *The Knickerbocker*, the *Southern Literary Messenger*, and the *New Yorker*, are typical of what literary editors were saying in the thirties, flattering words that seem effusive today and may have caused blushes on Cliff Street then. The brothers were "national benefactors"; their "wonted liberality" was well known and "their integrity as unimpeachable as their credit." That the fraternal partners worked as a unit with the strength of four reminded writers of the fable of the old man who demonstrated to his sons the strength of a bundle of rods. Their very success made them newsworthy, with editors saying that the extent and importance of their operation enabled them to "enjoy a higher distinction" and also "a greater reputation than any other bookselling house."

Modern writers who scan the eastern horizon for the dawn of American literature may expect too much of the 1830's. As the decade began, the *American Monthly* admitted that "there is scarcely a professed author in the United States. A few bright geniuses have arisen among us, but . . . they have generally passed away to Europe to shine." Irving, of course. And Longfellow, in his anonymous introduction to *Outre-Mer*, exclaimed, "What perils await the adventurous author who launches forth into the uncertain current of public favour in so frail a bark as this." Perils awaited the adventurous publisher, too, unless he had English reprints as ballast for *his* bark.

On June 22, 1838, John Quincy Adams (the ex-President was then in Congress) wrote to the young men of the Franklin Society in Baltimore in answer to their request for a list of suitable books for a library. After devoting four long paragraphs to the importance of reading the Bible, he recommended "other books of great worth and of easy acquisition." He began with the Harper *Family Library*, "a constant supply of profitable reading." Mr. Adams urged a reading of American his-

---

lect Novels, he says "all of them save some half dozen being foreign authors." He ignores the later 300-volume *Select Library of Valuable Standard Literature*, and the 187-volume *Family Library* in which the American ratio is more favorable; in fact, the latter series had at its early completion in 1845 at least 35 volumes of native authorship.

tory, the Constitution, and biographies of famous Americans, starting with those by Belknap and Sparks (works of both were soon issued from Cliff Street). He then turned to "fashionable novels and poetry of the present time," listing authors of the order of Scott, Byron, Moore, Southey, Wordsworth, two Montgomerys (James and Robert, the former represented in both the *Family* and *School District* libraries), Cooper, Paulding, Willis, Mrs. Hemans and Lady Blessington, Mrs. Sigourney and Miss Gould, "and worth them all, Miss Edgeworth." Travel writers recommended were "Dr. Dwight, Dr. Sprague, Mr. Bigelow, Lieut. Slidell, and Dr. Fisk." While his list had some surprising omissions, President Adams was representative of the average, literate, book-reading American who took it for granted that most of the books he wanted to read were written by English authors.

But the sales curve for American books was steadily moving upward. If Colonel Stone's 1836 figure for earnings of American authors was average for the decade (and it may not be because of the business depressions), the brothers paid out $300,000 as half profits and royalties between 1830 and 1839. The only extant Harper records are those showing Ingraham's earnings. But it is otherwise known, to give two examples, that Simms was getting $6,000 a year from his novels and Stephens had made nearly $6,000 on two books by midsummer, 1839. It is possible that American authors could have earned more had the brothers not been committed to low prices. Low prices meant small half profits to authors per unit of sale, but they also meant less risk on large printings, which kept the Harper pressmen and binders busy. Low prices also made it easier to tempt half dollars from the pockets of bookstore customers. "The Harpers are still continuing in their useful course," an editor wrote, "bringing down that knowledge, which was formerly confined to sages and to statesmen, to the reach of the poorest and humblest individuals." Their zeal to price books for the "poorest and humblest" was certainly commendable but it was to lead them into a hornet's nest of criticism over the way they treated Richard H. Dana, Jr.

As the decade ended, the brothers had a payroll of two hundred, of which seventy-five were girls ("very pretty ones, too!" a visitor noted). In ten years they had invested $280,000 in stereotype plates. These plates represented their belief in titles that deserved being kept in print. They had no idea how many different books they had issued and made no effort to keep at least one file copy of every work. If someone wrote from the West Indies or another distant part of the world for the last of the Waverley novels, for them still a topic of

conversation, some clerk would scrounge around the stockroom looking for what would satisfy the customer, even though what he found,
and reported finding to the brothers, was the last copy on hand. They
would rather sell it than keep it. Cash on hand was more important
than sentiment on a shelf.

But sentiment about people was another thing. No amount of business strain ever disturbed the warmhearted affection the brothers expressed toward each other and within their increasing families. Equally
noteworthy were their friendly and helpful relations with many of
their employees. Once James learned of a woman in the bindery who
was suffering from an inflammation of the eyes; a sister had written
urging a visit to the country, a trip she could not afford to make. James
went to see her and handed her a little book, saying, "There, there,
don't be troubled about your eyes. Go and visit your sister and here is
a little book to read on the way." After he left, she found ten dollars
between the covers, more than enough money to finance the trip.

Father Harper came around to Cliff Street occasionally to see "the
boys" and pick out a new book to read. "I saw him the other day,"
Park Benjamin wrote in the *Southern Literary Messenger* in 1839,

a fine, bluff, hale, hearty, ruddy-cheeked farmer, who has outlived the
allotted span of "three score years and ten," yet has he not known a day of
that "labor and sorrow" which the scriptures speak of as the doom of age. I
talked with him about the country and the crops, and, hearing every word
that I uttered as distinctly as I heard his, he told me stories about by-gone
times, and, in ready answer to my questions, related instances of the muta-
tions of our human affairs. It was truly an interesting spectacle to behold
the good, old gentleman,—standing like a sturdy oak, strengthened by the
storms of eighty winters—in the midst of his men-children—whose children's children may, as I warmly hope, "make smooth the pillow of his
final rest". . . .

In 1839 the brothers had as yet no grandchildren, but the "sturdy
oak" could boast, in the way of grandfathers, of fourteen. While James
then had only one son and Fletcher two, the other brothers had between them contributed four sons and seven daughters. And more
were to come. By 1837 Wesley had moved from 124 White Street,
Manhattan, into a large, new, two-and-one-half-story house at 105
Clark Street on Brooklyn Heights. A handsome white building with
brick-lined walls, its first floor contained two drawing rooms, a library,
a dining room, and, surprisingly for a Methodist home, a billiard room.
There were thirteen bedchambers above. Two ideas were obviously in
Wesley's mind: the new publishing business was making enough money

for him and his partners so that he could afford it, and he and Hannah were planning to have a big family. The other brothers restlessly moved about, John and Tammisin with their brood of five less so than the other two; in 1839 they were about halfway through a twelve-year residence at 30 Pike Street. James and Maria were soon to move to Rose Street, their residence during his mayoralty. In 1840 Fletcher and Jane moved to 155 Crosby Street after having lived in three houses on Cliff Street, where they had also made a home for boys who were apprentice printers.

CHAPTER IX

Before the Mast with Dana
1840–1841

Janu$_{ARY}$ 1, 1840, was the coldest day New Yorkers had suffered so far in what had already been an unusually frigid winter. Despite the cold, James Harper and other New York gentlemen went out to make New Year's Day calls, as custom decreed they should. They wore heavy cloaks over their frock coats and held tightly to their tall silk hats as they bent against the wind. James may well have reflected as he walked cautiously over the icy streets that the book business was equally hazardous—you had to watch your step. But the cold days would pass with winter and the dark years of the thirties would be replaced by good fortune in the forties. Always an optimist, he was also a Whig, and he could not but blame Jackson and Van Buren for the depressions the country had suffered. But now it looked as though the voters were ready for a change.

This pesky matter of newspaper reprints of English fiction was going to be a hard nut to crack. Park Benjamin was doing a foolish thing with that new weekly paper he edited, *The New World*. If he kept on reprinting whole novels in its columns the book trade would be demoralized. People would not pay even fifty cents for a Bulwer novel if Benjamin continued dishing out new stuff for a few pennies an issue. He had liked Benjamin.* If it had not been for this newspaper scheme he and his brothers would have gone ahead with their plan to bring out a collection of Benjamin's poems.

Behind Benjamin was a dangerous competitor, the tough and crafty Jonas Winchester, publisher of *The New World*. Winchester and Benjamin H. Day, who had bought control of *Brother Jonathan*, were out to challenge the Harpers as they had never been challenged before. Post office regulations made it possible for these "literary" newspapers —known to the public as "mammoth sheets"—to be distributed rapidly throughout the country at cheap postage rates.

James thought the Harpers should concentrate even more than ever on nonfiction and educational works. The American people were always ready to buy low-priced books that gave them more knowledge about themselves and the world they lived in. If his friends asked him what was ahead for the book business in the New Year, he could say that Americans were the most literate people of any nation and that there would always be a demand for more and better books.

As the old year ended, Epes Sargent was writing to Longfellow in Cambridge, "The fact is that all our publishers, whether of books or periodicals are desperately poor." Sargent had three books coming in the next three years and all of them were to be aimed at that best of all markets, the *School District Library*, where sales were assured and where there were no credit risks. That James encouraged the twenty-seven-year-old Sargent to write seems indicated by the testimony of another ambitious young man, Benson J. Lossing, who had come to New York from Poughkeepsie. Lossing was probably introduced to the Harpers by Joseph A. Adams, the wood engraver, under whom Lossing had been studying. "Many of the most eminent authors and literary men had become associated with the House, and their reminiscences of Mr. Harper's sage counsel and quaint humor would fill a volume," Lossing wrote later in recalling his early visits to Cliff Street.

* Park Benjamin was a talented young poet and journalist with a club foot and a violent temper. He had been born in British Guiana, attended Harvard, Trinity, and Yale Law School, edited *The New England Magazine* in Boston and worked for Greeley on the *New Yorker*. In 1839 he and Rufus Wilmot Griswold were co-editors of *Brother Jonathan*, which offered in its weekly editions and also in special supplements very cheap reprints of English novels. In effect, it began a price-cutting war against the older established "pirates" among the book publishers. The enterprise was so successful that Jonas Winchester, Greeley's partner, left the *New Yorker*, hired Benjamin as his editor, and started *The New World*, whose oversized pages ("mammoth weeklies") and large quarto supplements, selling eventually as low as 12½ cents, were crammed with the same reading matter as the 50-cent Harper books.

"But especially the young and as yet unknown author had occasion to remember the appreciation and encouragement received in the counting-room when he first met the oldest of the Harper brothers."

James had good reasons for encouraging young Lossing, who in 1836 had begun collecting literary gems (mostly excerpts from other publications) in the semimonthly *Poughkeepsie Casket*. Now he was displaying similar treasures in the pages of Mr. Redfield's weekly *Family Magazine*, where he could also publish his own engravings. He talked with James about doing a *History of the Fine Arts;* it was an ambitious project but he could get help at the Academy of Design, where he was studying. James thought it would make a good book for the *S.D.L.*, assuming that the office of the superintendent of common schools would approve. Approval was forthcoming and Lossing's first Harper book came out in 1840 with the backing of the *Family Library* as well.

What Lossing received for his book is not known. It was probably $200, since that was the amount paid about the same time to another comparatively unknown author, Dr. Charles A. Lee, for his book of a similar size, *The Elements of Geology for Popular Use*. Lee's book was also placed in the two libraries for quick sales and marked for him, as for Lossing, the beginning of a long and profitable author-publisher relationship. Dr. Lee was a successful New York physician and a frequent contributor to medical periodicals in the thirties and forties. His book on geology reflected the breadth of his scientific interest.

The Lossing and Lee books would not bring much profit, for the library margins were slight, but they could help keep the establishment going and meet the payroll. Were there any other books coming along that could be put on this production belt? Yes, Miss Sedgwick's new juvenile, *Stories for Young People*, for one. To be sure, Miss Sedgwick could go it alone, but the *S.D.L.* was safer and no one in Albany would question the author of *Linwoods*. Dr. Hawks's two manuscripts, *Uncle Philip's Conversations* on the states of Massachusetts and New Hampshire, were nearly ready, and Albany had approved four "Uncle Philip" books for the first *S.D.L.* series. Finally, and unexpectedly, there was the story of young Dana's trip round Cape Horn, the *Journal* they had thought they might publish the year before.

In *The House of Harper*, J. Henry Harper makes no mention of his grandfather Fletcher's negotiations for the publication of the work of Richard H. Dana, Jr. Perhaps Mr. Harper referred neither to the young Bostonian nor his book, *Two Years Before the Mast*, because he considered these negotiations a blemish on the bright Harper escutcheon, which they possibly were. The brothers had a trade reputation in Philadelphia and perhaps elsewhere for driving a hard bargain and the Dana story was repeated so often that this expertise was magnified out of all proportion. Their dealings with Dana, moreover, were to damage their reputation with authors and were effectively used against them by competing publishers, both in Boston and in New York, always eager to find another battering ram to thrust at the ramparts on Cliff Street.

Dana had returned in 1836 from his two years' seafaring trip to California, both ways round Cape Horn, and had taken his last year at Harvard before attempting to write the story of his experiences. His confidence in his literary ability was strengthened by a dissertation he wrote on the moral tendency in Bulwer's novels. Turned out in five days, along with other work, the dissertation won a "first" as well as a Bowdoin prize.

Inspired to make a book of his experiences at sea in order to improve the lot of the common seaman in the merchant service, Dana was not above thinking that whatever publicity the book received would help give a good start to his law practice. In fact, the first draft of his manuscript was completed while he was attending law school at Harvard, and by May, 1839, it had been read with approval by members of his family with agreement that they should first try Harper's, since the Boston publishers seldom sold "books abroad [outside New England] except upon order, so that there would be very little chance of the journal spreading throughout the country." Both he and his father professed that they were not interested in pecuniary returns from the book, Dana, Sr., writing to Bryant, "If he must choose between the two, a wide circulation, & a higher offer,—he would elect the wider circulation."

Professor Leonard Wood, president-elect of Bowdoin College, a friend of the Danas, agreed to take the manuscript of the *Journal*, as it was then called, with him to New York and deliver it to Cliff Street. Wood left the manuscript on May 14, the day of his arrival in New York, saying that Mr. Dana would like the Harpers to get Mr. Bryant's opinion. Bryant had long known Dana, Sr., as a fellow poet, and as a founder of the *North American Review*, to which Bryant often contributed. Bryant read a good part of the *Journal* aloud to his wife and daughter and recommended it enthusiastically to the brothers, who promptly accepted it, offering to pay a royalty of 10 percent after one thousand copies had been sold. This offer was reported to the elder Dana by Professor Wood on his return to Boston June 12.

But Dana wanted something better for his son, and with more emotion than judgment wrote Bryant to bargain for better terms. Bryant, who knew better than Dana the depressed conditions of the book trade and the characteristics of the brothers, might better have counseled Dana to accept their terms; however, he did as his friend requested, only to be met with a blunt refusal to publish. Perhaps the Harpers were offended that a fair offer had been spurned—or perhaps they had decided that their offer had been too generous and were looking for a way out. At any rate they were no longer "interested." Bryant then tried Appleton, Colman, and Wiley & Putnam in that order, but all of them rejected the *Journal*. He so wrote Dana, who replied that Bryant should try Lea & Blanchard. By the end of September the leading publisher in Philadelphia had also said No, a not surprising decision, in view of the bad times. Whereupon, in early October, Bryant returned young Dana's frostbitten *Journal* to Boston, where it went into hibernation for a few months.

In New York the following January to deliver a series of lectures on Shakespeare, the elder Dana decided to swallow his pride and call on the brothers. He took Bryant along for support. "They are sharp & vulgar men to all appearance," Dana wrote to his son on January 29, 1840, "but you could do nothing with anyone else. If I am down in town to-morrow—as I probably shall be—I shall call upon them to ascertain, if I can, what they will do:—They are famous for talking away off." Five days later he wrote further:

I have seen the Harpers again. Should they like the M.S. I think you may get a couple of hundred from them. They wish to have it sent to them. They are the publishers to the N.Y. School Library—wh', I believe, extends thro the state. Their plan is, if it would answer to go into this library, to publish it for that, as well as for the public at large. It will be necessary to submit the M.S. to the Sec^y of the Lib^y for him to determine whether it be suitable. His decision would, of course, help to fix the sum they would allow you. Now, sh'd you prefer retaining an interest in the copy-right—to selling out & out, I take it you c'd not have any in the Library editions. The Harpers did not seem to like the proposition to have you interested in the general copyright. . . .

Bryant told them that there was nothing in it wh' could be objectionable as a School book. You can run y'r eye over it, & see if there is anything objectionable wh' you could strike out without injuring the work—but don't sacrifice *any* thing going to the merit of the work in any way:—better take the smallest sum, than do that. If a bargain is made with them, I conclude from what they said, that they would wish to go to print now. Have you seen to your Sandwich Island words, & to your Spanish? And have you written your *first* chap. & closing one?

By the end of February, Richard had polished the manuscript and added a short preface and a concluding chapter. He had decided that he would call his book *Two Years Before the Mast, A Personal Narrative of Life at Sea* and that his name should not appear on the title page but at the end of the preface, and there indicated by initials only. Soon it was again being considered in Cliff Street, with a reader objecting to profanity in the book. The Albany people might not approve of the book unless the oaths were deleted, the brothers cautioned Dana, Sr., who had called again at Cliff Street. This word Dana passed on to Richard along with news of the publishing terms he had agreed to. ". . . they [Harper's] will give you two hundred and fifty dollars for the entire copyright, and allow you twenty-five copies to distribute. They will send you proofs for correction. These were the best terms I could make with them." Not their earlier offer of 10 percent royalty after one thousand copies had been sold, but $250 outright.

Even so the brothers considered the book something of a risk, since the author was unknown and in view of the close figuring they had to do on *S.D.L.* books, which were priced at from 30 to 33 cents per volume, wholesale, as they had reported to Jared Sparks in January. Sparks had written from Cambridge offering to prepare and stereotype ten new volumes of *American Biography* selling rights for $1,000 each. They replied that to earn back their investment they would have to sell ten thousand copies of each volume; yet despite the risk they would be willing to experiment with from one to three volumes. Sparks attempted to meet their offer by suggesting a limited contract for ten volumes but the brothers replied on March 3 that they were afraid to do so "on account of the disorganized state of business. . . . The low price at which we are compelled to sell our Library will not justify us . . . in paying so high a price."

Thus to finance the Dana book the brothers had to figure the cost of composition and plates, and of printing, paper, and binding on a per-copy basis to come within the price received of from 30 to 33 cents. But first of all the manuscript would have to be approved by the superintendent of common schools in Albany. Since their friend and author Professor Alonzo Potter of Union College was the key man in getting books approved, they sent the manuscript to him in Schenectady. But officialdom rarely acts speedily and it was May before the manuscript, properly approved, was back in New York, with plans being made to issue it in the third series of the *S.D.L.*, to be ready by autumn.

In mid-August the stereotypes were ready and a decision was

reached on Cliff Street to issue the book also in the *Family Library*. On August 20, Wesley wrote young Dana that this decision had been reached after consulting with "judicious friends," including Bryant. "It will be quite as respectable, and certainly much more serviceable to you, published in this shape than in any other," he wrote, "inasmuch as it will take it, forthwith, before five times the ordinary number of readers." Recognizing that Dana had hoped for a format similar to the volumes in Sparks's *American Biography* (12mo instead of the smaller 18mo), Wesley continued, "The volume, to be sure, will not be as *handsome* as it would be, if published independently—but the price will not be more than half—and in these times especially, the *cost* of an article, we find, is an important consideration with all classes of the community. . . . We hope you will be pleased with this arrangement, as it will enable us to get the work in Boston *earlier* than we should otherwise be able to do. . . ."

Wesley's logic was correct. Times were bad, and it would be easier to market a book at 45 cents (38 cents in the *S.D.L.*) than at the usual 75 cents or $1 for a "muslin gilt" item. And the "five times" normal printing (five times 1,000 copies) that the *Family Library* issues were enjoying would give Dana what he had said he mostly wanted—circulation. But there was another logic operating which the cautious brothers had overlooked in buying the book cheap and selling it at a slight margin of profit. They were not considering two facts: one, that the public never hesitates to buy quality books properly priced, and two, that the most valuable asset a publisher has is a happy author of a successful book. It is clear that the brothers did not know at the time that they were handling one of the great books of the century. (See illustration 9.)

Copyrighted September 1, 1840, *Two Years Before the Mast* was a hit from the day of publication and the most talked-of book during that fall and winter. Bryant gave it a big boost in the *Post*, wrote a seventeen-page review in the *Democratic Review*, and arranged for Theodore Sedgwick to write a criticism for the *New York Review*. Booksellers reordered stock, which necessitated a second printing before the year's end. Relatives, friends, and other publishers commiserated with the two Danas because the Harpers had paid so small an amount for the copyright. A month after the fact of publication, one publisher, possibly Ticknor, said he would have paid $1,000 for the book. And two months after publication a Boston publisher told the elder Dana that he had talked with Fletcher about the book's success; obviously on the defensive, Fletcher replied, "But suppose we had been the losers?" It was not so naïve an answer as it seemed. In his 1856 autobiography, S. G. Goodrich, successful both as a publisher and an author, estimated that two-thirds of the books by American authors lost money for their publishers.

Safe as it was to publish for the two libraries, there were not enough books coming through to keep the presses busy. And the margins were so slight that higher-priced "trade" books were needed to help carry overheads. There were three categories that the brothers could venture: fiction, textbooks, and standard works that had built-in sales.

They would publish American fiction by established authors only, and they would have to be "name" authors. And they would publish a few fiction reprints from England, if for no other reason than to show Benjamin and Winchester that they were not easily bluffed. So for 1840 they selected seven English novels, all by standard authors, including their favorites Bulwer and James. On the American side, they had to get the Fay novel out, Bentley having issued it earlier in the year. It might not sell but Morris was after them and Fay's debit account was alarming. Much to their surprise, *The Countess Ida* went into a second printing in July, a month after publication. Charles Fenno Hoffman's novel *Greyslaer*, also ready for early summer publication, did even better, with two editions quickly sold and *The Knicker- bocker* saying in August that a fifth edition was imminent. However, these editions were small, perhaps a thousand or less.

A dramatization of Hoffman's romance produced at the Bowery Theatre helped *Greyslaer* sales, as did generous reviews; Hoffman's kindly nature and obvious literary gifts endeared him to editors. Hoffman had chosen the popular Revolutionary times as the setting for his novel, with Joseph Brant, the Mohawk Indian chief, as a main character—a nice touch, since Colonel Stone's recent *Life of Brant* had aroused interest in this well-educated Indian who aided the British.

The book of fiction that really brightened that dark year, still a shining bit of Americana, was *Georgia Scenes*, by Augustus B. Longstreet. The book had been issued five years earlier in Augusta, Georgia, by Longstreet's States' rights newspaper, the *S.R. Sentinel*. The Harper edition reproduced the original text of "characters, incidents, etc., in the First Half Century of the Republic" and added twelve original illustrations. Longstreet depicted quaint and hearty scenes of country life with realistic, and sometimes crude, humor. Van Wyck Brooks called Longstreet's sketches "racy and crisp . . . reflecting . . . rough and virile pioneer life, destined, thanks to the acid and salt that preserved them, to survive whole shelves of contemporary romances and novels." *Georgia Scenes* was mined from that rich American lode that later yielded up *Uncle Remus* and *Huckleberry Finn*. Longstreet had followed his Southern friend John C. Calhoun to Yale College and the Litchfield (Connecticut) Law School, after which he returned to Georgia to practice law and politics, establishing the *Sentinel* in Augusta. Later he became a Methodist minister and, as the dignified president of the new Emory College, regretted publishing his most famous book. Long vanished with the Harper files—probably destroyed in the 1853 fire—were letters that might reveal how the brothers first learned of the book and also how the author tried to suppress it. But readership could not be suppressed. The constant demand for *Georgia Scenes* called for printing after printing for many years.

As far as new textbooks were concerned, there was always Professor Anthon to count on. The brothers had urged him the previous summer to prepare a *Greek Reader,* saying they had received many letters from schools asking for it. He replied that he had also been importuned to prepare the book but had always said No. He was talked into doing the *Reader*, which ran to 628 pages, and students paid $1 for it when fall terms opened. Perhaps Anthon had hesitated because of the hostility of the Boston scholars connected with the *North American Review*. As expected, that publication viciously attacked the *Reader*, with *The Knickerbocker* rising nobly to Anthon's defense. What did it matter, really, what Boston thought? Oxford and Cambridge universities were adopting Anthon's texts and some of his volumes had already attained their fourth British edition.

Two important new textbook authors joined up with the brothers in 1840, both "Professors of Mental Philosophy": Thomas C. Upham of Bowdoin College, Maine, and James Renwick, Sr., of Columbia College. Upham had been teaching at Bowdoin since 1824—with Longfellow, Hawthorne, Thatcher, and the brothers Jacob and John Abbott as students. He had been brought to the college to oppose Kantian philosophy. Unable to do so, he happily conceived a distinction between the intellect, the sensibilities, and the will, putting his three concepts into a "three-decker" work entitled *Elements of Mental Philosophy*. Soon it was being sold as *Upham on the Will*, one volume, and *Upham's Mental Philosophy*,* two volumes, with the latter work also abridged in one volume for academies. The Upham titles were

---

* An extant copy of the thirty-six-page Harper catalogue for 1840 opens with seven pages (mostly testimonials) on the "Upham Series of Philosophical Works for Academies and Colleges."

among the longest-lived texts ever issued by Harper's. Upham, and later his estate, received a 10 percent royalty.

James Renwick's contribution was an annotated edition of an English work, J. F. Daniells's *Introduction to the Study of Chemical Philosophy*. The book became known as *Renwick's Natural Philosophy* and was to be given top listing in the fifth series of the *S.D.L.*, while two other Renwick books, one on chemistry and one on mechanics, went immediately into the third series. *Outline of Practical Mechanics* paid Renwick a royalty of 12½ percent after a thousand copies had been sold. The memorandum of agreement covering this title is noteworthy since it is perhaps the first Harper contract to carry an option clause: ". . . it being understood that we shall have the refusal of any work on Scientific subjects which he may hereafter prepare for the press." In order that 1840 could establish Renwick both as a Harper property and a writer of versatile interests, two political biographies by him were put in the *Family Library*, one a life of DeWitt Clinton and one on the lives of John Jay and Hamilton. Renwick's blending of philosophy and science is today possible only with a man of Whitehead's towering genius. But in the 1840's scientific studies, such as chemistry and physics, were closely related to philosophy, and academicians such as he could write authoritatively on a wide range of subjects. Renwick had been graduated from Columbia in 1806 at the head of his class, and had married the eligible Margaret Brevoort, whose father, a close friend of Irving's, owned a small farm north of Washington Square, land which was rapidly increasing in value.

Of "standard" books with built-in sales potential, the one that caused most excitement on Cliff Street was Major General Winfield Scott's *Infantry Tactics*. When he called on the brothers on March 17 to draft a contract for the work, every employee who could think up an excuse went through the counting room to get a look at him. "Old Fuss and Feathers" had been a military hero ever since the War of 1812, and only recently he had arranged a truce between lumberjacks in Maine and Canada, ending the so-called Aroostook border war. His *Infantry Tactics* contract specified that the brothers should produce the three-volume work "at least equal to" an edition formerly published by George Dearborn, from whom stereotype plates were purchased. On his part, Scott promised to furnish revisions without delay; on their part, the brothers agreed to pay 8⅓ cents per volume royalty (25 cents on all three volumes). But "should Congress or the War Department or any state government, appropriate money, or subscribe for, at any one time, several thousand copies . . ."—a not unlikely prospect, in case of another war—the royalty was to be upped to 10 cents per volume. *Scott's Tactics*, listed year after year in the Harper catalogues, sold for $2.50, thus yielding its author the equivalent of at least a 10 percent royalty. The book got off to a good start in 1840 and the following year, when the author was made General-in-Chief of the Army, Scott wrote to Thaddeus Stevens that "the brothers Harper have taken a strange notion that I am not only one of their best authors, but a proper man for the presidency." James would have admired Scott not only as a valuable author, a national celebrity, and a staunch Whig but also as a writer and speaker for temperance, strongly opposed to the use of "ardent spirits."

On September 23, 1840, C. E. Lester of Utica, New York, called at Cliff Street, offering a manuscript entitled *The Glory and Shame of England*, to make another book with "built-in" sales potential. Lester would have come properly introduced, a necessary protocol by now, so that the Harpers must have known that he was a lawyer, a one-time theology student, and an antislavery lecturer. In fact, he had been a delegate to the World's Antislavery Convention in London the previous year, and while in England had come to some conclusions about the trouble ahead for that country unless it changed its protective policy, high tariffs, and monopolies. He also had a few frank things to say about the Church of England. Friends who had seen the manuscript were enthusiastic, saying that his book would sell because it was well written and controversial. Actually many people had already subscribed for the book, and Lester would need at least fifteen hundred copies as soon as possible to supply this demand, and might require another thousand copies soon—perhaps more. Those were pleasant statistics to contemplate as John began figuring costs. He drafted a contract based on printing a first edition to include fifteen hundred copies for Lester and a likely quantity for the trade at a cost permitting Lester to procure his lot for 30 cents a copy. For later printings of smaller quantities Lester would have to pay more; the next thousand copies would cost him 50 cents each, and any additional number 75 cents. How profitable the book was to either party after publication in 1841 is not known, although it may have helped Lester receive an appointment as U.S. Consul to Geneva, a post he was to hold for five years. But the brothers did not publish his later books.

In late October, a few weeks after signing the Lester contract, the brothers executed one with the Rev. Dr. Albert Barnes of Philadelphia, to whom they needed no introduction. They knew that Barnes's *Notes* on the Gospels, the Acts of the Apostles, and Paul's Epistles to the

Romans and Corinthians had been selling in large quantities. As a popular preacher, Barnes had also contributed to "Annuals," but he had given that work up two years earlier, even though he was paid two dollars a page; he had "two ponderous octavos to get ready for launching." These were launched in 1838 by William Robinson of New York. Now Barnes transferred the publishing rights of all the New Testament volumes to the Harpers with the understanding that they would issue revised and corrected editions in a more convenient 12mo size. Whereupon they got busy and produced three cloth-bound volumes averaging four hundred pages in length—in the short space of six weeks. Even more surprising than such speed, with proofs going to Philadelphia and back, was the small financial margin they allowed themselves, probably only a fraction more than what they paid Barnes, whose contract stipulated a per-copy royalty of 12½ cents, 16⅔ percent of the retail price. In the following year, Harper's brought out single volumes of *Notes* on Romans, First Corinthians, and Second Corinthians and Galatians. These three volumes were also "revised and corrected." They also contracted to bring out six "paper backs" of *Questions*, each averaging 164 pages, to be sold at 15 cents per copy, with 1 cent going to the author.

Barnes wrote his commentaries by rising at four o'clock in the morning and working till nine; thus he rationalized that his literary activities and consequent earnings did not interfere with his pastoral duties. Even so, he had other responsibilities than those connected with his own parish. During the early thirties, he had been a storm center of the "New School" movement stirring within the Presbyterian Church. Since he was minister of the First Presbyterian Church of Philadelphia, the denomination's "Mother Church," and usually the meeting place of the General Assembly, he was the scapegoat in heresy trials and a leader of the "New School" group after a schism in 1837-38. (Barnes lived to see the reunion of the schismatic groups that was consummated in his old church in 1870.) Thus he was frequently called upon to preach and lecture outside his own church and was a trustee of the Union Theological Seminary of New York almost from its beginning in 1836. In a book telling of Union's first fifty years, Barnes was described as having "a countenance marked in an unusual degree by moral thoughtfulness, benignity, sweetness, refinement, and manly dignity."

By 1843, Barnes had earned $4,000 from his Harper contract, and by 1847 his books were making him widely known abroad. Fletcher was to write from London in August of that year, "Mr. Barnes' future volumes must be copyrighted in England. They are selling enormously. Three or four different editions are published." The *London Church Examiner* commented, "The fame of Albert Barnes, of Philadelphia, has become European."

The Barnes *Notes*, nearly four hundred pages long, sold for only seventy-five cents each. Did their low prices and extraordinary value lead to a claim that the Harpers were making it impossible for other American clergymen to write and sell books? Or that the policies of Cliff Street were stifling the creative impulse in preachers' studies throughout the land? If so the charge would have been hooted down, for books by clergymen on religious topics sprouted from every publisher's list during the 1840's. Yet the argument has as much validity as those we have cited from literary historians Van Wyck Brooks and Earl Bradsher, in discussing the copyright controversy.

The policy of the brothers seems obvious: if the book had wide sales potential, they printed large quantities and sold to a mass market, regardless of the nationality of the author. Even if they had paid the same royalty to the Englishman Bulwer as to the American Barnes, it would have added only about 20 cents to the retail price, making a 70-cent book. And the book buyer would have paid the whole extra cost.

By the same token the Harpers could not afford to gamble large printings and low retail prices on unknown writers—British or American. No doubt they sometimes confused the record by using the availability of English reprints as an excuse for rejecting American manuscripts which they simply did not want. Such an instance occurred, apparently, when Washington Irving tried to persuade them to take a book by a friend of his—not known as a writer—and they refused. Writing in the January, 1840, *Knickerbocker*, Irving cited this as an argument for international copyright. Saying that he had "found it impossible to get an offer from any of our principal publishers" for the manuscript of his unidentified friend, Irving continued: "They even declined to publish it at the author's cost, alleging that it was not worth their while to trouble about native works of doubtful success, while they could pick and choose among the successful works daily poured out by the British press, *for which they had nothing to pay for copyright.*"

Irving's conversion to copyright reform was more laudable than the example he used. There was less risk in taking an American book whose author paid manufacturing costs than in taking an English book where the only saving was in not paying royalty. But a publisher cannot just say, "No, thank you," particularly not to a kindly, famous

Irving. The availability of English reprints offered an easy way out, and it was probably often used; if Mr. Clay's bill had become the law of the land, some other excuse would have been given.

On August 31, 1840, the brothers contracted with Irving himself for a book, when he and his brother Ebenezer called at 82 Cliff Street to discuss terms for a biography of Goldsmith with selections from his writings, two volumes that would join the Dana book in the *Family* and *School District* libraries. The terms agreed upon were an advance of $500 in lieu of royalty on the sale of 6,250 copies, and a royalty of 8 cents a copy thereafter. Since the two volumes retailed for 90 cents, the royalty rate covered by the advance was approximately 12 percent, to be reduced to about 9 percent. A declining scale of royalty seems surprising in view of today's practice of paying successful authors royalties on an ascending scale. Yet the Irving contract followed the logic of the Scott and Lester agreements: if you could market large quantities justifying large initial printings, you had more money to divide with the author. A likely assumption is that the 6,250 figure specified in the Irving contract of August 31 was the size of the first printing, 5,000 copies ("five times the ordinary number") for the *Family Library* and 1,250 for the *S.D.L.* Irving's *Goldsmith* came out in November. His biographer, S. T. Williams, says that Irving was never really interested in Goldsmith, and produced the book solely for financial gain, basing his work half on Prior's biography and half on ill-founded gossip.

Halleck and Bryant were also doing hack work that year to the benefit of the two Harper libraries, Halleck collecting an anthology of English poetry and Bryant one of American. Halleck's *Selections from British Poets* was a two-volume work and represented 106 poets; Bryant's *Selection from American Poets*, one volume, with 69 poets, including the two anthologists themselves and their friends (but not Poe). Bryant promised in his preface that if the book should have a favorable reception he would prepare another, possibly because all love and drinking poems had been omitted in order not to offend the school authorities in Albany or Hartford or Harrisburg.

Sam Ward, son of the wealthy New York banker, and brother of Julia Ward Howe, called at 82 Cliff Street on December 10 to look over a copy of Bryant's *Selections* and see what poems of his friend "Longo" Longfellow had been included. He was delighted with the choice and so wrote Longfellow, adding, "They [the brothers] told me that your publishers [John Owen] make too much money with your *Voices of the Night*—they give Halleck and Bryant 25 cents for every copy they sell of their poems." Realizing their mistake in not taking on Longfellow's *Hyperion*, the Harpers were trying to woo him back. (The royalty payments they cited to Ward were for the authors' own books, not the anthologies.)

Nearly everyone was writing poetry, and the publication of two anthologies of verse was found to bring even more songsters to Cliff Street. But the brothers would not catalogue the works of poets unless their names were well established. Hopefully Longfellow might have a book for them in the year just ahead; Mrs. Sigourney surely would. To publish the works of unknown authors just then was to risk too much. The winter closing in was as cold and disconsolate as the economics of the book business. James's optimism was running thin.

In New York that winter, the Dana saga was read by twenty-one-year-old Herman Melville, who, unable to find work, was a problem both to himself and his fatherless family. He began to dream about a sea voyage he too might take to far-off lands. The popularity of Dana's book abroad (it was published in England by Moxon) was attested by an order of the Lords of the Admiralty that a copy be placed in every library of the British Navy.

With his book a best seller, Dana wrote to the brothers in early March, 1841, to ask if they would sell him the copyright. Fletcher replied that they would willingly do so except for the fact that the book had been incorporated in the two *Libraries* and "our engagements with the public and the State render it necessary that they should ever remain there." But why did not Fletcher offer at that time to redraft their agreement, putting the book on a half-profits basis? He obviously had half profits in mind when he went on to say, "You have probably seen some of the paragraphs that have been going the rounds of the papers, magnifying the sale and profits of the work. We wish that they were well founded—but the fact is (between ourselves) we find upon a close calculation that we have not yet cleared a profit of two hundred and fifty dollars out of the sales of the work. The great demand has been principally from New England and some of the Atlantic cities."*

No doubt there were discussions in the Cliff Street counting room about the damage that unfavorable publicity was doing to the Harper name. Why not offer a half-profits contract now, admitting that the Dana work was selling better than anyone had ever dared to hope?

---

* In February Bryant had urged the brothers to give extra compensation to Dana. They said they had made nothing so far and offered to open their books to Dana's "friends" to prove it.

There was one strong argument against it—the very nature of a contractual agreement. You did not consider violating a business contract any more than you did a marriage contract. To be sure, you might be unhappy later on, but you did not go back on your pledged word. If the practice of rethinking and revising agreements ever started, there would be no end to confusion. Every author of a successful book would be knocking at your door asking for a better deal. Better to ride out the storm. Even though the brothers had so debated the issue, the question remains, why did they not issue a quality edition—then or later—based on a separate contract? Apparently they did not do so then because of their conviction that they could market only low-priced books, and by the time business conditions were better they had turned to other projects.

In 1862 Fletcher was dealing with another author who felt he was poorly paid. Anthony Trollope had written to the London *Athenaeum* to air his discontent over the Harper payment of £200 for early sheets of his novel *Orley Farm*. Fletcher may have had Dana in mind when he replied in a letter to the *Athenaeum*, "He [Trollope] is not the first man who, in the hope of selling his wares for a sovereign, has refused ten shillings, and has at last grumblingly agreed to accept a crown."

What was basically wrong with the Dana contract was not so much the amount the Harpers paid but that they purchased the copyright outright. Granted that they were contracting with other relatively unknown authors such as Lee and Lossing on the same terms. Granted that economic conditions were extremely unfavorable. Yet they might have renewed their original royalty offer when they reconsidered the work.

Actually the brothers were not buying American copyrights as frequently as London publishers were buying English copyrights, and were therefore less often in hot water over what was known as a "shrewd purchase." Even as late as 1875, George Bentley, Richard Bentley's son, was to purchase the copyright of *Comin' Through the Rye* by Helen Reeves for thirty guineas, and although he did make additional payments Mrs. Reeves claimed that she had lost £30,000 by selling her coypright. It did little good for Bentley to counter by saying that the firm's gross profit was only £3,000, or to moralize, "If I sold a horse or a picture tomorrow for an agreed amount, I should never receive another penny even if it won the Derby or was discovered to be an Old Master." Publishers had to learn the hard way of experience; today book rights to manuscripts are rarely, almost never, purchased outright.

During the winter of 1840-41, Dana had been writing a second book to be called *The Seaman's Friend* and arranged with Little and Brown to publish the book, they to assume manufacturing costs and pay a royalty of 10 percent on the retail price. By early June, the Boston publishers had the book in type and were proceeding with plates when they realized that Dana was angling for a better offer. On June 11, they wrote him that they had assumed they had a contract to proceed with the book, but they would "cancel" if he took over their liabilities to date. Whereupon Dana, now an author of some sophistication, wrote to the brothers to ask if they were interested in doing the book. Their reply in Fletcher's handwriting was dated June 14. "You say, 'be so good as to name your *highest price* as I shall take up with one of the other offers here, unless you go beyond them.' From this we infer that you have a preference for other publishers—If this is so, we respectfully decline making any offer. If, however, we are mistaken on this point, please let us know how much you have been offered and we will inform you by return mail whether we will *advance* on the offers that have been made." Dana's letter giving the Little and Brown offer was sent the following day and just as promptly rejected, Fletcher writing, ". . . upon reflection, we cannot bring our minds to go beyond the offer you have already received." He went on to say that they were about to go to press with a new edition of *Two Years Before the Mast* in which corrections that Dana had sent had been incorporated.

Years later when Parke Godwin was writing the biography of William Cullen Bryant, his father-in-law, he asked Harper's how many copies of the Dana book they had sold. They replied that they could not say, owing to the loss of their early accounts in the 1853 fire. Perhaps they did not know the precise answer but they could have given a fairly near guess. And they might in this instance have swallowed their pride to accommodate their friend Godwin and for the sake of generations to come who, having loved the book, were curious to know its publishing history. The only available Harper statistics relate to stock on hand, when, after twenty-eight years, the copyright expired, reverting to the author. On October 16, 1868, "Joe Brooklyn" Harper was to ask for an inventory count of *Two Years Before the Mast*. He noted in his memorandum book, "80 sewn sheets and 68 cloth bound copies." Demarest was to say in his *Catalogue* (1882) that the plates were destroyed, and closed the *Family Library* listing of 187 titles with a melancholy sentence, "The copyright of Dana's *Two Years Before the Mast* having expired, that work [No. 106] is withdrawn and nothing as yet substituted."

CHAPTER X

Publishing on Narrow Margins
1841–1842

Dana's second book did not add to his literary stature though it became at once a standard work on maritime law. Dana did not follow in John L. Stephens's wake, making other voyages to write about in further books. Stephens's third book was, in fact, a natural outgrowth of his going to the Caribbean in 1839, at the request of President Van Buren, who named him special ambassador to Central America. By spring, 1841, he had completed *Incidents of Travel in Central America, Chiapas, and Yucatan* and the Cliff Street establishment was setting the type and making the engravings, seventy-nine in all. The two-volume work, totaling 906 pages, was copyrighted on May 26 and contracted for as "now published" on July 19. Stephens retained the foreign market, the brothers agreeing to supply him with books to ship abroad at 10 percent over costs. The American retail price was $5.

The first printing of *Central America* was probably five thousand copies since the *Democratic Review* said in August that this quantity had been sold, with the demand so great that the Southern and Western markets could not be supplied. The October issue of the newly established *United States Literary Advertiser and Publishers' Circular* announced that the book was having a success "almost without precedent in this country," with more than ten thousand copies in circulation, and before Christmas the new Harper best seller had passed the twenty thousand mark. A French translation was under way, and an edition was about to appear in Germany. Langley, the editor of the new trade monthly, went on to share the latest gossip about the English edition. Apparently Stephens had purchased a quantity to be shipped to Murray in London. But Murray refused to pay "the expenses of duty, etc." until Colonel Thomas Aspinwall, the American Consul in London, came to Stephens's rescue by becoming security for the shipment. When these copies were bought up faster than Murray could supply them, he became really interested in the book and wrote to Stephens complimenting him on its deserved success. After relating all this to his readers, Langley said he was authorized to state that the story was altogether without foundation.

In October Stephens was off again to Guatemala. He had not said all he wanted to say about Central America, particularly Yucatán. Now he would be able to get more accurate detail for the illustrations. He took with him equipment for making and developing photographs, then called daguerreotypes, after Daguerre, the French artist who published the first description of his process in 1839. Stephens would have gone to Professor George W. Draper of New York University for instructions in this new art, since Draper in his experiments with Samuel F. B. Morse had made photography really feasible by creating a plate sensitive to a shorter exposure. Draper had taken the first photographic portrait of a human being—his sister, Dorothy—and also of the moon. With Draper's help, Stephens and his associate Francis Catherwood planned to take many daguerreotypes of artifacts in Yucatán, thus improving the quality of the illustrations for the next book.

Illustrations could also be used in book reviews. A woodcut, along with an extract from Stephens's *Central America*, was sent on June 11 to Rufus Wilmot Griswold for his use in the weekly Boston *Notion*. Griswold had left Philadelphia in early May and, en route to Boston, had stopped by Cliff Street to learn of forthcoming books to review. When Fletcher sent the Stephens publicity material, he assured its use by insinuating an exclusive feature. "Please keep this as quiet as possible," he wrote, "until your paper of the 19th inst. is published." In addition to performing his editorial chores, Griswold was busily collecting material for an anthology of American poets to be published soon by Carey & Hart. In Boston he would see Holmes and Longfellow and Lowell and Whittier in their homes or meet them at the Old Corner Book Store of "Jamie" Fields, who was a poet as well as a publisher. Dr. Holmes wrote, "What a curious creature Griswold is! He seems to be a kind of naturalist whose subjects are authors, whose memory is a perfect fauna of all flying and creeping things that feed on ink." Henry James was a child when Griswold called on his father, Henry, Sr. The son remembered Griswold as a man ". . . with lurid complexion, long, dark, damp-looking hair and a tone of conciliation."

Griswold was the sort of hack writer and compiler, not himself creative, who has always helped to keep publishers in business, both nourishing the tree of literature and being nourished by it. A few months before he left Philadelphia, where he was writing for the *Daily Standard*, Griswold received a letter from Horace Greeley, who sent him copies of his privately printed book *Science of Numbers*, to be distributed to newspaper editors just prior to the forthcoming Trade Sales. "Manage this neatly for me," Greeley wrote, "[even] if you have to write the notices or cut them from old papers, and I'll puff your book when it comes out."

About this time, Greeley was deciding that he should either sell or discontinue the *New Yorker*, which for seven years had earned him little either of fame or fortune. He was suffering from the financial distress of the times and from competition with the mammoth weeklies. "The great beasts murder me in the way of circulation," Greeley wrote Griswold in February, 1841. "Did you ever see such unmitigated humbugs?" Finding no buyers for the *New Yorker*, he discontinued it and, in April, established the New York *Tribune*.

The demise of the *New Yorker* was a blow to book publishers as was the failure a few months later of the much older *Mirror*. In addition to his own worries, General Morris was burdened with Fay's. Off in Berlin, Fay was wondering how much *The Countess Ida* had earned for him and how his Harper account stood. He kept after Morris to find out, and on January 2 Morris wrote in some exasperation, "I have had hundreds of talks with them, but to no purpose." Whereupon Fay turned to another friend, Daniel Fanshaw, to call at 82 Cliff Street on his behalf. On July 4 Fanshaw wrote Fay that he had talked with the brothers several times and expected to get a statement of account the following day. They had talked about having prepared two or three statements recently, but were concerned that they not "get in trouble from any mistake the clerk might make in carrying so many bills." They were also hesitant to release a statement without authorization from Fay. Whereupon Fanshaw produced the necessary letter from Fay and was given a partial accounting. The brothers were not willing, in view of the large debit balance against Fay's account, to release

Jones and Morris as endorsers of the note. Nor were they willing to divulge to Fay's "representatives" how large the debit balance was.

What they did not realize was that Fay had apparently forgotten about the five-year-old $1,000 advance, which was annually compounding interest. Or had he? In his Berlin office, Fay added up three credits to his account, which lacked but a few dollars of equaling the principal of his $1,500 note—and decided to write another novel. He would get word to Harper's.

This time he sent still another emissary, Mr. E. J. Detmold, who called at Cliff Street in November. Fletcher probably knew that Detmold was engaged in making surveys for projected railroads in the East and wondered why Fay had asked so busy an engineer to bother himself about literary matters. Of course he received Detmold courteously, saying he was pleased to hear that Fay was working on a new book, and asked its title. Detmold replied that Fay called the novel *Hoboken* and in turn wanted to know if Harper's would advance him $1,500 for it. "When it comes, we will submit it to our reader," Fletcher replied, "and then name the amount we can pay for it." This conversation Detmold reported to Fay in a letter on November 28, saying that he did not think Fay could count on so large an advance; he had heard a good deal of talk from the Harpers about the diminished sale of novels and general depression in their trade, as well as everybody else's.

To survive, a publisher had to count on a great deal more than fugitive fiction. Fortunately the brothers had the two *Libraries* to sustain their 1841 program, especially the *School District Library*. In his message to the New York State Legislature in 1841, Governor William Henry Seward stated that the productive capital of the Common School Fund was $2,036,625, its whole income being $261,073, and boasted of 10,886 school district libraries, with an estimated 630,000 volumes already purchased.

Of the total of fifty-three Harper titles published that year, twenty-three were issued in the *S.D.L.* Four titles were actually ready before the end of 1840 and went into the third series along with the Halleck and Bryant anthologies. Seventeen went immediately into the fourth series, issued during the autumn or winter of 1841* and three were held over for the two later series. At least ten titles in the fourth series were published in the early thirties; obviously someone had carefully

---

* See pp. 384ff for a listing of the series. *Letters from Abroad*, Vol. I (printed in July, 1841), carried an advertisement of the first three series, followed by the line, "The Fourth Series is now in Press." "In Press" was a phrase used by the brothers with considerable elasticity.

culled the back list for possible additions. Dr. Alonzo Potter, probably, for he was eating and sleeping the *S.D.L.* that year. His own
book, *Political Economy: Its Objects, Uses, and Principles: Considered
with Reference to the Conditions of the American People*, came out in
1841. He wrote an introduction to Abbé Maury's *Principles of Eloquence* and to Francis Lieber's *Essays on Property and Labor*. He may
well have rounded up Lieber for Harper's since they were teaching in
the same field, Lieber in South Carolina State College, Columbia. Born
in Germany in 1800, Lieber had come to America at the age of twenty-
seven, quickly establishing his name as a scholar; by 1832 he had completed for Henry Carey a thirteen-volume *Encyclopedia Americana*
(four years in the making) based on the Brockhaus *Konversations-
Lexikon*. His *Essays* were in immediate demand beyond the *S.D.L.*,
with reprints called for in 1842 and 1843.

Dr. C. S. Henry was another eminent scholar whose *Epitome of the
History of Philosophy* went immediately into the *S.D.L.* His two-
volume work was basically a translation from the French, giving concise biographies of leading philosophical writers of modern Europe
with brief expositions of their doctrines; to these he added about one-
fourth of new material. His book became a standard text and reference
title and was long in print. Dr. Henry had been a co-founder with
"Uncle Philip" Hawks of the *New York Review* in 1837 and was
professor of philosophy at New York University. He was a man of
great personal magnetism and an inspiring teacher.

Seven other American writers were represented in *S.D.L.* selections
in 1841, importantly Theodore Dwight, Jr., with a *History of Connecticut*. Two other authors contributed histories of the states of
Louisiana and Michigan, and Mrs. S. J. Graves produced *Women in
America*. Epes Sargent wrote *American Adventure by Land and Sea*,
heroic tales of the riflemen of the Chippewa Indians, of Daniel Boone
in Kentucky, of a forest on fire, of a tussle with a wildcat, of the wreck
of the whale ship *Mentor*, of the burning of the *Lexington*, and twenty-
seven more, showing American boys how enterprise and fortitude
could overcome hardship and terror.

That great naval hero of the Revolution, John Paul Jones, received
full biographical treatment in a two-volume work by Alexander Slidell
Mackenzie. This was Mackenzie's second venture in biography, for
which he had considerable talent, his life of Commodore Perry having
appeared the year before. The Perry biography, undertaken at the
request of the commodore's son, Dr. Grant Perry, was written at the
Mackenzie farm north of Tarrytown.

Successful as a biographer and with his new rank as commander,

Mackenzie left his rural retreat in May, 1842, to take charge of a U.S. Navy "school ship," the brig *Somers*. On his return trip from Africa a mutiny developed and a council of officers decided on the execution of the three leading malcontents, a decision carried out properly at the yardarm. One of the young men who were hanged was Midshipman Philip Spencer, son of Fletcher's Albany friend John C. Spencer, now in President Tyler's Cabinet as Secretary of War. Widespread publicity attended the return of the *Somers* in December and a Navy court of inquiry was instituted. This court found that the action of the officers was justified. However, at Commander Mackenzie's request a court-martial was held the following February and he was again acquitted. His trials also received wide publicity and his acquittal brought celebrations by friends in New York, Philadelphia, and Boston; his portrait bust, made by the sculptor Henry Dexter, was placed in the Boston Athenaeum.

Richard Henry Dana attended Mackenzie's trial and was impressed by the officer-author's bearing and testimony. He then visited the *Somers* and wrote a description of what he saw that was printed in many newspapers. Dana reported that the *Somers* was an unusually small brig, with low bulwarks and a single narrow deck fore and aft. Thus an ambush of the officers could easily have been managed by a handful of resolute conspirators before aid could come from below. Because the ship was laden with ammunition, Dana argued, it would have been too risky to attempt to imprison the mutineers, and the officers were endangered further by a surly crew. Hence extreme measures had been required to enforce discipline.

Mackenzie's first officer was Herman Melville's cousin Guert Gansevoort. Thus Melville's family was emotionally involved in the *Somers* affair, and in his later years Melville, haunted by the tragedy, was to write *Billy Budd*. While his cousin and Mackenzie were risking their lives with mutineers on the Atlantic Ocean, Melville was having a different sort of adventure on the Marquesas Islands in the South Pacific. What he observed there would later make a famous book.

Perhaps the most important work added in 1841 to both *Libraries* was the classic *Natural History and Antiquities of Selborne*, by the English cleric Gilbert White. Published in England in 1789, it was the first book to carry natural history into the realm of literature. White's acute observations of birds and animals and their habits are charmingly interwoven with anecdotes and comment. Thoreau was much influenced by White and he may have first read the book in the *Family Library* edition.

Income from the sale of Stephens's *Incidents of Travel in Central America* . . . and the two thriving libraries probably represented most of the accounts receivable at 82 Cliff Street in 1841. In addition, there was some income from the sale of five novels by those perennials Bulwer and James, but little profit because of newspaper competition. The big book from England for the year was written by James Silk Buckingham, the popular lecturer who had done so much to boost the sales of Stephens's first two books. After three years' sojourn in America, Buckingham knew that Americans, with a broad streak of narcissism in their psyche, enjoyed seeing themselves reflected in the literary mirrors held up by foreign authors. So he decided he would write a book which was eventually called *America, Historical, Statistical and Descriptive*, and asked the brothers if they would be interested in publishing an American edition. Indeed they were. They knew that his lectures had drawn huge crowds, and the newspapers had given him much publicity. Buckingham was for Americans the typical Englishman, having done the things that a distinguished Briton was supposed to do. He had spent several years as a young man at sea; he had lived in India, where in 1823 he established the Calcutta *Journal* and bravely fought the East India Company; returning to England, he had established the *Athenaeum*, destined to be the country's leading literary periodical; he had served in Parliament for five years. Furthermore he was a man of liberal views, of great friendliness, and of distinguished bearing.

At ten o'clock on Monday, November 22, 1840, the Hon. Mr. Buckingham had an appointment at 82 Cliff Street to make final arrangements for his book prior to his departure for London. He made six proposals to the brothers, five covering possible royalty payments, ranging up to 20 percent of the retail price, and one covering an equal division of profits after manufacturing costs, but not advertising, were deducted. The brothers naturally agreed to the half-profits arrangement, and asked for prior publication here as a precaution against the pirating of early copies from England.

By the summer of 1841, Buckingham had completed his book in London and stereotypes had been dispatched to New York. It was launched with great enthusiasm at the fall Trade Sales in New York and Philadelphia, and promoted with a generous distribution of newspaper releases and review copies. One copy was read by Poe, who was now reviewing books for *Graham's Magazine*. What he wrote was deflating both for author and publisher. After noting that on Buckingham's visit he was "feasted, huzzaed, followed by crowds . . . made a lion of," and that his two-volume work had been "ushered in by a flourish of trumpets from the presses on both sides of the Atlantic," Poe mournfully announced that not only was the author inane and egotistical, but also the book was exceedingly dull, not even worthy of being called mediocre. Despite Poe, there were enough Americans interested in what Buckingham had to say about them to keep the book in Harper catalogues through 1853.

Buckingham's book came out a few weeks after Miss Sedgwick's travel book in reverse: America's leading novelist published *Letters from Abroad* on August 1, giving her impressions of persons and places seen in England and on the Continent. In May, 1839, Miss Sedgwick had left her home in the Berkshires to spend fifteen months abroad. She went first to London. Willis was also there and wrote to the *Corsair* that visiting American ladies were a good deal the fashion; however, "Miss Sedgwick is here, but she seems to require a trumpeter." This accusation infuriated the *Southern Literary Messenger*, which asserted that Miss Sedgwick would not be interested in the frivolous English society to which Willis's "dandyism, affectation and servility" were suited. In her book two years later, Miss Sedgwick let it be known that she had attended theatres, balls, and dinner parties with titled personages, but her chief concern was to share with her readers her impressions of the literati of London, including the "two female writers most read in the United States, Miss Martineau and Mrs. Jameson." She was entertained by Lady Byron; Rogers, the poet; Joanna Baillie, the favorite both of Byron and Scott; Carlyle; and Miss Mitford. She also met Macaulay and Milman. Another Harper author, M. Sismondi, entertained her in Geneva; Sismondi, who wrote the *History of the Italian Republics*, had been her "long and intimate correspondent."

In addition to the books of travel on their 1841 lists, the brothers issued two books of poetry and two scholarly books by Anthon. The poets were Lydia Huntley Sigourney of Hartford, and Seba Smith of Portland, Maine. A veteran authoress whose work had been popular since 1815, Mrs. Sigourney soon discovered that in *Pocahontas and Other Poems* she had produced her most successful book to date. The lead poem was based on the early hsitory of Virginia and the career of the Indian princess who rescued Captain John Smith. Mrs. Sigourney did not dwell overlong on warfare between white men and Indians, but charmingly described the peaceful domesticity of Pocahontas's marriage to an English planter, John Rolfe, with frequent moralizing comments in her best style of iambic verse.

Oddly enough Mr. Seba Smith's poem was given the same historical setting, only he took Pocahontas's father for his hero, calling his "metrical romance" *Powhatan*. The subject was an odd one for Smith, who was famous for the political satires he wrote under the pseudonym Major Jack Downing. During the 1830's *The Life and Writings of Major Jack Downing of Downingville*, composed in twanging "Down-East" dialect, was one of the most popular books in America. It was aped by Charles Davis in the Harper best seller. (See p. 42.)

"Jack Downing" was a character somewhat like a modern-day "Kilroy," as illustrated in *Two Years Before the Mast*. The brig *Alert* bringing Dana home was off the Bermudas on September 11, 1836, when an outgoing vessel was sighted. In hopes of getting some fresh provisions the captain of the *Alert* signaled the other brig, the *Solon*, to heave to. After five months at sea, his crew was down to salt rations and two seamen were ill with scurvy. The *Solon* had an ample supply of onions, potatoes, and other fresh foodstuff, so the needs of Dana and his companions were quickly met. "We had supposed," Dana wrote, "that a new president had been chosen, the last winter, and just as we filled away, the captain hailed and asked who was president of the United States. They answered, Andrew Jackson; but thinking that the old General could not have been elected for a third time, we hailed again, and they answered—Jack Downing; and left us to correct the mistake at our leisure." (Dana's mistake was that he was thinking 1835 had been the year of a presidential election.)

The appearance, side by side, of two books of verse about early Virginia was naturally interesting to the ex-Virginian Poe, who took special note in his critical column in *Graham's*. He gave *Powhatan* elaborate praise as to paper and binding and typographical accuracy—after reading the book with the "greatest attention," he had not detected a single error. Then, with everyone's guard down, Poe delivered a knockout blow: "Your poem is a curiosity, Mr. Jack Downing; your 'Metrical Romance' is not worth a single half sheet of the paste-board upon which it is printed."

However, Poe had words of praise only for Professor Anthon, whose *Classical Dictionary* was published in the summer of 1841. His critical thrusts were on Anthon's behalf against the "clique of pedants in and about Boston" who had accused Anthon of plagiarism, "the most preposterous accusation in the world." Anthon had a right to claim the work as his own, although he did incorporate the writings of other scholars. Years before he had translated from the French Lemprière's *Dictionnaire*, a book revered by classicists, and made additions of his own; in 1833 he had prepared a subsequent edition of the work, rewriting nearly every article and making further additions. By 1839 he was contemplating a further and completely new work and asked the brothers to purchase the old plates from Messrs. Carvill for $4,500, presumably to get the book off the market. He asked them to charge him interest on the purchase price, he to own the plates and copyright. (See illustration 12.) The Harper edition was a completely reset royal-octavo volume of 1,467 pages and retailed for $4.75. Since it was published a little over two years after the old plates were purchased, the brothers used this period of time as the basis of a press release. It was immediately picked up by the *Democratic Review*, which charged that Anthon was vain to claim that he had produced such a monumental literary work in so short a time. Furthermore, Anthon was prudish to omit important information and to give Cleopatra but a few lines. And why should Christ, Paul, and others escape all mention? The *Democratic Review* also detected some inaccuracies. Anthon replied to this onslaught in *The New World*, hurling insults at the *Democratic Review* and defending himself badly. This counterattack shocked the *Democratic Review* and fomented further accusations on its part.

The most vitriolic attack on Anthon's *Dictionary* was made by Cornelius Mathews in his short-lived magazine *Arcturus*, who said that it was "not quite the original work the puff manufacturers of Cliff Street would have us believe." Mathews claimed falsely that Anthon's publishers had got the work for nothing and called its publication the "jobbing literature and book-making of Professor Anthon and the Harpers." He quoted an English notice saying that Anthon had stolen his material from the *Penny Cyclopedia*, an English work. However, Anthon did credit his sources and what he took from the *Penny Cyclopedia* he credited by its "less vulgar" name, *The Encyclopedia of Useful Knowledge*. All of this barbed controversy helped pleasantly to sell copies of the *Dictionary*.

Anthon's prolific output in 1841-42 included *Latin Prosody and Metre* and two companion textbooks on introductory prose composition, one Greek and the other Latin. While other reviewers were praising content, Clark wrote in *The Knickerbocker* to applaud the "externals" as worthy of the press from which they emanated. The paper, typography, and binding of the Anthon books should be an object lesson to other American publishers of schoolbooks. Perhaps Anthon himself insisted on quality in book production, for he was not a man to overlook details, and his love for books would include beauty of appearance as well as utility of content. He wanted students to share his enthusiam for classical studies, and for handsomely printed books.

Schmucker's Psychology was another textbook issued in 1842. Subtitled "Elements of a New System of Mental Philosophy," it was written by the Rev. S. S. Schmucker, professor of theology, and later president, at the recently founded Lutheran College at Gettysburg. The *Democratic Review* devoted a twenty-one-page review to the book, wholly negative. Likewise the *Messenger* said in its April issue that it had rarely seen a work that hit more widely of its mark, but by May it had completely reversed its view, commending *Schmucker's Psychology* highly; *The Knickerbocker* also gave its imprimatur to the book. What perhaps is most noteworthy about Schmucker is that a theologian writing on "psychology" was considered worthy of attention in three literary periodicals. Publishers today might find it difficult to interest reviewers in this intermixture of disciplines.

The year 1842 was one of the darkest in Cliff Street since the panic of 1837. Only thirty-six new books were published, and these moved out slowly; some works that were announced as in press in January were still there in March, sluggish as the icy waters of the Hudson. People who read for entertainment were buying Bulwer, James, and Dickens in the mammoth newspapers, intrigued by their novelty and cheapness. There they were also reading the works of Ingraham and other American authors whose copyright output was considered too risky for hard-cover publication. The brothers had often bragged of their ability to market books at low prices, but now they were being beaten at their own game.

In the meantime their good friend Dr. David M. Reese had dutifully fulfilled his commission to revise and enlarge Cooper's *Dictionary of Practical Surgery*, a steady seller since 1833. The new edition was an immediate success. Eleven physicians signed a letter to the Harpers (who no doubt inspired it) saying that they wished "to renew our thanks for the most acceptable edition [with] which you have just favored our profession . . . you have carefully embodied the great mass of original material . . . of the seventh and last [English] edition, and have also again commanded the talents of the same able and efficient editor, Prof. Reese, to enrich the book. . . . [after] a diligent investigation into the merits and services of American surgeons throughout the Union. . . ."

The most celebrated surgeon in America, Dr. Valentine Mott, turned in a manuscript this same year—not a medical tome, however, but another travel book. Entitled *Travels in Europe and the East*, this 452-page work did, of course, contain observations on the practice of medicine and surgery he noted while abroad. He was acclaimed wherever he went, for his fame had long preceded him. One eminent British surgeon, declared, "Dr. Mott has performed more of the great operations than any man living, or that ever did live." One such operation, as Dr. Mott himself admitted, was the most dangerous and difficult ever performed, the excision of the entire right clavicle for malignant disease of that bone, applying forty ligatures. Dr. Mott's surgery was the more remarkable since he did not use modern forms of anesthesia. He had lectured at the College of Physicians and Surgeons and in the Medical College of New York University, where he was professor of surgery and also relative anatomy, of which latter branch he was the founder. Dr. Mott was a large man and every feature of his face was big, excepting his brow and its receding hairline. The hair which was lacking on his forehead did, however, magnificently frame with sideburns the surgeon's prominent cheekbones.

From the medical point of view, the most significant event for New York City in 1842 was the completion of the aqueduct from the Croton Reservoir in Westchester County to the distributing reservoir at Fifth Avenue and Forty-second Street, where the Public Library now stands. The introduction of fresh water into the arteries and veins of the city was celebrated on July 4 with a parade that eclipsed anything since the 1825 procession at the opening of the Erie Canal. The Harpers' old friend General George P. Morris recited an ode he had written to commemorate the exciting event. A feature of the aqueduct was the 1,450-foot-long High Bridge across the Harlem River. This graceful structure with its fourteen arches was another cause for city pride, and people who lived nearby, including Poe (after 1844), loved to walk there for the view. Neighboring Fordham was also coming into its own; commuters could now live that far from the "city," taking trains on the Harlem Rail Road right to City Hall. Bishop John Hughes, the energetic Roman Catholic prelate, had established a college at Fordham the previous year.

Bishop Hughes had been much in the news because of his 1840 attack on the Public School Society of New York City. Organized in 1805, this society distributed to nearly one hundred city schools not only its own funds but what was allocated to it out of the New York State Common School Fund. Some of the funds went to buying Bibles, which were read in the classrooms. Bishop Hughes argued that it was unfair that Catholic children should be required to listen to daily readings from "the Protestant Bible" or to use textbooks containing hostile references to their church. Theodore Sedgwick, counsel for the society, replied that its trustees had expurgated such passages without aid from Catholic authorities, although such had been requested. Hughes appealed to the city's Board of Aldermen for relief, but the aldermen, after making an independent investigation, denied his petition on January 11, 1841; they were satisfied that the textbooks were inoffensive and that the Bible readings should continue. Whereupon Bishop Hughes carried his fight to Albany, advocating a completely secular system of education, with no Bible reading, under the control of the state. Governor Seward, an Episcopalian, informed the Legislature that there were some twenty thousand children in New York City, mostly children of immigrants, who were kept out of public schools because of alleged Protestant emphasis. His solution was state aid to Catholic schools as well. While the Legislature did not support him in this request, it did pass a bill which practically extended the state's system to New York City and closed the books of the Public School Society.

The Harpers watched these political goings-on with the greatest of interest. While only a few of the schoolbooks they published were likely to come under criticism, their investment in the *School District Library* was extensive and profitable. They feared censors might be going through all these books to demand withdrawals or expensive plate corrections. Furthermore, they were in the early stages of planning the most ambitious Bible project ever undertaken in America and public schools would be an important part of the market. Fletcher would soon jokingly suggest to James that maybe he should get into politics to help protect their interest in the Bible. The brothers and their families were hearing the school religion issue discussed in the pulpits of the Sands Street Church in Brooklyn, and in the John Street Church in New York. Their friend Sidney E. Morse, editor of the New York *Observer*, the oldest religious journal in the state, was writing vigorous editorials on the issue, and his brother Samuel Finley Breese Morse had, in 1841, established the American Protestant Union. Harper authors were exchanging gossip about possible political repercussions. The Rev. Dr. Barnes had received a letter from Lyman Beecher, written from Indianapolis, on the urgent need to support the Protestants in the West against "the infinitude of depraved mind here bursting forth, and rolling in from abroad upon us like a flood."

Another friend who was much concerned was Thurlow Weed. He considered the *School District Library* his baby, claiming later that he had induced the State Legislature to pass the law imposing a small tax on each school district to help establish its own collections of books.

Equally influential was the educational philanthropist James Wadsworth of Geneseo, New York. Weed brought Wadsworth to Cliff Street to meet the brothers in the early days of the *S.D.L.* In 1842, Wadsworth did a good turn both to the Harpers and to the schools and academies of the state by buying and distributing, free of charge, a large edition of *The School and the Schoolmaster*, a Harper publication. The book was sent to all school districts, county clerks' offices, to deputy superintendents in the several counties, and to governors of other states. All in all, a sizable order of twelve thousand copies.

The book was written jointly by Alonzo Potter and George B. Emerson, Potter contributing the first part, "The Education of the People," and Emerson, well known in Boston as a teacher, contributing the second part, "The Schoolmaster." Wadsworth drew up a suggested contract on June 9, which the brothers accepted with but one change, substituting the word "muslin" for "linen" in the binding specifications. They agreed to produce a book "not exceeding" 450 pages at a cost to Wadsworth of 31 cents a copy. Unfortunately, to satisfy Potter, Emerson, and Colonel Young of Albany, the new superintendent of common schools, the book ran 118 pages over the estimate, adding 8 cents to the per-copy cost. This increase annoyed Wadsworth as did the authors' "tampering with the publication." On receiving a bound copy in October, he detected some printing errors and thought the volume looked "cumbrous." It was not up to what he considered Harper standards. His unhappiness was the more regrettable since he had chosen to place the work with the brothers in appreciation of the service they had rendered the public in getting out the *School District Library*.

The Wadsworth-subsidized volume was the only new publication sent to school districts in the uneasy year of 1842. The ten 1842 additions, along with one late 1841 issue, were held over till 1843 for the fifth series, which included a larger number of that year's books. Two holdovers were by Epes Sargent, one of them an anonymous novel, *What's to be Done*. On May 19, 1842, Sargent wrote Griswold that he had asked Harper's to forward a copy—Griswold was to keep his authorship secret. What he called "my little book" revealed his love for American customs, manners, and institutions. It was termed "strictly national" by the *Messenger* in July, two months after the demise of the monthly *Arcturus*, which Cornelius Mathews and his friend Evert Duyckinck had started in December, 1840, to champion the cause of literary nationalism. Other 1842 books of American authorship destined for the *S.D.L.* included a three-volume edition of that old standard *Belknap's American Biography*, with additions and notes by J. M. Hibbard. After being "in press" in January and March, it was issued in July. Miss Sedgwick's *Means and Ends* followed in August, and in a foolhardy challenge to Winchester and his crowd they reissued *Hope Leslie*, the novel that had first made the Sedgwick name famous.

The only versifier on the 1842 list, was a Virginian named Robert Tyler, whose long poem about the Wandering Jew was entitled *Ahasuerus*. It apparently did well, for the *Messenger* reported that a large edition had been rapidly exhausted; sales were not hurt a bit when the public was informed that the author was none other than the son of President John Tyler. Longfellow was a more elusive poet to snare. Learning that he had sailed for Germany in April for a "water cure," the brothers asked Sam Ward if he thought Longfellow would write a book about Germany. "I hope you will," Ward wrote his friend. "The growth of that nation is so rapid and their intellectual phases so constantly changing that I am sure you will observe and hear many things worth noting and valuable to us." He went on to outline a possible book, but failed to convince Longfellow, who replied curtly, "I have no such intention. I am here for my health." Then he added a postscript, "What will the Harpers give for the Play?" Longfellow was referring to *The Spanish Student*, partly inspired by the European dancer Fanny Elssler, earning $500 a performance, and "consequently [making] with her heels in one week just what I make with my head in one year," as Longfellow had written to his father. But he could not find a publisher for his play. William D. Ticknor had said No, and John Owen was thought to be on the verge of bankruptcy. And a slightly wicked play, even by the desired Longfellow, was not for the Methodist brothers.

In January, 1842, Charles Dickens received a hero's welcome on his arrival in Boston, and his first American trip was a continuous toasting to Boz and his wonderful creations. Determined to make an issue of international copyright at once, he was astounded to find the Americans not only apathetic but openly hostile. They would gladly pay to hear him lecture but liked getting what he wrote in cheap books or in the mammoth weeklies for pennies. The Hartford *Times* was typical of the bristling press, saying bluntly that America did not need Dickens's advice on copyright. George Bancroft, the historian, went so far as to assert that there could be no exclusive property rights to intellectual creations, an argument Henry Carey was to develop in *Letters on*

International Copyright (1853 and 1868). On the night of February 18, Dickens was honored in New York at a civic dinner given at the City Hotel. Washington Irving was in the speaker's chair. After everyone had drunk too much wine and listened to too many speeches, Cornelius Mathews got to his feet to plead the cause of international copyright and American authorship. In *The Raven and the Whale*, Perry Miller suggests that Mathews was hitching a ride on the Dickens bandwagon in thus speaking up for copyright; it was well known that Mathews had imitated Dickens in a story called *Puffer Hopkins,* and allowed his friends to call him the "American Boz." The Dickens dinner was his opportunity to push the analogy further. Responding to a toast of Irving, Mathews called out, "What, Sir, is the present condition of the Field of Letters in America?" His answer was "anarchy" because of the lack of a copyright law, with foreign publications sown broadcast across the land. He then took a crack at the Harpers, particularly James, saying that Irving might be coming from Tarrytown to the city by boat bringing a manuscript to submit to a publisher and find himself in the company of a neighbor who had farm produce to sell. His neighbor would soon market his poultry, while "you call, sir, on certain traders in Cliff Street; you suggest the Mss. 'For Heaven's sake, Mr. Irving,' is the response of the blandest member of the firm, the one that talks to the authors, 'don't plague us just now; we have a profound respect for your talents, an ardent affection for American literature: but Mr. Bulwer's *Zánoni* has arrived, and we must have a hundred hands on it before night. Call again, we shall be happy to see you!' . . ." Greeley, who had been converted to the cause of international copyright, published Mathews's address in full in the *Tribune* on February 21, giving it editorial support. But Clark, of *The Knickerbocker*, who was also supporting copyright, detested Mathews and thought the issue should not be made "a piece of Indian jugglery, performed by Cornelius Mathews."

That his might not be the only British voice crying in the American wilderness, Dickens appealed to friends in London for support. This reached him early in May at Niagara Falls in the form of a "memorial" signed by twelve distinguished English authors. He sent a copy to Bryant along with a covering letter, both of which Bryant published in the *Evening Post* on May 9. The memorial appealed to a common brotherhood, played down the argument of a just monetary reward, and made two points: one that the consequence of inundating the American market with English works must be "the extinction of American literature as an adequate, honourable and independent profession," and two, that copyright protection for foreign authors should not cause an increase in retail prices of books. Bryant gave editorial denial to their first argument. Sympathetic to the cause—in fact, a foremost leader—his pride in American authorship could not admit its early demise. He listed nine outstanding native writers, four of them Harper authors (himself excluded) and made the extraordinary claim that "within the last year the number of books written by American authors which have been successful in Britain is greater than that of foreign works which have been successful in this country." A short time later, Cooper wrote to Griswold, "I see that [Bryant] begins to fire a little at Dickens. . . . This country must outgrow its adulation of foreigners, Englishmen in particular, as children outgrow the rickets."

But Cooper was voicing a minority opinion, at least with regard to books Englishmen wrote. Both George Putnam and Appleton's senior partner were then resident in London to procure the best of Britain's literary output for sale in America. The Appleton firm advertised that they had taken this step in order the better to serve the literary interests of the home market, purchasing books "advantageously for export by the custom of the London trade." To this advantageous wholesale price, however, the cost of transportation and a tariff of thirty cents per pound had to be added before books could be priced and marketed at home. Margaret Nicholson, a modern commentator, writes in *A Manual of Copyright Practice* that the freedom to publish foreign works in this period "actually was a service to book-hungry Americans, as the cost of importing enough copies to supply the demand would have been prohibitive."

Most American book buyers in the forties would have said Amen to that statement, desiring few things less than an international copyright law. But the brothers were no longer opposed to the measure—or at least one of them so assured Simms in the summer of 1843. And in 1844, Wesley was a member of the American Copyright Club, of which Bryant was president, and thus one of the signers of a petition to Congress favoring a change in copyright status. Apparently, however, the Harpers were unwilling to take a more aggressive stance than this. Their dilemma was a difficult one. As printers they still believed heartily in tariff protection for home manufactures. But as publishers they could now see, in the fierce competition of the mammoth newspapers, that their old argument for free editorial matter was reduced to an absurdity.

CHAPTER XI

Fighting the Mammoth Weeklies

1842–1843

Eᴀʀʟʏ ᴏɴ ᴛʜᴇ ᴍᴏʀɴɪɴɢ of June 1, 1842, burglars broke into the Harper bindery and set it on fire. Hand-drawn fire engines raced into Cliff Street and red-shirted volunteers soon controlled the flames, confining damage to the upper stories, which housed the bindery, and the gabled roof. Some old bookkeeping records were destroyed and all bound stock on hand was burned or spoiled by water, including copies of G. P. R. James's new novel *Morley Ernstein.** When this book almost immediately came out as a "supplement" of *The New World*, it was generally believed that the bindery had been broken into to snatch copies of the Harper edition and to destroy what was left. Demarest in his notes blamed Jonas Winchester.

Realizing $45,000 from insurance—"placed comfortably in funds," according to Demarest—the Harpers began a spirited retaliation. They had earlier purchased from Phillips, Sampson and Company the stereotype plates of twelve Bulwer novels, presumably to keep them off the market; the Boston publisher had issued them in two-column, royal-octavo size, packing the twelve works into two volumes of 1,724

* William Cullen Bryant wrote to Richard H. Dana on the day of the fire saying "their establishment, with nearly everything it contained, [was] destroyed by fire."

pages. What was once a liability was now suddenly an asset. They could fight Winchester and the other newspaper pirates with these plates. They would start with *Pelham*, the first Bulwer novel they had published back in 1828. The original work ran to 453 pages in two volumes; the "new" plates repackaged it in 172 pages of small type. At 25 cents it was easier on the purse than the eyes. The brothers announced to booksellers and literary periodicals that *Pelham* would be issued in July as Number 1 in a new series to be called *Harper's Library of Select Novels*, a rejuvenation of an older series they had abandoned in 1834. Two more Bulwer titles were released in August and three in September, Number 6 being the ever-popular *Last Days of Pompeii*. *Rienzi* came next in October, with *Ernest Maltravers* and *Alice* following in December. And since they did not want the series to be ridiculed as a wastebasket of old Bulwer titles, they put in three new English reprints in September and November, Mrs. Hofland's *Czarina*, Miss Campbell's *Self-Devotion*, and the anonymous *Nabob at Home*. By the year's end they had launched twelve cheaper-than-cheap fiction reprints. The text of each was printed in eight-point type, in two columns on deckle-edge paper, and the sheets were side-stitched and bound in paper covers, the covers glued securely to the spine. But they were books, not magazines—books with a vengeance—and published at a loss, as they were to tell Simms a year later.

Their opponents were not disposed to run away from this counter-attack. They too were out to supply literate Americans with reading matter at minimum prices. On the afternoon of Christmas, the day of peace and good will, the Harper establishment was again raided, this time to steal a copy of Bulwer's *Last of the Barons*, which the brothers had been announcing for three months as forthcoming and for which they had paid Bulwer £200 (nearly $1,000) for early sheets. The newspapers reported the thievery, and in the warmth and seclusion of his study at 20 Clinton Place Evert Duyckinck moralized, "What a compliment to English authors that every new book of more than usual attractiveness sends forth a whole brood of felony."

Having the advantage of cheap postage, the mammoth weeklies were in fact riding high. *Brother Jonathan* welcomed the brothers' competition, hoping they might "turn their money quick," as did the bright lad who purchased apples at two for threepence and sold them for three at twopence. So the game continued with the Harpers trying to outwit and outsell John Neal, who was for a short period editing *Brother Jonathan* for Wilson & Co., and Park Benjamin, who did the editorial chores for Winchester's *New World*.

Could it be that books were really too expensive, or that serious book publishers were an anachronism? Some people thought so and said as much. Hilliard & Gray of Boston, Jared Sparks's publisher, and a much older firm than Harper's, had recently gone into bankruptcy. J. & H. G. Langley of New York was in obvious difficulty.

Literary periodicals bemoaned the low state to which the book business had fallen. Lieutenant Matthew F. Maury, editor of the *Messenger*, who had never cared for Bulwer's output, declared that at twenty-five cents a copy his novels were "dirt cheap—little enough . . . for so large a dose of moral poison." In January, 1843, the *Democratic Review* observed, "The causes of this great [literary] sterility, if we except perhaps the discouraging influence upon the bookselling business of the recent revolutionizing of the press by the mammoth extras, is to be attributed to the pecuniary pressure of the times. . . ." This thought was repeated almost verbatim in the February issue of the *U.S. Literary Advertiser and Publishers' Circular* when Langley apologized for having issued only one other number since October. After noting that conditions in the book trade were bad, "unparalleled in the history of the bibliographic fraternity," Langley went on to say, "The revolutionary new system of cheap periodical issues of works of all kinds seems to have checked, for the present, all enterprise . . . as to the production of *new* books. We hear that the Harpers are about reissuing the volumes of their 'Family Library' at one half the original price."

Lieutenant Maury, down in Virginia, who had a passion for low-priced reading matter, said in January, "Any European work that is at all popular . . . is snatched up by one or the other of these enterprising papers, and before the royal ink is fairly dried upon it, it is pushed through our Yankee presses, and hawked about the towns and villages in the remotest corners of the republic, at one-twentieth of its European cost." Four months later, he was prophesying a "complete and popular" literary revolution if this strife between the "mammoth weeklies" and book publishers continued, observing that "Harpers have put themselves at the head of the opposition and are leading the way far in advance of their line."

The rumor about the *Family Library* was true. By May, 157 volumes were out in cheap bindings at 25 cents a copy. According to the *Messenger*, they were being issued weekly, the sales were immense, and the publishers were accomplishing wonders in the way of cheap literature. This venture was soon dropped for the *Family Library* was made up of *books*, books neatly bound for a *library*, not dispensable maga-

1. Fletcher, James, John, and J. Wesley Harper as photographed by Mathew B. Brady (ca. 1850). (See Notes on Illustrations, p. 379.)

2. The Harper establishment, 82 Cliff Street, in 1825.

3. Calling card of the brothers after Fletcher was made a partner.

J. & J. HARPER, will hereafter transact business under the firm of HARPER & BROTHERS, at No. 82 Cliff street, New-York.

JAMES HARPER,
JOHN HARPER,
J. W. HARPER,
F. HARPER.

oc 29

MRS. SHERWOOD.——HARPER & BROTHERS, No. 82 Cliff street, have in press—
THE WORKS OF Mrs. M. M. SHERWOOD, Authoress of "Henry Milner," "Little Henry and his Bearer," "The Lady of the Manor," "Roxobel," &c. It will be published in an economical, uniform, and beautiful form, illustrated by numerous splendid engravings on steel. The first volume will be issued in a few days, and the whole work will be completed with all possible despatch.   oc 29

HARPERS' FAMILY LIBRARY.—HARPER & BROTHERS, No. 82 Cliff street, will publish To-morrow, Wednesday, 30th instant, No. LXI of the Family Library, entitled—
NUBIA AND ABYSSINIA; comprehending their Civil History, Antiquities, Arts, Religion, Literature, and Natural History. By Rev. Michael Russell, LLD. Author of "Egypt," "Palestine," "Connexion of Sacred History," &c. Illustrated by a Map and Engravings.   oc 29

4. Advertisements from the New York *Commercial Advertiser*, October 29, 1833.
Above, left, the card giving change of the firm's name.
Below, left, the initial appearance of "Harper & Brothers" as a publishing imprint, a "first announcement" of English reprints.

5. James Harper (1844) by Henry Inman and Daniel Huntington.

6. John Harper (ca. 1830) by Samuel Lovett Waldo and William Jewett.

7. J. Wesley Harper (ca. 1830) attributed to John Paradise.

8. Fletcher Harper (ca. 1830) attributed to Samuel Lovett Waldo and William Jewett.

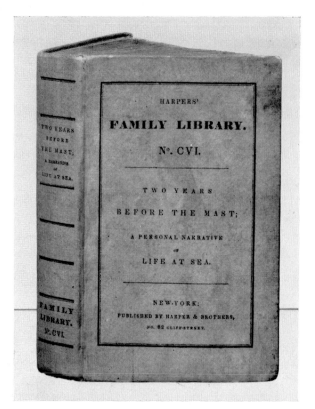

9. First edition of *Two Years Before the Mast* in the Family Library Series.

Know all men by these presents that I he
appoint constitute and appoint John P Forda
my full and lawful attorney to do any thi
that he should judge expedient & proper in relation
to the writings of my late husband James M
now in the hands of Messrs Harper & Brot
of New York and by his acts on this subje
I bind my heirs Executors Administrators &
assigns as well as myself to carry into
full effect accordingly his acts on this head

Signed Sealed & delo
this 14th day of Sep 1844

Witness
Ann Payne

D P Madison

10. Letter of Dolley Madison to Harper's, September 14, 1844.

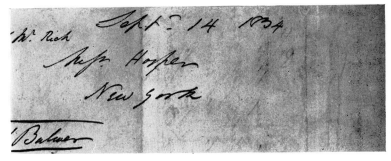

11. Cover of letter from Edward L. Bulwer conveying proofs of *Last Days of Pompeii* to Harper's via Obadiah Rich. Left margin cropped by a previous owner.

12. Professor Anthon's authorization for Harper's purchase of the plates of *Lemprière's Classical Dictionary*.

13. Closing paragraph of the contract for *History of the Conquest of Mexico* showing signatures of author and publishers.

HARPER'S

CONDENSED CATALOGUE

OF

Valuable Standard Publications,

IN THE SEVERAL DEPARTMENTS OF

GENERAL LITERATURE.

NEW YORK:

HARPER & BROTHERS,

82 CLIFF STREET.

MDCCCXLVII.

14. Title page used in Harper catalogues for 1846 and 1847.

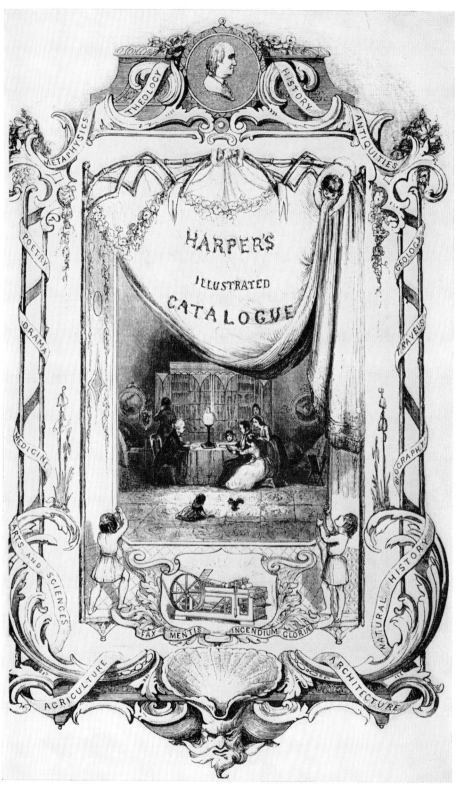

HARPER'S
ILLUSTRATED
CATALOGUE

THEOLOGY · HISTORY · ANTIQUITIES · METAPHYSICS · POETRY · GEOLOGY · DRAMA · TRAVELS · MEDICINE · BIOGRAPHY · ARTS AND SCIENCES · NATURAL HISTORY · AGRICULTURE · ARCHITECTURE

FAX MENTIS INCENDIUM GLORIÆ

15. Title page used in Harper catalogues for 1847 and 1848.

Declined

Pittsfield Nov 24th 1853

Gentlemen :— In addition to the work which I took to New York last Spring, but which I was prevented from printing at that time; I have now on hand, and pretty well on towards completion, another book — 300 pages, say — partly of nautical adventure, and partly — or rather chiefly, of Tortoise Hunting Adventure. It will be ready for press some time in the coming January. Meanwhile, it would be convenient, to have advances to me upon it /\$300. — My acct: with you, at present, can not be very far from square. For the abovenamed advance — if remitted me now — you will have security in my former works, as well as security prospective, in the one to come, (The Tortoise-Hunters) because if you accede to the aforesaid request; this letter shall be your voucher, that I am willing your house should publish it, on the old basis — half-profits.

Reply immediatly, if you please,

And Believe Me, Yours

Herman Melville

16. Letter from Herman Melville to Harper's.

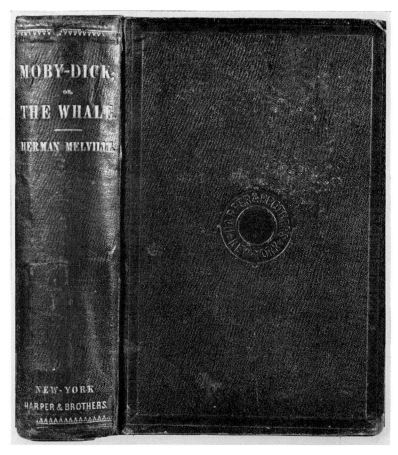

17. First edition of *Moby Dick* showing on the front board the Harper imprint blind-stamped within a sailor's life preserver.

How many copies of have
been sold of Melville's three
last works?

Typee	1779
Omoo	6328
Mardi	2574
Redburn	4516
White Jacket	4115
Moby Dick	2771
Pierre	1916

18. Memorandum of Fletcher Harper, November, 1853, on which William Demarest listed sales of Melville's books.

IMPORTANT NEW WORKS

IN COURSE OF PUBLICATION BY

MESSRS. HARPER & BROTHERS, NEW YORK.

I.

Mr. Macaulay's New Work.

The History of England

FROM THE ACCESSION OF JAMES II.

By THOMAS BABINGTON MACAULAY.

Beautifully printed in the Octavo Library form, from New and Legible Type.

VOL. I. *Nearly Ready.*

The work of so eminent a scholar as Macaulay cannot but be a priceless treasure to posterity. We may look for a gallery of brilliant portraits from this Vandyke in literature.—*Western Continent.*

Macaulay has transmuted vast learning and varied accomplishments into one sweet and subtle thing, which really deserves the name of genius. He is the poet of facts, and the most rhetorical of writers.—GILFILLAN.

He is a master of every species of composition.—SIR JAMES MACKINTOSH.

Behind the external show and glittering vesture of his thoughts, beneath all his pomp of diction, aptness of illustration, splendor of imagery, and epigrammatic pomp and glare, a careful eye can easily discern the movement of a powerful and well cultivated intellect, as it successively appears in the well-trained logician, the acute and discriminating critic, the comprehensive philosopher, the practical and far-sighted statesman, and the student of universal knowledge.—E. P. WHIPPLE.

II.

Melville's New Work.

Mardi; and a Voyage Thither.

By HERMAN MELVILLE.

AUTHOR OF "OMOO," "TYPEE," &c.

This new book is characterized by that rare brilliancy and graphic power which have rendered the author's previous works such general favorites; it is even more stirring in its narrative, more glowing and vivid in its pictures, and will be found altogether a more unique production than either of its predecessors. Thus preserving the idiosyncrasies of his style, it cannot be doubted Mr. Melville's forthcoming work will add even to the illustrious literary reputation he has already attained in the world of letters.

III.

The Life and Letters of Thomas Campbell.

Edited by Dr. BEATTIE.

WITH AN INTRODUCTORY LETTER

By WASHINGTON IRVING.

This work presents the true character of the illustrious poet; rendering, in the words of Mr. Irving, "a great act of justice to the memory of a distinguished man, whose character has not been sufficiently known. It gives an insight into his domestic as well as his literary life, and lays open the springs of all his actions, and the causes of all his contrarieties of conduct. The biography does more: it reveals the affectionate considerateness of his conduct in all the domestic relations of life. Above all, the crowning romance of his life—his enthusiasm in the cause of suffering Poland—a devotion carried to the height of his poetic temperament, and, in fact, exhausting all that poetic vein, which, properly applied, might have produced epics; these, and many more traits set forth in his biography, bring forth his character for the first time in its true light; dispel those clouds which malice and detraction may at times have cast over it, and leave it in the full effulgence of its poetic glory."—*Extract from Mr. Irving's Introductory Letter.*

IV.

New Volumes of Mr. Jacob Abbott's Illustrated Historical Series.

1. The History of Alexander the Great.

1 volume, 12mo., with Illuminated Title and numerous Engravings.

2. The History of Hannibal.

1 volume, 12mo., with Illuminated Title and numerous Engravings.

V.

Volume V. of Chalmers's Posthumous Works.

Horæ Biblicæ Sabbaticæ;

Or, SABBATH SCRIPTURE READINGS.

By the late THOMAS CHALMERS, D.D., LL.D.

Volume Second, completing this work, forming the fifth of the series.

It is full of piety and prayer, and the fervent author earnestly extracts a moral gious lesson from every passage or event to which he alludes. We might truly him to the bee gathering sweets from every object, and building up a hive of w construction and everlasting richness.—*London Literary Gazette.*

The outpourings of a spirit in which simplicity and deep wisdom are be combined.—*London Examiner.*

VI.

New Work on California and Oregon.

Oregon and California in 1848.

By J. QUINN THORNTON,

Late Judge of the Supreme Court of Oregon.

This work comprises some intensely thrilling incidents; a very interesting narrative of a journey across the Continent to Oregon, and thence by sea to the States via California, during the years 1846, 7, 8; together with much valuable ge statistical, and practical information, designed for the use of emigrants, &c. &c.

VII.

The Caxtons; a Family Picture.

ATTRIBUTED TO

SIR EDWARD BULWER LYTTON.

VIII.

Chapman's Illustrated Life of Franklin.

Benjamin Franklin.

HIS AUTOBIOGRAPHY, WITH A SKETCH OF HIS PU LIFE AND SERVICES.

Splendidly Embellished by numerous exquisite Designs by Ch

The Work, which will be elegantly printed upon fine paper, will be comple Eight Parts, at 25 cents each, issued at brief intervals.

This pictorial Life of Franklin will, it is believed, be regarded as the *classi* being in all respects worthy of the advanced state of art in this country, as w the fame of the distinguished "patriot, printer, and philosopher."

IX.

Lieut. Ruxton's Posthumous Work.

Life in the Far West.

By the late

GEORGE F. RUXTON, ESQ.,

Author of "Adventures in Mexico and the Rocky Mountains."

WITH A BIOGRAPHICAL SKETCH OF THE AUTHO

This work possesses value and strong interest as a fresh, life-like picture of life. In the opinion of *Blackwood's Magazine*, its style is as remarkable for terseness and vigor, as its substance everywhere for great novelty and original

MESSRS. HARPER'S LATEST PUBLICATIONS.

THE FORGERY. By G. P. R. James, Esq. 8vo. paper. 25 cts.

THE GREAT HOGGARTY DIAMOND. By W. M. Thackeray, Esq. 8vo. paper, 25 cts.

By the same Author.

VANITY FAIR; or, Pen and Pencil Sketches of English Society. With Illustrations by the Author. 8vo. muslin, $1 25; paper, $1.

This rich, racy, humorous, picturesque, inimitable book. We know not when we have been more truly grateful to an author for keeping our spirits in good humor point, and our blood to life heat, than when under Thackeray's influence.—*Union Magazine.*

COWPER'S POETICAL WORKS. Illustrated by 75 exquisite Designs. With a Biographical and Critical Introduction. By Rev. Thomas Dale. 2 vols. muslin, gilt edges, $3 75.

An edition beautifully appropriate to the purity and exceeding excellence of Cowper's writings. We have no other such elegant edition among us.—*Evangelist.*

THE ROMANCE OF YACHTING. VOYAGE THE FIRST. By Joseph C. Hart, Esq. 12mo. muslin, 60 cts.

A book of smartness and spirit; the author appears to have roamed over the seas with his eyes open.—*Tribune.*

HISTORY OF CHARLES THE FIRST. With an Illuminated Title Page and numerous Engravings. By Jacob Abbott. 12mo. muslin, 60 cts.

The subject is on many accounts one of the most interesting in all history; and the writer carries a pen so graceful and graphic, that all the scenes which he describes become to the mind of the reader undoubted and strongly felt realities. This book, by its thrilling details, will prove irresistible to the young.—*Albany Argus.*

MODEL MEN, WOMEN, AND CHILDREN. With numerous Comic Illustrations. By Horace Mayhew, Esq. 2 Parts, 18mo. paper, 25 cts. each.

Sketches of various characters smartly executed, and one of the steamboat and railway class of belles-lettres. The embellishments are very clever.—*Literary Gaz.*

THE MORAL, SOCIAL, AND PROFESSIONAL DUties of Attorneys and Solicitors. By Samuel Warren, F.R.S. Author of "Now-and-Then," &c. 12mo. muslin, 75 cents.

The author is universally known as a writer of great power; and in this little work he has set forth, strongly and impressively, in a clear and condensed form, much of interesting and valuable suggestions, useful not only for lawyers, but for all classes.—*Courier.*

MARY BARTON, A Tale of Manchester Life paper, 25 cents.

Gladly do we hail the advent of a true pen can interpret faithfully between the operatives masters—between the low and the high—betw starving and the well-fed.—*Jerrold's Newspaper*

ARABIAN NIGHTS' ENTERTAINMENTS. ed with Six Hundred Exquisite Engravings, &c. Translated and Arranged for Family Reading, planatory Notes by E. W. Lane, Esq. 2 vol muslin, gilt edges, $3 75.

It is a precious gallery of Oriental pictures. title-page to the last engraving, it is a casket of beautiful gems, and from the palace to the hu bare all that is interesting to know of the foll Mahomet.—*New York Sun.*

THE IMAGE OF HIS FATHER. A Tale of Monkey. Illustrations. By the Brothers M 12mo. muslin, 75 cents; paper, 50 cents.

A very witty production of those distinguished the Brothers Mayhew, two of the most celeb ciples of the "Punch School."—*Spirit of the T*

BIOGRAPHICAL HISTORY OF CONGRESS Portraits and Fac-simile Autographs. By H Wheeler, Esq. 8vo. muslin, $3 per volume. II. now ready.

19. Full-page Harper advertisement in the *Literary World* for December 16, 1848, an example of many, generally with a back-page position.

20. The Custis mansion, Arlington, Virginia, engraved by Lossing, a typical illustration in *Harper's New Monthly Magazine*.

21. Home of James Harper, 4 Gramercy Park, before which he placed the two lamps emblematic of his mayoralty.

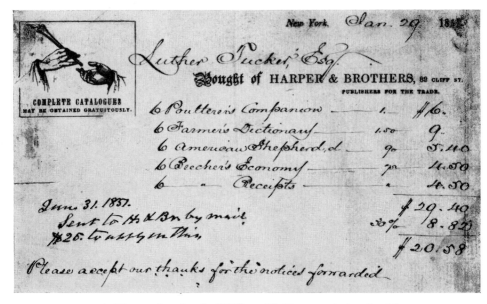

COMPLETE CATALOGUES
MAY BE OBTAINED GRATUITOUSLY.

New York, Jan. 29 1841

Luther Tucker, Esq.

Bought of HARPER & BROTHERS, 82 Cliff St.
PUBLISHERS FOR THE TRADE.

6 Poulterer's Companion	—	1.	$6.
6 Farmer's Dictionary	—	1.50	9.
6 American Shepherd, d	—	90	5.40
6 Beecher's Economy	—	70	4.50
6 " Receipts	—	"	4.50

Jan. 31. 1851.
Sent to H & Bn by mail
$25. to apply on this,

$29.40
30% 8.82
$20.58

Please accept our thanks for the notices forwarded

22. A Harper invoice in William H. Demarest's handwriting.

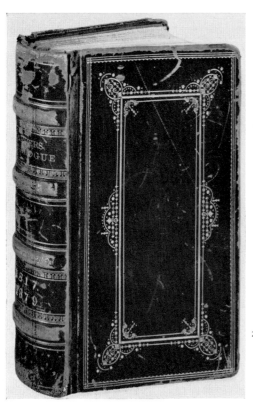

23. Above, "Pirate's chest." A late eighteenth-century iron chest probably rescued from the 1853 fire with its contents
of valuable papers. Long lost is a large
key which could be inserted in a secret
keyhole on the top and turned to move
an elaborate mechanism of eleven bolts
below.

24. Left, the leather-bound, tooled and
embellished ledger book containing
Demarest's catalogue of Harper books,
1817-1879.

25. First draft of a letter to Thurlow Weed, written by James and corrected by Fletcher. An early use of the Franklin Square address.

26. Engravings by Benson J. Lossing shown on the cover of the new *Monthly* and on

27. A New York Trade Sales in the auction room of Bangs Brother and Co. on Park Place. Mayor Harper, hatless, sits in front of Andrew Merwin, the auctioneer. Horace Greeley is seated on the bench looking at the catalogue through heavy-rimmed glasses.

SENECA'S MORALS.

BY WAY OF ABSTRACT.

TO WHICH IS ADDED,

A DISCOURSE,

UNDER THE TITLE OF

AN AFTER-THOUGHT.

BY SIR ROGER L'ESTRANGE, Knt.

FIFTH AMERICAN EDITION.

NEW-YORK:

PUBLISHED BY EVERT DUYCKINCK,

NO. 68 WATER-STREET,

J. & J. Harper, printers.

1817.

28. Title page of the first book produced by the Harpers. On the facing page each of the brothers signed his name to a brief historical account penned to William C.

zines that cluttered up a house. How better could the brothers under-score their point that books were here to stay?

But in the meantime they harassed the mammoths with their own paper-wrapped weapons. Some time after the Cliff Street fire the Har-pers decided to publish important works of nonfiction in paper covers like the newspaper "supplements," at twenty-five cents a number.* By November, 1842, they were ready to serialize an English dictionary of science, literature, and art, later known as Brande's *Encyclopedia of Science*. After appearing in twelve "numbers," it was published (August, 1843) as a single quarto volume of 1,358 pages for $3. "Mes-srs. Harper, 'how is it done?' " queried Clark. "Be so good as to men-tion." Maury reprinted ten pages of excerpts in the *Messenger*, also praised "these extensive publishers," and said the work was having an immense circulation. Another English tome, a geographical dictionary, was launched in numbers before the Brande work was completed. Called *McCulloch's Gazetteer*, it was issued in twenty numbers and was later available in two volumes, running to more than two thousand pages. It was edited by Daniel Haskell, formerly president of the Uni-versity of Vermont. Haskell, whom Clark thought opinionated, re-wrote and expanded the articles relating to the United States. Using the old Dearborn plates, the brothers published Shakespeare's plays and poems in eight numbers between March, 1843, and February, 1844.

The most popular of their serials was Archibald Alison's *History of Europe* (1789-1815), which came out in sixteen numbers, the last one in December, 1843, at which time they also issued the complete work in four volumes, totaling 1,358 pages. "The Messers Harper, in their public-spirited enterprise, have commenced publishing a series of *Standard Works*," Maury wrote in an eight-page review of Alison in March. "These works are published at wonderfully cheap rates and we consider the scheme of the Messrs Harpers as an undertaking fraught with incalculable public and national advantages. It is nothing less than a plan for placing within the reach of every American, however hum-ble, the most valuable and instructive books in the language." Pointing out that Englishmen had to spend about $40 for Alison, ten times what American readers were paying, he reminded *Messenger* readers that here was a

striking illustration of what this country would lose by the establishment of any plan of international copy-right. . . . Had the Messers Harper pub-lished this work under the restrictions of copy-right, its price here instead

---

* Since the Brande and Alison "numbers" are known to have retailed at 25 cents each, it seems fair to assume that this price applied to other works as well.

of $4 would have been at least $15 or $20. . . . We owe the foreigner abroad nothing but comity. If he will come among us we have guaranteed to him certain rights. Is there any more reason why we should protect, and that by a direct tax upon our citizens, the monopolies of Englishmen in the written or printed letter of books, than there is for granting in the manufacture and sale of printed calicoes and figured muslins? . . . Suppose the circulation of the History in the United States to be 100,000 copies. In order to secure Mr. Alison the benefit of copy-right, the readers of the work would have been taxed from one million to two millions of dollars upon this single book.

Maury went on to argue that by limiting the extent of readership, international copyright would impose a tax upon Americans' "general knowledge and popular instruction."

Unfortunately no Haskell was employed to rework Alison's chapter on America and its inaccuracies brought a storm of protest. But fortunately Alison's provincial notions of American literature and culture inspired George Putnam to write an eight-page rebuttal in the *American Book Circular*, issued in London in April, 1843, a pamphlet which with its facts and statistics is now an important piece of bibliographical Americana. Acknowledging Alison's *History* to be "an Elaborate work of high character," Putnam nevertheless was piqued by such statements as "Literature and intellectual ability of the highest class meet with little encouragement in America," and "so wholly are they [Americans] regardless of historical records or monuments, that half a century hence, *its* history, even of these times, could only be written from the archives of other States." Such false deductions as these and other anti-Americanisms characterized the work as a whole; they may have even contributed to its popularity. For popular it was, quickly running through ten editions in England and being translated into many European languages and into Arabic and Hindustani. This work of the Scottish historian was termed "lasting" and "unrivaled" by *The Knickerbocker*, which also called attention to the fact that the completed work was available through Harper's at one-tenth the price charged by the English publisher. Jared Sparks wrote to Putnam in London congratulating him on the pamphlet, saying, "Mr. Alison's ignorance is astonishing." Sparks was piqued that Alison was apparently ignorant of his own monumental work on Washington's *Papers* and of his ten volumes of American biography, the stereotype plates of which had "gone into the hands of Harpers, who diffuse the work far and wide."

Tucked away in the Putnam pamphlet is a sarcastic bit on Dickens, who was so keen about international copyright. "Mr. [Joseph Clay]

Neal, of Philadelphia, published about 1839, a volume, called 'Charcoal Sketches,' with illustrations; his name appended in full. This volume appears entire, plates and all, in the middle of 'Pic-Nic Papers, etc.,' 'edited by C. Dickens, Esq.,' 3 volumes, London, 1841. Mr. Neal, no doubt, would have been proud of his company, if his patron had not introduced him as a *nameless* person! 'A volume has been appended,' (to make the orthodox *three*) 'from an American source,' says the editor . . . !"

Charles Dickens, so able at picking up a good American work to publish in London in 1841, could hardly have objected strenuously when the Harpers issued his *Martin Chuzzlewit* in New York in 1843. Beginning in January, they published seventeen numbers at sixpence each, the last number and the bound book coming out in July. According to Demarest, the numbers were sold chiefly by newsboys, "then a new institution," and once James gave them a good rousing speech before they spread out through the city to sell the latest number. *Martin Chuzzlewit* was the last of Dickens's great character novels and the second book by him on the Harper list. In November, 1842, they had issued *American Notes* in paper covers at 12½ cents. Heretofore, they had respected Lea & Blanchard's "rights" to Dickens, but the floodtide of newspaper competition had washed away all the ground rules so painfully marked out in the thirties. Anyway, Lea & Blanchard either were not sufficiently concerned about the new danger or were lacking in combativeness. They did, however, issue books in numbers, and the *Messenger* for May carried a review of their *Encyclopedia of Geography*, sold at 25 cents a number, and said that it was printed on better paper and in larger type than the New York publications. "Formerly Philadelphia was the great mart for books," Maury wrote. "But New York with her greedy appetite that is swallowing up everything, has stretched forth her hands, through the Messrs Harper, after this branch of the trade also." Isaac Lea was encouraged by Maury's pat on the back and warned the public that reading very small type was dangerous to the eyes, a warning that Maury soon passed on to his readers in needling the Harpers for printing reading matter in tiny type. But Clark, always ready to go to bat for the brothers, was applauding them for the serial works "which they continue to publish with their wonted regularity and in their accustomed style of excellence."

By far the most significant and ambitious work that the brothers projected for serial publication was *Harper's Illuminated and New Pictorial Bible*. It was not originally their idea but that of Joseph Alexander Adams, the engraver. On April 4, 1843, their discussion with the forty-year-old Adams was consummated by a contract; by that time he had completed 206 woodcuts, and the contract called for 1,359 additional, a figure that was later increased to make 1,600 in all. Fortunately for Adams, the contract called for an equal division of profits; he was to earn $60,000, enough to take him abroad three times and enable him to retire at an early age. It is the work by which he is now chiefly remembered. The contract did not specify any deductions from the wholesale price beyond manufacturing costs at the "market price" other than 5 percent for "guaranteeing the sales."

Adams was the outstanding engraver of his time, had done the engravings for the *Fairy Book, Pilgrim's Progress*, and other Harper books, and was a popular teacher of his art. The possibility of a bountifully illustrated Bible had occurred to him in 1837 when he was seeking work for his pupils. Thinking then of an octavo-sized Bible, he procured transfers of some forty English cuts after designs by John Martin and Richard Westall, who together had produced a set of Bible illustrations. These engraved, he proceeded to make more. He was also concerned with the problem of printing wood engravings, especially to find a border that would both support and protect the blocks. In 1839, he developed a galvanic process whereby an electric current passing through a solution holding copper would coat a wax mold of his border engraving with a shell of copper. This shell, when affixed to a block, gave the necessary support to the engraving itself. This discovery, now known as electrotyping (see p. 359n.), was simultaneously developed that same year by two Englishmen and a Russian.

Another mechanical aid was the development of the six-roller press by Isaac Adams (not related to the engraver) and his brother Seth of Boston. This press was first put into operation at 82 Cliff Street in 1840. Since the Adams press could take a larger sheet than other presses, this may have been the reason for the decision to issue the Harper-Adams Bible in folio, rather than the smaller size. Adams wanted to supervise the printing (he wrote this provision into the contract) because, perfectionist that he was, he knew of no printer whom he could trust to overlay his blocks.

But excellent engravers are generally not original artists, their competence being that of exact copyists. Thus the question arose, who should be engaged to draw the pictures? The obvious choice was John G. Chapman, who had worked with Adams on the *Fairy Book* and *Pilgrim's Progress*. Chapman agreed to supply the designs—more than 1,400—and was paid $2,121.80 for his work. (A few years later he painted "The Baptism of Pocahontas" in the national Capitol rotunda.) Excited over the Bible project and the teaming of Chapman with Adams, the brothers got busy with a release to the papers and book trade. They bragged of an initial expenditure of $25,000 and promised that those who subscribed early would have "proof impressions." Fifty numbers were projected. Each one in its beautifully colored paper cover would cost only 25 cents. This new *Illuminated Bible*, they said, would be "the most splendid and rich-illustrated Bible ever published in the world." Winchester could not challenge that.

Not all were convinced. "We think it questionable taste," John L. O'Sullivan of the *Democratic Review* grumbled, "to print the edition in the obsolete form of folio, as well as to incorporate the Apocrypha," a criticism that was again echoed by the *U.S. Literary Advertiser*. But the brothers knew they had a winner. It would require their best efforts, their utmost skill. Looming ahead were long months of typesetting and proofreading, of page make-up, of printing and binding the numbers, of promoting and selling the best of all good books. It might be 1844 before they could issue Number 1. First of all just to handle the production of the Bible they would need to put up a new building on Pearl Street, backing up one of their Cliff Street buildings.

In the world of publishing, Bibles and dictionaries make good companions since they are basic works that respond to similar merchandising methods. Eight weeks after signing with Adams for engravings for the *Illuminated Bible*, the brothers contracted with White & Sheffield for the abridged royal-octavo edition of *Webster's Dictionary*, edited by Chauncey A. Goodrich, a work this New York firm had earlier issued. The contract was to run until July 10, 1857, the life of the copyright, with provision made for further revisions. White & Sheffield agreed to transfer their stereotypes to the brothers for $10,000, receiving negotiable notes in payment. In addition they were to receive 90 cents a copy for all copies printed. The dictionary retailed for $3.50, with a wholesale price of $2.80 (equivalent to a discount of 20 percent, although 22 ½ was to be given on orders of a hundred or more). Allowing 2 ½ cents for "guaranty," 75 cents for the specified manufacturing cost, and 90 cents to White & Sheffield, John could figure on more than $1 as the Harper gross profit. The contract called for an equal division of profits on a revised edition. (Presumably White & Sheffield allowed the Harpers an extra 10 cents a copy more than their share to amortize their plate investment.) To determine manufacturing costs a separate memorandum was to be drawn up every three years, with paper figured at the lowest previous six months' price, and printing and binding figured at "a rate not exceeding what other respectable printers and binders would charge."

Three days before the May 26th agreement with the brothers,

White & Sheffield had contracted for publication rights with Professor Chauncey A. Goodrich, Noah Webster's son-in-law and the editor of the abridged dictionary. They apparently paid him a royalty of slightly more than 10 percent of the retail price and pocketed the difference between that amount and their share of the profits. The payment of 37 cents a copy to Goodrich and other Webster heirs is spelled out in a later White & Sheffield–Harper contract, dated June 21, 1847, for the revised edition. It was to appear in 1851. (See p. 328.) Noah Webster died of pleurisy two days after the first Harper contract was signed. He probably did not know that the brothers were to be entrusted with the manufacture, promotion, and sale of his famous dictionary. Following his death, the heirs were involved in bitter feuding over his literary estate, largely stemming from William G. Webster's jealousy of his brother-in-law, Goodrich. Even though it may be believed that William Webster helped his father considerably, it is clear that the lexicographer's mantle fitted more snugly on the shoulders of Goodrich, who had been for many years professor of rhetoric at Yale.

The furor created in the forties over Webster's Americanizing of English words can hardly be imagined now when the spellings of *center* for *centre*, *traveler* for *traveller*, and *practice* for *practise* are taken for granted. But at the time there were endless debates over Webster's orthography, with uncounted hours spent on checking Webster's inconsistencies, to show, for example, that he did not always follow the principle that a primitive should be spelled consistently with its derivative (*defense* because of *defensive*). But such controversy helped to sell dictionaries, and Wesley dutifully styled manuscripts to conform to Webster, a practice that was to prompt Edward S. Gould, New York author and critic, to write in 1850 protesting that for years he had "refused to buy any of Harper's books, because I *would not* encourage their abominable orthography." And in that same year, in a poem delivered before the Phi Beta Kappa Society of Yale, Oliver Wendell Holmes was to mock the New York critics for their airs and pretensions, including a couplet aimed at Cliff Street:

> When our first Scholars are content to dwell
> Where their own printers teach them how to spell.

The *Dictionary* was sold with great enthusiasm that autumn at the thirty-eighth New York Trade Sale. Dealers were asked to bid on lots of 150 copies instead of the usual 5 or 10 for a $3.50 book. For any one bookseller to invest more than $400 in one title—with hundreds of others demanding representation in his total order—says a great deal both for public interest in the *Dictionary* and for booksellers' confidence in what the brothers would do to promote it. Ten years later Henry Carey was to say that the $3.50 abridged edition had sold 250,-000 copies, a figure that probably included pre-Harper disposals as well. The sale of from 10,000 to 20,000 copies a year both inspired and necessitated an expansion of manufacturing equipment and publishing facilities during the forties. And for 1843 the profits on this new publishing property were a token of the return of good times after nearly six years of financial uncertainties.

Shortly after the Christmas Day burglary, Evert Duyckinck called at 82 Cliff Street. He was, as always, immaculately dressed, reflecting, as Poe commented, the "instantaneous conviction of the gentleman." Duyckinck was a somewhat slender man of medium height and his eyes and hair were light. Perhaps his most striking characteristic was his air of serenity and self-possession. He was both attracted and repelled by the brothers. He admired their industry and square-handed competence. He shared their eagerness for a look at first proof sheets and their pride in rich gold leaf on muslin or half-calf bindings. Printer's ink was in his blood, too. But they were merchants and books were their merchandise. Authors were important to them to the degree that their books would sell, add prestige to an imprint, and both serve and improve the moral and cultural needs of the American people. While Duyckinck would admit that these editorial claims had merit, yet they tended to prostitute literature. Books should be loved for their own sake and not be used as means to a commercial end. Being an Episcopalian, he would have little interest in a sublimated Methodist evangelism catering to and improving the reading habits of the Republic. His Americanism was focused on authors who could interpret the nation to itself. He would have to look elsewhere to find literary companionship where there was leisure for sophisticated talk of books, clever gossip about authors, and cultivated laughter over writers' jokes—even a pun, such as the one James Russell Lowell had told him of the Biblical servant who had the hardest duty, the valet of the shadow of death. He considered James Harper's humor crude and called "stupid waggery" one story that he heard James tell about John Wesley at Oxford. Such a story he would think inappropriate for a Methodist.

Returning to his home on Clinton Pace, Duyckinck recorded in his diary his visit with the brothers on January 5.

Dropped in at the Harpers in Cliff St. where business is carried on like some of the modern plays—a rich drama in four acts. They are remarkable men, the Harpers, and have undoubtedly been raised and sustained in their position by their energy and enterprise. They are keen and wary, with little compunction and scent a falling author very rapidly though he be one of their own. John Harper is the more godly, for the firm is religious, some people requiring more of this article or what passes for it than others. James is the mountebank and a very useful part he serves. Wesley has the best serious part and Fletcher is a kind of curly pated fellow with the least. The present system of publishing they confessed was an exclusion of American authors. They had a novel of Fay which they could not publish at the old rates, for nobody would pay for it and which could pay the author nothing if published at the new. The new edition of Hope Leslie fell stillborn.

The brothers' pessimism regarding Fay's new novel, *Hoboken*, is extraordinary in view of the enthusiasm they had expressed for it five weeks earlier. Detmold, Fay's agent, received the manuscript from Fay in November and carried it dutifully to Cliff Street. On the 29th they sent a note to Detmold saying, "We think it would be well to put Mr. Fay's novel in hand immediately,—as there have been but few good American Novels published lately." On the following day Detmold passed on the good news to Fay. "The Harpers think well of your book," he reported, "think it may yield you $1,500 and upwards and are willing, in three weeks after its first publication, to make a liberal advance, if the book nets $1,200. You are entitled to a set of their 'Family Library' complete which costs $70—or its equivalent in other books." Detmold negotiated a half-profit contract with an agreement that *Hoboken* would be published the following spring, "so soon as navigation opens."

But in April, 1843, neither the steamboats that plied the coastal waters and rivers nor the slow boats on the network of American canals carried many copies of *Hoboken*. American readers were saving money by reading novels in cheaper format, and the brothers were left wondering if they ever could see an end to the troubles with their author in faraway Germany. Instead of a nice profit, from a cautious printing of nine hundred copies, *Hoboken* had failed by $186 to earn expenses, as they told Detmold in late May. When Fay in Berlin heard the bad news, he was wishing that the book might have been delayed a year or two till book publishing in America had recovered from its economic indigestion. A delay would have helped but little for it was not a very good novel and its threadbare plot was based on a duel between two fashionable young men on the Jersey meadows—hence the title.

In point of fact, April, 1843, marked a turning point in the conflict between books and literary weeklies. *Brother Jonathan* was frank to admit that "literature is now a drug. All the markets are overstocked." One reason for this pessimism was a directive issued that month by the Post Office Department. Thereafter newspaper "extras" would be charged postage at book rates. The official order may well have been inspired by letters or visits to Washington from Cliff Street. According to Frank Luther Mott's *Golden Multitudes*, the increase in postage rates "was a body blow against novels in newspaper form; and though the publishers continued to issue them, their sales declined."

One disappointment with a work of American fiction was enough to affect Cliff Street policy. No more novels this year by American authors. Even Maria Brooks, famous under her pen name María del Occidente, as author of the long poem *Zóphiël*, was turned down when she submitted her novel *Idomen*. "It is too elevated to sell," the brothers told her. Southey had called Mrs. Brooks "the most impassioned and imaginative of all poetesses" (before Elizabeth Barrett Browning became famous) but this work was a somewhat autobiographical novel, not poetry. Even poetry was frowned upon and only one volume was issued in 1843—Robert Tyler's *Death; or, Medorus' Dream*. An autumn publication, it was favorably reviewed by Clark, who said it was being praised widely by the newspapers. Tyler was a special author, however; his 1842 book had been a success and he was not only the son of the President of the United States but also his father's private secretary—a valuable pipeline to the White House. Two books by A. G. Abell on President Tyler resulted, one on his "History, Character and Position," and the other a short biography and a selection of his speeches and writings, a paperback. This contact may also have brought two books by Joseph Scoville on John C. Calhoun, one a 554-page book of speeches and other writings, which the *Democratic Review* applauded. These books were among the few nonfiction titles issued in 1843 from Cliff Street—these plus a half-dozen small religious books concerned mostly with issues within the Episcopal and Anglican churches. One was Dr. Pusey's famous sermon *The Holy Eucharist, a Comfort to the Penitent*, delivered that year at Oxford, a sermon that caused his suspension as a university preacher, made him the most influential Anglican divine for a quarter of a century, and was a contributing factor to Newman's leaving the Anglican Church for the Roman Church.

However, the brothers did offer their hard-pressed friends in the book trade three best sellers of nonfiction, published in the good old-fashioned way of muslin bindings without advance issue in numbers. Two were in the dependable category of travel books, the first *Travels in Egypt, etc.*, by Stephen Olin, who had succeeded to the presidency of Wesleyan College on the death of Dr. Fisk. When Olin, following Fisk, published his book, people were saying that in order to be a success at Wesleyan the president should become ill, travel abroad for his health, and then, returning, write a book for Harper's on his travels. Olin did much of the proofreading during the winter vacation of the college while staying with Fletcher and Jane on Crosby Street. Six months earlier Fletcher had succeeded in publishing a biography of President Fisk even though other publishers were after it; Olin may have helped influence the author, although the Harper offer of half profits was better than any other. While Olin was abroad, the office of president at Wesleyan was taken over by Fletcher's old friend Dr. Nathan Bangs, formerly publishing agent for the Methodist Book Concern. Just the man, Fletcher thought, to revise for American readers an English book he had bought, a biography of the Dutch theologian Arminius. When that book came out at the year's end, Fletcher's batting average with Wesleyan College presidents was a perfect 1,000.

Olin's *Travels in Egypt*, "an excellent work" according to *The Knickerbocker*, was published in May and soon went into a third printing, a success due in part to the fact that people are always eager to read a first book by a popular and eloquent preacher. The *Democratic Review* observed that Olin's work struck "the mean between the popular books by Stephens and the scholarly ones by Dr. [Edward] Robinson.*" Other reviews were linking the names of Olin and Stephens, for the latter's *Incidents of Travel in Yucatan* was also a spring, 1843, publication.

On April 17 the brothers signed a contract with Stephens for the book "now published." As soon as Stephens had returned from Central America, the brothers—all four of them—called on him to urge that he lose not a moment before beginning his book. Langley had announced a forthcoming book on the Mayan ruins and other competition could be expected because of the publicity that had been given Stephens's explorations. With that aplomb characteristic of one who knows himself to be a publisher's best-selling author, Stephens replied that he could promptly deliver a manuscript but certain conditions must first

* Dr. Edward Robinson's *Biblical Research in Palestine* was also being widely reviewed. Dr. Robinson of Union Theological Seminary, New York, was to switch from Crocker & Brewster, the Boston publisher of this book, to Harper's in 1850.

be agreed to. The octavo size and $5 price of the two-volume *Central America* should be retained. (Other works on archeology had far exceeded the common reader's purse; i.e., Lord Kingsborough's eight volumes, at $150 the volume and Waldeck's folio, at 3,200 francs.) Furthermore his fellow traveler to Yucatán was to have charge of making the illustrations; Francis Catherwood was not only scientifically trained and a railway surveyor but also an artist. Catherwood should be given the responsibility of selecting the engravers, who would work from daguerreotypes, supervising their work and designing the binding. The brothers readily agreed to Stephens's conditions and in the contract stipulated that $5,707 should be a first charge against profits to reimburse Stephens and Catherwood for expenses they had incurred. After this amount plus the cost of plates had been amortized, Stephens was to be credited with $1.04 per copy (equivalent to a royalty of more than 20 percent of the retail price of $5). Since the contract specified the manufacturing cost (paper, presswork, and binding) and is based on the assumption of an equal division of profits, it is clear that the brothers were figuring a discount of 20 percent to the trade, as in the case of Webster's *Dictionary*:

Wholesale price $4.00		
"Profit" to author	$1.04	
"Profit" to publisher	1.04	
Manufacturing cost	1.78	
Guaranty (3%)	.12	3.98

Other publishers were giving booksellers and agents a discount of 25 percent. Many of the more than eight hundred booksellers* who were stocking Harper books certainly argued for a better discount; if they called at Cliff Street, it was Fletcher's job to mollify them. Years later an anonymous Boston bookseller was to write of his visits there in the early forties:

"I always calculated that if I wanted the lowest terms, or to perfect a new arrangement, I had to pass Uncle James's jokes, John's genial growling, Wesley's studious questionings and go to Fletcher. His

---

* In the January, 1842, issue of the *U.S. Literary Advertiser and Publishers' Circular,* Langley advertised that he had "the most extensive and complete list of the American Book-trade," amounting to more than eight hundred names. The brothers could hardly have had fewer names since they were carrying on a much more extensive operation. They soon stopped "trade" advertising in the *Literary Advertiser,* although Langley gave them the preferred position in his first issue; no doubt they recognized, as it now appears, that in its short life this periodical grew to be a Langley house organ, and they would spend money better promoting their books to the trade by mail, as they had previously done.

words were verily, Yea, yea, and Nay, nay. . . . Their wisdom, their counsel, their business ways, and their unvarying courtesy during my thirty-five years' business relations with them, have aided my advancement, added to my prosperity, strengthened the Christian in my business and in my life. . . ." Another bookseller, D. B. Cooke, recalled that in the early forties "the great publishing event of the period was the famous 'Harper's Pictorial Bible,' far in advance of the times." In 1844 H. W. Derby, for whom Cooke worked, moved from Columbus to Cincinnati, locating his bookstore at Third and Main streets. The trip (not unlike that of Dickens two years earlier) took Derby and Cooke several days of weary travel "in one of Neil & Co.'s old-fashioned stages."*

When word got around that the "American Traveler" was soon to publish another work, people began talking about how much money Stephens was making from his books—$10,000 on *Egypt* and $20,000 on *Central America,* while the most that Cooper had ever earned on one of his novels was $5,000. The *Democratic Review,* which passed these figures on to its readers, decided not to publish an ordinary review of *Yucatan,* "since everyone has read the book anyway." Editor O'Sullivan did chide Stephens gently for his reasoning on the origin of the Mayan ruins, but this metaphysical bent in Stephens was one of his appealing qualities. His feeling of awe and his sense of the sublime were infectious, and the thousands who were reading *Yucatan* that year felt that they intimately shared Stephens's travels (the most extensive to date of any outsider) to these forty-four ruined cities or places where ancient peoples had lived and worshiped. In April *The Knickerbocker* claimed that *Central America* and *Yucatan* would take their place "at once among the foremost achievements of American literature, not only in the estimation of his own countrymen, but in that of the enlightened world." It was not an extravagant prophecy since *Yucatan* would soon be translated into six languages, with two English and one Irish edition; Murray had already sold 2,500 copies of *Central America* in England. Queen Victoria was among Stephens's enthusiastic readers.

The Boston historian and author of *Ferdinand and Isabella,* William H. Prescott, was another admirer. After reading *Central America,* Prescott had written Stephens, "I cannot well express to you the satis-

---

* Like the Harpers, there were four Derby brothers, all in the book business. J. C. Derby, who figures most prominently in the Harper story, was the eldest. H. W. Derby (born in 1820) was his junior by two years. In 1840 he was married to a Columbus girl in Trinity Episcopal Church. It was the first church wedding ever held in the Ohio city and the crowd of gaping spectators was so great that the wedding party had difficulty in reaching the altar. The third brother, G. H. Derby, established a bookstore in Buffalo and the youngest, C. L. Derby, conducted one in Sandusky, Ohio.

faction and delight I have received from your volumes," and assured Stephens that his return trip to Yucatán would not be in vain if the resulting book were half as good. Eager for Prescott's approval, Stephens forwarded one of the first copies of *Yucatan* by Harnden Express. It was sent on March 24 and the following day Stephens wrote Prescott that the book was forthcoming.

But that was not Stephens's chief reason for writing Prescott. He was anxious for his friend to share in his good fortune by having a publisher who could get books widely publicized and sold. *Ferdinand and Isabella*, published in 1837, had got off to a bad start when the Boston publisher, American Stationers' Company, failed the following year after selling a first printing of 1,250 copies and launching a second. Prescott had then signed a contract with Little and Brown giving them exclusive rights till November 1, 1843. By the time Stephens was writing to Prescott, Little and Brown had printed seven editions of five hundred copies each, one of which had been shipped to Paris. In all, hardly a quarter of the American sales of Stephens's *Central America*, and reviewed equally well, if not better. Bentley in London had been more generous with Prescott than Murray had been with Stephens, paying him £1,000 for *Ferdinand and Isabella*, and the *Edinburgh Review* had said that "Mr. Prescott's work is one of the most successful historical productions of our time." Obviously, Stephens thought, Prescott should be prodded to transfer this book and his new work to Cliff Street. He wrote:

. . . I have spoken to the Messrs Harpers about the publication of your next work. They are desirous to undertake it and of course offer their usual best terms i.e., half of the nett profits,—or they will allow you to have it stereotyped in Boston, and to keep the plates under your own control, they will pay the cash, and will allow the same rate per copy that would be allowed by your Boston publisher. They consider that with their capital and business connexions they have the means of making larger sales than any other publishing house in the country. Their principle is, small profits and large sales, and in allowing you the same rate they would sell at $1 or $1.50 less per copy. It is my belief that they would sell of such a work as yours at least 2500 copies more than any other house, and I feel persuaded that after a years trial of them with the new work you would find it to your interest to put Ferdinand & Isabella into their hands. Their responsibility is beyond all question, they pay out $3000 per week in cash to workmen, never give out notes when they can get a deduction of interest, and to make all sure, would pay cash for your books as they receive them. I do not like to be urgent in advising you to make any change, but I cannot help wishing that your new work should have the full benefit of the widest profitable circulation, which I sincerely believe can be effected only by placing it in the hands of the Messrs Harpers. Carey & Lea* of Philadelphia stand next to them in extent of business relations, but as I believe at considerable distance behind. I am sorry I had not spoken to them before, as I find them more interested than I supposed they would be. Publishing for American authors forms but an inconsiderable part of their business, but they say that with myself, Professor Anthon and yourself they would have the three best, or at least the three most available, (this is between ourselves), the credit of which would operate indirectly upon their general business and upon us individually. In fact, but for my being the go between, I believe they would be disposed to treat with you with quite as much regard to the credit of publishing your work as to the profit. If you should wish to communicate with them and should think the sales of my works any criterion please let me hear from you. . . .

Prescott replied promptly. He would be pleased to have Stephens inquire what Harper's would offer for *Conquest of Mexico*. While he felt kindly toward Little and Brown, he had not promised them the book and would not be obligated to "give them the business at a great pecuniary loss to myself." He planned to speak to them about the book and would have their offer by the time Harper's proposal was forthcoming. So that the brothers might know what to figure on, he gave the length of the manuscript, discussed the subject matter and market, and said he would like a three-volume work to sell at $6 and to pay him a royalty of $1.50. He would supply the stereotypes, which he would own ("I am now . . . up to the eyes in stereotyping") because years before he had been given what he thought was good advice by Jared Sparks, that he should supervise the design, composition, and plating of his works. Furthermore he had good working arrangements with Charles R. Metcalf, head of the Cambridge firm that had the reputation in the first half of the nineteenth century of turning out the finest books printed in America.

Pleased to be a go-between in so important a publishing deal, Stephens hurried to Cliff Street with Prescott's letter. All the brothers needed to do, if they could meet Prescott's terms, was to tempt him with sizable quantities they thought they might sell during the first and subsequent years. The brothers listened carefully to what Stephens had to say and John worked out costs on 5,000 copies. They could agree to Prescott's proposal and advance him $7,500 on publication; they could almost guarantee the sale of 7,000 or 8,000 copies the first year and confidently expect to reach in four years not the 8,000 or 10,000 figure

* I.e., Lea & Blanchard.

Prescott mentioned, but 15,000. They also agreed that Fletcher should write the letter setting forth their views. This he did on April 3. Good salesman and editor that he was, he followed up the letter with a call, knowing that the best way to sign up an author is to go to see him. And he was not the first salesman or the last editor to get cold feet. Before he could ring the doorbell of the famous author's house on Bedford Street in downtown Boston, he had to walk around the block two or three times to work up his courage.

The man Fletcher met was nearly blind. Shortly before he was graduated from Harvard in 1814, Prescott had lost the sight of one eye when a prankish student threw a crust of bread that pierced the eyeball. The other eye becoming inflamed, Prescott visited oculists in London and Paris in the hope of restoring his vision. While he obtained little help for his eye, his two years abroad did strengthen his general health and helped him to learn to live with his affliction. He returned to Boston with two resources, one a resolve to devote his life to intellectual pursuits—eventually literary ones—and the other a writing case, or noctograph, which contained wires to guide a stylus as he wrote on carbon paper. He was to say later that the characters he formed were a near approach to hieroglyphics, but reader-secretaries, for years his daily companions, became skilled in transcribing them.* At first he wrote but little for publication, averaging about an article a year in ten years for the *North American Review*. That decade, as planned, was devoted primarily to a study of the literature of France, Italy, and Spain. His contemporary George Ticknor, the first professor of modern languages at Harvard, was his frequent companion and later wrote of Prescott, "His industry never flagged; his courage never faltered; his spirits, buoyant by nature, never sank under the burdens imposed upon them. It was the period when he laid deep and sure the foundations of his coming success." Ticknor's growing library of Spanish books, many procured through Obadiah Rich, was a godsend, and by the time he was thirty-one Prescott knew that his literary career would focus on Spanish-American themes. Ticknor was one of the few intimate friends of Prescott who knew of the grueling, yet exciting, hours of research that streamed like a hidden river under the surface life of this handsome, sociable, wealthy young Bostonian. Prescott acknowledged his great indebtedness to Ticknor in his preface to *The Conquest of Mexico;* he was later to dedicate his *Miscellanies* to Ticknor, reminiscent of "studies pursued together in earlier days."

* Prescott described these "embarrassments" of his historical work in the preface to his *Conquest of Peru* (1847).

History does not disclose what the distinguished historian and the aspiring publisher discussed that April day. Prescott would have asked questions about the Harper establishment, the distribution of review copies, sales promotion in the West and South. He would have asked questions to which we today should like to know the answers. Whatever Fletcher said, he was successful in convincing Prescott that it would be to his advantage to entrust his book on Mexico to Cliff Street promotion. But it was not easy for Prescott thus to admit the superiority of New York over Boston. "I am sorry to transfer the work to New York," he wrote on April 30 to his friend Edward Everett, then American Minister at the Court of St. James's, but on April 19 he notified Stephens that he now felt himself "at liberty to accept the terms of the Messrs Harper." Prescott himself apparently drafted the contract. It was signed and witnessed on April 25 and forwarded to the brothers with a covering letter expressing Prescott's hope that it "conformed to the desire of your note." This agreement, which was duly and appropriately copied in the Harper leatherbound contract ledger right after the Stephens agreement for *Yucatan,* specified that the work should be published in November; to that end Prescott was to deliver the stereotype plates "in season," unless prevented "by ill health or any other cause." (See illustration 13.)

Proud of their new acquisition, the brothers immediately sent out press releases, only to find them backfiring in one curious respect. On May 31 Wesley wrote Prescott "there seems to be a great deal of uneasiness among several writers to publish something on the same subject, in anticipation of your work," going on to recommend early publication in three monthly installments beginning in August. Obviously Wesley was worried about some real or imagined competition from Jonas Winchester and company, and the best way to squelch it would be the announcement of early serial publicaton. This would also increase sales, Wesley thought, since many would thus subscribe to the work who would find it difficult to spare so large a sum as $6 at one time.

Prescott wrote back immediately to say No to such a proposal. He was arranging with Colonel Aspinwall in London to sell the English "copyright" to Bentley or Murray (although Everett wrote from London to remind Prescott that copyright was not possible). Even so it was desirable that the English edition be published at least a fortnight before the American edition to give the authorized publisher a head start on London pirates. Early three-part publication in New York would make any such deal impossible. Aspinwall had apparently decided on Bentley but was getting bids from Longmans as well as Murray to pry a larger sum out of Bentley. Mr. Thomas Longman hurried to Aspinwall's office, offering to publish on half profits, to take Harper sheets on commission, or to pay £300 down and £200 more after 1,500 copies had been sold. John Murray* wrote that he would do no more than he did with Stephens—half profits and no advance. Bentley finally agreed to pay £650 for the copyright, which amount Aspinwall later forwarded to Prescott after deducting a 10 percent commission.

The concern that Wesley expressed over the competition of the weeklies and over high book prices may explain why, out of twelve books announced as "in press" in April, only two were ever issued. Serial publication of *Life of General Jackson* by Amos Kendall, who had been Postmaster General in Jackson's second term, began in the autumn but ceased after about half of the numbers had appeared, even though the *Democratic Review* was prophesying it would sell in the tens of thousands. Yet the Harpers were obviously not short of funds, for in June they paid Commander Mackenzie $2,900 for all rights to his three earliest books and boasted to young Henry David Thoreau, in New York that summer looking for a publishing job, that they were making $50,000 a year and their motto was to "leave well enough alone." In November the *Messenger* reported that the brothers used $2,000 worth of paper every week and valued their plates stored in subterranean vaults at $250,000, adding a laconic comment, "Verily it is a good thing for young men to begin with Morals."

Moses Y. Beach, proprietor of the New York *Sun*, pioneer penny newspaper, also testified to their wealth. Beach was titillating New Yorkers with occasional issues of a pamphlet on the *Wealth and Biography of the Wealthy Citizens of New York City* whose fortunes could be counted in six figures or more, and his fourth edition, published in May, 1842, had estimated the assets of the brothers at $200,-000. Out of 44 columns listing 646 names of individuals or families, Beach devoted nearly a column to the story of the brothers, a lineage exceeded only slightly by what he gave to John Jacob Astor. In his biography of the brothers (see Appendix 3) Beach associated their enterprise with the competitive rise of the mammoth weeklies. He prophesied: "The lightning-like rapidity with which the choicest coinings of the brain in foreign lands, are almost immediately made the common property and universally circulating cheap commodity of our own people, threaten in time to make the book-business, if not peri-

---

* John Murray II, Byron's close friend and publisher. A few weeks following this exchange of letters with Aspinwall, Mr. Murray died.

odical literature, also a *dead letter* and destructive pursuit to those
who embark in it."

As the year 1843 drew to a close, it became increasingly clear that if
a "dead letter" publisher were to be buried, it would be Jonas Winchester and not Harper's. But Winchester was still kicking. He won out
in the year's competition over Eugène Sue's *The Mysteries of Paris*, his
translator, Demming, being considered by *The Knickerbocker* much
superior to Town, for whose translation the brothers paid $500.* Ac-
cording to Duyckinck, the Winchester work "made a hit." Arranging
to publish Sue's *The Wandering Jew* the following summer, the Harpers worked this time with an English translator, paying slightly more
than £180. Finding that *The Wandering Jew* was the most popular of
the Sue titles, the brothers later published an illustrated edition from
plates imported from England, an edition called the only decent one,
typographically speaking, available. Here again, the work was first
issued in numbers, and as issues of the "Illustrated Sue" began appearing in 1845, they helped to decorate the grave of at least one of the
"mammoths." Jonas Winchester sold *The New World* in November,
1844, and it died soon after, marking the end of what Duyckinck
called Winchester's "bold but rash conflict with the Harpers."

Contributing to that end, the *Library of Select Novels* continued to
mark up huge sales but not profits. By September, when Mrs. Gore's
The Banker's Wife was issued, the brothers had brought out two new
novels by James,† and one each by Bulwer and W. J. Neale. Also
Adam Brown by Horace Smith and three novels by the Swedish
authoress Fredrika Bremer, including *The President's Daughters*.
Smith was not a newcomer to the Harper list; since 1829, five of his
works, mostly fiction, had been taken. He was a friend of Leigh Hunt,
Shelley, and Southey, and well known to American readers. Miss
Bremer was making her Harper debut and a rather impressive one at
that.

The Bremer novels had been translated by Mary Howitt, an English

---

* "James and Sue, Forever" was the heading of an advertisement of S. W. Pearse, a
Cincinnati bookseller, who announced G. P. R. James's *The Smuggler* and Sue's *Mysteries of Paris*.

† *Forest Days* in February and *The False Heir* in June. *The False Heir* was given a
five-page review in the *Messenger* for August, the last issue to be edited by Lieutenant
Matthew F. Maury. Maury was a writer and editor only by avocation, his chief interests being navigation, astronomy, and hydrography. In 1855 he was to give the brothers
The Physical Geography of the Sea; five years later it was in its eighth and greatly enlarged edition. In 1843, the *Messenger* suffered the loss by death of its founder and
publisher, T. W. White. One of the last letters White wrote was addressed to Griswold suggesting that he go to "my friends, the Harpers" to get an enclosed check
cashed and a note discounted.

writer who was also the first to translate the fairy stories by Hans Andersen. This translation the brothers did not undertake, probably because of their own staple, the book of fairy stories that James had rounded up. But they were to publish five of Mrs. Howitt's own books; the first one, *Who Shall Be Greatest*, was earmarked in 1843 for the *School District Library*. For the same series they also acquired two titles by Miss Maria McIntosh, popular author of juvenile stories under her nom de plume, Aunt Kitty. The books were *Conquest and Self-Conquest* and *Woman an Enigma*. Moving to New York from Georgia in 1835, Miss McIntosh had lost most of her inherited wealth in the crash of 1837 and began earning her livelihood as a writer. Although she was to give the Harpers two additional books for young people in 1845 and '46, she switched to Appletons for her further books and for later reissues of Aunt Kitty. The brothers may have taken her on in the hope of eventually getting the Aunt Kitty books, but by 1847 they had signed up Jacob Abbott, author of the more popular Rollo books. Miss McIntosh's books sold well in England, introduced there by W. C. Macready, the popular English actor, who, in 1844 after a prosperous American tour, took copies home to his childen.

In addition to the names of Mrs. Howitt, Mrs. Mary S. B. Dana, and Miss McIntosh as authors of *S.D.L.* books, there appears, surprisingly and enigmatically, the name of Harriet Beecher Stowe. Entitled *The Mayflower*, her 324-page book contained fifteen sketches (one of them "Uncle Tim") of scenes and characters among the descendants of the Pilgrims. Mrs. Stowe's elder sister, Catharine Beecher, who wrote a preface for the book, was the more desirable author because she was widely known for her outstanding work in the nascent movement for female education. The brothers probably accepted *The Mayflower* at the urging of Catharine, whom they soon signed up. For a period of nearly thirty years beginning in 1845, they were to catalogue ten books by Catharine Beecher and to publish her articles in their *Magazine*. Why, then, did Miss Beecher not try in 1852 to interest her publishers in *Uncle Tom's Cabin*, as she did Phillips, Sampson & Company? Or did she? It was reported that Mr. Phillips turned it down because the firm enjoyed, as the Harpers did, a large Southern trade.

In this time of conflict with the mammoth weeklies, a few books were being added to the *Family Library*. By 1844 it had grown to 171 volumes and sold for $75.70.* Included in the *Library* were the

* That year the brothers printed an annual catalogue and also a broadside listing all their titles. This sheet, 27 by 20¼ inches, could be folded for convenient letter-size mailings. It was made up into four pages, the bottom of one page being left blank for addressing. One such, now held by the American Antiquarian Society, was mailed on

seventy-two volumes that were placed that summer on the frigate *United States*, which Herman Melville, a young Navy recruit, had boarded nine months earlier in Honolulu. Recent additions were titles that would have interested Melville, such as the two-volume history of the Lewis and Clark expedition, edited with updating on the present condition of the Oregon territory, by Archibald McVicar. A new volume that he would have read with misgivings was the Rev. Dr. Michael Russell's fifth *Family Library* work, *Polynesia*. By this time Melville had formed some opinions of his own about missions and missionaries in the South Sea islands. While Dr. Russell was a liberal Scottish clergyman, he wrote with appreciation of the introduction of Christianity there, and Melville was returning to his homeland with grave questions about natives, as he was to write later, who "had been civilized into draft horses, and evangelized into beasts of burden." As Melville looked over the *Family Library* volumes, some of which, like *Two Years Before the Mast,* he had already read, he probably thought that if he too should write a book after he got home he knew what publisher he would seek out. Here was proof that the Cliff Street brothers could get their books round the world. On October 3, 1844, the *United States* dropped anchor in the Boston Navy Yard and before the month was over Melville was out of the Navy and reunited with his family. Before leaving Boston, he had dropped into the Charles River a quilted white canvas jacket which he had made for himself. The white jacket had come to symbolize his own individuality among the mass of Navy seamen.

More profitable than books published for the *Libraries,* four text-books and one scholarly reference book rounded out the year on Cliff Street. Two were modern-language grammars—one German and one French—and another, *Elements of Algebra,* presaged a vigorous pro-gram of publishing mathematical textbooks. The perennial Anthon produced an edition of the *Aeneid of Virgil* and also edited a big, 1,126-page *Dictionary of Greek and Roman Antiquities.* The latter was based on a work by William Smith, the English lexicographer; Anthon added "numerous articles relative to the Botany, Mineralogy, and Zoology of the Ancients."

Anthon had a strange bedfellow on the year's Harper list—Cornelius Mathews. He had not only poured vitriol over Anthon's *Classical Dic-*

May 12 by Gerherdus Demarest to Charles W. Brewster of Portsmouth, N. H., quoting "one-fifth for the Cash" on orders from the Benevolent Association, which was espe-cially interested in the *Family Library*.

tionary but had also lampooned Stephens's *Central America* in an earlier issue of *Arcturus*. On October 19, 1843, John signed "Harper & Brothers" to a contract, drafted by Mathews, for a 370-page book, stereotype plates of which were to be supplied by Mathews. Entitled *Various Writings*, the book contained an essay on international copyright. The brothers heaped coals of fire on Mathews's head, for the essay was based on his speech at the Dickens dinner and included the hypothetical anecdote of the James Harper rejection of Irving's manuscript, although this time Cliff Street went unnamed.* The contract specified that not more than a hundred copies would be distributed for review, including a dozen to foreign editors. Mathews also agreed to purchase 750 copies to supply orders he already had or expected to get. These would be without royalty; on regular sales he would receive 20 percent of the retail price of $1. But he did not earn much. Demarest penned a sarcastic note after his listing of *Various Writings:* "It was a favorite joke among the clerks, in allusion to the extremely small sales of this book, that the Fire of 1853 destroyed many more copies than were originally printed."

The truly big book of the year was Prescott's *The Conquest of Mexico*. During the summer, it was anticipated and publicized, having been sold to booksellers at the Spring Trade Sales in New York and Philadelphia. Its appearance strongly emphasized the fact that real books were not "dead letters." It also helped the Harpers recoup some of the prestige they had lost in Boston for paying so small a sum for *Two Years Before the Mast*.

Long summer days supplied the many necessary hours of daylight that Prescott had counted on for the tremendous job of proofreading his work. There were 1,484 pages of type to be read in first proofs and again in corrected proofs, to make sure that all corrections had been properly made and no typos introduced; the same readings followed on proofs of the plates. Finally the job was done. Perfectionist Prescott happily dispatched a set of final proofs to London, and Bentley's edition appeared on October 24. Early that month the completed stereotypes had been forwarded to New York. In the meantime word had come from Cliff Street that "unforeseen delays" might keep *Mexico* from being published in early November; "we hope not for the sale might be affected unfavorably by the lateness of the season." But the brothers were delayed, not able to issue Volume I till December 6. Six

---

* Nine days after dating his introduction to *Various Writings*, Mathews signed his name to a pamphlet, *International Copy-right*, in which he referred to "the barony of Cliff-Street . . . which included the Pelham vineyards."

days later they wrote Prescott, sending a copy of Volume II and referring to publicity that Volume I had received in the New York press.
Issuing the three volumes at short intervals would multiply notices and
distributing copies to editors "*throughout* the United States" would
yield a good harvest, the brothers wrote, "unless the 'cheap literature'
has used up entirely good taste and intelligence." A total of 150 review
copies were sent out, royalty being paid on 80; in addition, Prescott
received 25 free copies, some of which he used to aid sales. On December 11, he wrote Cliff Street that he would give editors of the two
leading Boston dailies proof sheets containing "the most showy & striking passages." Perhaps the brothers should consider sending out similar
clippings from proofs for "newspaper editors do not like to spoil their
own copies & have not time to copy extracts themselves." This suggestion was made diffidently ("You may smile at the idea of my pretending to give you any assistance in your own business") but the brothers
were learning early that their new author was not one to hide his
literary lantern under a basket of humility. A few weeks later he was
proposing that they use an English quote in advertising. "You will see
the London Quarterly contains a long favorable notice of the Conq. It
is fr. the pen of Milman the historian of the Jews. The last paragraph
might furnish a good extract as coming from the highest foreign authority."

Praise for book, author, and publisher was widespread in America.
The Knickerbocker said that the printing and publishing job was better than the best of the Boston press and the equal of any books published in London. The *North American Review* pulled out all the
double trumpet stops on its organ to announce their friend's book, "a
noble work, judiciously planned and admirably executed. . . . It will
take its place among the enduring productions of the human mind."
Such reviews moved copies out of the Cliff Street warehouse into
bookstores and libraries but not so swiftly as the brothers had anticipated. While the first printing of five thousand copies was exhausted in
four months, the hoped-for sale of eight thousand copies was not
reached during the first year of publication.* Six dollars was a lot of
money even for three large octavos, and people were still spending a
lot of time reading the cheap weeklies.

---

* The 1844 sales of the *Conquest of Mexico* amounted to seven thousand copies according to *Harper's New Monthly Magazine*, June, 1850.

CHAPTER XII

His Honor, the Mayor of New York

1844–1845

O<small>N MAY</small> 24, 1844, Samuel Finley Breese Morse was able to establish the practicality of the electric telegraph when wires strung up between Washington and Baltimore began transmitting almost instantaneous messages. That the first words ticked off did not spell out "What hath Morse wrought" but gave Divinity the credit was a testimony to the depth of Morse's religious convictions. He and his brothers had been reared in a home where spiritual concerns were primary. His preacher-father, Jedidiah Morse, a friend and contemporary of Timothy Dwight, the Calvinist president of Yale, had fought against the growing religious liberalism around Boston, and Morse was largely responsible early in the nineteenth century for ejecting the nonorthodox from the Congregational Church, who then established Unitarianism. Jedidiah Morse was also famous as the father of American geography. In 1784, shortly after his graduation from Yale, he wrote *Geography Made Easy*, a school text, the first of its kind in America. The book was much revised and reprinted and Morse's *Geography* became almost as famous as Webster's *Speller*. At his death in 1826, his copyrights were inherited by his son Sidney E. Morse, Samuel's younger brother, an obvious bequest because Sidney had

worked with his father on revisions and, in founding the New York
Observer three years earlier, Sidney had learned how to deal with
printing and publishing problems.

A few weeks before his brother telegraphed the famous four words,
Sidney Morse went to 82 Cliff Street with his cousin Samuel Breese, a
cartographer and then part owner of the copyright to the Morse
School Geography. They drew up a contract with the brothers
whereby the *Geography* was to be published on a half-profits basis.
The cousins were to supply the color plates for the maps and the
brothers were to pay them $1,500, or one-half the estimated value. Fur-
thermore the brothers agreed to manufacture each edition at the going
rate or allow Morse or Breese to do so. This, the twenty-seventh edition of the *Geography*, published well before the opening of schools
that autumn, was given vigorous advance advertising and promotion to
schoolteachers and trustees, with upward of one thousand free copies
being distributed, each party assuming one-half the cost, to promote
text adoptions of the *Geography*. The book was quarto size in order to
accommodate the fifty-three cerographic maps. ("Cerographic" was
the name Sidney Morse gave to a process he had developed to make
engravings on wax molds, from which by a process akin to electrotyping metallic plates resulted, plates that could be used on the common printing press. The brothers were to learn considerably more
about "cerography" the following year.) This 9-by-12-inch size, established by Morse because he wanted detailed maps, made the *School
Geography* the largest book that generations of American boys and
girls were to carry home from school, always a problem, for smaller
books were forever falling out when strapped in with it. In addition to
the maps, there were 72 pages of text and 143 wood engravings. Bound
in "muslin," the book retailed for 50 cents. On orders of one thousand
copies or more, the brothers were to give a discount of not less than 30
percent. Did school district or statewide adoptions of textbooks account for such large group sales? At any rate, the new "cerographic"
process for producing the maps brought costs down to a point where
the brothers could claim that their edition of Morse's *Geography* was
priced lower than any competing book.

Sidney Morse was also using maps as premium offers to subscribers
of the *Observer*. He now had more time for experimenting with color
plates and investigating new printing processes since he had turned
over editorial responsibility four years before to a young Presbyterian
minister named Samuel Irenaeus Prime, who showed much promise.
Also he had the responsibility of managing the six-story Morse Building at the corner of Nassau and Beekman streets. The building was

pointed out to sightseers for on its roof Professor Draper, aided in his laboratory work by S. F. B. Morse, had made those famous photographs. Anyone who could afford it wanted to have a daguerreotype made, willing to undergo the mild torture of the head vise which Draper developed to keep a man from blurring his own image.

But there was another image now getting blurred that Draper could do nothing about. It was the image of the typical American. There had been no question up to recent times. He might be a Yankee by his accent ("to guess betrays the Yankee"), a New Yorker or Philadelphian with easy city sophistication, a Virginian or Carolinian with drawling speech and courteous manners, even a Westerner with the ruggedness begot by frontier living, but the image was clear. An American was white, of native stock, and presumably a Protestant. Now this picture was being changed by the influx of foreigners, many of them Irish Catholics, who quickly asserted the rights of citizenship, eager also to be known as Americans. They were creating political blocs, particularly in New Orleans, Boston, and New York, often inspired by Roman Catholic priests who also were challenging Protestant dominance in the prevailing culture.

As a reaction to this assertiveness, Protestants began talking about "native Americans" and the very present danger to their faith. The Morses and the Dwights were among the first to become articulate. As Jedidiah Morse and Timothy Dwight had fought the left-wing Calvinists in their day, so their descendants would attack the right-wing challenge of Catholicism. This attack took two directions, one political and one literary. Samuel F. B. Morse had a leading part in each. In 1832 he had returned to New York after three years abroad, some of that time spent studying painting in Italy. There he developed an antipathy to the Roman Church that was aggravated when he became aware of the rapid increase in the number of Irish immigrants (by 1832 over 25,000 a year, and by 1842 over 50,000). The political movement was expressed through a new party based on "native Americanism" and on its platform Morse ran unsuccessfully for mayor of New York in 1836.

The literary movement took the form of pamphlets, books, and a magazine, the *American Protestant Vindicator*, with offices adjacent to the Morse Building. Morse wrote several tracts and a book called *Foreign Conspiracy Against the United States*, published by Van Nostrand & Dwight. Theodore Dwight, Jr. (cousin of Van Nostrand's partner, nephew of President Dwight, and author of the Harper book on the history of Connecticut), put out *Open Convents, or Nunneries and Popish Seminaries Dangerous, etc.* George Bourne, editor of the *Vindicator*, published *Lorette, the History of Louise, Daughter of a*

Canadian Nun in 1833, a book of fiction that was in its sixth edition the following year.

With this best seller to his questionable credit, Bourne must have been delighted in 1835 to meet a woman who called herself Maria Monk. Brought to New York by the Canadian fanatic William K. Hoyt, "Maria" told a story of seductions, infanticide, and other wicked events within the walls of a Montreal convent. It was quickly ghostwritten, apparently by Bourne and the Rev. J. J. Slocum, and published in January, 1836, by Howe & Bates, a New York bookselling firm with offices at 76 Chatham Street. Apparently Van Nostrand & Dwight had first planned to publish it, and the Harpers may also have had it under consideration, deciding not to allow their imprint on such a book. However, they were not above manufacturing it for Howe & Bates, and on quantities printed they evidently paid out royalties, as revealed by papers they saved, along with an affidavit signed by Maria Monk swearing that her disclosures were true. Royalty payments and the copyright itself had rival claimants and the brothers were involved thereby in suits brought against them by Slocum and Maria Monk in the New York Vice-Chancellor's Court and by Hoyt in the United States District Court. They were successfully represented in these suits by attorney William Emerson, brother of Ralph Waldo Emerson, whose receipted bills were also saved.

Some commentators on this mysterious affair (mysterious because it involved persons and firms that are now but names only), importantly Professor Ray Allen Billington, noting the Harpers' litigation over royalty payments, have assumed that they set up two employees as a dummy firm to exploit the book and safeguard their own imprint. Such chicanery is disproved by the fact that Timothy A. Howe and Joseph T. Bates are listed in the New York City Directories from 1834-35 to 1837-38 as booksellers on Chatham Street, with the firm name of Howe & Bates. Furthermore they were issuing other books—one on phrenology—during these years and are listed as publishers in O. A. Roorbach's *Bibliotheca Americana: Catalog of American Publications, etc. 1820-1852*. A more likely assumption is that the brothers contracted to manufacture the book as another outside job and paid royalties on printings, either because they were considered by those who controlled the work more reliable than the small firm of booksellers or because the brothers wanted to control the financing of the book until their printing work was paid for.*

---

* In *The Protestant Crusade 1800-1860. A Study of the Origins of American Nativism*, Billington cites *Cases in the Vice-Chancellor's Court* (Edwards), Volume 3, p. 109

That they even made a manufacturing profit on *Awful Disclosures* must have embarrassed the brothers when Colonel Stone, himself a Protestant, returned from a visit to Montreal that summer and published facts in the *Commercial Advertiser* to prove that Maria Monk was a fraud. She had sworn to her affidavit falsely and the Harpers had been taken in. Stone was vilified by the *American Protestant Vindicator* and other reactionaries but his findings were substantiated by other investigators. He summed up his case a year later in the New York *Observer*: Maria Monk's story was "the most stupendous imposture of modern times."

In *Freedom's Ferment*, Alice Felt Taylor writes, "Suspicion of the naturalized citizen and fear of the Catholic Church have never been entirely absent from the American mind, and outbreaks due to such fears have always accompanied periods of rapid increase in immigration." Thus the winds of prejudice turned into a cyclone in American cities in the mid-1840's. Philadelphia had the most violent outbreak, a series of riots in which scores of persons were killed and two downtown Catholic churches burned. The reaction was mostly political in New York and Boston, where Nativist candidates (called American Republicans) were elected to the office of mayor.

To be sure other forces were at work to elect James Harper mayor of New York on Tuesday, April 9, 1844. Particularly, the time was ripe for a reform in the government of a city that had the reputation, partly through Charles Dickens's recent acrimonious digs, of being the most-prosperous and worst-managed city in America. And burdened with smelly garbage. "New York, I perceive, still can hold her own," a recent visitor had commented. "She's had, as far back as I can remember, the reputation of being the dirtiest city in the Union." James also received the tacit support of many Whigs, who knew he was a kindred spirit and were giving him support as a kind of protest to Henry Clay's leadership of the party. Thomas McElrath, Greeley's partner, wrote James on March 25 that his "peculiar position" prevented him from taking a "public stand," but he was sure that many Whigs, including himself, would vote for Harper for mayor.

James took little active part in the campaign. He was not at his best before an audience. People knew that he was an honest and successful

---

ff. and the New York *Observer* of November 26, 1836, as authorities, but neither speaks of Howe & Bates as being a dummy publisher. Several issues of the New York *Observer* in 1836 and 1837 discuss Maria Monk and the book. The only reference to Howe & Bates appears in the issue of January 23, 1836, "A little 18 mo. volume, of 231 pages, entitled 'Awful Disclosures by Maria Monk,' has just been published by Howe & Bates of this city."

man of business, that he was of native American stock, and that he took his stand on the Bible. If people wanted to elect him on these qualifications, he would do his best. His handwritten speech of acceptance indicates that he was a man of few words: "Gentlemen: I feel highly complimented that the mayoralty convention of the American Republican Party have honored me with a nomination for the office of mayor—I may add that such high honour I never expected—Gentlemen, if our fellow citizens confirm the nomination by electing me it will be my study to discharge the duties in conformity with the principles of our party—being a plain Mechanic I have rather been accustomed to doing than talking—you will therefore excuse my brevity." Some of his supporters were less restrained. One orator claimed that there were dangerous dungeons under St. Patrick's Cathedral and these were intended for no other purpose than the imprisonment and torture of the Protestant clergy when the Catholics gained the ascendency. Bishop Hughes may himself have been partly to blame for such accusations, for he made the tactical error of organizing, rather belatedly, a Catholic party of opposition. He was challenged by Stone in the *Commercial Advertiser* and by Bennett of the *Herald,* whose criticisms stung so bitterly that the bishop later arranged with Jonas Winchester to publish "A Letter on the Moral Causes that have produced the Evil Spirit of the Times, addressed to the Honourable James Harper, Mayor of New York. Including a vindication of the author from the infamous charges made against him by Jas. Gordon Bennett, William L. Stone, and others." Bishop Hughes's biographer claimed that on the night of the election some twelve hundred yelling Native Americans bearing "No Popery" banners attempted to provoke a riot in two almost wholly Irish Catholic wards. Diarist Duyckinck did not report any such provocative goings-on, but he and his friend Cornelius Mathews did stroll "through some of the more noisy electioneering quarters of the Five Points [Bowery].... The lower part of Mulberry Street and the Points—'Dickens' place' presented a very squalid London-like admixture of fog and mud. . . . In the green moss-roofed huts in the triangle sat an Irish family as unselfconsciously as if in their native bogs."

George Templeton Strong recorded the election by saying, "Hurrah for the Natives! They've elected Harper by a majority of 4000* and stand two to one in the Common Council. . . . I'm just from the Native Headquarters, the Aboriginal gathering place. Not an exile of Erin

---

* James Harper received 24,510 votes, the Democratic candidate, 20,538, and the Whig candidate 5,297.

ventures to show his nose in the neighborhood and the row and the bonfires and the popping of small arms of every denomination and the whiz of the rockets from the roof of 'Military Hall' are altogether imposing and tremendous."

That night the new mayor and his wife were cheered by their neighbors on Rose Street. He spoke to them from a balcony while a friend on each side held tallow candles that dripped grease on his coat. He said, "I feel like the boy who had made a kite, the pride of his life, and set out to fly it. Higher and higher it went till it caught in the limb of a tree. He climbed up to release it. He passed branch after branch, and then began to creep along the one on which his kite was hanging. On he went till further advance was dangerous. He resolved to go back, but found he could not. In fact he was stuck. And that is just what I am now, fellow-citizens."

James, Maria, and Philip had moved to 40 Rose Street, not far from Verplanck's residence, just three years before. Their house was five stories high, each story embellished with rows of four large windows— windows that had featured in a riot in 1834. The house was then owned by abolitionist Lewis Tappan, a wealthy merchant who had helped Lyman Beecher establish a new theological seminary in Cincinnati. A mob of anti-abolitionists formed on the street one night, broke into the house (Tappan barely had time to escape with his family) and threw furniture out the windows to feed a bonfire in front.

After James was elected mayor, the house was more discreetly lighted by two gas lamps, the double lampposts being a quaint tradition dating back to the early settlement of New Amsterdam when Dutchmen needed to know where they could find their chief magistrate after dark. Rose Street voters had hoped to get the lampposts ten years earlier when Verplanck ran for mayor during the city's first mayoralty plebiscite, but he lost out to Cornelius W. Lawrence, the candidate of the Democrats.

The day after the election the counting room at 82 Cliff Street was crowded with friends and well-wishers, including the Rev. Dr. John M. Wainwright* of Trinity Church and Evert Duyckinck, who noted how the new mayor skillfully parried congratulations—"a perfect Brutus for nonsense in himself and antihumbug for others." No doubt he was asked if he was sending numbers of the *Harper Illuminated Bible* to Bishop Hughes. Everyone there to greet the successful candi-

---

* On April 18, Dr. Wainwright entertained for Prescott, who was in New York. Fletcher, rather than the Mayor, would have been invited. "All of the literary men of the city were there," according to Hone.

date would have agreed that the monthly publication of fifty thousand numbers of the big Bible was perfectly timed to aid his campaign. In fact, the advance publicity which the *Illuminated Bible* was receiving had made James Harper the obvious choice when the American Republican party was considering who should be their standard bearer in the coming municipal election.

Not that all Bible readers approved the new Harper venture. Some New Jersey clergymen had publicly protested the printing of illustrations in the Inspired Book, asserting also that some of the illustrations were obscene. The clergymen were embarrassed by the Adams engravings of naked cherubs and scantily clothed Adam and Eve. This criticism the *Messenger* answered with an *argumentum ad hominem*: the principles of the brothers Harper and their habits were of the highest order. A year later the short-lived *Broadway Journal* was to be sharply critical: "Harpers Illuminated and New Pictorial Bible . . . may be old to somebody else, but it is new to Harper . . . it may not be 'illuminated' to another person, but it is to Harper." Editor Charles F. Briggs was saddened by the thought that the publishers had missed their opportunity to give impetus to American art, win the nation's lasting gratitude, immortalize themselves, and make a lot of money.

Presumably Briggs desired something less florid and ornate, but that was just what the American people wanted and the sale of numbers was enabling John to bank $10,000 a month, some of which went to pay for the new building. And Adams was giving his best, inspired by such accolades as the one conferred by the *Democratic Review*, "the highest excellence to which the graver's skill has yet ministered this side of the Atlantic."

While supervising the *Illuminated Bible* was taking many hours of every workday, the brothers had many other publishing irons in the fire during 1844 and 1845. Chief among these were medical books which were being forged with the help of the medical faculty of New York University. In 1841 Dr. Martyn Paine founded the university's Medical Department and soon he and his six associates were translating, editing, and writing medical books for Cliff Street publication. Dr. George W. Draper's college text, *Chemistry of Plants*, ten years in preparation, came out in 1844.* In addition, there were Drs. John

---

* The full title of Draper's book was *A Treatise on the Forces which produce the Organization of Plants*. Although Demarest gives August, 1845, as the date of publication, it was reviewed by *The Knickerbocker* in December, 1844, as already published. "This is one of the *very few* original scientific treatises published in the United States," Clark wrote, commenting on its format, "unusual for an American book," printed in quarto size on fine paper with steel engravings, some beautifully colored.

Revere, Gunning S. Bedford, and Granville S. Pattison. Associated with the founding, but not on its first faculty, were Drs. Charles A. Lee and A. Sidney Doane, who had worked so assiduously for the brothers in 1835 and 1836. And on his return from abroad Dr. Valentine Mott had joined the faculty, becoming its president in 1845.

The brothers, being patriotic gentlemen, were proud to have as friend and author Dr. John Revere, the youngest son of Colonel Paul Revere. Making a fortune on copper plating, Paul Revere was able to send his son through Harvard and abroad to Edinburgh for further study of medicine. In addition to teaching and practicing medicine, John Revere was reading the important new French medical books and offered to translate the fifth and latest edition of Magendie's *Précis Elémentaire de Physiologie*. The 539-page book was published in 1844, with Dr. Revere saying that his aim was "to present a system of human physiology which shall exhibit in a clear and intelligible manner the actual state of the science, and adapted to the use of students of medicine in the United States." For his translation Dr. Revere received a royalty of 10 percent. This same royalty was specified in a contract with his colleague Dr. Gunning Bedford, for his translation of a book of similar size, published the same year. Dr. Bedford linked his name to Chailly's *Practical Treatise on Midwifery*, a long-lived textbook. Dr. Bedford was the first professor of obstetrics to hold an obstetric clinic in the United States, and was to write two textbooks of his own in this field (one in 1855 and one in 1861) that went through many editions and were translated into French and German, making him one of the most widely known authors of medical textbooks of his time. But they were published by William Wood and not Harper. Is it possible that they lost so promising an author by switching from the royalty contract for Chailly's *Midwifery* to an outright purchase of copyright agreement? Nine months after the contract was signed, it was canceled by mutual consent and Bedford was paid $500 for all rights. To be sure Bedford may have needed the cash and himself have proposed the sale of his copyright, but this later Esau, having sold his copyright for a mess of pottage, would have turned against his benefactor when his book became successful. It was the Dana story all over again.

The physician who worked the hardest for the brothers in these years was Charles A. Lee, whose earlier book on geology had reflected his enthusiasm for the physical sciences. He lectured widely and also

---

Clark also noted, probably in response to a publicity release from Cliff Street, that whole chapters from the book were being reprinted in England, Germany, France, and Italy.

carried on a profitable medical practice in New York City. But over-work took its toll from his own health, so in 1840 he moved to Geneva, New York, to teach. There, with more leisure, he began editing three English books for the Harper presses: *Pharmacology* by Paris, *Dictionary of Practical Medicine* by Copland, and *Principles of Medical Jurisprudence* by Guy. Dr. Lee and Wesley discussed what legal authority in New York they should ask to advise Lee on the Guy book and agreed on Chancellor James Kent, a friend of the brothers and famous for his commentaries on the law. The title was changed to *Principles of Forensic Medicine* and the *New York Medical Journal*, which Lee had helped to establish, was to extol Lee posthumously for his "extensive and valuable notes and additions" to the British edition. For his editorial work on *Pharmacology* he received, at his own request, the sum of $100. His letter proposing these terms was written in his hand and signed by each of the brothers, one of the few extant documents carrying the four signatures.

Dr. Lee's greatest contribution to medical literature was his work on the American edition of Copland's *Dictionary of Medicine*. This work had first been spotted by J. & H. G. Langley, who engaged Dr. Lee as editor. Their contract with Lee was dated June 24, 1844. Soon there-after these enterprising publishers, who had so hopefully started a book trade monthly, went out of business, failing presumably because of the competition of the mammoth weeklies, which had admittedly fright-ened them.* The Langley contract had been witnessed by Frederick Saunders (Saunders did not mention a Langley association when he dictated his brief biography). Thus Saunders would have followed the Lee-Copland book to Cliff Street after Langley had issued the first three numbers. Numbers 4 and 5 of the Copland *Dictionary* came out with the Harper imprint in March, 1845, and by the end of the year a total of twelve were in the hands of American physicians. The series eventually grew to nine bound volumes and was not to be completed till 1862, owing to Copland's tediously slow but careful work. The *Medical Journal* was to boast that the *Dictionary* "forms the most complete and valuable work on the theory and practice of medicine, including etiology, pathology, and therapeutics, ever issued from the English or the American press." Dr. Lee was heartily thanked by Dr. Copland for the able and satisfactory way he had made the *Dictionary* available to the American public. He might have thanked Harper's, too, for they rightly decided that the pocket size and small type face of

---

* Apparently the business was carried on for a short period under the H. G. Langley imprint. *Cf.* New York Trade Sales catalogues, spring, 1845, to fall, 1847.

Longmans' edition would not do, and chose a royal-octavo size with a larger type face, a format that by 1858 Longmans had copied for England. And the tens of thousands of doctors throughout America were grateful, too. Who knows how many children and adults were saved from death as country doctors, puzzled by symptoms of disease, searched in these volumes for help in diagnosis and treatment? To the brothers' publishing perspicacity and to Charles Lee's zeal for the dissemination of medical knowledge, nineteenth-century America owed a great debt. Lee died in 1872 and his body was laid to rest near Washington Irving's in Sleepy Hollow Cemetery.

Rounding out their medical program for 1844-45 were two further English reprints, sufficiently revised to justify American copyright. (Historians of American medicine have not been so suspicious as their peers in American literature that English reprints were muzzles on authors of original works.) Dr. Granville Pattison edited *The Anatomy of the Human Body*, which the French anatomist Jean Cruveilhier had recently published. It made a book of 923 pages, and contained 302 engravings but not the colored plates available in the French edition. Dr. Pattison was a Scotsman by birth and education and had the distinction of being the first professor of anatomy at London University as well as at New York University, where he came later. Also the indefatigable Dr. Reese edited Neligan's work on the use and administration of medicine. He figured his time at six weeks and his honorarium at $100. However, he stipulated that if more than 750 copies (first edition?) were sold in six months, he should receive a further payment of like amount. Reese also edited an English work, *Encyclopedia of Domestic Economy* by Webster, adding a closing section on American medicine. He estimated that he would have to give three months' time to this job, offered his services for $500, and finally agreed to accept half that sum. Reese also received $125 in 1845 for another work which for some reason the brothers never published.

The five-line agreement that Dr. Reese signed on August 24, 1844, agreeing to take $250 for his work on *Domestic Economy* appears to be in Mayor Harper's handwriting. About the same time the Mayor was given a publicity note in *The Knickerbocker:*

Our friend Mayor Harper, who does not lack a shrewd common sense, but who, like Necessity, "knows *no law*," illustrates this by a little anecdote. His firm were about publishing a work by a popular writer. A brother of the author waits upon James, with a contract filling 3 or 4 ms. pages, setting forth, that "whereas on this day, etc." Our Mayor-Publisher wiped his "specs," looked at the document a moment, and stepping to his desk wrote on a piece of paper, "We agree to give —— 25¢ for each copy sold of any editions which we may hereafter publish of the book entitled So-&-So." The time of payment was specified; and these four or five lines, being dated and signed by the firm, were as binding and as "good in law" to all parties as the long and half-unintelligible document for which it was substituted.

The story may have been apocryphal, or incorrect as to amount of royalty paid. The only author with a known brother who was published in 1844 was Catherine Sedgwick; her 392-page book of tales, *Wilton Harvey*, for which no contract is extant, was priced at 45 cents, hardly suitable for a 25-cent royalty.

But most of the Mayor's time was being spent at City Hall, four short blocks from 82 Cliff Street. He was being paid a year's salary of $3,000, and there was much for a reform administration to do. He liked the idea of reform and refused to hand out favors to politicians or remove from city employment any competent man just because he was not "native" or Protestant. Receiving an anonymous letter saying he should fire a Roman Catholic woman working in the Harper bindery and "replace her with one of your own faith and land," he looked her up, found she was a good worker in straitened circumstances, and at once ordered that she be given a better job with more pay. Another letter to the Mayor protested that in his administration native Americans were being removed from the Customs House, and their jobs being given to Irishmen; the Mayor saved the letter but not his reply. He got pigs off the streets, and forbade cattle driving, in the daytime, below Fourteenth Street. He gave jobs to 350 men to sweep the streets and put through an ordinance for a contract system whereby garbage could no longer be left indefinitely to accumulate. He suppressed the customary "entertainments" put on by the Common Council, thus saving money for the city and arresting a practice which was said to be more of a debauch than a seemly assemblage of representative citizens.

The Mayor's most noteworthy reform was to divide the city into police districts, with a headquarters for each district, and to require the city's two hundred policemen to wear uniforms. The uniform, never before worn by the New York police, consisted of a blue cloth coat with the letters M.P. (Municipal Police) on the stand-up collars. Soon the wags were calling the dressed-up officers of the law "Mayor's Pups." The reform of the Police Department was approved by the Common Council in the autumn, and it was high on the Mayor's agenda, an enabling act by the State Legislature having been passed the winter before.

Once on his return from a trip to Albany, he saw an opportunity to put through still another reform. As his overnight steamboat was docking that morning, it was boarded by hackmen, who greeted the passengers with loud cries of "Carriage, sir!" and began carrying off designated luggage. The Mayor immediately engaged seven or eight, saying to each, "Yes, my son. Certainly! Give me your card." As he beamed on them benevolently through his spectacles, they thought they had captivated a most affable gentleman who was taking carriages for a large party. But the affable gentleman had something else in mind: the city ordinance that forbade hackmen boarding a steamer at dock. Getting into one of the carriages, he ordered the drivers whose cards he held to follow him to City Hall, where he ordered fines imposed and licenses revoked.

As Mayor he seemed to enjoy his opportunities to perform marriage ceremonies, even getting up early one morning to be at City Hall by 6:30 to marry a couple in time for them to make the 7 o'clock boat to Albany. "Our old friend Mayor Harper ties the mystical knot to great edification," Clark wrote. "His Honor has numberless customers; and they are as enthusiastic in his praise as those who love order in the metropolis and affect clean streets."

The allotment of municipal jobs was for James more of an administrator's headache than a politician's opportunity. Could he always be sure that favors requested were worthy? One job seeker wrote to John asking for help; John penciled a note of approval and passed it on to City Hall. People wrote not only asking for appointive positions but also begging for help. One man knew he could get money because the Mayor was known as a philanthropist. Another wrote from Cincinnati for financial aid. A woman needed his support in starting a religious magazine. And there were complaints. Citizens were upset that pigs and rubbish were still on the streets, that fires were being started near their homes, that boys were pitching pennies at all hours near their door stoops.

But there were also pleasant letters to read. One man wrote thanking the Mayor for the engraved portrait he had received; he had placed it where he could see it while at his dining table, a reminder "to lead me forward in the path of rectitude and industry." The Lord Mayor of London wrote to acknowledge the receipt of a chair that had been forwarded by the Mayor-publisher in the name of the booksellers of

New York City; he would be proud to present it to Miss Jane Porter, the British novelist so much admired by the New York book trade. (The brothers had also admired her; one of her three Harper books, *Seaward's Narrative*, had been abridged the preceding year for the *School District Library*.)

The Mayor cracked down on disorderly grog shops and got an ordinance passed closing saloons on Sundays. Poe was among those who protested, although his argument published in the Columbia (Pennsylvania) *Spy* was against Sunday closing per se—if saloons were bad (and he could well believe they were) why were they not closed on weekdays too? The Mayor also decided that New Yorkers should have a dry Fourth of July and forbade the erection of booths where celebrating citizens had been accustomed to find stimulating liquid refreshment. Diarist Hone, himself a former mayor, noted that James had put his temperance principles to constructive use: ". . . His Worship, in depriving the sovereigns of the means of getting drunk in public, with a laudable foresight provided them with other and more innocent draughts to quench their thirst. The large basin of Croton water in the park was cooled with divers cartloads of ice, and tin cups were chained to the banks from which thousands of parched lips were cooled during the day. One bad consequence of the reform was that the fountain did not play during the day." The Mayor was waited upon that evening at his home in Rose Street by a delegation of thirsty people whom he mistook to be partisans. Presenting himself at a front window prepared to respond to cheers, he was greeted instead with nine long groans.

The most amusing temperance story about the Mayor resulted from a call that George Wilkins Kendall, senior editor of the New Orleans *Picayune*, made at City Hall one fine May morning. John, who happened to be outside the Mayor's office, told Kendall he should go right in; James was receiving a delegation of lady officers of the Martha Washington Temperance Society, of which he was honorary president, and would likely welcome an interruption. Clark passed the story on to his readers: "George was received, beyond a slight greeting from the Mayor, with ominous silence; but he 'knew his course.' 'Come, Harper,' said he, 'let's go out and get *another* drink: it's eleven o'clock,' he added, taking out his watch; 'ain't *you* dry ag'in? *I* am!' The Mayor says he had been 'taken aback' before; but the coolness and outrageous impudence of that 'tack' couldn't be beat." Clark then quoted the Mayor as saying, "The women looked daggers while Kendall was pretending to be hurrying me to go with him to take a drink called 'moral suasion.'"

Kendall had likely come to New York because of the publication a few weeks earlier of his *Narrative of the Texan Santa Fé Expedition,* a two-volume work based on articles that he had written for the *Picayune.* By December the fourth (or fifth) edition, slightly revised, was out, according to the *Messenger,* and nine years later the book had sold forty thousand copies. Kendall prided himself that he had written without literary affectation but in the homely, everyday language which any reader could grasp. This fact plus the exciting story of adventure he told makes the first edition of *Santa Fé Expedition* a high-priced item in antiquarian bookshops today. He described the tour he and his companions made through Texas, across the southwestern prairies and over the hunting grounds of the Comanche Indians; and told of sufferings his party underwent from lack of food, and of the cruelty of Mexicans who marched them as captive prisoners to Mexico City. Daniel Webster, then Secretary of State, sent long letters to the Mexican government protesting this treatment of Kendall, which letters the brothers were to publish in 1848 in Webster's *Diplomatic and Official Papers.*

In writing his book, Kendall seemed to be more angry with Marryat than with the Mexican government. He accused Marryat of having published in *Narrative of Monsieur Violet* blocks of material that he had stolen from Kendall's articles in the *Picayune,* material that he himself was now issuing in book form. Kendall's *Sante Fé Expedition* contained a frontispiece engraved by Jordan and Halpin after a painting by J. G. Chapman, entitled "A Scamper among the Buffalo," and a vignette from this picture was made into a die and stamped in gold on the spine. The work is also interesting bibliographically because it is one of the first Harper books to carry the publisher's name at the bottom of the spine.

In the spring of 1846, Kendall was off again to the Southwest. With war declared against Mexico, he accompanied the American forces under Generals Taylor and Scott, sent stories of the Mexican campaign back to the *Picayune,* and supplied Washington with intelligence often in advance of official dispatches. The successful termination of the Mexican War was to make both generals presidential prospects in 1848.

Scott, with one ear always tuned to politics, wrote a four-page letter to James Harper in November, 1844. Scott had called at 82 Cliff Street a few weeks earlier but had missed seeing the Mayor; he wanted to discuss an order he had recently come across in which General George Washington took a position that clearly made "*The Father of his country* . . . the first member of the *Native American* party of which you are, if not the founder, the present *type* & *capital*, in New York." (The alleged order of Washington's was, "Put none but Americans on guard.") Scott went on to claim, in fact, that he himself was the founder of the party. "I conceived the idea at hearing the cry *Down with the natives*, during the spring election of 1834, when sent for to meet the Common-Council, about the means & the manner of suppressing the riot. I heard the same cry, from the Astor-House, at the election of Nov. 1840, & the very night that Harrison electors were chosen. James Madison, Wm Whetton and I sat down in my parlour to draw up an address designed to rally such a party."

The novelist-politician John Pendleton Kennedy, of Baltimore, was also drawn to Cliff Street during James's mayoralty. The brothers had tried unsuccessfully to sign him up in 1835 (p. 81). Now he came with his manuscript, *Defense of the Whigs*, knowing that James would be sympathetic both to him and his subject. His 152-page book was dedicated to his fellow Whigs in the 27th Congress.

Another Whig, Colonel Stone, had published in August, 1843, what was to be his last book. *Border Wars of the American Revolution* was issued in two volumes and was placed at once in the two Harper *Libraries*. It included the story of Joseph Brant, the Mohawk chieftain, whose biography Stone had written earlier. Stone's interest in Indian life stemmed from a boyhood spent in upstate New York, where he became acquainted with the Indians of the forest. For many years his hobby was collecting letters and documents relating to the Revolutionary War, talking with surviving soldiers, and reading source material on the Revolution. Duyckinck said that Stone had "the habit of systematizing the retentiveness of a powerful memory by a time-saving process entirely his own." After writing *Border Wars*, he turned to what he thought would be his *magnum opus*, a book on colonial America centered on the life of Sir William Johnson, that extraordinary Irishman who emigrated to America in 1738 and spent most of his life with the Mohawk Indians. (He became so beloved by them that they made him sachem and so respected by the British government for his management of Indian affairs that King George II gave him a baronetcy, a yearly salary of £600, and 100,000 acres of land, on which he lived with his Indian wife, a sister of Joseph Brant.) But Stone had completed only 350 manuscript pages of the Johnson biography when he died on August 15, 1844, while vacationing at Saratoga Springs, and it was left to his son and namesake, William Leete Stone, Jr., to complete the definitive biography of Sir William.

About a month after Stone's death, the brothers were visited by John Payne Todd to arrange for the publication of a portion of the correspondence of his stepfather, the late President James Madison. Todd may have been accompanied by Professor Henry St. George Tucker of the University of Virginia since it is known that the latter called at Cliff Street regarding the posthumous books of Madison. It was not the first time that the brothers had been dealing with the famous Tucker family of Virginia and they would have asked at once for news of his cousin, Nathaniel Beverley Tucker, whose novel, *George Balcombe*, they had published nine years earlier. There would have been talk of the *Southern Literary Messenger*, and how they still missed the genial T. W. White, and what did Tucker think of Benjamin B. Minor, who had replaced Lieutenant Maury as editor of the *Messenger?* Neither was it the first time that the brothers had been dealing with the writings of Madison. For eight years they had been deeply involved in plans for publishing these historical papers.

Shortly after Madison's death on June 28, 1836, efforts were made to interest publishers in Philadelphia, Boston, and New York in bringing out three volumes of Madison's *Debates*, which included letters of Madison in the 1780's and notes on debates in the Articles of Confederation Congress and in the Constitutional Convention, papers that Madison had edited for posthumous publication. These three volumes and enough material to make an estimated six additional volumes comprised what Madison thought to be his most substantial bequest to his widow, Dolley. In fact, Professor Tucker had then represented Mrs. Madison in talks with Carey, Lea & Blanchard. He placed a value of $30,000 on the *Debates*, figuring a royalty of $1 a copy on a printing of ten thousand copies of the three volumes. Presumably the same proposal was made to the American Stationers' Company in Boston by Jared Sparks, and to the Harpers by John Payne Todd, Dolley's son by her first marriage. Afer every likely publisher had either declined to publish or made unattractive offers, Mrs. Madison sought publication of the *Debates* by Congress. On November 15, she wrote to President Jackson that she could not get a publisher to undertake them "without advances of funds & involving of risks which I am not in a situation to make or incur." Early in 1837 Congress agreed to pay Mrs. Madison $30,000 for the original manuscripts and to publish the first three volumes.

While these negotiations were under way, Mrs. Madison and her brother, John C. Payne, were preparing four additional volumes of the President's papers for publication. Mrs. Madison told John Quincy

Adams, as he noted in his diary on March 15, 1838, that she hoped to have the fourth of these additional volumes "published immediately by the Harpers at New York." Obviously the brothers had shown the greatest interest, for she said three months later, "Considering myself bound in the first instance to allow the Harpers to print them, I lately wrote to know if they would immediately publish the volume on Constitutional subjects [Volume IV] and have not received their answer." She did not hear because the Cliff Street operation was shrouded in the black and forbidding gloom of the financial panic. However, they tried to appease her by promising publication in 1838 and again in the spring of 1840 (this time they had been holding the manuscript for a year). Both the brothers and the Congress dragged their feet, with the government edition of the *Debates*, known as the "Gilpin edition," not ready till the spring of 1840.

In the meantime Bentley in London had promised to publish the first three of the additional volumes and to send proofs as ready to America "to enable the publisher there to produce the volumes at the earliest day." Demarest says that the brothers sterotyped the three volumes in 1840 but did not publish. Since the manuscript copy for the hoped-for American edition was in Mrs. Madison's possession in April, it seems likely that the Harper edition was set from Bentley's proofs.

But why did the brothers not publish the three volumes? The answer may be that Mrs. Madison would not accept their terms— presumably a half-profits arrangement. In a letter of April 20, 1840 (to Richard D. Cutts) Mrs. Madison referred to a publishing partnership which friends had urged her not to accept. It may well be that a failure to come to terms on Volumes I-III caused the brothers to delay their work on Volume IV. According to *Dolly Madison, the Nation's Hostess*, by Elizabeth Lippincott Dean, Mrs. Madison was excitedly making plans in April, 1842, for her first and only trip to New York "in order to attend to the business of offering the Madison papers for publication." Even though Demarest does not mention Volume IV, the brothers did set it up and in 1842 Richard Rush of Philadelphia was reading proof. He wrote to Mrs. Madison about what seemed to be missing sections that Harper's had apparently lost, and Dolley in turn asked her son, John Payne Todd, if he could find the originals to fill in the gaps. This may have been a hopeless quest since he had sold— sometimes with his mother's consent—portions of the Madison papers to pay off gambling and liquor debts. In January, 1844, Mrs. Madison was again to urge her son to busy himself with Volume IV, and that same month Paulding (who had been urged to undertake a Madison biography) wrote to her that he had talked to the brothers, assuring them that nothing was needed but a preface and a title page. But by then she was deciding to offer all four volumes to Congress in return for cash. While it is known that Volume IV was printed at Cliff Street, it was never published. (See Appendix 4.)

Congress adjourned in June without acting on the matter and Todd came to Cliff Street to revive Harper interest. He was prepared to say that his mother would now agree to a half-profits arrangement. This agreement was dated September 24, 1844, and was eventually placed in an old iron chest for safekeeping along with a letter that Mrs. Madison had written ten days earlier. The letter said in part that she authorized John P. Todd "to do anything that he should judge expedient and proper in relation to the writings of my late husband, James Madison, now in the hands of Messers Harper and Brothers." (See illustration 10.)

The brothers soon filed also any hopes of combining profits and patriotism by issuing these four volumes of the papers of President Madison. When Congress reconvened that December, the Senate voted to purchase all of Madison's unpublished papers. Thus the Harper edition was stopped even though the House of Representatives failed to act. Not until 1848 was Dolley Madison to receive more money. On May 31 President Polk signed a bill authorizing the purchase of the papers for $25,000.

No half-profits contract the brothers ever signed was quite that promising. Except the one with Professor Anthon. And Anthon was more dependable than John Todd, who as a public figure had in some ways as bad a reputation as Edgar Allan Poe.

It was to Anthon that Poe turned when he needed a friend at the Harper court. He was inspired to write to Anthon in June, 1844, knowing he could appeal for help from a man for whom he had genuine admiration. He liked Anthon's bold, frank, and cordial manner, his bonhomie, his scholarship, and his freedom from cant. The letter Poe wrote to Anthon is one of the most moving ever written by an author eager to be in the good graces of a publisher. "It is true that I have no claims upon your attention, not even that of personal acquaintance, but I have reached a crisis of my life in which I sadly stand in need of aid, and without being able to say why—unless it is that I so earnestly desire your friendship—I have always felt a half hope that, if I appealed to you, you would prove my friend. I know that you have unbounded influence with the Harpers, and I know that if you would exert it in my behalf you could procure me the publication I desire."

Anthon waited five months to reply. He then wrote that he had seen the brothers, who had asked to keep Poe's letter for further perusal. However, he could not hold out much hope since they had "complaints" against Poe grounded on "certain movements" of his when they had published for him several years previously. He urged Poe to call on them in person since a talk would surely remove difficulties now standing in his way. He closed his letter by saying, "The Harpers also entertain, as I have heard from their own lips, the highest opinion of your talents, but—."

"But—" needed no amplification for Poe. He knew it implied criticism of his personal behavior. This criticism he had also detected in Frederick Saunders, whom he met on Broadway shortly afterward. Saunders was now working for the brothers. Poe rushed up, clasping Saunders in his arms. "Saunders, I am delighted to see you. People are beginning to appreciate real genius. I have at last written a poem that will bring me undying fame. It is the greatest poem that was ever written!" "And pray, what is it called?" " 'The Raven,' " Poe replied. But Saunders gave him no encouragement. He was repelled by Poe's maudlin manner and what he later called Poe's "unfortunate habit that so often degraded him below the commonplace." Evert Duyckinck was willing to overlook the manners and habits of genius and talked Wiley & Putnam into publishing *The Raven and Other Poems*. It came out November 1, 1845.

In 1844, however, Poe was yearning for Harper backing for a literary magazine to be called *The Stylus* that would make his name as an editor. He had moved from Philadelphia in April, found a home for his wife, Virginia, his mother-in-law, Mrs. Maria Clemm, and himself at 130 Greenwich Street, and set about assiduously to show the prospectus of his magazine to possible publishers. Failing to interest any, he then set out to sell his services or contributions to other magazines. But he was an outsider and his frank criticisms had cut the sensitive literary fingers of several who might have held out helping hands. Gaylord Clark, for one, would not easily forgive a gibe that *The New World* had flung at *The Knickerbocker:* "The present condition of this periodical is that of a poorly-cooked-up concern, a huge handsome-looking body, but without a soul." He suspected with good reason that piece, signed "L," was written by Poe. Duyckinck proved sympathetic, but he too had just failed to get a publisher for a magazine that he and Mathews wanted to edit, to be called *The Home-Critic*. And while O'Sullivan in the *Democratic Review* (publishing Poe's first "Marginalia" in 1844) was sympathetic to those writers who were self-consciously "Young America," he wanted literature to be yoked up with Jacksonian democracy.

By January, 1845, Poe found an outlet in two new periodicals, the *Broadway Journal*, with Charles F. ("Harry Franco") Briggs as editor, and the *American Review*, often called the *Whig Review*, piloted by Clark's cousin George H. Colton. Colton challenged O'Sullivan's assumption that the new literature should be equated with the Democratic party and set about to show that an organ holding to conservative theories could also spot literary genius and give it column space. These periodicals were soon publishing Duyckinck, Lowell, Walt Whitman—and Poe. Colton accepted "The Raven," had it set up in type, but failed to receive the kudos of history in being the first to print it; he kindly gave proofs to the *Evening Mirror*, which printed the poem a few days before the *American Review* appeared. The *Evening Mirror* was edited by N. P. Willis and General Morris, and they also issued a weekly *Mirror*, largely but not wholly made up of articles from the daily. Poe was a "regular ally" of both, but quit early in 1845 to devote more of his time to the *Broadway Journal*, of which he became sole literary editor in July and proprietor late in the year. Another associate on the *Mirror* was Hiram Fuller, a bookseller from Providence trained by Morris; he succeeded Willis and Morris as editor of the *Mirror*.

It was probably Briggs, still in charge of the *Broadway Journal*, who wrote "The Author's Tragedy, or The Perfidious Publisher" that appeared in the April 19 issue. This twelve-hundred-word drama in six acts was a shaft of sophomoric satire obviously aimed at Cliff Street. Two well-fed publishing brothers, one a bespectacled wag, were discussing a manuscript submitted by an impoverished American author who was soon to appear. On being asked whether he had read the manuscript, the humorous brother replied, "You know I always reed all manuscripts that come to hand; I stick a reed in them, so I can always say with a clear conscience (for you know I hate lying), 'Sir, I have been *reeding* your manuscript. . . .' " The trembling author comes in, is offered $10,000 for his work and leaves in a delirium of joy to share the marvelous news with his family, while the brothers and their clerks have a good laugh over their joke, and a porter is ordered to remove the reed and pack up a case of Bibles.

The fourth act shows the author on his tenth trip to the counting room for news of his book. Ready now to have them print it for nothing, he is told that so valuable a book could not even be accepted for nothing; in fact, they were so busy that they would have to install another steam press "*ex*-pressly for it." Whereupon the author retrieves his manuscript, finds the seal of the wrapper unbroken and in anguish finds a cheap publisher who issues the book. He dies heartbroken just before news comes that Bentley is issuing it in London at two guineas, but rises from his coffin on hearing his wife exclaim, "O, strange unequal world, that secures to the meanest laborer, the mechanic, the merchant, the farmer, the fruits of their toil, the full extent of their possessions, but leaves the author destitute of the protection, a prey to every mercenary wretch that chooses to appropriate his belongings. . . ." Alive again, the author vows he will write no more, but will cobble shoes that he may enjoy the fruits of his own labor.

A much more subtle dig had appeared in the February 1 issue. Briggs wrote, "Mayor Harper has refused to sign the bill giving the use of The Rotunda in the Park to the New York Gallery of Fine Arts because he thinks it would be establishing a bad precedent.* The reason is a good one. To show the Common Council that it was not owing to hostility to the cause of art, the Mayor informed them that he was a member of the institution. The price of life-membership is One Dollar."

The Mayor would have chuckled over that one as he did over the story that was told about his driving one day rather faster than regulation speed. An officer held up a hand in warning, whereupon the Mayor stopped his carriage, gravely beckoned the officer, and, as if to reward him or buy him off, reached ostentatiously into his pocket. He brought forth a peppermint from a supply he always carried for children, gravely passed it to the officer and drove off.

Henry Clapp, who was known as something of a Bohemian, delighted to tell a story about the Mayor that had its setting at the Tombs, the city prison with its Egyptian-inspired architecture, recently built at a cost of $250,000. It was always pointed out to visitors. One day Clapp and the Mayor were riding past it in a Fourth Avenue horsecar when the Mayor called to the conductor, and, pointing to Clapp, said, "My friend, here, from the country would like to know who lives in this building." The conductor, annoyed, ignored the question, but was urged again for an answer. "I don't know who lives there now, Mr. Mayor," he replied, "but I know who ought to."

Another story that got around told of a call that the Mayor made

* Two weeks later the Board of Aldermen overruled the Mayor by a vote of 14-0.

one day at the home of his brother John on Pike Street. The family were at dinner and a new servant asked what name she should give. "Colonel Jones of Nebraska," he replied. The name was taken downstairs and someone suggested that since they knew no one by that name from the far West their visitor was likely a sneak thief. One of the boys darted out a back door to summon the police from a nearby station, and John with other members of the family in tow walked stealthily to the parlor. A look inside that room showed no one there. Surely a thief was loose in the house. What should they do? Wait for the police? The maid bravely offered to look in the library. Opening the door cautiously, she saw the suspected thief helping himself to a book from the shelves. "Well, Mary!" said the Mayor, using a common appellation. The shock was too much for "Mary," who screamed and collapsed on the floor. The family rushed to the room. The sedate John surveyed the scene. "Colonel Jones of Nebraska, here is your work," he said severely as he pointed to the prostrate form. "But, John, I didn't do it," the Mayor retorted. "She did it to herself." Just then John's son appeared at the door with two policemen and two reporters who had just stopped by the station. One of the officers, an appointee of the Mayor, took the situation in at a glance. "It's only one of the Mayor's jokes," he said.

The few hours in any week that the Mayor could devote to his business in nearby Cliff Street were spent in the engraving and pressrooms of the new building. Work on the *Illuminated Bible* was progressing on schedule in the spring of 1845, but his was the final word on Biblical episodes that still needed to be chosen for Chapman's drawings. Wesley's desk was piled high with proof sheets to be looked over and freshly printed signatures of the latest number to be admired as they came off the new Adams steam presses. There were problems of personnel and the proper use of space in the new building to be examined. The eldest brother was not only the chief magistrate of the city, but on Cliff Street he was the court of last resort when counsels were divided or when the authoritative final decision had to be made. In the counting room there was a hearty slap on the back for twenty-seven-year-old William Demarest, recently brought in from the pressroom to help his elder brother Gerherdus keep the books. But what James most enjoyed was his walk through the pressroom. Here he would shake hands with Henry Marsh, now the superintendent, and reminisce a bit about the old J. & J. Harper days. Marsh would introduce him to the new apprentice and journeyman printers, added because of the spurt of new work now that times were better. And, as the admiring men gathered around him, James would tell of a funny thing that happened to him when he was working a hand press for Jonathan Seymour and say that he would rather be helping them operate the brand-new presses than sit behind his desk over at City Hall.

Besides the Bible, there were two other big projects under way that James needed to be informed about. One was the Verplanck Shakespeare and the other the Episcopal Prayer Book that Fletcher and Dr. Wainwright were giving so much time to. Verplanck was coming often to Cliff Street since he was seeing his dream of many years come true: the first fully annotated and illustrated edition of Shakespeare's plays to be issued in America. A portrait of Verplanck hangs in the Century Association of New York, of which he was the first president. It shows him in his later years, a well-fed, tousle-haired old Dutchman who would enjoy a mug of beer or a few draws on a long-stemmed pipe. Poe wrote a contemporary description of the affable Verplanck, saying that he was short in stature, not more than five feet, five inches, and stoutly built. He described Verplanck's head as square and massive, with "thick, bushy and grizzly hair; the cheeks are ruddy; lips red and full, indicating a relish of good cheer; nose short and straight; eyebrows much arched; eyes dark blue."

The Verplanck *Illustrated Shakespeare* came out in 136 numbers, priced at 25 cents each. The first nine numbers were issued in 1843-44 by the engraver H. W. Hewet, who also published an occasional book, but by March, 1845, the enlarged printing facilities which had been procured for the Bible were producing both the Shakespeare and the *Book of Common Prayer*. Since Hewet was also making the engravings for Dr. Wainwright's edition of the Prayer Book, it seems likely that he could not carry the double load of engraving and publishing. The April *Messenger* noted the receipt of Numbers 39 and 40 of Verplanck's work, saying, "It does not and cannot suffer any decline from being transferred to the Harpers. They double the matter each issue and charge 25 cents."

Verplanck's compensation was $3,000, paid by Hewet out of his half-profits contract with the brothers. His Harper contract mentions only "one dollar by him to them paid," which would permit Verplanck, after two years from the completion of the Harper edition, to issue elsewhere any or all of his copyrighted material. Hewet was also charged with half the cost of stereotypes and regular advances on account. But these advances were to be insufficient to see him through evil days that autumn when the red devil of fire, always dogging the footsteps both of Verplanck and the brothers, attacked Hewet's premises at 11 Spruce Street. On November 15, the brothers agreed to advance Hewet $800 to reproduce engravings for the early numbers that were entirely or partially destroyed by fire and up to $1,400 to reproduce engravings that had been made but not yet delivered to Cliff Street. Hewet figured he could turn out 490 wood engravings in a year's time at a cost of between 25 cents and $33 each, with the total cost of his engravings amounting to $2,707.50. The fire also caused a loss of time and the last of the 136 numbers was not issued until 1847.

In 1838 the General Convention of the Episcopal Church had authorized a revision of the *Book of Common Prayer*, and in 1844 Bishop Onderdonk of New York in turn authorized Dr. Wainwright to "correct and compare" with this revised text "such editions . . . as may be published by the Messers Harper and Brothers of the City of New York." The composition and plating of ten editions (ranging in type size from five point to twelve point and in trim size from 48mo to quarto) occupied many months, with the first three out in January, March, and May of 1845 and the last one in June, 1847. The illustrated edition with nearly 700 wood engravings by Hewet was to be a featured gift-book item in the bookstores at Christmastime in 1845.

What was called Dr. Wainwright's most celebrated work on his own account was his 1844 publication with Dr. George D. Potts, a leading Presbyterian clergyman of New York, of *No Church Without a Bishop*, an early Harper paperback. The book grew out of a phrase used by Senator Rufus Choate in a December, 1843, address in New York to the New England Society. Choate's phrase, "a government without a King and a Church without a Bishop" was challenged by Dr. Wainwright, who had Anglican sympathies, at the Astor House dinner which followed the oration. Dr. Potts in turn challenged Dr. Wainwright in the New York *Commercial* and the widely publicized controversy led to the book and helped make Wainwright Bishop of New York in 1852.

One who followed the Choate-Wainwright-Potts controversy with great interest was Dr. John O. Choules, an exuberant authority on the early Puritans and an avid collector of books on the subject. While he earned his board and keep by running a boys' school in Providence, he was all over the country lecturing and hobnobbing with famous people. Few men knew as many celebrities or a better stock of jokes and anecdotes about them. Choules called at Cliff Street one day and talked the brothers into reissuing the old classic history of the Puritans by Daniel Neal and into paying him $300 for contributing revisions, corrections, and notes. After coming out in eight numbers, it was long to be listed in Harper catalogues as two volumes in both muslin and sheep bindings.

A less jolly author writing on a more tolerant theme was the Reverend Dr. Joel Parker, whose current book was called *Invitation to True Happiness*. Dr. Parker's Philadelphia colleague, Dr. Barnes, was also on Cliff Street seeing his seventh volume of *Notes* through the press. Almost as popular in the bookstores and acclaimed in the religious press was *Religion in America* by Robert Baird. Also a Presbyterian, Dr. Baird, as general agent for the American Sunday School Union, had traveled all over the settled portions of the country, founding thousands of schools, before going to France, in 1835, to aid the cause of Protestantism in the south of Europe and to promote the cause of temperance in the north of Europe. He was probably the most traveled clergyman of his day, but was home often enough to sire a few children and more than a dozen books, two of them written in French. His 343-page history of Evangelical churches in America, still an important source book, went through many printings and was to be revised and enlarged in 1856. One of Dr. Baird's precocious sons, sixteen-year-old Charles, was also around Cliff Street in 1844-45. His translation from the French of Malan's *Can I Join the Church of Rome while my Rule of Faith is the Bible?* came out about the same time as his father's book. And to encourage the young and not to overlook the Nativists' worry about the Catholic Church, the brothers published Charles E. Anthon's *A Pilgrimage to Treves* to show that church relics were unimportant. This Anthon was a nephew of the classicist and a brother of George Strong's best friend.

Strong's diary does not mention this book but it relates another of the Mayor's jokes. Somebody was recommending to James and Professor Anthon that they publish a Greek Testament with English notes "mainly for the benefit of Harper's friends of the Methodist clerical corps, who, being men of rather limited education, would find it much more convenient than the . . . [usual] Latin notes. . . . 'Don't' said Harper; 'they're nice people, they are—but they all think the New Testament was written in English, and it would only unsettle their minds and throw them into horrid perplexities to be undeceived; they do well as they are—let 'em alone.' " Strong would have relished the newspaper editorial, published nearly a century later, in which Goodspeed's translation of the New Testament was attacked because it tampered with what "St. James" wrote. Strong's entry was dated March 31, 1845, and he referred to James as "the immortal Harper, the

Mayor that wants to be, but won't be after his present term runs out."

This prophecy was grounded on the knowledge that Polk's election and recent inauguration had put new life in the "Locos," the Democrats. Furthermore, the Whig and American Republican parties would divide the opposition, and no reform administration is long popular with voters. In late February, the Mayor had written a short letter accepting the nomination of the American Republicans for a second term, "though I cannot but feel that a more worthy candidate might be selected." But he was determined not to campaign. On April 1 he wrote to the editor of the *Sun:* "I see by the *Sun* of this morning that I am represented as addressing political meetings in the several wards as a candidate for the mayoralty. It is possible that you were only playing an April joke at my expense, but lest some of your readers should take it in earnest, I must beg you to make the proper retraction. I have no time to attend to political meetings and no inclination to speak at them, most assuredly not as a candidate." He said that he had never sought for office and if granted an "honorable discharge," he would lay aside a heavy weight of responsibility and gain financially since "the expense is easily made to exceed the salary. I have eaten but one meal at the expense of my constituents and have not driven a mile at their charge and have allowed myself but one day of recreation since last May. Not one cent of the public money has been wasted, the waste of which I could prevent. Fifteen hours of every twenty-four have been zealously, however imperfectly, devoted to the service of my fellow-citizens, and in a word, I have endeavored in the fear of God to do my duty, to reclaim the vicious, to maintain peace and good order, and to promote the cause of virtue and morality."

But virtue and morality in a candidate for public office are qualities that rarely endear him to an electorate. The Mayor and his reform administration were bitterly attacked during the campaign.* That these attacks cut deeply is shown by his April 25 letter to R. L. Schiefflein, declining an escort of the American Republican Association at the close of his administration on May 12, ". . . we have not accomplished all that we desired and intended but we have made a beginning; and we have a right to expect that the same severe judgment which took note of all our mistakes and failures, making little allowance for our inexperience, and the magnitude of the task we had undertaken, will watch with still sharper eyes and more unsparing scrutiny the doings of those who come after us . . . who have so loudly proclaimed

---

* Referring to politicians, a New York taxicab driver recently philosophized, "It's a thankless job. No matter how good you are, you're bad."

their ability as well as their intention to excel us in wisdom, integrity and action."

The Mayor, who dearly loved a joke, had one played on him one cold night. He was awakened about 2 A.M. by the violent ringing of his doorbell. Presently he opened his second-story window to ask querulously what the trouble was. He saw several heavily muffled young men below but did not recognize them as his nephews, who were on their way home after a dinner of their Columbia University fraternity. Nor did he recognize the disguised voice of "Joe Brooklyn," who said they had lost a yellow dog who answered to the name of Cato, and they would like to know if the Mayor could give them any information as to where they might find him. The Mayor replied that if they didn't clear out immediately he would have them arrested and slammed down the window. The next morning when he arrived at his office he found pictures of a yellow dog with a notice that a reward would be paid for Cato's return. By now he suspected who the jokers were and vowed he would get even with them. Fletcher's elder son was probably one of the group of pranksters, but Fletcher, Jr., was then sailing somewhere "before the mast." His passion for the sea and obsession to visit China had finally obtained his parents' reluctant permission to spend his seventeenth year aping Dana, whose book he had read. Fletcher, Jr., entered Columbia on his return from the trip that had washed away all romantic notions of life aboard a brig.

Father and Mother Harper were making their home with James and Maria on Rose Street, living to see their farm-boy son serve his year as Mayor of the city to which thirty-four years earlier they had tearfully permitted him to go to seek fame and fortune. But the infirmities of age left but a few more months on the calendar of Elizabeth Kolyer Harper's years. She died on November 4. Her husband, "the stalwart oak," was to survive her by two years. "Perhaps the most notable things about him [Joseph]," the *New York Times* was to say later, "were his devoted Methodism, his extreme temperance principles, his absolute uprightness, and his desponding temperament. The sons inherited much from him that was good; but the general sunny parts of their natures came from their Dutch mother."

CHAPTER XIII

Mr. Fay Issues a "Statement"

1844–1845

In october, 1844, Prescott wrote to remind the brothers that earlier they had expressed an interest in taking over *Ferdinand and Isabella*. Were they still of this mind? If not, he would renew his contract with Little and Brown, who had now only fifty copies on hand. Fletcher's pleased and affirmative reply brought a contract from Prescott dated November 6. It specified a first printing of 1,500 copies, the use of the author-owned stereotype plates containing revisions, and a royalty of $1.50 per copy sold. The Harper edition came out early in 1845, at which time the brothers sent Prescott their note for $2,250, payable in three months.

About this time Prescott, through Aspinwall in London, was closing with Bentley for a volume of essays, to be called *Miscellanies*, most of which had appeared in the *North American Review*. For some reason he did not also notify the brothers and they first learned of the new Prescott title in a printed announcement of Bentley's. This announcement would have been issued and read in New York in late March or early April. In his book, *Prescott and His Publishers*, Gardiner says that the brothers, not having heard from Prescott, discounted the Bentley announcement. Even so, why did they not write to the historian to find out for sure? The likely reason seems to be that by that time they knew they were being attacked by Theodore Sedgwick Fay and suspected that Prescott was knowledgeable of Fay's criticism. They probably knew that Fay was buying books for Prescott and acting as agent with German publishers for translations of Prescott's works. If they were to ask Prescott about his new book and if he, in turn, queried them about their troubles with Fay, they would be put on the defensive by their most prestigious author, the one whose respect they probably cherished more than any other.

L'affaire Fay was important then because it subjected the brothers to criticism of their business dealings with a novelist, a criticism potentially able to harm them with other authors. It is important today because Fay's privately published *Statement* is known to bibliographers, even though it is likely none have read it. Also the story of this literary altercation has never been told and a story is all the more interesting when it tells about those who create stories for others to read. Furthermore, the financial dispute, even though the amount involved was comparatively small, did involve a good many people who were well known at the time.

Fay had not seen his American publishers since June, 1836, when he had left New York believing that *Norman Leslie* and his next book would earn him nearly $1,000 more and that he could soon liquidate his $1,500 note. What he had not counted on was the financial panic and its aftermath of years so depressing to American authors of fiction. Letters and newspapers that passed over his desk at the embassy office in Berlin told how others had suffered, and he had some consolation in knowing that he was not alone in carrying debts. He had managed, however, to pay off everything but the Harper indebtedness, which was a frightful annoyance. While his publisher had a better reputation than most, you heard so many stories about gullible authors being the prey of crafty printers that you could not be too sure even of the Methodist brothers on Cliff Street. The few letters he had received from them were short and businesslike; to be sure they answered his questions but they revealed no interest in him or his concerns as a writer. There were times when an author needed an editor if for no other reason than that of knowing his worries and frustrations were shared and sympathized with. He was the more frustrated because Berlin was worlds away from New York. He had sent Fanshaw and Smith and Detmold to Cliff Street to act for him, but there was a limit to what you could ask even of the best of friends.

In the winter of 1843-44, as Fay in Germany was confronted with the failure of *Hoboken* in America, his literary temperature fell below zero centigrade, matching the thermometer outside his house in Berlin. He talked the matter over with Mrs. Fay. They decided he should send Mr. A. M. Burt to see the brothers. They were surprised they had not thought of him before since he was not only a brother-in-law but a New York attorney as well. Confronted by a lawyer, the brothers would know he meant business. Whereupon Fay wrote Burt to see what could be done to release Morris and Jones as endorsers of the old note and to get a statement of his account. On March 30, 1844, a few days before James was elected mayor, Burt sent word to Fay that after several calls at 82 Cliff Street he had been unable to get a statement. They would not know exactly until they had re-examined their records; they wanted to be sure that their bookkeeper had not made an error. About this time Fletcher turned the Fay account over to the Harper attorney, Mr. H. E. Davies, determining that, if Fay distrusted them to the extent of sending a lawyer around, then he should be given a dose of his own medicine. In June Burt was finally able to send Fay a statement. It showed that the Harper indebtedness amounted to at least $1,200. Until that was paid, the endorsers could not be released.

Whereupon Fay decided to appeal to His Honor, James Harper, the Mayor of New York. As a servant of the people who was also an author he would appeal to a servant of the people who was also a publisher. Fay's 2,500-word letter to the Mayor was dated July 11, and recounted his publishing relations with the brothers, quoting copiously from letters he had received from Messrs. Detmold and Burt. He argued that the note should have been liquidated by what Morris had paid plus earnings on *Norman Leslie* and *The Countess Ida*. Why, then, should he be indebted to the Messrs. Harper for $1,200? He appealed to the Mayor even amid his multifarious and important public and official duties to find time to repair a private act of injustice.

Shortly after the Mayor received Fay's letter he had a call from Burt, who asked His Honor what he thought of Fay's complaint. The Mayor replied that he had sent the letter over to Cliff Street since his brothers were handling the affairs of the business principally. He assured Burt that there should be no difficulty in settling the matter in a "business way." Reporting this conversation to Fay, Burt wrote that the Mayor was "considerably elated by his political elevation, in as much that he treated me with most marked politeness, professed the highest respect for that 'clever fellow Fay,' and perfectly overpowered me with a superabundance of the *suaviter in modo*. . . ." Burt followed the Mayor's advice, called twice at 82 Cliff Street, the second time receiving a detailed account, showing advances made to Fay, including the partially liquidated note, half profits on the three books (by this time *Hoboken* had earned $61.44 for its author) and additional credits and debits due to interest accruing to Fay for his half profits, and interest accruing to Harper's for advances. The long, detailed statement, as of October 4, 1844, showed a debit of Fay, not of $1,200 but $2,197.15. It also disclosed what Fay had long since forgotten—two cash advances amounting to $1,000 made in the spring of 1836 over and above the $1,500 note. (See Appendix 5.)

On November 14 at his Berlin office in the U.S. Legation Fay sat down at his desk to go through the mail just in from New York. He opened a large envelope that he saw was from Burt. The letter was long and detailed: about Burt's call on the Mayor, then about his calls at Cliff Street. Of his decision not to draw on Fay's account to settle his indebtedness since the amount was so much more than Fay thought it would be. Then came the statement itself. Fay was appalled. He could hardly believe what he was reading. He reached for his pen. "I have not the *slightest recollection* of these [$500] payments," he wrote Burt. "Are the Messieurs Harper so ready to lend their money, and so backward in requiring payments? . . . I have sent them Mr. Fanshaw, Mr. Detmold, and yourself—and never have I succeeded in procuring from them one [statement] alluding to these pretended loans, thus lying in the background, at heavy interest, unmentioned by them, and unsuspected by me." He asked Burt to settle his account by the sale of copyrights, plates, and stock to the brothers and to get the note paid off, once and for all time.

On the day that Burt received this and still a further letter from Fay, he also heard from Jones (so-signer, with Morris, of the note) that the sheriff had levied upon his goods by a court order ensuing from a suit of John's father-in-law, Abner Higgins. Immediately Burt rushed over to Cliff Street to ask in Heaven's name why, and to show them Fay's letters. Fletcher thought that the Higgins-Jones matter was not their affair (Higgins had reportedly said it wasn't his affair either) and assured Burt they were in no hurry for their money. Whereupon Burt drew drafts on Fay's account to pay off the note and get the sheriff off Jones's premises. He went back to Cliff Street to get an explanation of the two $500 advances. What evidence did they have of payments made to Fay of which he had neither remembrance nor record? At first Fletcher refused to show him their books, saying that they could prove their account if they had to in order to collect it. But why, Fletcher asked, had not Mr. Fay written to them? He had not treated them well, always sending in a third person. Could not Mr. Burt see that they were always on the defensive? How did he know but that Burt had come as a spy, to ascertain their weak points, preparatory to a lawsuit? As to Harper & Brothers making an offer for Mr. Fay's copyrights and plates, No, that was not the usual procedure. However, if Fay wanted to offer an amount they would no doubt be able to close without difficulty.

Realizing that he had to satisfy Fay with some explanation of the two $500 payments, Burt returned several times to press as tactfully as he knew how for permission to see what evidence their books disclosed. Obviously annoyed at being so pestered, with everyone in the counting room busy with the year's end rush of business, Fletcher finally said they would put their bookkeeper, Gerherdus Demarest, to looking for the two vouchers that would substantiate the charges. He set a day for Burt's return. On the appointed day, Fletcher apologized that they had so little to show him since their books and papers were still in confusion because of a fire.* Later on they expected to locate the vouchers, but in the meantime Burt could see their 1836 ledger showing the debit entries against Fay's name made on April 23 and May 16. Gerherdus told Burt that he had made the entries, copying them (in reverse order) from the cashbook of the year, still not located. Fletcher also brought out stubs of two checkbooks for 1836. That of the Leather Manufacturers Bank showed a check drawn to Fay for $500, and that of the Manhattan Bank showed a check drawn to Fay for $200.

On December 30, Burt mailed another long letter to Berlin detailing these matters. When the distraught Fay read it, he determined to write a pamphlet. It would be nonfiction and short—just thirty-two pages. He would preface it with a "Statement," followed by all pertinent correspondence, including his lengthy July letter to the Mayor. He would then present his arguments in an effort to show that his publishers were in error, to procure a settlement on his behalf either voluntarily on their part or by arbitration, and to vindicate his own character. He would close his pamphlet with a short letter of appeal to the Mayor. This "open letter" he would date March 1, 1845.

That he was preparing such a statement must have been known to attorney Burt, who wrote to the brothers on February 25 to say that Fay had no intention of instituting legal proceedings, but he did de-

---

* Presumably the fire of June, 1842. Demarest lists five fires: "When doing business on Dover St., when on Fulton St., when at 230 Pearl St., partially at 82 Cliff St. in 1842, and wholly in December, 1853. . . ." *Catalogue*, p. 3.

mand a full explanation of the two $500 charges, backed by evidence; if no explanation was forthcoming or insufficient evidence produced, Fay would *"immediately lay the whole case before the public."*

The steamship *Great Western* brought copies of Fay's privately printed pamphlet to New York in mid-April. Burt and Morris each received copies, Morris at once apprehensive that the pamphlet if widely broadcast would be bad publicity for all concerned and endanger prospects of an amicable settlement of the dispute. He and Burt hurried down to City Hall and Morris went in alone to see the Mayor, hoping against hope that a copy of the pamphlet had not preceded him. The conversation between him and the Mayor—immediately afterward related to Burt and by him conveyed to Fay—went as follows:

"Mr. Mayor," Morris said, "there's this unpleasant business with my friend Fay—it ought to be settled some way. Can I do anything?"

"Yes, go and talk to the Colonel [John]—or the Captain [Wesley]. Avoid Fletch! He's a Turk!—He wants the bowels of compassion— He's got his back up in this business some way or other, but I don't know how. I don't understand the business. It was all transacted while I was in Europe and has never been explained to me. I think you can settle it if you go to the Colonel or the Captain."

"I received a letter from Fay by the *Western*. I suppose you had one of the same kind."

"No," the Mayor replied, "I haven't had a letter from him in nine months."

After reporting this conversation to Fay, Burt wrote that Morris was going to burnish his recollections so that he could serve as a witness if a lawsuit developed. However, Burt was hopeful that the dispute could be arbitrated, as was Detmold, with whom he had just talked. Detmold had read the pamphlet and thought it made a strong case; he had visited Cliff Street the day before and Fay would be glad to know that Detmold reported a friendly interview, with the brothers' saying they would be willing to investigate with any friend of Fay's, *"other than a lawyer . . . provided my note of 25 Feb., which they consider offensive in its terms be withdrawn."* Burt concluded his letter by saying that Detmold also thought the letter offensive and enclosed a copy of his own letter to the Messrs. Harper withdrawing it.

The brothers had not yet seen the more offensive pamphlet, but their leading author, Prescott, had read it. Fay had mailed a copy to his Boston friend, Charles Sumner, with a request that he pass it along to Prescott. Prescott read what Fay had written with obvious interest although his reaction is not recorded. At any rate he was not disposed to write to the brothers about his volume of essays—at least not yet.

Sumner's immediate reaction was to have the dispute arbitrated and to do so quickly before the contents of the pamphlet became common knowledge. He immediately wrote to Detmold expressing concern and urging Detmold to try at once to bring about settlement. He thought Joseph Cogswell might help, and Cogswell knew about the matter, having just been in Sumner's office before returning to New York. (The planets were in a good position for both Sumner and Cogswell that year. Orator for Boston's 1845 Independence Day celebration, Sumner discovered his power to sway audiences and began the political career that soon led to his twenty-five years in the U.S. Senate. Cogswell was busy buying books for what was to become New York's first public library, having convinced the aging John Jacob Astor to put up the money and to start plans for a building to house them.)

Sumner's letter reached Detmold on April 28. That same day he went to Cliff Street and found Fletcher eager for arbitration. They quickly agreed that the brothers would submit to Messrs. Detmold and Cogswell their evidence as to the correctness of the two debit charges of $500 each; if the arbiters were convinced by the evidence, they would so certify and Fay would be bound to admit the Harper claims; on the other hand, if the arbiters found the evidence unsatisfactory, Harper's would pay Fay the amount he claimed; should the arbiters disagree, they would call in a third party whose decision would be final.

Two days later Detmold and Cogswell met with Fletcher and John in the Harper counting room. After discussing the matter for an hour or more, they saw what Detmold called "damning proof," two checks made out to Fay and endorsed by him, equivalent, Detmold thought, "to receipts for the amounts carried on the face of the checks." A clue to the disposal of the checks was given by initials appearing under Fay's endorsement of each. The $500 check was endorsed by initials "J. S. and S.," and the check for $200 carried the initials "G. P. M." "For the balance of the second charge of $500, viz $300," they wrote in their signed statement, "no other evidence was furnished, but the averment of the Bookkeeper [Gerherdus Demarest] that the original entry in the waste,* April 25, was for $500; the rest as the Messers Harper think probable having been paid in cash at their office, and as it was included in the original entry in the waste, and as their charges in other respects were found correct, it may be inferred that this was so

* In bookkeeping, a waste book is a daybook.

also." The statement of findings ended by saying, ". . . satisfactory reasons are assigned by them for not having presented their account more seasonably."

Detmold immediately forwarded a copy of their findings to Fay in Berlin, with an accompanying letter saying, "Grieved as I am, my dear Fay, to find our investigation adverse to you . . ." Like a doctor sympathetically explaining an illness to a patient, Detmold outlined what he thought had taken place during Fay's last weeks in New York before his departure for Europe in June, 1836. The two $500 payments were advances on *Norman Leslie,* which was enjoying a rapid sale, "as everybody in those days bought new books at any price." (See p. 76.) The $1,500 note was *not* an advance on further books he would write; Harper's considered the note a "special loan" and had entered it in their books as "Bills receivable," their usual method of handling discount notes for authors and others. With the proceeds of the loan Fay "bought a Bill" on Wiggins, London, and took it to Europe for traveling expenses, so the Harpers and Mr. Burt thought. The initials "J. S. and S." stood for Jonathan Seymour and Sons, with whom Morris did business in those days and "G. P. M." obviously were the general's initials. Perhaps Fay could remember why he had passed money over to Morris; when Detmold had seen Morris that morning, the general confessed himself staggered by the evidence, but had no recollection whatever of having received the sums. When Detmold had asked Fletcher why in frequent interviews they had not mentioned the $1,000 advances, Fletcher replied that they had not wanted to frighten an author who would be giving them books that by profit sharing should easily wipe out the indebtedness. "This shows that they have played throughout a very shrewd and cunning game," Detmold observed, and as to the *Statement,* he was collecting what copies he could and giving them to Burt, who would destroy them. Fay should call back whatever copies he had mailed to different parties.

Detmold's letter conveying the bad news to Fay was dated May 6. Nine days later, also in time to catch the steamer *Boston,* Burt wrote a short note to say that "the Messers Harper have astounded us all," and that he had seen the checks which had all the appearances of being genuine. "We are suppressing the pamphlets," he added in a postscript.

This letter with the arbiters' findings reached Fay on June 7. He was staggered by what he read—by Morris's acknowledgment that the checks had passed through his hands. His astonishment was only surpassed by disbelief. The checks were perhaps forgeries or, if they were genuine, why had he made no record of such amounts of cash

received? He was soon in a shadowy world of wonderment. He began
to think that perhaps his sense of right and wrong might, by some
wicked enchanter, be as sadly confounded as his memory had been.
After discussing the letter and statement with his family and several
friends, he was reassured that, while he had lost his money, he had not
lost his power to distinguish between right and wrong.

Yes, he knew now that right was on his side, and he would set about
to prove it. And if New York was destroying his pamphlets, he would
write a rebuttal and add to the record. He would go through his
journal, begun in 1834 and devoted particularly to entries regarding
money matters; he would also review all pertinent letters he had received since 1836, fortunately preserved in bound volumes. He would
detail the whole tedious record and get confirming statements from his
wife and from his brother-in-law, Captain Gardenier, also fortunately
in Berlin.

For five hectic weeks early that summer Fay worked through his
journal and bound letters. Removed by thousands of miles from the
Cliff Street evidence his friends had seen, and by nine years of elapsed
time from the events themselves, he attempted to reconstruct what had
taken place. Restudying his tabulation of receipts for the winter and
spring of 1836, he saw only two Harper payments, one "Norman Leslie
—$650." and one "Advance on Andre, Harpers—$1500." He totaled
his receipts for the period as $3,800 and then noted that in addition, "I
had a credit for $1040 opened at the London Bankers, Messers Wig-
gins, by Asa D. Fitch, at my request, and on the account of Gen.
Morris who by agreement, now before me, signed by him, May 1,
1836, had contracted this, my usual yearly salary for contributions to
the Mirror, I had thus received in cash during my visit in N. York
$4840."

Since he had entered the $1,500 as an advance on his next book and
not as a loan, he proceeded to write out arguments to show, as he had
in his first pamphlet, that the two checks, if genuine, were given him
on account of the $1,500 note. He refused to acknowledge, as Detmold
and Cogswell had, that the two $500 items had been *debited* to Fay in
the Harper ledger. He furthermore overlooked Detmold's important
point that the $1,500 loan was not likewise a ledger entry but placed
among "Bills receivable." In fact Fay was so convinced that the $1,000
was a part payment to him of the $1,500 for which he signed the note
that he proceeded to advance two further arguments. One was that the
brothers would not have been so generous as to have advanced him as
much as $1,000 after giving him $1,500 for which he had to sign a note

and procure endorsers and satisfy everyone by taking out a year's life insurance policy. The second argument, hashed and rehashed, was that if the brothers had known through the years of this additional amount why had they not revealed the fact instead of talking only about what was still due on the note? He devoted many pages of his extended pamphlet to quoting passages from letters that spoke only of manuscripts to be published or accounts rendered to pay off the note plus accumulated interest.

As a brief Fay's second pamphlet leaves much to be desired, since no effort was made to develop a logical argument or to make use of evidence to create a cumulative effect. As a literary production it hardly rates its New York Public Library classification, "Ephemeral American Literature." Its only structure is a roughly chronological one. Repetitious and disorganized, it intersperses documentary material with commentary in so confusing a manner that the reader is lost in speculative deductions. Occasionally a sentence sparkles with an apt simile or illuminating phrase but, for the most part, the writing is dull and uninspired. Full of typographical errors and containing several inaccurate and self-contradictory statements, the pamphlet evidences hurried writing and first-draft publication. Perhaps its chief interest is its portrayal of a distraught and deeply disturbed mind searching to find evidence that will prove its own integrity. Fay is baffled that his business relations with the brothers could have been so misunderstood by them and misinterpreted even by close friends. His frequent outbursts of disbelief or sarcasm are tempered by a conscientious effort to understand the brothers and by one illuminating sentence of charitable feeling.

To read the pamphlet today is to indulge in a bit of historical detection. Could Fay have spent the $1,000, which he undoubtedly received, in so obvious a way that he would not have thought it important enough to note in his journal? Could he have spent the money in a way so clearly unrelated to the purpose of the advance that his memory would never relate the receipt and the expenditure? His considerable indebtedness is a possible clue. With complete candor he quotes from his journal to list the six persons to whom he was indebted in 1836. (He arose at three o'clock one cold March morning to name the six persons to whom he owed $2,201 and to calculate means of repaying them.)

Or could it be that the $1,000 was spent by Fay and Morris in stock speculation? Among the receipts noted in his journal for May 24, 1836, is an item "Stock—$500." In an explanatory note Fay says it "was cash received on certain stock procured for me by Colonel Morgan L. Smith" (see page 98). For a while Fay himself wondered whether he and Morris had spent the contested $1,000 on stock. After he completed his rebuttal, soon to be added to the original *Statement* in a seventy-eight-page pamphlet, Fay appended a closing paragraph. It reads: "Query. Is it possible that the $500 mentioned in Smith's letter as refunded to him by the *stock*, the profits on which Smith *advanced* to me through Morris, just as I was about to leave, *may have any connection with the two checks?*" (Fay's italics.)

It is tempting to think that Fay was his own best detective and honest enough in his final "Query" to admit that he and Morris had speculated in stock, making investments to be wiped out in the panic a year later, and long since rationalized and forgotten. His own record of 1836 expenditures lists, without annotative comment, a payment to Morris of $226.

There is, however, a more likely explanation of where the money went: loans to Morris. The $226 payment along with an entry made in his journal April 27 provide a clue. His entry reads, "April 27. Wednesday. Lent Morris 350 D. Harpers object about life insurance." This loan to Morris was made two days after his first $500 advance. However, the real evidence lies outside the pamphlet itself. On November 10, 1845, Fay was to write to Prescott that he had heard from Morris that the general had found "an old account book which shows that he *borrowed these two checks* [Fay's italics] with the residue in cash to the exact amount of $1500 less the discount (& $4) and repaid the same." But why did Fay lend so much money to Morris and make but one record of the transactions? It was his own searching question raised on page 57 of his pamphlet, when he wrote, "I seriously and carefully considered the possibility whether I might not have endorsed the checks for Morris, as a mere temporary accommodation, on his promise to return the amount to the Harpers immediately, and whether *in this way* [Fay's italics] I may not have had the money and forgotten it." If Fay, instead of immediately discarding that lead, had followed it up with a diligent study of his own records, he would not have been under compulsion to develop his long, pertinacious argument with the brothers.

For one thing, in addition to his April 27th entry he would have discovered (unless he was intentionally attempting to deceive, which seems unlikely) that he had made duplicate entries for earnings he expected to receive from Morris during the ensuing twelve months as salary for work on the *Mirror*. One entry which he considered, significantly enough, as *cash received* was the Wiggins-Fitch-Morris *credit* for a year's salary of $1,040. (That the words "year's salary" related to the coming year is indicated both by the fact that he was being paid regularly during his six months' stay in New York and by the phrase itself, "my usual yearly salary," not "my year's salary past due.") In another paragraph in his journal Fay wrote out a sort of budget of expected income during his first year abroad. The first entries under "Expectations" were quarterly payments to come from Morris beginning in August. Why did Fay fail in 1845 to see this duplication, for Morris would obviously not "credit" him with a year's salary in May and also pay him quarterly sums beginning in August. Thus his faulty bookkeeping in 1836 led to his faulty reasoning in 1845.

What happened probably went as follows: In April, 1836, Fay knew that if he and Mrs. Fay should carry out their plan of leaving in June for at least a year's stay abroad, he would need more money than he could easily put his hands on. He went to Cliff Street to see whether he could get a loan, hopefully of $2,500. The Harpers agreed on April 20 to loan him $1,500. They apparently paid him $1,395 (discounting one year's interest) at that time, although obtaining a second endorser and procuring a life insurance policy delayed the execution of the note by several weeks. Three days later the brothers said they would be glad to help out further by advancing $500 on *Norman Leslie*, then stereotyped and selling well in its second edition. In fact, as they had told him the previous November, they felt a bit conscience-stricken since only by chance were they prevented from printing 2,500 or 2,800 copies of the first edition, which would have earned him at least $500 more. Needing more money, Fay went to his broker, Smith, and got a loan of $500 with his and Morris's stock as collateral. Morris had to agree to this transaction. He also agreed to endorse the Harper note, after insisting on another endorser and a life insurance policy. Morris would then have confessed that he was in need of funds, with Seymour pressing him to pay bills past due. How about Fay's doing him a favor? If out of his present advance from Harper's and the Smith loan Fay could let Morris have $1,000, he, Morris, would use the money to pay off debts and within six months be able to refund the temporary loan. He would repay him with interest and send the amount, $1,040, to the Wiggins bank in London. Asa D. Fitch could act as agent. This made sense to Fay since he needed funds partly as a backlog to keep his London fire burning.

Whereupon Morris drew up an agreement on May 1, 1836, to guarantee Fay that this sum would be so deposited. By coincidence it was exactly the amount of a year's salary. A month later when Fay picked up his journal to enter his receipts and expenditures for the preceding six months, he had the Morris agreement in front of him. He entered as part of his cash receipts the $1,040 "credit" on the London bank "contracted" for by Morris. A careful reading of his explanation (see page 219) reveals that he implies rather than states that this was his yearly salary. Actually it was less than he was to receive later; beginning in August he was to be paid $221 per quarter for his work on the *Mirror*.

Fay was pleased to be able to help out his good friend Morris. But in order to pay so much money to Paul he had to get some more from Peter. Back he went to Cliff Street to ask if they believed in him enough to advance him another $500 on his next work, which, as he had said in the preface to the stereotyped edition of *Norman Leslie*, would be a fictional treatment of the life of Major André. The brothers needed to think that one over. The loan was no doubt safe, what with endorsers themselves protected by the life insurance policy. The $500 advance on the stereotyped edition of *Norman Leslie* was also safe enough and in good conscience they had to do that for him. However, he was going abroad again and might not complete his book. True, he had a good theme for a novel. Both Simms and Ingraham were showing what could be done with historical novels. Actually the Harpers had confessed to Fay that one of their authors (in his journal Fay identified him as "S"—Simms?) received $400 for his first book, $700 for his second, and had declined $1,200 for his third. Furthermore, Hoffman was praising them for what they were doing to encourage American authors. Yes, they would advance him $500 on his next book. Fay picked up the check on May 16. Easy come, easy go—Harper to Fay to Morris to Seymour.

It was not so easy to satisfy Cliff Street on the $1,500 note. Fay complained to his wife about the delays and frustrations in his dealings with the Harpers, Morris, and Jones. Mrs. Fay remembered that the note "was a frequent topic between us, but I never heard of any other [Harper] loan." Neither did Mrs. Fay know of her husband's loaning $1,500 to Morris unless he showed her the letter from Morris, the news of which he shared with Prescott in November, 1845. Perhaps Fay did not want his wife, Laura, to know how freely and forgetfully he loaned money to the general.

On July 11, 1845, Laura M. Fay signed her name to the *Statement*, and five days later Fay swore in an affidavit before a Prussian magistrate that his representations were sincere and true to the best of his knowledge and belief. He then had the pamphlet printed and bound. That he attempted to circulate it widely seems unlikely. Of the two known copies, the one in the Library of Congress carries the handwritten notation, "*Confidential.* Theo. S. Fay to C. C. Lewett, Esq. Providence." (Lewett was then librarian of Brown University.) However, Fay was determined that Prescott should see a copy.

During the time that Fay was writing and printing his enlarged *Statement* in Berlin, however, Prescott was busy with his own affairs in Boston. Chief of these was the publication of his *Miscellanies*. There were several exchanges of letters in early May between Prescott and Fletcher with no mention of this new book. On May 1 Fletcher wrote sending Prescott a copy of the Cogswell-Detmold findings, saying that they had not seen Fay's "printed circular . . . and as you intimate that it contains some aspersions upon our character, we feel that you cannot in justice refuse to transmit it to us without delay. . . ." Prescott replied that he had seen only Sumner's copy, which copy had been delivered to Cogswell. On the 13th Fletcher wrote again, "Since our last we have seen Mr. Fay's 'Statement'—and shall await his apology, which we doubt not . . . will be full and spontaneous." How much the self-confident Fletcher misjudged the reaction of the self-righteous Fay. But Fletcher was writing to Prescott not about Fay but to ask Prescott whether he wished to have corrections made in the plates of *Mexico*, as they were soon to reprint. He did not deign to ask about the *Miscelanies*.

Or had the brothers decided that a book made up of old reviews and articles would be hard to sell, even though by a famous historian? A book of collected essays and its prestigious brother, the *Festschrift*, rarely show a profit. Even Prescott had his doubts and wrote to Edward Everett, "I am about to commit a folly, which you will think savors of mental blindness; that is, the publication of some of my periodical trumpery, whose value, or rather little value, you know."

The Fay matter arbitrated, Prescott was satisfied that he could now take the initiative. His letter offering *Miscellanies* brought a prompt rejoinder on May 27: "We should be proud to be the publisher of the work in this country." Correspondence followed as to whether to publish on half profits, which the brothers preferred, or by purchase of copies that Prescott would have produced in Boston, or by the Harper purchase of the copyright for $2,000, which two alternatives Prescott preferred. But he finally agreed to the half-profits arrangement. He could hardly have done so had the Fay pamphlet caused him to doubt the brothers' integrity. A printing of twenty-five hundred copies was to be ready for December publication.

Their June correspondence over publishing arrangements was carried on in the best of spirits. To Prescott's query as to why they were reprinting only five hundred copies of *Mexico*, Fletcher replied that they had a perennial problem of warehousing—"our buildings are already crammed with stock." Prescott retorted: "I should think that 1000 copies of such light stuff as an author's wits might be packed in fairly small quarters." Fletcher sallied back: "If the quality of our authors' brains generally were like yours we should not be cramped as we now are . . . to keep on hand a decent supply of each [title] requires, we find, nearly a whole block of storehouses. Had all our books sold as well as yours have we should have plenty of room for the storage of 'gentlemanly' editions and means to pay for them too." Noting that in the English edition of *Ferdinand and Isabella* Prescott had permitted Bentley to print an engraving made from a recent portrait of the author, Fletcher wrote that Americans had "more cause to feel interest in you than the 'beef-eaters' of England have. If you would gratify the public, by all means give the Portrait." Fletcher succeeded in getting it for *Miscellanies*. To the half-profits proposal for this work Prescott wrote, "I don't much like the idea of publishing on shares. When publishers and authors hunt in couples—the author is not apt to share much of the game—or, at least, not to bag much. But I see the difficulties in the present instance—and you make just the kind of offer I expected." He would be glad to have them set from corrected English proofs and stereotype. "Your Bible shows what you can do—an' you like—in the way of stereotype." Even Boston could admit by now that New York knew how adequately to design a format, set type, and make plates.*

The economist-author Francis Lieber had either seen the first Fay pamphlet, which seems probable, or heard of his attack on the brothers. Lieber wrote Prescott for his opinion of the firm. Prescott's reply was dated August 6.

I make very simple and explicit contracts with them and have no complicated accounts, advances &c. They agree to take a certain number of copies of a stereotype work [of the two histories] & pay me so much a copy—one dollar, fifty cents therefor. They have paid me punctually. My contracts give them also the right to print as many more copies as they please, within the specified time, they paying at the same rate as before. This put me to

---

* The brothers had obviously been challenged to improve the physical quality of their production by such criticisms as that of the *Southern Literary Messenger*, which had said in 1841, "In nothing has there been so decided an improvement in this country within the last few years as in . . . publishing . . . Messers Harpers, in the number and cheapness of their publications, surpass any other house . . . but . . . they have given the public but few specimens of beautiful typography. The Boston publishers took the lead in presenting good books in a good style."

a certain extent in their power, as they certainly may cheat me in regard to the number of copies they strike off. But I do not think there is much danger of such a gross fraud in a house of their standing and character, and where it must be known to the four partners, and to some of the subalterns in the establishment,—at least if carried to an extent. This would be supposing rogues to be more plentiful than usual, even among publishers. I have found, too, that the report of the Harpers from persons who have dealt with them, and know them best, has been, almost always, favorable to their integrity. I have had the opinions of such men as Catherwood and Stephens, who have dealt with them long and largely, & who think them shrewd and sharp in their bargains, but faithful in the execution of them. They have no chivalry, and will not send you a horse or a butt of wine, as Scott's publishers did him, if your book should make a fortune for them. I should recommend you to be precise in your *written contract*—and to leave as little in said contract, as possible, to contingencies. Downright sales for an edition are the best thing. But it is not easy for an author to do the best, always,—only the best, his publisher will agree to. I should add in conclusion, that Mr. Fay of Berlin thinks very ill of the whole concern. His case is a difficult one to explain—& he has another pamphlet on the anvil, he writes me, anent the matter. I should easily believe they could be guilty of considerable blunders in their rapid wholesale way of doing business. But I should be very slow to suspect them of intentional fraud.

While writing to Lieber, Prescott had at hand a letter from Fay which he had received a few days earlier. Fay had written, "I do not ask you, on my assertion, to believe them unscrupulous scoundrels, but I ask you not to put much confidence in them, till you look through my other pamphlet. . . ." This letter Prescott acknowledged on August 11. His noctograph copy leaves many words and phrases blurred, although a few sentences are decipherable: "I am sorry to hear that you are having trouble [?] with the Harpers. I do not ever put too 'much confidence' in men [?] or any publisher, I assure you. . . . an honest publisher may sometimes be found with the help of a lantern. . . . When others are in ruins they [?] accumulate millions. . . . There is great danger of error without intending it. . . ."

That very same August day Fay was also writing Prescott, this time to say that he had posted his second pamphlet to Sumner with a request that he pass it along. He was still angry. Stock speculation or not, he had to save face. What mattered now was his pride. He had been proved wrong and his publishers right. He could strike back at them by turning one of their best authors against them. His letter to Prescott continued, "From a very careful examination of all the points of this singular controversy I am satisfied that they are swindlers, that their impudent attempt upon me will eventually be placed in its right light. ... I think you ought to know with whom you are dealing—and the imputation under which I lie by their account & the unscrupulous manner in which they have attempted to silence me, and their adroit style of managing and using Cogswell and Detmold, have, I confess, excited in me an indignation quite refreshing in our dull diplomacy and monotonous town."

On November 10 Fay wrote again to Prescott both to discuss a matter of business and to give him the news that General Morris had found the old account book which showed that Morris had borrowed $1,500 from him. While Fay still believed himself somehow to have been the victim of a knavish piece of work, he was forced to admit that the checks were not spurious. Morris, he said, had come out on his side.*

Two questions remain: Why did the brothers not admit to faulty bookkeeping, and why did they charge Fay (and themselves) interest at 7 percent? The answer to the second question is that such was the pleasant practice of the day. Today authors would be horrified and agents out of business were publishers to charge interest on advances. However, financial outlay in those days was considered risk capital and anyone who could was doing a bit of banking on the side. An 1844 Cliff Street publication, popular for years, was Stansbury's *Interest Tables* (at 7 percent). At the same time that John was figuring interest due on the Fay account, Henry Noble Day—on his way to becoming one of mid-century America's leading business entrepreneurs—was expecting a 25 percent return on risk capital. (Day graduated from Yale in 1828, while his uncle, Jeremiah Day, was president. In his Biblical studies at Yale young Day must have skipped the first Epistle to Timothy.) Writing in this same period, Thomas Low Nichols asked, "Why the universal and everlasting struggle for wealth?" His answer: "Because it is the only thing needful; the only secure power, the only real distinction. . . . The real work of America is to make money for the sake of making it. It is an end and not a means." As Grund pointed out in his *Aristocracy in America* (1839), Bostonians could conceive of no greater ambition than that of "making dollars in a neat, handsome, clean manner," and New Yorkers could hold "no higher rank in society than that of a rich man," the wealthy Mr. Astor having a greater reputation than the learned Chancellor Kent. Thus to criticize

---

* Morris does not appear to have been estranged from the brothers. In the 1850's he was to address letters "My dear Fletcher," closing them with such sentiments as "I remain, my dear old friend, with kind regards to your brothers," and "My best love to you *all*, old friends," and "With love for all 'the brothers.'"

the brothers for their business practices is to criticize their times.

Fletcher made one of the great mistakes of his career when he told Detmold and Cogswell that Fay had never been notified of the full amount of his indebtedness because the firm did not want to frighten a productive author. Fletcher's comment was construed by Detmold as evidence of their having played a "very shrewd and cunning game." Talk about frightening a productive author was sheer rationalization. Fletcher should have admitted what seems more likely to have been true, that they also had forgotten about the $1,000 advance. As late as November, 1842, they were equating Fay's indebtedness with the old note (see p. 168). Actually Fay's indebtedness was then more than $2,000. In the summer of 1844, after Burt began pressing them for a statement, they apparently found the checkbook stubs and entries in the 1836 ledger, entries made according to the arbitrator's statement "in the handwriting of Mr. [Gerherdus] Demarest, Messrs Harper's book keeper, who stated to us that he transferred [them] from their waste book, which could not be produced, having been lost when the printing office was destroyed by fire." Also a receipt book was lost in the fire and during the arbitration proceedings John did testify that he remembered seeing there Fay's receipts for the two payments. Fear that an admission of inadequate records would have given Fay an easy way out of his indebtedness and a hope that time was on their side might have led to evasions and delays when Burt was importuning them. Actually the two endorsed and canceled checks were found just a few days before the Detmold-Cogswell arbitration.

There is other evidence that the brothers kept their books with something less than vigilance, as when Lemuel Haynes had to remind them that they had failed to credit his payment for plates with a $100 banknote, "yellow paper or reddish." It was not until 1857 that William Demarest succeeded in talking John Harper into introducing double-entry bookkeeping. The whole dispute was partly due to a failure to keep increasingly complicated records in a rapidly expanding business. More importantly it was the partners' refusal to keep their own participation equal; if they had drawn up annual profit-and-loss statements to determine partnership earnings, they would have kept better books.

That the Fay affair involved faulty bookkeeping seems further indicated by a notation made by William Demarest thirty-five years later. After wrongly listing *Sydney Clifton* in his bibliography of Fay titles, Demarest wrote, "There was a long feud between the author and the firm: the merits of the dispute I know nothing of." Not know? How could he have helped knowing? Two years before the Fay ink was spilled William had taken a desk in the counting room alongside his elder brother Gerherdus. With Gerherdus so deeply involved in keeping the books, searching the records, and testifying before Cogswell and Detmold, it follows that William once knew what his memory later erased, the shame of poor bookkeeping. To be sure, by 1880 he had few records to refer to. The brothers obviously did not save the Fay pamphlets, and if they saved the Cogswell-Detmold report, it was not for long. Apparently all that Demarest saw was three letters exchanged with Detmold regarding *Hoboken* and two papers relating to the 1854 transfer of publishing rights of the four Fay titles to Bruce & Brother of New York, who paid $500 for existing stereotypes. At that time Fay was American minister to Switzerland. He was to retire in 1861 and spend the closing decades of a very long life in Germany.

CHAPTER XIV

Big-Name Authors

1846–1849

THE YEAR OF James Harper's term as mayor marked the turn of the tide for publishing on Cliff Street. The long years of bad times, starting with the 1837 panic, had ebbed away, as had the fantastic competition to mass produce cheap literature. The brothers were the acknowledged leaders in the rich field of English reprints, with British publishers eager to sell them early proofs of their most likely books. Their extraordinary success with the *School District Library*—half salesmanship and half diligence—and the *Family Library*—good editing and good pricing—had built up their back list and helped them not only to survive but to pile up hefty capital resources as well. Frugal living and conservative management had enabled them to plow profits into new equipment and buildings. The prestige of the office of mayor had reflected brightly on nearby Cliff Street. The Fay episode may have taught them to keep better books; it certainly gave them renewed confidence and self-esteem, always a part of the victor's spoils.

No merchants kept a closer watch on the economic barometer than those operating from 82 Cliff Street. Their agility in retreating when a storm center was approaching was matched by their speed in advancing when the rising mercury promised fair skies ahead. The mood of national expansion which had elected President Polk in 1844 found a response in the expansionist program on Cliff Street. After issuing an average of fifty-five new titles a year for the preceding four years, they jumped to seventy-five in 1844 and eighty-seven in 1845. While others, such as Duyckinck and Mathews, were dreaming of a new national literature, the brothers were busy purveying literature to the nation. In this effort they were aided by several factors, as they well knew. By 1848, books could be shipped by rail from New York as far as Wilmington, North Carolina, and across most of New York State—a total of more than six thousand steel miles. Even though the competition between books and newspapers had piled up losses on both sides, it had encouraged people to read. A literate people with a desire for knowledge and entertainment were ready for the best and most that the Cliff Street brothers could get to them. The telegraph, with the large-scale transmission of news, was calling for background information that books could best give the people. The school population was exploding as frontiersmen bred large families and young immigrants married and began having children. Evangelical churches were establishing an increasing number of academies and colleges throughout the land and Sunday schools were increasing with astounding rapidity. Perhaps never before or after did America reach a more generous and eager hand to book publishers than in the ten years beginning in the mid-forties.

The brothers were better able to grasp that hand than any other publisher. Boston publishers were still moribund with tradition and provincialism. Young Jamie Fields, who was to give them real competition later, was a $800-a-year junior partner of Ticknor. Little and Brown was satisfied with its profits on law books and its conservative publishing policy. The old and prestigious name of Hilliard was gone and that of Phillips, Sampson & Company was better known later. Marsh, Capen, Lyon & Webb, friends of Horace Mann, were soon to go out of business, many of their titles going to Cliff Street. In Philadelphia the two firms that carried on the work of Mathew and Henry Carey lacked the drive and genius of their founding father and his sons. The Quaker Lippincott* was less interested in publishing than in selling books at retail, as was true of Appleton in New York. Wiley & Putnam were handicapped by lack of capital and back-list titles. There were scores of small publishers, some, like Redburn, to flourish awhile

---

* However, Gregg, Elliott and Company had become important publishers, and their back list was basic to the establishment in 1849 of what eventually became known as the J. B. Lippincott Company.

and die, some, like Scribner, just aborning. New York, however, had become the center for American publishing as it had for finance and other commercial activities. And the center of publishing was located at 82 Cliff Street.

How did the brothers merchandise their books? J. Henry Harper was twenty-seven years old when his grandfather Fletcher died; he was his grandfather's favorite, spent much time in his home, and gave up college at Fletcher's insistence to start in the family business. Whatever stories the grandson heard about the sale of books in the forties and fifties he forgot or thought to be of little reader interest when he wrote *The House of Harper*. However, Moses Yale Beach of the New York *Sun* wrote a contemporary account of the means and extent of the Harper sales efforts. The fifth edition of his *Wealthy Citizens* booklet out early in 1845 listed the brothers by name and described their start as publishers. With a sweet-sour mixture of praise and frankness, he wrote:

They are now the most extensive publishers in this country, and their names in the history of publishing will be associated with Galliane, Constable, Murray and Longman. They have in different parts of America, from twelve to fifteen hundred booksellers acting as their agents, besides a large number of travelling clergymen and other itinerants. So extensive is their business connexion that should they dispose of but one or two copies to each agency, they would be sure to pay the expenses of publication, and no matter what work they may publish, (and they have published several of the worst and most stupid books ever issued) they are sure to dispose of an average more than two copies to each house with which they deal. They have a correspondence established not only with every considerable place in this country, but with cities abroad, where books are published, informing them of every work worthy of publication. They have besides in this city, and other parts of the United States, many literary men in their employment, to pronounce their opinion of manuscripts submitted for publication, to revise those that are imperfect, and to write notices and puffs for the more important newspapers and magazines which they have either directly or indirectly subsidized to their interest.

Citing this pamphlet as its authority, the New York *Herald* gave the brothers' wealth as $1 million. James probably told Beach that he was exaggerating, for Beach's sixth edition, out a month later, eased the figure back to $500,000, a more propitious sum for authors to contemplate. Among such authors were Verplanck ($200,000), who, Beach said, "holds the most polished and classical pen in American literature but wants the pathos and feeling of Irving, and the strength and energy of many other of our native writers."

Little is known about advertising expenditures that book publishers made during this period. The brothers were said in 1849 to be spending $4,000 a year. Newspapers gave space freely to list new books, sometimes with "puffs," as well as to review the important ones. Books and authors were important sources of stories for news columns and subject matter for editorial comment—perhaps more so than today. Publishers did not pay for what they could get free, a fact that infuriated Moses Yale Beach. On October 1, 1847, he wrote to Fletcher, "Some few weeks since I particularly requested of your brother James a sett [*sic*] of your Shakespeare offering to pay him to satisfaction in our business. He thought we could do nothing which would compensate you and refused. Today I see a particular request from you to insert a notice in a style which readily commands from other businesses than yours from $16 to $20—certainly a little more than the book sent is worth to us. For a long time we have favored your house more than others in the way of notices, taking up room in noticing a 50 cent book which is actually worth from $2 to $5 to us and it would be fair if the compliment were returned once in a while." Fletcher filed the letter without noting his reply.

Beach knew that the brothers could well afford to be generous with free copies of new books. A few months after writing Fletcher, he issued another pamphlet, entitled *The Aristocracy of New York, etc.*, giving the brothers' wealth as $2 million. In his series of pamphlets Beach now listed Charles Anthon—able to add up his dollars in six figures—with the icy comment, "In his Classical Dictionary, and other works, he has been charged with having made free use of the labor of others." This was changed in still a later pamphlet to the gossipy kind of gibe that made his pamphlets good table talk: "He has a popular reputation as a scholar, and is a most learned man. He is in the strictest sense a bachelor and is said not to have looked a pretty woman in the face for 20 years."

When Beach spoke of booksellers as "agents," he probably used the term loosely, although it is known that in 1848 the brothers had a financial interest in at least one bookstore, that of H. W. Derby & Co., of Cincinnati. By the mid-forties Harper catalogues were being imprinted for the trade. Two such catalogues—probably not the first ones—were imprinted in 1847 and 1848 for G. B. Zieber, a Philadelphia bookseller doing business at 141 Chestnut Street. And colportage was at its height. During the forties and early fifties the Rev. W. H. Milburn, a blind Methodist colporteur, traveled more than 200,000 miles throughout the Middle West and the frontier country. Colporteurs rode horseback with saddlebags crammed with books.

Stopping at log cabins or small settlements and using rush-bottom chairs for pulpits, these dedicated men were selling tracts, books, and Bibles. Their chief sources of supply were the Methodist Publishing House, The American Bible Society, and Harper & Brothers. Subscription bookselling was also beginning, with Henry Bill of Norwich leasing or buying Harper plates to issue big fat books that salesmen sold from door to door.

Thus the brothers entered upon the last four years of the decade with everything in their favor: book-hungry Americans in the twenty-eight states (Texas and Florida having been admitted to the Union in 1845) and the several territories; a mammoth book manufacturing establishment paid for and money in the bank; nearly 1,000 titles catalogued and stocked in bulging warehouses; a network of review media and sales outlets; more than twenty-five years' experience of what books people would buy; an imprint so well known that for most aspiring authors it was the first to come to mind. These authors, both native and foreign, supplied them with 94 titles in 1846, with 113 in 1847, with 89 in 1848, and with 70 in 1849. Some of these authors came by the purchase of rights and plates from other publishers, notably in 1847. Some of the four years' total of 366 titles were, as Beach so candidly stated, of questionable value and soon interred in the ample burial ground of American literary history. The ephemeral book of fiction or collection of sermons found its quick market and was soon forgotten, yet a surprising number were in sufficient demand to deserve stocking and cataloguing for many years. Among these were a large number of big-name authors, some of whose books were more important then than they appear to be today.

The best seller of them all was Morse's *School Geography*, the revised edition of which came out in 1847 after two and a half years of work on the cerographic maps. On April 17, 1845, Morse spent the day at 82 Cliff Street supervising the drafting of contracts for the revised edition. (This was less than two weeks before Detmold and Cogswell were to come in to arbitrate the Fay dispute.) April 17 was a field day for the lawyers. Not only were the brothers Harper involved with the cousins Morse and Breese, but also both parties had to deal with a man named Henry Munson, who knew how to make the cerographic plates. This process was top secret and all parties pledged themselves several times to keep it so. The cerographic maps were also to be used in an *Atlas of North America*, which was to depict the states, the Indian territory, Canada, Mexico, the West Indies, etc.—thirty-five plates in all. (The *Atlas* was first published, folio size, in nine numbers and then bound in half roan leather and sold for $2.75.)

By these contracts the brothers purchased Breese's interest in the *Geography* for $5,000 (in cash) and in the forthcoming *Atlas* for $3,000 (payable in three years with interest at 6 percent); they also promised to pay Breese a royalty on the *Atlas* of 10 cents a copy after 20,000 copies had been sold. They agreed to pay Munson $1,000 a year for three years to superintend a "Cerographic Establishment," Munson to have some of his ten-hour day, six-day week available for doing experimental work for Morse at Morse's expense. Breese also promised to use his skill as a cartographer to produce *Harper's Map of the United States and Canada*, a wall map three feet by four in size. When the map was printed in color by "the Cerographic art," showing canals, railroads, and principal stage routes, it was mounted on rollers and published a week following the revised *Geography*. Schools could choose one of four "editions" of the wall map, priced from $2 to $2.50 according to the amount of cerographic color desired.

The major Morse-Breese-Harper contract ran to four and one half foolscap pages. The Morse-Harper contract was shorter and is more interesting today since it specified the amount of manufacturing overhead that was figured in the half-profits contracts. The brothers agreed to purchase their interest in the plates by compensating Morse for "labor, rent, fuel, light & materials," plus 33⅓ percent of such cost, which was called "profit." (Today it would be called "overhead.") This cost-plus-33⅓-percent formula was mentioned three times in the contract, and a reasonable assumption is that it was used as a matter of course in figuring manufacturing costs in other half-profits agreements. In this case it was accepted by a man who knew his way around a printing plant as well as the brothers did. In fact, Morse stipulated that he should have the right before any reprint was undertaken to manufacture it himself if he wished.

Having had nearly a year's experience with the *Geography*, Morse and the brothers had learned that the earlier contract stipulation of a discount of 30 percent on orders of a hundred or more was on the low side competitively. The new contract specified a discount of 40 percent on such quantities of the *Geography*, as well as the *Atlas*, which was also published on a half-profits basis. A reputed $20,000 went into making the cerographic maps and wood engravings. How many copies of the Harper edition of the Morse *Geography* were sold is not known. By 1853, the Cliff Street presses were printing 70,000 copies a year. Loss of Harper records in the 1853 fire may be the reason that it was not included in the Boston *Post's* 1859 series of articles on publishers and best-selling books.

Five important authors in the closing years of the decade were women: Miss Beecher, and Mesdames Farnham, Hale, Embury, and Sigourney. By 1845 the brothers had signed up Catharine Beecher, whose introduction to her sister Harriet's *Mayflower* they had considered so essential. At that time Catharine was perhaps the best-known member of the Beecher family. While her father, Lyman, was struggling to establish his theological school in Cincinnati (he failed to get Dr. Barnes to join the faculty), Catharine was getting publicity everywhere through her lectures and because of her leadership in the cause of education for women and the "female seminaries" that she had established. One of the manuscripts she left at Cliff Street was an address, "Evils Suffered by American Women and Children," which she had given in Indianapolis and Cincinnati, in Washington and other cities on the Eastern Seaboard; all agreed that it would help to sell the 12½-cent pamphlet to give title-page listing to the more important cities. (Whether these were the cities in which women and children suffered the most evil is not recorded.) The *Address*, as it became known, was published in August, 1846, two months after *Miss Beecher's Housekeeper's Receipt-book*, 322 pages of recipes, illustrated by forty woodcuts. The year before she had arranged with the brothers for the reissue of a revised edition of her *Treatise on Domestic Economy, for the Use of Young Ladies at Home and at School*, and the publication of her new book, *The Duty of American Women to their Country*. The brothers kept a beautifully handwritten, five-page contract with Miss Beecher for her three book-length works. The contract was unsigned and undated except for "1845," but carried penciled corrections in John's handwriting. Were it not for the date, a reasonable guess would be that this is the "whereas" contract for which the Mayor substituted a short-form agreement (see pp. 193f). The "brother" part fits since Charles Beecher was then pastor of a church in Newark, New Jersey. In 1849, Charles got his own name on a Harper contract. His book, *The Incarnation*, was subtitled "Pictures of the Virgin and her Son." This time the sibling introduction was written not by Catharine but by Harriet.

Like Catharine Beecher, Mrs. Elizabeth Farnham was concerned about the evils done to American women. She also lectured on the subject but with less oratorical flourish and more practical knowledge than Catharine. Mrs. Farnham's interest was prison reform. In 1846 she was matron of the female department of Sing Sing Prison, working at the problem of rehabilitating as well as punishing the women who had been convicted of crime. However, Mrs. Farnham's book, *Life in Prairie Land*, had nothing to do with prison reform. It was written out of remembered experiences in Illinois, where she had lived as a young woman.

Sarah Josepha Hale was also demonstrating how much a woman could do in a man's world. She began making a living as an author and editor after being widowed at the age of thirty-two, with five children to support. For their pleasure she wrote a poem about a girl named Mary, whose pet lamb followed her to school one day. After conducting the *Ladies' Magazine* in Boston for nine years, she was hired by Louis A. Godey to become literary editor of *Lady's Book,* and from 1837 till she was ninety she completely identified herself with this magazine, helping to make it the best known of all American periodicals for women.* Her 1846 Harper book was entitled *Boarding Out; or, Domestic Life,* a companion volume to *Keeping House and Housekeeping,* published the year before.

Mrs. Emma Embury was the wife of a wealthy Brooklyn physician. Her poetry, for which she was noted, was not published from Cliff Street, but her *Constance Latimer,* the story of a blind girl, was the book, according to Poe, by which she attained most of her reputation. He considered Mrs. Embury "the most noted and most certainly one of the most meritorious of our female *littérateurs.* . . . Her style is pure, earnest and devoid of verbiage and exaggeration." Along with this title the brothers were getting good sales on an 1846 reissue of an older title, *Pictures of Early Life,* called "fresh and glowing" by the *North American Review.*

Next to Mrs. Hale, the real pro in this 1846 Harper group of five lady authors was, of course, Lydia Howard Huntley Sigourney. It was said of Mrs. Sigourney that one reason famous men dreaded death was the knowledge that their demise would move the "sweet singer of Hartford" to write a poem extolling their virtues. When she herself died, this widely read versifier and essayist had sixty-seven volumes to her credit. Her new Harper book, *Myrtis,* contained twelve poems in addition to the one that gave the three-hundred-page book its title. A slightly larger book than *Pocahontas,* it sold for less—for 75 cents as compared to 90—perhaps because the stereotypes cost less—$257 as compared to $410—and because, at her request, she was receiving a 10 percent royalty instead of the more remunerative half-profits. Rufus Wilmot Griswold, always favoring the ladies, gave Mrs. Sigourney a big boost in his *Poets and Poetry of America;* the best that Duyckinck

---

* Mrs. Hale persuaded President Lincoln to make Thanksgiving Day a national holiday, helped to establish Vassar College (as did Mayor Harper), started the first day nursery, saved Mount Vernon as a national memorial, raised the money to finish Bunker Hill Monument, and sent off the first woman missionary.

could say of her poems was that they possessed "energy and variety."

A frequently reprinted engraving made in the mid-nineteenth century by A. H. Ritchie shows forty-four American literati posed formally in a classical setting, a blending of Greek revival and Italian Renaissance architecture. (Many of these ladies and gentlemen had seen their names on title pages of Harper books, several in 1846 and 1847.) At a table at the left in the picture the chaste and beautiful Mrs. Sigourney sits opposite the benign and handsome Mr. Longfellow, each looking away from the other. Their averted faces are symbolic of the fact that Longfellow's growing popularity as a poet was giving him the highest Nielsen rating in the 1840's. On February 6, 1846, Longfellow noted in his journal, "Putting together a cheap edition of my poems, complete in one volume, double columns." This edition contained antislavery sentiments which had not appeared in a more sumptuous volume issued by Carey & Hart a few months earlier. Placing a retail price of 50 cents on the book, the brothers soon sold 5,300 copies, doing for Longfellow's popularity and pocketbook what they had recently done for Bryant's. Longfellow, like Prescott, produced his own stereotypes and had copies printed and bound locally, the printing by Metcalf & Company, Cambridge. The brothers bought books at half off, thus netting something under 15 cents a copy, little enough figuring that at least 150 copies had to be sent out to reviewers. One letter went off to Longfellow carrying a postscript to ask if this expense should not be charged in whole or in part to his account of "Stereotype Plates & Copyright."

In 1847 the brothers tried unsuccessfully to publish Longfellow's *Evangeline*, offering to take bound copies from him at his price. What the price was is not known, but Ticknor wrote Longfellow that he and Fields would make a better offer—40 cents a copy, or $800 for a two thousand printing. So Ticknor & Fields got the book, issuing it at 75 cents. Two years later, however, Longfellow added the long, popular poem to his Harper paperback, and the brothers took this occasion to ask if they could try their hand "at publishing a new poem from your pen, to see what we can do, having the *freshness* of the market to operate upon." They also asked if they could bring out a matching paper edition of his prose works. But Longfellow was not interested. By now he had married into one of the best Beacon Street families and had become a close friend of Jamie Fields, who was eagerly promoting the poets.

Longfellow's Harper book was promoted in the market that had recently been freshened by an 1845 reissue of Halleck's *Alnwick*

Castle. It had been published first in 1827 by Carvill and again in 1835 by Dearborn. Out of print for several years, its Harper format made room for one added poem and its Harper promotion took it quickly into a second printing. Demarest says that still a further edition came out in 1852, with more than twice the number of pages, but it does not appear in the 1853 catalogue. By 1847 Halleck had arranged with Appleton to issue his collected poems. While he was only fifty when the Harper edition of *Alnwick Castle* appeared, Halleck was being stereotyped "old Knickerbocker," and he retired to his home town of Guilford, Connecticut, following the death of John Jacob Astor, whom he had served for many years as a confidential clerk.

"Halleck is out," Charles Fenno Hoffman had written Griswold after seeing the Harper book. Griswold was conniving with Hoffman to get the brothers interested in reissuing Hoffman's *The Vigil of Faith and Other Poems,* on the 1842 list of S. Colman. James and John consented, one of them saying to Hoffman on September 25, 1845, "Let Mr. Griswold send on the plates to us. We will print it on handsome paper with a large margin and do our best with the book and make what we can for you and Griswold out of it. . . ." This conversation Hoffman detailed in a letter to Griswold, urging action and warning him that "if the Harpers dream of any other [publishing negotiation] being attempted after their offer, they will turn the cold shoulder." The slow-moving Griswold finally arranged to get the plates delivered but overlooked a bit of publishing protocol. Hoffman wrote to him again on November 11, "Calling in here [82 Cliff Street] today to see if a certain volume was likely ever to see the light, the Messers Harper tell me that the plates have been deposited with them for a week or more—But that they hold them subject to the order of the stereotyper having no right to publish save with his written permit." The book finally went to press, with bound copies available before Christmas.

Hoffman had a loyal friend in Griswold, who promised the brothers that if they did not make enough profit on *The Vigil of Faith* to pay for the plates, he would make up the difference out of his own purse. He had chosen more poems by Hoffman than by any other writer for his anthology of American poetry. Poe did not care much for Hoffman's verse and was nettled by the *Dublin University Magazine's* verdict that Hoffman was "the best song writer in America . . . a better fellow than the whole Yankee crew." However, Poe admired Hoffman as a man, spoke of his graceful and winning manners, and described him as "quiet, affable and dignified, yet cordial and *dégagé*. He converses much, earnestly, accurately, and well. In person he is re-markably handsome."

Knowing of Hoffman's Harper connections, Dr. E. B. O'Callaghan of Albany asked him to speak to the firm on behalf of his own manu-script on the early settlement of New York. Hoffman's letter to Fletcher is a model for all who write letters to editors on behalf of friends. First, it states why the author is significant (O'Callaghan had spent five years of research and writing on the Dutch settlement). Second, it shows that the work is important (despite many books on the settlement of New England, here is the first one to show that a "Spirit of Liberty" existed earlier in New York). Third, it flatters the editor with a bit of humor (Fletcher himself should read it and not let the dust of a pigeonhole thicken on it). Fourth, it makes an intelligent suggestion of an outside reader ("not Mr. Trisman [?] but Mr. Ver-planck"). Good as the Hoffman letter was, it failed to convince Fletcher, who had some of the freedom-loving (and stubborn) Dutch blood in his own veins. He declined *History of New Netherland,* which Appleton published in two volumes in 1846-48, with a second edition to be called for in 1855.

The brothers' willingness to favor Griswold on the Hoffman reprint followed soon after they had tried to interest Griswold himself in doing a book for them. But it would not have been cricket for them to ask him directly. They turned to Henry J. Raymond, now reading manuscripts for them in addition to his work with James Watson Webb on the *Morning Courier and New York Enquirer.* Raymond dutifully wrote about the biographical dictionary that Griswold was rumored to be undertaking, saying, "The Harpers are in the way of publishing a good many valuable books of reference, and would be anxious, I should think, to secure that. Could you not make better terms with them than elsewhere?" But Griswold was then too busy working on *The Prose Writers of America* to give much thought to the biographical dictionary. Not until February, 1847, two weeks after Carey & Hart had published this companion volume to *Poets and Poetry,* did he get around to signing a Harper contract to prepare a *Cyclopedia of Biography* based on *Biographie Universelle* by Rose. Immediately a Cliff Street publicity release was sent out. It brought one unexpected response—an offer of editorial help from William Allen of Northampton, Massachusetts.

"Receiving a notice," he wrote, "that you have in press a translation of the great biographical dictionary . . . now in course of publication in Paris, to be issued by you in monthly parts—it has occurred to me that you might wish to associate with it a complete American Biography."

He then went on to say that his large work, *The American Biographical Dictionary*, had gone through two editions and that he was preparing a third. He hoped that Harper's would either annex his to the Rose translation or engage him to supplement that with selected American names he would write up. He listed several persons, including Bancroft and Cogswell, who could speak a good word for his work. The offer may have been tempting, for the brothers asked Saunders to send a fishing sort of letter to Griswold. Saunders wrote: "Friend Griswold, I send you copy of two letters which came to hand today: what reply are we to make? Write me by the earliest post on the subject. Have you the same sources open and at command as Allen had or has? If so of course we can do without him: if you have not, what then do you suggest?"

Apparently Griswold said No to the Allen proposal. He did not want to divide either the honor or the honorarium—$1,250 a year. Anyway he could have the aid, if he wished, of a translator; the total Harper obligation was not to exceed $2,500. Griswold also agreed in the contract to "devote his entire attention to the work until its completion," and wrote to James Fields in Boston that he would thus be occupied constantly for a year and a half or two years. By late May or early June, he had left Philadelphia for New York to begin the job. But he dragged his feet. He had first to finish another Carey & Hart book, *Washington and His Generals*, although he expected "little money and no reputation" from it. He arranged with Bayard Taylor to translate portions of the French text of the *Dictionary*, for which the brothers advanced $500. By 1849 they had also paid Griswold $1,100, had enough material at hand to make 1,000 stereotyped pages, and in the December issue of *Holden's Dollar Magazine* again announced the work as forthcoming. But before the print of that issue was fairly dry the project had been abandoned. Griswold pleaded ill health but the more likely reason seems to be that he had more interesting literary projects. He had taken time out to edit *The Female Poets of America*, a selection of poems with introductory puffs to their authors, and also to see through the Carey & Hart presses a book of his pet female poet, Mrs. S. S. Osgood. More importantly, after Poe's death in October, 1849, Griswold had set himself up as Poe's literary executor to publish an edition of Poe's collected works, to which he prefixed an acrimonious biography of Poe. Also, by that time Griswold had probably heard rumors that the brothers were planning to start a monthly miscellany. Maybe he could interest someone in backing a periodical that he would edit.

Griswold had Simms and Ingraham working with him in the hectic

weeks he gave to finishing *Washington and His Generals*. At the same
time, Simms was finishing his last Harper volume, *The Life of Cheva-
lier Bayard*, and was soon to contribute articles for the *New Monthly
Magazine*. Having sold his unprofitable *Southern and Western
Monthly Magazine*, published for a while in Charleston, to the *Southern Literary Messenger*, Simms now had more time for his New York
literary friends, among them Evert Duyckinck, whom he considered
the ablest and most honest of editors. Simms's testimony was inspired
by the new venture Duyckinck had talked Wiley & Putnam (for
whom he had begun to edit books) into financing, a monthly to be
called the *Literary World*. The first issue appeared in February, 1847,
with Hoffman associated with the brothers Duyckinck as editor.

The *Literary World* was launched as New York, "the focus of
American letters" (Poe's phrase), was at the height of a literary con-
troversy over "Americanism." Even though Duyckinck was on the
Wiley & Putnam payroll as a book editor, he was convinced that a
magazine rather than a book was the best form of literary expression.
The *Literary World* would be the best of all possible pulpits from
which to preach his and Cornelius Mathews's cult of "Americanism."
This preachment Griswold considered absurd; in *Prose Writers of
America* he said there was not and never could be an exclusively national literature. The mild-mannered Duyckinck threw caution to the
winds at this thrust and in one of his early issues gave the Griswold
book an angry review. "It looks very much as if Mr. Griswold were
usurping some nationality throne," he wrote, "and like an Eastern
monarch bow-stringing all rival claimants to feel himself secure." Attacks provoked counterattacks, all of which depressed Duyckinck. In
July he wrote in his diary, "The editorial world is discharging its bile
... in the old-fashioned, classical style of personal polemics," and moral-
ized that American literature badly needed a few "noble authors."

One such noble author, Herman Melville, had come to him unrecognized and by default. In the early summer of 1845, Melville had
completed a first draft of his manuscript, a combination of fiction and
fact to be called *Typee: A Peep at Polynesian Life*. He left it at Cliff
Street, probably with Frederick Saunders, and waited hopefully for a
decision. Saunders recommended publication, saying that the work, if
not so good as *Robinson Crusoe*, seemed not to be far behind it. But he
was overruled, the brothers deciding that it was impossible that the tale
could be true and it was therefore without real value. In the meantime
Gansevoort Melville, Herman's elder brother, had been named secretary to the American legation in London as a reward for his strenuous

political activities in the Polk campaign. Sailing for England on July 31, Gansevoort carried the rejected manuscript with him; prior publication in England might be important from the copyright point of view and would surely give the book prestige among Amerian publishers. In New York Herman busied himself making revisions and additions and posting them to London, where they arrived in December. By January *Typee* had been accepted by Murray and proof sheets read in London by George Putnam. Putnam was enthusiastic, accepted it at once, and in February dispatched corrected proof to New York. (The proofreading had been done by Gansevoort Melville, then suffering from a fatal illness.) Duyckinck read the proofs apathetically and saw the book through to publication on March 17, a volume in Wiley & Putnam's new project, the *Library of American Books*.

Henry David Thoreau, another young and noble author, was hopeful in 1847 that the Harpers would take his first book, *A Week on the Concord and Merrimack Rivers*. William Emerson, who had served as counsel for the brothers when they were sued by Maria Monk, was trying to place the book for Thoreau. He wrote to his brother, Waldo, on September 29, "Please tell Henry Thoreau that I . . . am daily expecting an answer of some sort from the Harpers." The answer was that they would publish it at the author's expense, an answer that tempted neither the Emersons nor Thoreau. Emerson also submitted the manuscript to Wiley & Putnam and two other publishers, but with no success. It was finally published in 1849 on the Harper terms by James Munroe and Company of Boston. The Harper rejection of Thoreau tended to confirm Ralph Waldo Emerson's somewhat contemptuous opinion of their operation. He had attempted in 1846 to befriend a Scandinavian author, Harro Harring, whose novel, *Dolores: A Novel of South America*, had been translated into English and quickly accepted on Cliff Street through the recommendation of Sam Ward. What happened then is related by Emerson: "Some *foreign* or religious influence came in and they [Harper's] sent the manuscript back to him [Harring]. He prosecuted them, being assured that he could recover $1000. or the like damages and in his absence at London . . . his counsel compounded the matter with Harpers and according to H.H., paid themselves [the counsel] and gave him nothing. Meantime the offended Harpers have effectually prevented any chance of sale for it in N.Y. or any city where they have correspondence, and no paper dares mention the book."

The brothers' opinion of Ralph Waldo Emerson can only be guessed. It is likely that they shared the prevailing New York disdain for his transcendentalism and doubts of his Christian conviction. They were cultivating Professor Thomas C. Upham of Bowdoin College, who found Emerson's ideas distasteful. On January 20, 1846, Upham had contracted for the Harper publication of his manuscript, a life of the French mystic Madame Guyon. The work was stereotyped in Boston, at a cost of $875, and published the following year. In 1848 the brothers took over the plates and publishing rights of three earlier Upham titles, including *Principles of the Interior or Hidden Life*. Upham could establish and the brothers publish works that would uphold the life of the spirit without going to Emersonian extremes. And even though he had been dead for nearly thirty years President Timothy Dwight could still speak the authoritative Christian word. In October, 1845, the Harpers contracted with Benjamin W. Dwight for the publication of his father's *Theology Explained and Defended, in a Series of Sermons*. Using the plates of a New Haven edition issued in 1836, with a memoir and portrait added, they published the four volumes in 1847.

The brothers' final answer to all "isms" was, of course, the Bible. After appearing in fifty-four numbers,* *Harper's Illuminated and New Pictorial Bible* came out in all its morocco-bound, hand-tooled, gold-embossed, and gilt-edged glory in the early part of 1846. The *Democratic Review*, no longer critical, claimed that the *Illuminated Bible* was "a credit to the city as well as indicative of a new era in the progress of publishing science," and *The Knickerbocker* cheered for what was "by all odds the most magnificent production of the publishing art in the United States." In *The Illustrated Book*, Frank Weitenkampf, the graphic arts historian, gives a twentieth-century accolade: "the Harper Bible . . . is the first richly illustrated book in the United States, the first attempt to produce a fine piece of book-making." Weitenkampf also quotes W. J. Linton, a noted nineteenth-century wood engraver and author, who knew "no other book like this, so good, so perfect in all it undertakes." By 1858 the *Illuminated Bible* had sold 25,000 copies at more than a half million dollars retail.

Verplanck's three-volume *Shakespeare*, published in 1847 after being delayed by fire, was almost as good. It was issued in three volumes (Histories, Comedies, and Tragedies) containing over 2,200

---

* Each number contained twenty-eight pages. The sheets were hand sewn before the cover was glued to the spine. The highly ornate front cover, printed in two colors, was standard for all issues, but beginning with No. 33, "Critical Notices" were carried on the back cover with a description of the project itself. From that number to the last one, the inside covers, heretofore blank, were used to advertise the two important libraries and miscellaneous current titles.

pages and over 1,400 engravings. It was priced at $18 in muslin, $20 in half calf extra, and $25 in morocco, gild edges. Using the editorial "we," W. Gilmore Simms nevertheless spoke for many when he wrote, "We may say with pride that the American additions and comments, from the pen of Verplanck, are of a sort to render the publication unique, and quite superior to any other." It was the first scholarly edition ever attempted in America and showed the gradual development of Shakespeare's genius. The text was accompanied by sensible and useful notes, including references to Shakespearean words still extant in America though no longer used in Britain. However, the Shakespeare suffered in comparison to the Bible, for Hewet was not quite so good an engraver as Adams, and Weir was not so excellent an artist as Chapman (although two of Weir's students, Whistler and Grant, are world famous). Chapman also made seventy-six drawings to illustrate the *Autobiography* of Benjamin Franklin, the man who inspired fifteen-year-old James Harper to become a printer. The brothers asked the Rev. Horatio Hastings Weld, of whom little is now known, to edit the work. It was first issued in eight numbers, and in book form in April, 1848, available in three bindings, including half calf.

Five additional "big name" American authors added nonfiction luster to the Harper output in 1846-49: J. Ross Browne, Donald G. Mitchell, William H. Prescott, Daniel Webster, and George Ticknor. Browne's *Etchings of a Whaling Cruise*, published in August, 1846, is read today by advanced students of American literature, since Melville so obviously depended upon it for his whale story. But it deserves a wider reading as an authentic and realistic account of men's adventures on distant seas in pursuit of excitement and profit. Reviewers were saying that it was almost as good a sea story as Dana's, a comment that pleased Browne, since he had written, "I am very confident the public know little or nothing of the detestable cruelties practiced on board our whalers, and to show these in their true colors is my main object." The *American Review* thought Browne's book superior to Dana's.* These two books, along with Melville's *Typee*, were, according to the *Weekly Mirror*, "three of the best books on nautical life which the language can boast of." In *The Raven and the Whale*, Perry Miller says that Duyckinck worked with Browne to help make his book a work of "unvarnished facts" (he also blue-penciled some profanity)

---

* But *Two Years Before the Mast* was then and destined to be the public's favorite. In 1847, according to the annual report of the New York City library, Dana and his book were second in popularity only to Miss Sedgwick and her output.

but Miller wrongly assumes that the book was published in Duyckinck's *American Library*. Perhaps Duyckinck pushed Browne too far
—over to Cliff Street—for it was a Harper, not a Wiley & Putnam
book.

The late Thomas B. Wells, shortly before he retired in 1931 as
editor of *Harper's Magazine*, commissioned an article (which he paid
for but did not publish), from T. R. Glover, when the Cambridge
historian put his idea for an article in Latin verse, and Wells responded
in like manner. Such erudition always impresses editors and may be the
reason that Donald G. Mitchell's letter to the brothers got attention in
March, 1847. He threw in a Greek quotation from Herodotus after he
had outlined a projected travel book, *Fragments of Travel* (published
as *Fresh Gleanings*). Moreover, he knew what he wanted and said so
succinctly—also impressively. "Leaning in style to the later French
Thomists, as Dumas and Hugo," he wrote, the book would have "an
eye to the peculiarities of Sterne." He also asked for—and received—a
royalty contract, which was signed in John's handwriting. *Fresh
Gleanings* was published under the pseudonym of Ik. Marvel. Shortly
after it was published, Mitchell returned to Paris and was there during
the Revolution. He wrote up his experiences, entitled his manuscript
The Battle Summer, and presumably took it to Cliff Street. If so it was
rejected, for his 1850 publisher was Baker & Scribner. According to
Duyckinck, Mitchell unfortunately imitated Carlyle's *History of the
French Revolution*, and Derby says the book was almost a total failure.
In 1850 Mitchell published two other books, one with Stringer and
Townsend, *The Lorgnette; or, Studies of the Town by an Opera Goer*,
and one with Baker & Scribner, *Reveries of a Bachelor; or a Book of
the Heart*. The latter book was a great success and made the Ik. Marvel
name famous.

The polished, debonair Mitchell was five years younger than the
rough, seafaring Browne; both of them belonged to an oncoming generation of writers. *Fresh Gleanings* was Mitchell's first book, published
about the same time as *The Conquest of Peru*, which William H.
Prescott thought might be his last. Prescott had written to the brothers
in December, 1846, to announce the completion of *Peru* and to say
that stereotype plates would be ready for shipment by April 1. The
first printing of *Conquest of Peru* crowded the block of Harper storehouses with 15,000 volumes of the two-volume work and reduced the
Harper bank balance by a hefty $7,500. Both author and publisher
were too sanguine regarding sales, even though they predicated the
likely demand for *Peru*—and the consequent size of the first printing—

on the excellent record of *Mexico:* 7,500 copies, in a total of five impressions. But *Peru* was not reprinted till 1849. Perhaps the usually cautious brothers did not think that the failure of *Miscellanies* (in one nine-month period copies returned from bookstores exceeded sales by nearly 250 copies) had darkened the bright light of Prescott's name. Or maybe they believed that another *Conquest* would restore its luster. One of the most difficult decisions a publisher makes is the size of the first printing of a new book about ready for press. To guess the likely number of copies the book trade and the book-buying public will ingest within one year, the publisher must consider such factors as the fame of the author, the success of previous books, if any, the best possible retail price—always and of necessity figured on size of printing and royalty percentages—the state of business generally, and of professional readers' opinions particularly. If business is good and readers' reports enthusiastic, the publisher may discount a previous dud and gear his sales, promotion, and advertising efforts to put over a relatively large first printing. Perhaps the brothers so reasoned when they printed 7,500 copies of *The Conquest of Peru.*

Daniel Webster, the most celebrated of nineteenth-century American orators, belonged like Prescott to a generation beginning to step aside. Yet Webster would not have called himself an author. What he created was verbal effects to move the minds and hearts of those within the range of his powerful voice. If he had been asked to arrange his words in a form to reach people's intellects through the narrow sense gate of the scanning eye, he would have been wise enough to know that considerable revision and editing were called for. For such work he had neither the time nor the inclination. Yet he did agree that what he had written as diplomatic papers, particularly while Secretary of State under Tyler, could well be put into a book "for the record." It would be more appropriate to have someone other than himself compile and edit it. A fellow Bay Stater, young George Ticknor Curtis, could do the job; he was himself a jurist with some experience as an author. He was also well placed, being a nephew of George Ticknor and married to Justice Story's daughter. The chief value of Webster's *Official Papers* is its record of Webster's diplomacy in effecting a settlement in 1842 of the disputed boundary line between Maine and Canada and of his great speech in the Senate in 1846 defending this diplomacy. Handsomely bound in black muslin, stamped in gold, the book discloses a new imprint die at the bottom of the spine; two volumes topped by a scroll, lamp, and pen, with a flowing ribbon at the bottom carrying the words "Harpers New York."

Handsome book that it was, and handsomely promoted, it did not induce Webster to publish his six-volume *Works* from Cliff Street. The brothers were disappointed when Edward Everett, who edited them, carried the manuscript, presumably with Webster's approval, to Little and Brown for 1851 publication. But George Ticknor Curtis was soon to come to Harper's again with a two-volume history of the Constitution of the United States. And George Ticknor was there himself in 1849, following his nephew and one of his closest friends, William H. Prescott.

Ticknor's *History of Spanish Literature* was perhaps the most important American work of literary criticism of its time. Ticknor's writing style was as direct and unpretentious as his scholarship was exact and exhaustive. His translations from the Spanish of selections of prose and poetry were made with accuracy and felicity. It was not only the first scholarly work ever attempted on Spanish books and authors but also a complete record of Spanish civilization, as Prescott pointed out in his review in the January, 1850, issue of the *North American Review*. Prescott's 25,000-word article probably set an all-time record for length of a book review. Since he had gone over the manuscript to suggest revisions to Ticknor or to rewrite portions himself, Prescott scarcely needed to read the printed volume.

To reflect on Ticknor's work today is to wonder why authors so often feel impelled to publish quickly. Perhaps a seminal work should always take root slowly and over a long period of time. Ticknor's three-volume work—over seventeen hundred pages—followed roughly the outline of courses he had given at Harvard before he resigned in 1835, to be succeeded by Longfellow. Ticknor then spent three years in further research in England and on the continent—it was his second trip—and, returning to Boston, gave ten years to writing and rewriting. To be sure, he had business interests to attend to—insurance and banking—but his *magnum opus* was his *History*.

He gave equal thought and attention to the production of his book. In the tradition of Sparks and Prescott, he supervised its design, composition, and plating at the University Press in Cambridge. As this job was nearing completion, he planned ahead for its publication in London and New York, and for translations that would soon appear in Spain, France, and Germany. Plate proofs were dispatched probably to Aspinwall and a contract negotiated with John Murray. Having notified the brothers of his desire to publish the American edition from Cliff Street, he sent them a contract on October 19, when the plates were ready for shipment. Wanting publication by Christmas (a new book is an author's best possible gift), he stipulated that the volumes should be issued between December 14 and 25. (The Harpers bettered their promise by getting Volume I out on the 12th and Volumes II and III on the 20th.) He preferred the Little and Brown edition of *Ferdinand and Isabella* to the Harper edition and so specified it for quality of paper and binding. He asked for a list price of $6 for the work, a wholesale price of $4.80 (restricting booksellers to a 20 percent discount) and a royalty of $1.50 a copy on a guaranteed sale of 3,500 copies. He asked for payment of the $5,250 thus due him in three months or on publication less three months' interest. The brothers were to have rights for one year, to indemnify him for any damage to or loss of plates, and to give him 25 copies free. Knowing something of the costs of printing, paper, and binding, Ticknor also stipulated that he might purchase copies for personal use at $2 the set without royalty. A pretty stiff contract. The brothers had met a man of their own metal. They not only agreed promptly but set about at once to give the work top priority. They decided to promote the work as a quality production and bound quantities in sheepskin and half calf as well as cloth. They were confident they could satisfy Ticknor and make a profit for themselves because business was definitely improving.

Weather conditions in New York were observed with no greater diligence on Governors Island than business conditions were observed on Cliff Street. This willingness to be influenced by the business barometer had both good and bad effects. Obviously it helped the brothers to survive when less alert competitors collapsed. On the other hand it gave them the reputation of vacillation, of mercurial ups and downs, "famous for talking away off," in Dana, Sr.'s, phrase. Those who did not know the business sensitivity of the brothers would criticize them for parsimony over *Two Years Before the Mast* and congratulate them for prodigality over the *Illuminated Bible*. But the brothers did not exhibit either trait for the sake of being capricious. If you sailed a boat, you trimmed sail in rough weather and you let out sail before a good wind. Their correspondence with Prescott in the late summer of 1849 shows how the Cliff Street barometer was being read:

> August 2 -"business of every kind is very much depressed"
> September 15 -"business is just beginning to look up"
> October 11 -"business is good"

This bettering of business conditions in that particular autumn was to have profound effects on their enterprise. It not only led to a more confident approach to new book publication, as indicated in their eagerness to push ahead on Ticknor's *History*, but it also crystallized their decision—for long months a maybe-yes and maybe-no—to establish a new monthly miscellany. Such a magazine could not have been started in 1849 since business in 1848 had been only moderately good, the country not yet recovered from the doldrums of the Mexican War.

However, an upward trend of business began after the election of Zachary Taylor in November, as Ralph Waldo Emerson reported in a letter to Dr. John Carlyle. On December 12, 1848, he wrote, "Since the election [of Taylor] our people are in better spirits, and trade and, at last, booktrade will revive, it is believed." Emerson was reporting a reading of the Harper barometer to Dr. Carlyle, whose translation of Dante's *Inferno* had for several months been under consideration.

In the summer of 1848 Emerson had taken the proofs of *Inferno* to the Old Corner Book Store in Boston to interest Ticknor, who promptly said No and recommended Harper's. Whereupon Emerson posted the proofs to his brother William, on Staten Island, who did not mind doing literary chores for the younger and more famous Ralph Waldo. Would William try to interest the brothers? William dutifully took the proofs to Cliff Street. Saunders wrote on September 7 to reject the book but he was promptly overruled by Fletcher, who possibly saw his opportunity to get on better terms with the sage of Concord. The brothers had recently purchased from Putnam the plates of three works of Thomas Carlyle. The two-volume *History of the French Revolution* had been issued in August; *Letters and Speeches of Oliver Cromwell* was due to be ready in October, with *Past and Present*, a book of essays, to follow in November. Fletcher knew that Emerson had first published Carlyle in America, underwriting books which London publishers had turned down. Fletcher probably reasoned that if they should take on the book of Carlyle's brother, John, then Emerson could hardly criticize them for putting the Putnam plates on their Cliff Street presses. On the day following Saunders's letter, Fletcher wrote to William Emerson, addressing him "Dear Judge."

I think it is likely that we might reprint Dr. Carlyle's "Dante," and get back our investment, provided we were not required to give anything more than a few presentation copies for the translation—And we would probably venture upon it, if informed that it would be agreeable to your Brother and the Doctor for us to do so. Of this, you can advise us at your leisure. At the same time, if there is any probability of your getting it republished by any other House, and realizing from it something, in addition to "glory," or "reputation," for the Doctor, we should be better pleased.

Our Reader has been out of the City ever since you left the sheets with us, and has not yet returned. We are therefore still without his advice in the premises. But taking it for granted, that the Doctor has done himself and his author all possible justice, still the abundance and cheapness of the old edition would necessarily prevent the enterprise from proving very profitable.

Weeks passed without further word from Fletcher and the Indian summer in Concord found Emerson restive rather than serene. He was worried that some pirate might already be setting the book, but William reassured him on October 27 that Fletcher was only waiting for final proofs of the front matter and that he had announced their intention to publish in time so that no other publisher would interfere. But in his next letter William referred to some misunderstanding and wondered whether he should take the Carlyle to Appleton's. Emerson replied that Wiley & Putnam had acted the same way over Thomas Carlyle's *Cromwell* two years earlier and he was ashamed to be forced to tell the Carlyles what was happening. "I shall be wiser, I am sorry to say it, in the future." But Saunders wrote in late November giving reassurances and Fletcher was saved the embarrassment of Emerson's apology for American publishers being sent to London. In fact, Fletcher may have been in London himself that winter. If so, his absence and the likely separation of Saunders from the firm at that time explained why Emerson did not hear from Cliff Street for two months after the December news that the book trade was reviving. In the meantime he sent down a copy of the English edition.

By March, 1849, Emerson's patience was nearly exhausted. On the 13th he wrote from Concord to his brother William, "If you should meet this 'Fletcher' again, I wish you would tell him that if he has never printed, & only destroyed my copy (which he was to take special care of), I will forgive [him] if he will only own it at once and let me go with the book to Somebody who prints with ink instead of air." The book finally got printed with Fletcher's ink and was published on June 21. Ten years later, however, it was to be out of print; the 1859 catalogue carried instead four other titles of Thomas Carlyle, including the first two volumes of a projected four-volume life of *Frederick the Great*. Writing of this edition's being published by "our obtuse reprobates of Cliff Street," Emerson was probably annoyed because

Fletcher was paying £250 to Chapman & Hall of London for first proofs and not paying royalty directly to his friend, the author. The brothers had ceased using the Cliff Street address even before the 1853 fire, but no matter; Emerson had from the beginning of his writing career found publishers suspect, paying too little to authors, giving too large discounts to booksellers, and on the whole a "vanity & vexation."

Several important New England authors—but not Ralph Waldo Emerson—were added to the Harper list by the purchase of some thirty copyrights formerly published by the defunct firm of Marsh, Capen, Lyon & Webb. Chief among these in terms of prestige was Justice Joseph Story's famous work familiarly known as *Story on the Constitution*. It was an abridgment of a larger work first issued by Hilliard, Gray & Co. in 1833. Long a member of the United States Supreme Court and an intimate friend of Chief Justice Marshall, Story was also famed as the father of the Harvard Law School. Other works taken over from the defunct Boston firm included Washington Irving's *Life of Columbus*, Paley's *Natural Theology*, Francis Lieber's *Great Events*, and Alonzo Potter's *Principles of Science*. Also *Letters on Astronomy* by Professor Denison Olmsted of Yale, *The Useful Arts* by Dr. Jacob Bigelow of Harvard, and *The Importance of Practical Education* by Edward Everett, then president of Harvard. Included in the purchase were several phrenological works, in great demand at that time, and *The Farmer's Companion* by Jesse Buel, whose book *The Farmer's Instructor* had been issued from Cliff Street in 1839. Several names on juvenile books came home again, including Miss Beecher, Mrs. Embury, Mrs. Hale, Mrs. Phelps, and Dr. John Aikin. (Dr. Aikin's books helped make little financiers out of boys and girls with the *Juvenile Budget Opened* and the same *Reopened*.)

All of these titles except the phrenological works had been selected by Horace Mann for the *Massachusetts School Library* and were so grouped in subsequent Harper catalogues. There had been some give and take between this library and the *School District Library* so the brothers well knew what they were buying. Being series-minded they added another one in 1847, the somewhat abortive *Fireside Library*, "expressly adapted to the domestic circle, Sabbath schools, etc." Its interest lies today in the conscientious effort made to issue quality books by royalty authors at a low price. For 45 cents they offered 192-page books (on the average) illustrated with engravings, and bound in cloth with gilt edges. Four of the eight titles were by Dr. Joseph Alden, professor of English at Williams College. His first, *Alice*

Gordon, contained ten engravings; his second, *Lawyer's Daughter*, contained eight, certainly by Hewet; his last two, *Young Schoolmistress* and *The Dying Robin*, carried no illustrations. Two or three English reprints were added, and fifteen months after its beginning the series was adjourned *sine die*.

In 1847 Henry Howe, an important figure in the annals of nineteenth-century American publishing, brought the plates of his book, *Memoirs of the Most Eminent American Mechanics*, to Cliff Street, hoping for a wider circulation than a small New York publisher, named Blake, had been able to obtain. "Published by the Harpers [it] went through many editions," Howe said later. His life was largely devoted to subscription bookselling, which he learned in the early forties while compiling and issuing *Historical Collections* in volumes by states—Connecticut, New York, New Jersey, and Virginia. In 1847 he settled in Ohio and during the next thirty years developed one of the country's largest enterprises in selling books from door to door and farmhouse to farmhouse. Once Howe advertised, "Twenty-thousand agents wanted." He was respected by his agents and honored by the unnumbered thousands who placed his books alongside their family Bibles.

Among their plate and copyright acquisitions, probably at a trade book auction, was *The American Poulterer's Companion* by Caleb N. Bement, an early "gentleman" farmer. In 1837 he had purchased "Three Wells Farm" near Albany and devoted his considerable energy and ingenuity to agricultural theory and practice. It soon became a showplace. Bement invented and manufactured a corn cultivator and a turnip drill; he also developed blooded stock by importing and breeding cattle, sheep, hogs, and poultry. In 1844 he leased the American Hotel in Albany, where his farm-supplied kitchen and dining room became famous among gourmets. His illustrated *Poulterer's Companion* was the most complete and practical manual available. In 1856 it was to appear in a revised and enlarged edition with 120 illustrations, 16 in color. This reissue of Bement's and other older books, including the Boston titles, were treated as new books. They were vigorously promoted to the trade, and publicity notes and review copies were mailed to newspapers and magazines.

Bement was not a big-name author but he is typical of the literary producer who turns out bread-and-butter titles that stave off hunger pangs for publishers and booksellers. Such sturdy authors do not get listed in Jacob Blanck's magnificent series, *Bibliography of American Literature,* but they do write the "how to" books that often subsidize the creative stars such as are being listed in those volumes. Another Harper "staple" book was Joseph Blunt's *The Shipmaster's Assistant,* which gave merchant owners and masters of ships all they needed to know about marine administration. Its eighty-word subtitle listed nearly forty subjects, from Averages (marine losses) through Quarantine Laws to Weights and Measures. It went into a new edition three years later. For still another such book, *Dyeing and Calico-printing,* the author-editor, Clinton Gilroy, supplied the engravings and stereotypes. The brothers reimbursed Gilroy with $2,000, which they charged to the first printing of 2,000 copies. Thereafter they paid a royalty of 50 cents a copy, slightly less than 15 percent. Demarest remembered that Gilroy professed a great friendship for him, one time borrowing $15 which he neglected to repay.

The all-time best seller of Harper staple books was Haswell's *Engineers' and Mechanics' Pocket-book.* By 1848 it had proved its worth, celebrating its fourth birthday by going into a revised edition. It was to bring pride and profits to Charles H. Haswell and to Fletcher, who had known him since they were young volunteer firemen on the engine *Lafayette.* By 1867 *Haswell's Engineering,* as it was called, would be in its twenty-eighth edition, revised and enlarged to 663 pages, more than twice its birth weight and length. Even though Haswell lived to be nearly a hundred years old, his book was to outlast him, not dropping out of the Harper catalogue till 1935. According to a 1912 *Prospectus* for the sale of Harper mortgage bonds, written by Colonel George Harvey, *Haswell's Engineering* had gone through 73 editions and grown in length to 1,100 pages. For a book that established a record in catalogue longevity, it is amusing to note that, in contracting for it in 1843, the brothers were willing that Haswell should be free after three years to crate up his stereotypes and go elsewhere. Because he owned the plates he received a 20 per cent royalty, or 25 cents a copy. By 1854 he would be paying only for alterations and additions; thus he took 5 cents less per copy. Now he was willing to trust his publishers for six years. By 1867 he was receiving a 15 percent royalty and the brothers had publishing rights for the life of the copyright.

After the war with Mexico was won in 1847, the brothers began looking for likely authors of war books, always a post-bellum publishing bonanza. Henry J. Raymond spotted one in Burlington, Vermont. He wrote to Saunders that he was somewhat out of line in reporting on a manuscript that had not been officially submitted to 82 Cliff Street; nevertheless he could recommend it highly: "I have no doubt that the book would make a decided hit, without interfering at all with your Boston friend, should he accept your offer or with Kendall's book should he write one. . . ." The book was *Campaign Sketches of the War with Mexico* by Captain W. S. Henry, later made a brevet major for "gallant conduct at Monterey, Mexico." The 331-page book sold for $1 and was ready before Christmas. The "Boston friend" to whom Raymond referred may have been Captain James H. Carleton, a hero of Buena Vista. Carleton's book, which told of the army of occupation as well as of the battle, was published in August, 1848. The brothers apparently printed a first edition of 2,000 copies.

The most satisfactory book on the war for its time did not come till a year later, when Major R. S. Ripley contracted for his two-volume *War with Mexico*. Published on December 8, 1849, this work of 1,164 pages embellished with 14 maps and plans of battles gave American armchair warriors all they needed to know about what later catalogues listed as "Ripley's War with Mexico." If he also had a war with his publishers before signing up, the major won pretty good terms: volumes of the quality of Prescott's *Mexico*, and because he paid for the stereotype plates, a royalty of 70 cents, 17½ percent on the cloth price of $4. To meet the demand for more expensive bindings, the work was available also in sheep and half calf.

On February 2, 1848, the treaty of Guadalupe Hidalgo settled matters between Mexico and the United States. The southwestern boundary of Texas was established at the Rio Grande River, and the New Mexico and California territories were purchased for a total of eighteen and a quarter million dollars. Only a few days before the treaty was signed, gold had been discovered at Sutter's Mill in California and Americans soon began getting their money back. Despite efforts to keep the discovery a secret, word soon got out and by February, 1849, Americans thirsty for fortune and adventure could read in a Harper book "recent and authentic information on . . . the gold mines of California, and other valuable matter of interest to the emigrant." For some reason the author, J. Quinn Thornton, gave it the perfunctory title of *Oregon and California in 1848*—perhaps neither author nor publisher realized what a gold mine they had right on Cliff Street. It would be pleasant to note that the book (with its two-color, 18-by-20½-inch, folded and tipped-in map) spark-plugged the rush for gold, with forty-niners begging, borrowing, or stealing copies to take with them, but historians agree that newspaper stories, government documents, letters, and oral reports largely stimulated what was the most wonderful, colorful, and adventurous westward movement in the history of the Republic.

Four other Harper books were being read and reviewed because of the new excitement westward, two by a young Englishman named George Ruxton. His *Adventures in Mexico and the Rocky Mountains* came out in February, 1848, followed by *Life in the Far West*, in June, 1849. The third, *Los Gringos*, was written by thirty-year-old Navy Lieutenant Henry A. Wise, recently returned from the Mexican War and married to Harvard President Everett's daughter. "Los Gringos" was the epithet used by natives in Mexico and California to describe those of Anglo-Saxon descent. It meant "Greenhorn," a term hardly applicable to the handsome, gay, and gallant officer who wrote of experiences aship and ashore, of hunting deer and being hunted by grizzly bears, of shooting brigands, of dancing fandangos, of swimming with Sandwich Island girls. The fourth "true Western" of this period, and the only one turned out by a professional writer, was *Old Hicks the Guide* by Charles W. Webber, published in April, 1847. At that time Webber was contributing articles to the *Literary World*, having completed two years as editor of the *American Review*. *Old Hicks* was an account of Webber's adventures during the late thirties on the troubled frontier of Texas. His narrative style was rapid and impulsive, reflecting the stirring action he described.

Not the least among newspaper editors who were creating and sustaining interest in California was Horace ("Go West, young man") Greeley. He was often at Cliff Street during this period, once with his former associate Henry J. Raymond to discuss terms with the brothers for their joint work, a small book called *Association Discussed*. It amicably presented the economic and political differences between them, Greeley being the more liberal of the two. Greeley also talked the brothers into publishing a work to benefit a Kentucky friend. It was entitled *The Life and Writings of Cassius M. Clay*. Greeley's friend was a leading figure in Kentucky politics and journalism. He had been a captain in the Mexican War and helped get his general, Zachary Taylor, elected President.

While these two books are of some interest as journalistic Americana, the works by Thornton, Ruxton, Wise, and Webber bring better prices today at rare book auctions. Also in demand by collectors is a somewhat different book, *The Trees of America*, by Daniel Jay Browne. A civil engineer, Browne spent long months in Maine surveying wide acres of virgin forest, trudging unrecorded miles among tall, first-growth timber, and sharing the rough, hazardous life of the lumberjacks. Back home in Brooklyn in 1844 Browne began writing his book, which impressed the brothers, who signed him up on a half-profits contract. He thought he could complete his writing, supervise the work of the engravers, and produce the stereotypes in two years. This he did, and the brothers liked him and his workmanship so much that they gave him $30 for an editorial chore that would take a few days' time—the preparation of copy for an *Almanac for 1847* to be printed along with their 1846 book catalogue. *The Trees of America* made a volume of 553 pages, including 346 separate engravings, and was handsomely printed on the same quality of paper as used in the *Illuminated Bible*. American trees were described both scientifically and popularly, with the text also discussing trees in relation to geography and history, soil and situation, propagation and culture, accidents and diseases, properties and uses. Browne wrote with a literary grace that engineers can rarely boast and revealed both his scientific training and aesthetic interests. The book is also important bibliographically since it is an early example of publishers' use of several colors and patterns of cloth in the same edition of a book. Apparently the variations made possible a more interesting display on booksellers' tables and gave a choice to buyers who fancied certain colors more than others. One collector has first-edition copies of the *The Trees of America* bound in five different colors of cloth.

These were some of the more interesting and important books being published from 82 Cliff Street during the closing years of the decade. America was expanding rapidly and American authors were depicting its political, social, economic, aesthetic and religious life in readable books. Many of them were big-name authors; all of them left a record of how men and women reacted to the exhilarating life of the Republic, a country growing up with the speed and self-consciousness of an adolescent boy. Nearly every interest of literate Americans could be satisfied as they browsed in stores and picked up new books carrying the Harper imprint.

CHAPTER XV

Books from Overseas and Textbooks

1846–1849

IN DECEMBER, 1846, Fletcher and Jane sailed for Europe, Dr. Wainwright sending his regrets later that he had not known of their departure so that he could have seen them off. They planned first to take a holiday; it was high time, the other brothers had said, that Fletcher get away for a needed rest. There would also be leisure for sightseeing on the continent, places to visit that James and Maria had been enthusiastic about. Places where John and Tammisin had stayed, they having been over a few months earlier on account of John's health. By late spring Fletcher was in London calling on publishers, a bit conscience-stricken for having been out of touch with business for so long. There were negotiations to complete that had been initiated by correspondence, such as the deal for books in the Bohn library. The book business was languishing in London and Bohn was eager for cash in exchange for stereotype plates. Some beautiful editions of classical works were being issued, such as a twelve-hundred-page *Arabian Nights*, with engravings by Harvey, whose work was highly praised. Fletcher arranged to take some of these plates back to New York with him; already he could see it issued in numbers and then published in two or three volumes—in muslin for sale to schools and libraries and in

Turkey morocco for gift use. Harvey had also made the drawings for a two-volume edition of Milton's poetical works, which should do even better. And there were rich-looking single volumes of Goldsmith's *Poems* and Thomson's *Seasons* with designs and engravings by Cope, Creswick, Horsley, Redgrave, and Taylor, famous members of the Etching Club. Plates of these books could reach New York in time for books to be produced well before Christmas. Fletcher thought that one of the prettiest books he had ever seen was this edition of *Seasons* by James Thomson, the early eighteenth-century poet who was the precursor of Cowper and Wordsworth.

There were other books to be negotiated for. Fletcher was not a man to wrangle over prices. He had a good instinct for values and would quickly say Yes to an offer that seemed reasonable and as quickly say No if it seemed high. If he really wanted the book, he sometimes found that when he went back, perhaps to say goodbye before sailing, the price for sheets was down to a reasonable figure. Often he could offer a *quid pro quo*. The popular Dr. Barnes would soon have his *Notes* on the General Epistles ready; Fletcher promised that it would be first published in England, hopefully to obtain copyright and to give Longmans a head start on pirates. He sold early proofs of the new edition of Webster's *Dictionary*, concerned that their late arrival might be harmful. He found the Messrs. Longman eager purchasers of sheets of Anthon's *Xenophon*, paying £25, and thus disposed to offer him a good book in return. The eight titles purchased that spring—first proofs, not stereotypes—totaled £100, averaging $60 apiece.

Did Fletcher also call on some of Harper's best authors—say James and Bulwer? (It was now Bulwer-Lytton, the surname added at the recent inheritance of family property on his mother's death.) If such calls were made, it is likely that they were perfunctory and concerned with business. Because of their temperance principles and their compunctions about the theatre, Fletcher and Jane would not have been easy to entertain. Wainwright had written to introduce them to some of his friends and these may have included the Anglican clergyman Charles C. Southey, son of the late Robert Southey. The Rev. Mr. Southey had just finished working over his father's *Life of John Wesley*. Fletcher would have asked him whether he had minded their getting Dr. Daniel Curry, an American authority on Wesley and pastor of the Methodist church near the Yale campus, to add some material. By this means they could claim American copyright for the book that was Coleridge's "favorite among favorite books." Fletcher would also have asked Southey if there was to be a biography of his father—it would sell in America—and the reply would have been Yes, he was already working through his father's correspondence.

Lemuel Bangs and his wife were also in London, and there were sightseeing trips to take together around London and a weekend down at Bath to hear the famous Dr. William Jay preach; three volumes of Jay's works had been published from Cliff Street three years earlier. Fletcher also told Lemuel that they had arranged with Sampson Low, well spoken of around London as a publisher, to act as their British representative. He would be glad to introduce Lemuel if he wanted representation too. Lemuel took him up on that, for he had not been able to get enough consignments off to New York for auctioning at the August Trade Sales and such an arrangement would be good insurance for the future. The Bangs and Harper couples arranged to return to New York together on the S.S. *Washington*, sailing July 10.*

There had been a family reunion in London a few weeks earlier, with young Joe coming over to spend a year abroad. Fletcher had said that traveling around Europe would be a good way for his elder son, just past twenty, to top off his formal schooling. Before sailing for New York, Fletcher took time to arrange for a young man with a knowledge of languages to accompany Joe as his tutor. But the tutor was not employed for long. Soon after their return to New York, Fletcher and Jane were receiving letters from Joe telling more about an attractive young lady he had met than of his tutor and educative travels around England. One letter told of his engagement to Ellen Urling Smith, and soon Fletcher and Jane could say that by Joe's marriage they now claimed a daughter.†

Back in New York that summer of 1847, Fletcher found William Demarest especially interested in the books he had arranged for in London. As head bookkeeper, Demarest now was the one to whom people came to ask for information about stock and news of forthcom-

---

* Two years later Mr. and Mrs. Lemuel Bangs named a newly born son Fletcher Harper Bangs; he was to be remembered in Fletcher's will with a bequest of $500. Six others outside the immediate Harper family—including two sons of employees—received similar amounts because they perpetuated the Fletcher Harper name. Lemuel Bangs was by nineteen years the senior of his brother, Francis Nathan Bangs, who was made a member of the New York Bar in 1850, and soon began doing legal work for the brothers. He was a close friend of the second generation Harpers, and his son, John Kendrick Bangs, was identified with Harper periodicals and wrote books of humor and verse for the Harper firm in the 1890's.

† The following year their first grandchild, Urling Harper, was born and Jane began wearing a lace cap, insisting that she should look like a grandmother. Thereafter Fletcher brought her a new one from Europe on each of his many trips, some of them taken on the spur of the moment.

ing books. By October, he was making memoranda of publication dates; these memoranda were to be of invaluable help to him years later when compiling his *Catalogue*. His memoranda of English fiction reprints were soon piling up. During 1846, twenty-four titles had been added to the *Library of Select Novels*, bringing it to a total of ninety-one. Demarest was to list additional titles for the next three years in the descending order of eighteen, sixteen, and eleven; half of the *L.S.N.* titles for 1848 were by G. P. R. James. Possibly the loyal Demarest wondered if they weren't overdoing the popular James. Mrs. Catherine Gore was even more prolific than James, but of her two hundred volumes the brothers bought only thirteen, the last three being added to the *L.S.N.* in 1846. Fredrika Bremer and her translator, Mary Howitt, were more popular with American women readers.

In her autobiography, Mrs. Howitt recalled that after her translation of the first Bremer novel, *The Neighbors*, she could not find a London publisher who would undertake it. She and her husband, William, printed it and other Bremer novels at their own risk, "when such became the rage for them that our translations were seized by a [London] publisher, altered, and reissued as new ones. The men in our printer's office were bribed from America, and in one instance pirated sheets appeared before those we ourselves sent over. Cheap editions ran like wildfire through the United States, and the boys who hawked them in the streets might be seen deep in *The Neighbors, The Home,* and *The H—— Family*." In 1848 and 1849 the last of the *L.S.N.* editions of Miss Bremer's novels came out, *Brothers and Sisters* and *The Midnight Sun*. With two of Mrs. Howitt's own novels already in their series of cheap reprints, the brothers had thus staked their claim to her works when they bought first proofs of her three new juveniles, *Tales of Natural History, Tales in Prose,* and *Tales in Verse*. What they paid in 1847 is not known, but in 1859 her two-volume *Popular History of the United States* would cost them £200. Eighteen forty-seven was a "Howitt year" on Cliff Street, for the brothers also issued their fourth title by William Howitt, *Homes and Haunts of the Most Eminent British Poets*. The work came out in two fat volumes with forty-two illustrations for which they engaged Hewet to make the engravings.

Through 1853 the Harper catalogues were to group separately the works of six novelists—all of them, with the exception of Miss Bremer, English novelists. The select five were the earlier Miss Edgeworth and Mrs. Sherwood, the everlasting James and Bulwer-Lytton and the emergent Mrs. Anne Marsh. To be sure the brothers had published

Mrs. Marsh in the thirties, but in 1845 they began in earnest, reissuing an older title after a new cheap one took hold. In the following eight years, through 1853, they were to publish eleven Marsh novels, most of them costing £15 for the proof sheets, and all assigned to the *L.S.N.* except the 1848 issue of *Angela* (paper at 75 cents and cloth at 90 cents).

Also appearing on the Harper list, magnificently so, was William Makepeace Thackeray. In 1848 *Vanity Fair* made its bow to American readers, Volume I on July 29 and Volume II on August 19. For proofs of this author-illustrated work, they probably paid £100 (a later Thackeray price). Certainly more than the average of £10 for an *L.S.N.* title.* Later a one-volume edition came out, selling in paper for $1 and in cloth for $1.25. *The Knickerbocker* devoted six pages to *Vanity Fair*, Clark saying that it was Thackeray's best book yet. He also apologized for giving the book only six pages—no more effective (he said) in showing the quality of the book than the few bricks the Irishman brought over to show the superiority of the architecture of Dublin. *Vanity Fair* was followed in December by *The Great Hoggarty Diamond* (an *L.S.N.* item), which became the first of twenty Thackeray works the brothers were to issue as books, some of them after serialization in their *Monthly* or *Weekly*.

Except for Thackeray, the year of 1848 was clearly the year of the English Bells, insofar as Cliff Street fiction reprints were concerned. The brothers published three of them: Acton, Currer, and Ellis. Acton Bell, whose real name was Anne Brontë, wrote *The Tenant of Wildfell Hall*. Currer Bell, whose real name was Charlotte Brontë, wrote *Jane Eyre, an Autobiography*, and Ellis Bell, whose real name was Emily Brontë, wrote *Wuthering Heights*. All of the Brontë novels were turned down by several British publishers before *Jane Eyre* was accepted by Smith, Elder & Company of Cornhill and published in October, 1847. It was immediately acclaimed by reviewers, and Sampson Low quickly dispatched an early copy to Cliff Street. Another copy was sent to Wilkins, Carter & Co. of Boston; it seems likely that this may have come from the British publisher, being issued in what the *Literary World* in April was to call a "handsome and convenient edition." Both the Boston and New York printings appeared in January. The Harper *L.S.N.* volume, priced at 25 cents, was pub-

---

* This figure is based on known payments made between 1846 and 1850 for first proofs of Mrs. Gore's novels. An old record book, *Priority List*, gives payments for first proofs between 1846 and the late 1890's. It was probably begun after the 1853 fire since the earlier records are incomplete. If as much as £50 was paid, as in the case of Bulwer's *The Caxtons* and Charlotte Brontë's *Shirley*, the books were placed (in paper) in the *L.S.N.* but priced at 37½ cents instead of the usual 25 cents.

lished on the 4th and reviewed by the *Literary World* on the 29th, Duyckinck saying that it would "create a deeper interest and seize more strongly on the hearts of the reading public than any work of fiction that has appeared since Miss Bremer's *The Neighbors.*"

Wuthering Heights and *The Tenant of Wildfell Hall* were published in London in December by T. C. Newby, who claimed that they were by the author of *Jane Eyre*. Fletcher may have negotiated for American "rights" directly, for he was in London in the latter part of the month. If so, he believed what Newby claimed, and *Wuthering Heights* came out on April 21 with title-page credit to the author of *Jane Eyre*. That he paid at least £50 for the book (or proofs) is indicated by the high retail price of *Wuthering Heights*, 75 cents in cloth and 50 cents in paper. In reviewing *Wuthering Heights*, Duyckinck pointed out that it was being advertised in England as written by *Ellis* Bell. By what authority did the American publisher claim it to be written by the author of *Jane Eyre*, who was named Currer Bell?

The Boston firm apparently protested to Smith, Elder & Company, since they had been promised sheets of the next Currer Bell book. Whereupon Smith, Elder & Company wrote to their pseudonymous author complaining of the problem they faced over mixed identities. "The very day I received Smith & Elder's letter," Charlotte Brontë wrote later, "Anne and I packed up a small box . . . and whirled up by night train to London with the view of proving our separate identities to Smith and Elder and confronting Newby with his *lie.* . . ."

Thus by early summer at least two British publishers knew the identity of the three Brontë sisters. *The Tenant of Wildfell Hall* came out from Cliff Street on July 28 as written by Acton Bell. All three novels were reviewed in the October, 1848, issue of the *North American Review*, with *Jane Eyre* credited to the Boston firm. "Not many months since," the reviewer wrote, "the New England states were visited by a distressing mental epidemic, passing under the name of 'Jane Eyre fever,' which defied all the usual nostrums of the established doctors of criticism. . . . The book which caused the distemper would probably have been inoffensive, had not the same sly manufacturers of mischief hinted that it was a book which no respectable man should bring into his family circle. Of course, every family soon had a copy of it, and one edition after another found eager purchasers. . . . The whole firm of Bell and Co. seems to have a sense of the depravity of human nature peculiarly their own."* Charlotte Brontë saw the

---

* James Fields, then in charge of the Old Corner Book Store, Boston, returned copies of *Wuthering Heights* to Cliff Street saying that customers would not keep the book in their homes because of its profanity.

review and was both amused and perturbed by it. The same thing was being said at home.

The Harpers were the sole American publisher of *Shirley*, Charlotte Brontë's next novel. It came out on November 22, 1849, in 12mo size and cloth binding to match her sisters' books, and in the *L.S.N.* format to match *Jane Eyre*, which was also reissued that same day in the smaller-sized cloth edition. It takes a lot of juggling of sizes and retail prices when payments for sheets and manufacturing costs must be balanced against what the public will pay for a title. It always makes the tightrope act more interesting when books of permanent worth, such as *Vanity Fair*, *Wuthering Heights*, and *Jane Eyre*, are being balanced.

Forgotten now, the name of Grace Aguilar was one to please mid-century booksellers' hearts and purses as much as Charlotte Brontë's. Like the Brontë sisters', Miss Aguilar's short life permitted but a few books to be written. Her American fame as a best-selling author came after her death in 1847 at the age of thirty-one; however, she had received a testimonial from an organization known as "The Women of Israel," which was fame enough. Her books were religious novels. *Home Influence: A Tale for Mothers and Daughters* came out in 1848. Paying £10 for sheets, the brothers issued the 419-page book for 75 cents in paper and 90 cents in cloth binding. This book had a sequel entitled *The Mother's Recompense*, but, as often happens, the author's second book did not begin to approach the success of the first one.

Important books of nonfiction from abroad included *The Statesmen of the Commonwealth of England* by John Forster, famous later as the biographer of Dickens. Also a *Pictorial History of England*, which came out in 44 numbers during two years, after which it was published in March, 1848, as a four-volume royal-octavo work of 2,731 pages and 1,259 engravings. It was edited by George L. Craik, an English man of letters who also wrote much of the text. The plates for this massive work cost $4,375, a sufficiently high figure to discourage pirating.

But the brothers ran into plenty of mutineers the next year when they issued the first two volumes of T. B. Macaulay's famous *History of England from the Accession of James II*. They had hoped for fair play by paying Longmans (early in 1848) £200 for first proofs and by announcing the book (according to protocol) well ahead of time. But early proofs did not give the brothers much advantage. The London two-volume edition was published November 23, 1848, and the best the brothers could do was to get their volumes out on January 6 and

February 7, 1849. Anticipating trouble, they issued a cheap 12mo edition in cloth for 40 cents simultaneously with the octavo "library" edition, priced at 75 cents. And trouble there was—plenty of it. The pirates sailed in eager for booty—at least four of them eventually—two from Cincinnati, one from Boston and one from Philadelphia. There was an immediate counterattack from Cliff Street, another cheap edition printed to match the octavo size of Alison's *Europe*. The volumes were rushed through composing room, pressroom, and bindery by mid-March, and thence, thinly clad in paper covers, to booksellers, to retail for 25 cents a copy. E. H. Butler of Philadelphia attempted to undersell by offering two volumes in one at 30 cents (how much lower could you go?). The competition did not damage the brothers, for in another month they were writing Macaulay, "We beg you to accept herewith a copy of our cheap edition of your work. There have been three other editions published by different houses, and another is now in preparation; so there will be six different editions in the market. We have already sold over forty thousand copies, and we presume that over sixty thousand copies have been disposed of. Probably within three months of this time, the sale will amount to two hundred thousand copies. No work, of any kind, has ever so completely taken our whole country by storm." One thing that helped to sell the *History* was the controversy raised in American newspapers as to whether the Messrs. Harper were justified in altering Macaulay's spelling to conform to Webster's *Dictionary*. The issue is still debatable.

The Harper "Library Edition" was handsomely bound in half calf as well as in the customary muslin and sheep for quality books. All three bindings were stamped on the spine in real gold and boasted marbled edges and end papers.* While American readers were storming book stores by the tens of thousands, selecting their editions of Macaulay for reasons of taste or of purse, English readers were going more sedately to purchase their thousands. Longmans did issue a second printing at the end of 1848, with two more following in 1849, and

---

* The "marbling" process used for dressing up end papers was a forerunner of offset printing. Colors were separately mixed with water and kept in shallow paint pots, each of which was equipped with a brush of stubbly bristles. These mutually repellent colors—perhaps six or more—were then sprinkled over the surface of a gummy liquid contained in a shallow tank until a solid pattern of distinct and intermixed colors resulted. Over this surface a sheet of paper was carefully placed and then withdrawn. The "printed" sheet, the colors immediately fixed, was hung up to dry and later burnished. Before the "printing," a pattern of color was often made by drawing a copper comb across the surface, or the operator would create a pleasing "wave" pattern by gently and dexterously causing ripples across the surface of the liquid as he laid down the sheet. Marbled edges of sewn sheets were similarly produced.

while the size of these printings is not known the three subsequent ones (1850-53) were of two thousand copies each. Such success for Macaulay in America left Prescott somewhat bitter. On April 2, 1849, he wrote the brothers in reply to their request for his choice of excerpts of reviews of his works to be used in advertising. He complied and added a closing thrust, "But who will give two dollars a volume for Prescott, when they can buy Macaulay for seventy-five cents? This was a hard cut for us all."

During this period, the brothers also published the works of a Frenchman, Alphonse de Lamartine, who was making history as well as writing it. The *History of the Girondists*, his most important work, came out in three volumes, the last two published in January and May, 1848. Often the success of a book is due to perfect timing; by luck or foresight a first edition comes out while news events focus the spotlight on an author or his writing. Luck was with the brothers when the last two volumes of the *Girondists* came off press. Newspapers were then carrying stories of the Revolution of February, 1848, the abdication of the elderly King Louis Philippe, and the proclamation of the Republic by Lamartine himself, as head of the dominant faction in the Chamber of Deputies. Stories of Louis Philippe's residence in America (1796-1800) were recalled, and Lamartine's position and influence discussed. Suddenly the author was front-page news, and the sale of his book benefited. Like the Girondists of the first French Revolution, of whom he wrote, Lamartine was more the theoretical thinker than the man of action, more the poet than the politician. After a few glorious months of leadership, he quickly lost power and position and returned to the comparative obscurity of authorship. But his name had been made. During the ensuing three years seven Lamartine titles were issued from 82 Cliff Street, some of them earlier titles, one of them his account of *The Past, Present and Future of the Republic*.

During this time English works of nonfiction were also placed in a new library, started in late 1845, called the *New Miscellany*. With 187 titles in the *Family Library*, apparently the time had come to start a new series. The *New Miscellany* was advertised as "Popular Sterling Literature," but books being chosen were of the same sort that had gone before into the *Family Library*. A noteworthy change was one of format, the new series shifting from 18mo to 12mo size. Perhaps the buying public now preferred larger books. Anyway a new series would bring new publicity and people could say that they stayed out of ruts on Cliff Street.

The honor of starting the *New Miscellany* went to William Whewell's *Elements of Morality.* (It also had the lead position in the sixth and last series of the *School District Library.*) The Harper title page reproduced a vignette showing a hand passing on a flaming torch to a waiting hand. This emblem was soon appropriated as the Harper colophon (see p. 377 and title page). It was probably designed for Dr. Whewell by Sir Francis Chantrey, English sculptor, one of whose works, a statue of George Washington, is in the State House, Boston Massachusetts. Whewell was master of Trinity College, Cambridge, and this 1845 title was the best of his books in moral philosophy, his special field. The fifth title in the *Miscellany* series was *The Practical Astronomer* by the Scottish scientist and author Thomas Dick. It was the third volume which the brothers had issued by this popularizer of astronomy, following *Celestial Scenery* and *The Sidereal Heavens.* Both of these books had been puffed by Clark, proud that they added prestige to the name of *The Knickerbocker's* Scottish correspondent. *The Practical Astronomer* is of special interest today because it contains a significant forecast of the importance of celestial photography.

A most significant scientific book came out in 1846 as Numbers 10 and 11 of the *New Miscellany*, although the brothers probably took it on as another book in that most salable of categories, "Voyages and Travels." It was entitled *Journal of Researches into the Natural History and Geology of the Countries Visited during the Voyage of H.M.S. Beagle round the World, under the command of Captain Fitzroy, R.N.* The first American edition was published in two volumes of 350 and 324 pages. Known as *Voyage of the Beagle*, it was written, of course, by Charles Darwin, and the nearly five-year voyage it described was Darwin's real preparation for his life's work. His careful observation of animals and fossils led him to think profoundly on the modification and transmutation of species, and to publish, in 1859, *The Origin of Species.* But one looks in vain for a first American edition of this later and greater work with the Harper imprint. Perhaps the brothers backed away from it because it charted a voyage too hazardous for them to venture, a voyage into heavy theological seas, risky even a century later for Teilhard de Chardin and his publishers.

Other volumes of importance in *The New Miscellany* included two translations of Frederic Schiller, *History of the Thirty Years' War* and *History of the Revolt of the Netherlands.* Also *Expedition to Borneo*, in which Captain (later Sir Henry) Keppel told an exciting story of chasing real pirates in the Malayan seas while in charge of H.M.S. *Dido.* The last of the twenty-two volumes in the *New Miscellany* came out late in 1848. By that time the brothers were beginning to think of still another new venture, James saying that they might try their hand at a *Monthly Miscellany* since people obviously liked to buy paperback issues in regular installments.

In 1847 the great Scottish preacher Thomas Chalmers died. A spiritual heir of the reformer John Knox, Chalmers continued the work of reformation that led to the so-called "Disruption" and the founding of the Free Church of Scotland, of which he was the first moderator. Throughout his adult life Dr. Chalmers had devoted some time in each day to writing, often in the field of political economy. One of his works had been printed for Kirk & Mercein by J. & J. Harper during the early months of their career as printers, with another one off their hand presses in 1821. In 1840 they had published another Chalmers work on their own account. Learning that Constable had purchased the Chalmers copyrights for £10,000 from the Rev. William Hanna, his son-in-law, who would also be writing a *Memoir*, the brothers immediately negotiated with Constable for the purchase of first proofs for £100. The *Literary World* took note of the Harper contract, saying that the literary and religious world would await the works "on tiptoe" and that there would doubtless be a prodigious demand for them. Beginning in December, 1847, and continuing through March, 1850, the brothers published five of the posthumous Chalmers titles, and through 1853 nine more volumes—biography, miscellaneous writings, and correspondence—altogether a hefty lot of Chalmers reading matter.

Two more books for the theological list were translations of important works by German scholars. One was John K. L. Gieseler's *Kirchengeschichte*. In 1824 Gieseler had published the first volume of his projected history of the Christian Church, and the fame of the work led to reprints and revisions in Germany and to the English translation in 1846 of the fourth German edition. The work of the English translators was revised and edited in America by Henry Boynton Smith of Amherst College, who was paid $375. The publication of an important literary work often helps a professional man, such as a clergyman or a teacher, to get a better job. Smith's work on Volume I, published from Cliff Street in January, 1849, led the next year to his being named professor of church history in the Union Theological Seminary, New York. The whole of Gieseler's vast work was not to be published till 1854, and American sets of the work were not to be completed till the 1860's.

While Gieseler was teaching at Bonn and at Göttingen, August Neander was professor of theology at the University of Berlin.

Neander, who had studied under the great Schleiermacher, also wrote a church history, but this work was not to be translated and published till after his *Life of Jesus Christ*, which was translated—similarly from a fourth German edition—by Professors John McClintock and Charles Blumenthal of Dickinson College, Carlisle, Pennsylvania. This was an American first and the brothers, having paid translation costs, sold or traded proofs in London, where the book was published also in 1848. Gieseler and Neander were leaders in the spreading movement to apply to the Biblical record those scientific principles of historical study and research that were used in secular studies. This "higher criticism" of the Bible was to present a greater challenge to the presuppositions of the Christian faith than the Darwinian theory of evolution.*

Germanic studies contributed four further works that were eagerly picked up by English and American scholars. The German of a German-Latin Dictionary compiled by C. E. Georges was translated by two English clergymen, named Riddle and Arnold; these names—not Georges's—were used to identify the American edition, which Anthon revised and amplified to the tune of $500. For $400 he applied the same treatment to a Latin grammar by Karl Zumpt of the University of Berlin and made an abridgment for younger students; in this case Zumpt's name was kept in the title, not that of Leonhard Schmitz, the translator. Anthon did not, however, share in the biggest Latin project of the mid-century, although surely it had his blessing, the famous *Andrews Latin-English Lexicon*. On June 9, 1846, the brothers contracted with E. A. Andrews of New Britain, Connecticut, to prepare what turned out to be a 1,689-page dictionary of the Latin language. Andrews was paid $6,000 for his labor, most of which was based on the work of the German philologist Wilhelm Freund. More than one-third of this amount was recovered over a five-year period from Sampson Low, who printed a British edition from a duplicate set of plates. Whether the brothers made some payment to Freund is not known, but they did send him £400 in the 1850's for supplying Andrews with new material basic to a later revision. The *Andrews Lexicon* has served several generations of Latinists by staying in print almost to the present day.

Another book that the brothers launched in 1846 likewise still stands as a monument to their contribution to scholarly studies. It is the *Greek-English Lexicon* of Liddell and Scott, whose work was based on

---

* Neander died in July, 1850, and the September issue of the new *Monthly* devoted three pages to his life and work, including an engraving showing Neander standing before his lecture desk.

the German of Franz Passow, who in turn reworked a lexicon by Schneider. And the American who put the finishing touches on Liddell and Scott was Anthon's twenty-eight-year-old assistant, Henry Drisler. He was paid $1,800 for his work. In seven years the $5 royal-octavo work of 1,735 pages sold 25,000 copies and must have been a thorn in the flesh to Dean Henry G. Liddell of Christ Church College, Oxford. Years later—in 1877, actually—Joe Brooklyn Harper was to make a special trip to England to see Liddell about further revisions that Drisler had made in association with others, importantly Professor W. W. Goodwin of Harvard. Arriving in Oxford, he went to Dean Liddell's residence.

Mr. Harper's presence announced, there was a great rumpus upstairs. "Tell that New York pirate I'll not see him," the reverend gentleman shouted down to the butler. "But, Dean Liddell," Harper protested, going to the staircase, "I've come to buy ten thousand copies of your *Lexicon.*" To which inducement Liddell replied, "Oh, in that case, I'll come down directly." That staircase is still known as the "Lexicon Staircase" because the dean used some of his royalties to build a new one that was solid, substantial, and Victorian, replacing a lovely two-centuries-old Jacobean staircase.

The many generations of divinity students who have used the *Lexicon* have passed along a jingle about it, sometimes found inscribed in second-hand copies. The verse is palpably unfair to Liddell, since he did more of the work than Robert Scott, but the rhymesters found Scott an easier word to play with, "Liddell" being pronounced to rhyme with "fiddle":

> Liddell and Scott gave much thought
> To writing a Lexicon,
> Part was good and part was not.
> The part that was good
> Was written by Scott.
> The part by Liddell was not.

Dean Henry George Liddell's name has achieved a certain immortality because of his *Lexicon*, but his greatest contribution to literature came through his daughter, Alice, who inspired the Oxford don Charles L. Dodgson to write *Alice in Wonderland.*

Basic to the study of law, *Blackstone's Commentaries* was universally used in law schools and "read" by ambitious young men in all well-established law offices. The Harper edition of *Blackstone* was reprinted from the twenty-first London edition. They employed John L. Wendell, reporter for the New York Supreme Court, to supply notes to adapt the work to American students. It was already updated to 1844 by English barristers, so the brothers could claim in 1847 that their edition of *Blackstone* was the best. They bound the four-octavo volumes—2,200 pages—in sheepskin and priced the set at $7. While Chancellor Kent's *Commentaries* (for which he was publisher as well as author) were in some ways more useful to the American profession, they never supplanted *Blackstone*. English law was so deeply embedded in America that even the descendants of those who defied King George III clung tenaciously to the law of their forefathers. *Blackstone* was the lawyers' Bible.

Medical schools and physicians also profited by a rich assortment of medical books brought over from England and the continent in the late forties. Two of them were French originals. The English translation of Masse's *Anatomical Atlas* was edited for American students by Dr. Pattison, who had done such a fine job on the Cruveilhier tome. The new work was pocket size and contained 442 figures; the volume with colored plates cost $7—uncolored, $3. Another French work in pediatrics by Villard was sufficiently rewritten to merit its being catalogued only under the name of Dr. James Stewart of New York, with the title *Diseases of Children* (1845), 584 pages. Dr. Stewart nine years later was to establish the city's first children's hospital, the New York Nursery and Child's Hospital. Another New York physician and friend of the brothers, Dr. John W. Corson, produced a book of travel, *Loiterings in Europe* (1848) which contained observations on European charities and medical institutions. In London, Fletcher followed up leads on forthcoming medical literature that Dr. Corson had given him.

In 1824 J. & J. Harper had printed Dr. Robert Hooper's *Lexicon Medicum*. In 1829 they reissued this important dictionary on their own account and in 1846 they brought out another edition. Dr. Samuel Akerly's name helped to revitalize this old staple; it was appearing frequently in medical and scientific journals. Also in 1846 they issued Dr. Hooper's manual on the principles and practice of medicine, entitled *Vade Mecum*. A Scottish author, Dr. Andrew Combe of Edinburgh, provided two further titles: *A Treatise on Infancy* and *The Physiology of Digestion*. Apparently Dr. Combe had royal bedside manners. He was for a time physician to Leopold I, King of the Belgians, and later one of the physicians extraordinary to Queen Victoria in Scotland. Dr. Combe's brother, George Combe, had three books on phrenology in the Harper catalogue, a part of the Boston purchase of plates.

The phrenological craze that excited so many headhunters in Europe and America in the 1830's and 40's was due largely to George Combe and to his immediate predecessor, the German phrenologist J. C. Spurzheim. Both lectured in America (the latter died in Boston) and by their books helped to show where in the brain the various mental faculties were located and how the size (and consequent power) of these faculties could be determined by careful measurements of the outer surfaces of the cranium. The several charts in the Harper books, all carefully diagrammed and numbered, helped locate propensities, sentiments, and faculties. Baldheaded men were suddenly popular at dinner parties and people got used to being stared at by strangers. Phrenology had its influence on authors of the time, notably Edgar Allan Poe.

Medical books from England, especially the works of Drs. Hooper and Grant, were drawn upon by Dr. D. Pereira Gardner of Philadelphia for still another Harper medical dictionary. His 682-page book, despite its apparent competition with the Hooper-Akerly *Lexicon Medicum*, was published the following year, in October, 1847. A man of broad interests, Dr. Gardner had given them *The Farmer's Dictionary* the preceding year; for his work on the *Medical Dictionary* the industrious and omniscient doctor drew upon that of four English authors, all named, and "the most eminent" but unnamed American authorities. He walked—as do all compilers of such books who must use the work of earlier authors—the tightrope between plagiarism and the scholarly use of source materials.

Dr. Martyn Paine, the organizing head of the Medical School of New York University, put the date January 1, 1847, at the end of the preface to his *Institutes, or Philosophy of Medicine* and took the manuscript down to Cliff Street to get the year off to a good start. Through 1870 Dr. Paine was to incorporate revisions and additions to eight more editions, and while the printings were small, the book grew from 826 to 1,151 pages. *Institutes* was prominently listed in the medical section of the 1847 catalogue as was "*Revere's System of Practical Medicine*. 8vo. (In Press)." This entry troubled Demarest years later while compiling his *Catalogue* because he could not remember the book —for the good reason that it was never published. Dr. Revere died before his projected fifteen-hundred-page tome was completed. Four hundred pages of proof were left but the balance of the manuscript could not be found. Dr. Revere loved his students as his father had loved his country. He died of an illness aggravated by the strain of almost constant attendance on a young medical student who was dying of typhoid fever. The boy had incurred the disease while giving medical aid to Irish immigrants among whom typhoid was then endemic.

Two years later, despite fresh Croton water, New York City suffered another epidemic of cholera. In July, 1849, the disease took Horace Greeley's beloved five-year-old son, "Pickie," described by N. P. Willis as the most beautiful child he had ever seen. In August Fletcher wrote Prescott to explain why they had not reported on "your French friend's volume"; their reader had escaped to the country taking it and other manuscripts along. "After the prevailing epidemic has left the Country," he wrote, "we hope trade will revive. . . . In fact, the taste of the people generally does not incline that way. The bowels instead of the brains are now most cared for—and this is not to be wondered at." (In an aside Fletcher wrote, "Your letter was directed to 'Boston.' We beg to inform you that notwithstanding adverse surrounding circumstances, we still hang our flag in 'New York.' ")

In September Fletcher was declining a request to reissue Noah Webster's two-volume work on pestilential diseases. William G. Webster had written to ask if Fletcher would consider taking over the plates and printing an edition since his father's suggested treatment of cholera would be helpful. Fletcher replied that they were "not caring to increase our engagements in this [medical] department" and recommended Lea & Blanchard, whom Fletcher knew to be moving ahead with strength and confidence in this field. This firm was gradually to cease trade publishing and specialize in medical works, with its imprint established as Lea & Febiger. Thus the tree that Mathew Carey set out in Philadelphia in 1785 now stands as the oldest in the forest of American book publishers.*

The brothers were uninterested in moving ahead with medical books just then for the obvious reason that they were finding textbooks a more profitable venture. In 1846-49 they were adding at least thirty books to their list of titles for schools, academies, and colleges.

Many of these texts and reference works were siphoned from overseas. There was a *French Grammar* by Noel and Chapsal and a *First Book in Spanish* by Salkeld. In 1846 John Stuart Mill's *Logic* was a featured addition to the textbook list. Apparently it was also sold to the

---

* The Methodist Publishing House, with its trade name of Abingdon Press, dates its origin as 1789, although it could possibly claim an earlier year. The Harper start in 1817 makes it the oldest *general* publisher that continues the name of its founders.

general public and was reprinted at least fifteen times through 1883. Mill's *Logic* was followed in three years by Archbishop Richard Whately's *Elements of Logic.* Both books had appeared earlier in Britain—Whately's book early enough to have influenced Mill. Whately's *Elements of Rhetoric* was issued from Cliff Street, also in 1849; for decades those Americans who sought to be more skillful in their use of words found no better modern tool than the *Rhetoric* of the Anglican Bishop of Dublin. Whately's episcopal peer, Bishop Connop Thirlwall, supplied a two-volume *History of Greece* which was also a standard work for decades. Whately's intimate friend the German expatriate Leonhard Schmitz made a condensation of the work which the brothers also published six years later (1851). It matched the one-volume Schmitz reprint, a *History of Rome.*

Schmitz and Anthon were two of a kind in their devotion to classical studies. One wonders whether they ever met. They must have corresponded over the Zumpt *Latin Grammar* and other German works on which Anthon leaned heavily in preparing his *New Greek Grammar, Anabasis of Xenophon, Memorabilia of Socrates,* and *Tacitus.* He gave credit where credit was due and seemed generally to be choosing the best from several foreign sources. When Wesley made up the 1847 catalogue, he devoted nearly four pages of the textbook section to "Prof. Anthon's series of school classics." This caption is followed by a blurb, chosen obviously for prestigious reasons from the London *Athenaeum:* "Dr. Anthon has done more for sound classical school literature than any half dozen Englishmen; his books are admirably edited [the first to have notes and explanations for the student]. His merits, as an editor of school classics, are so well understood and appreciated in this country, as well as in his own, that commendation would be superfluous." Wesley could well have had a copy of the catalogue bound in sheepskin for Professor Anthon, or at least have taken him to dinner at the Astor House, the best hotel the city could boast, a proper place to take an author who gets top billing in a new catalogue. (See illustrations 14 and 15.)

And one or all of the brothers might have dined, if not wined, Professor John W. Draper, who gave them a *Text-book on Chemistry* in 1846 and a *Text-book on Natural Philosophy* in 1847. The bulky manuscripts that he took from Washington Square down to Cliff Street made four-hundred-page books and each retailed for 75 cents, a price that included a royalty of ten cents per copy. The brothers paid for making the illustrations, three hundred in one and four hundred in the other, as well as for the stereotypes. But they got their investments back quickly enough. *Natural Philosophy* was in a third printing by 1850, at which time *Chemistry* was in its sixth printing, with major revisions to come in 1853 and 1859. And the printings must have been unusually large to justify such low prices—as cheap as English reprints. In fact, cheaper. Four years before the Draper *Chemistry* was published, the brothers had brought over from England Dr. Robert Kane's *Elements of Chemistry*, which Draper edited for student use. They continued to catalogue this English "reprint" at $1.50, twice the price of the American "original." To be sure it was three hundred pages longer and of somewhat larger trim size. But the two books taken together could hardly be used as an illustration of the thesis that low-priced English reprints always undersold American books and discouraged native authorship.

Since the retail price of a book is to some extent determined by the size of a first printing, the brothers seemed to have followed what is now common practice in charging the cost of the composition of type and plates against the first printing. If these charges (now called "plant costs") amounted to $500, the brothers would add fifty cents a copy to their "manufacturing cost" of printing, paper, and binding on an edition of one thousand copies, or only five cents a copy on a printing of ten thousand copies. Thus they obviously estimated a comparatively small sale for an elementary textbook on mechanics when they priced it at $1.50; the volume contained fewer pages and illustrations than either of the Draper books and carried a lower royalty (10 percent of retail). Its author, Augustus W. Smith, was professor of mathematics at Wesleyan; when the college was to look for a new president in 1852, it chose, not surprisingly, another Harper author, Professor Smith.

The brothers were giving Boston publishers competition for favorite schoolbook authors in the mid-forties, one of them being William Russell, a popular teacher in the Andover Theological Seminary and the Newport (Rhode Island) Female Seminary. Russell, who had come to America after graduating from Glasgow University, loved teaching elocution and enjoyed writing textbooks. Two Boston firms, Munroe and Ticknor, employed him at the rate of $125 a month, and early in 1846 the brothers signed him up at this rate for six months to do *Harper's New York Class Book*. They also agreed to pay him $100 to cover travel expenses and book purchases so that he could properly inform himself about the geography, scenery, and natural history of the Empire State as well as collect stories about its famous men and institutions. His book of 650 type-crammed pages came out the following year. The reading of so much small type must have been hard on the eyes of the older boys and girls who used it as a reader and it deserved its fate of going out of print in a few years. A curious announcement of the book is extant giving credit to the publisher as "Messrs J. & J. Harper."

Another Boston publisher, Robert L. Davis, lost an author, Richard G. Parker, to the brothers in May, 1845, when Parker came to Cliff Street with the second edition of his book *Aids to English Composition*. Davis was enraged and claimed that the Harper edition would be an infringement on his own copyright of Parker's *Progressive Exercises in English Composition*. He threatened action and the brothers were upset. Parker mollified them by agreeing to assume any expenses involved in defending the copyrights, but the threat hung over his head for a year. The brothers paid him $1,000 for revisions and the copyright itself and might have been satisfied with fewer revisions, but Parker was concerned to make his book as adequate as he knew how and worked assiduously to perfect it, even though he would not thereby profit financially. "I cannot say of myself," he wrote the brothers, "as Johnson said of Dryden that 'when he had no pecuniary interest, he had no further solicitude.' "

The brothers may have been secretly amused at Parker's having to worry through twelve months of legal insecurity, for Parker had brought suit against them the year before when they published *Elements of Rhetoric and Literary Criticism*, by James R. Boyd. Parker then claimed infringement of his copyright on *Aids* and he may have had just cause. Certainly the Boyd title page laid author and publisher wide open to claims of literary trespass, for Boyd, after giving credit to two Englishmen, Reid and Cunnell, added the words "with large Additions from other Sources." But the quarrel was settled out of court and Parker agreed to assign his literary children to the brothers. In 1846 he shipped to Cliff Street the revised plates of a small book, *Questions in Geography*, getting a release for this one from still another Boston publisher named Dickinson. That same year he gave them a big new book, also developed as a text in his Boston grammar school. It was called *Outlines of General History*. In the meantime Boyd had re-established his ethical position and issued a book for "literary institutions" entitled *Eclectic Moral Philosophy*—for which no one was sued.

Parker's book of geographical questions was advertised as adapted to any one of nine different collections of maps then on the market. Of course the Morse name, like Abou Ben Adhem's, led all the rest. The revised edition of Morse's *School Geography* in all its cerographic splendor was issued in 1847—on October 7, a bit late for some schools.

With the *Geography* made new the brothers faced the perennial problem of scheduling a revised edition in order not to be caught with quantities of the old edition still on hand.

A book issued for grammar schools in 1848 was an English reprint, *History of France*, by Elizabeth Penrose, first published in England twenty years earlier. Mrs. Penrose was the daughter of Edmund Cartwright, inventor of the power loom. She became celebrated in the early part of the nineteenth century as the author of history books for children, writing under her pen name of Mrs. Markham, and her books were acclaimed because she eliminated the "horrors" of history and the machinations of politics and included fictional "conversations" between a teacher and pupils bearing upon the subject matter of each chapter. To the Cliff Street reprint Jacob Abbott added maps, notes, questions, and a concluding chapter to bring the book up to date. Eighteen forty-eight was a banner year on Cliff Street, for it marked the beginning of a long partnership with Jacob Abbott, who was already famous for his "Rollo," "Lucy," and "Jonas" juveniles, which were to reach an estimated sale of 1,250,000 by 1860. In addition to his work on Mrs. Markham's reprint, his *Summer in Scotland* came out in February. He got the brothers' agreement to print in the book four pages advertising his older books, he to supply the plates. His *Mary, Queen of Scots* came out in October; his *King Charles the First of England* and his *Alexander the Great* in December. These three titles were the first in a Harper series to be known as *Abbotts' Illustrated Histories*. By 1853 the series had grown to eighteen titles, a few of them written by Jacob Abbott's brother John S. C. Abbott, with a total sale of 400,000 copies. The volumes were being read by Abraham Lincoln of Illinois, who wrote a moving tribute to the authors: "I want to thank you and your brother for Abbotts' Series of Histories. I have not education enough to appreciate the profound works of voluminus historians, and, if I had, I have no time to read them. But your Series of Histories gives me, in brief compass, just that knowledge of past men and events which I need. I have read them with the greatest interest. To them I am indebted for about all the historical knowledge I have."

In addition to schoolbooks, the brothers were issuing in the late forties an impressive list of texts for academies and colleges, mostly original American works. Professor Elias Loomis, recently come to New York University from Western Reserve, gave them four college mathematics texts: an algebra, a geometry, a trigonometry, and a book of logarithms. His contract for the geometry book contained a new provision: "The premium on the first thousand copies thereof to be paid in books, which the said Professor Loomis is to distribute gratuitously." The brothers had already signed up Professor Charles W. Hackley of Columbia to do an elementary algebra and an elementary geometry, but Loomis was to be their star author of mathematical texts.

Elementary books in Latin and Greek—two of each—came from Anthon-recommended Professor John McClintock, who was currently translating the Neander work from the German. In 1848 he left Dickinson College to become editor of the Methodist *Quarterly Review* in New York and was thus able to give more time to his scholarly publications from Cliff Street. He was to become one of Fletcher's close friends and advisors, and in 1860 to contract (along with James Strong) for an eight-volume Biblical encyclopedia, known to generations of seminarians and clergymen as "McClintock and Strong." A Greek New Testament with notes in English—"critical, philological, and exegetical"—was prepared for colleges and seminaries by Jesse Ames Spender, a former student of Anthon's and a graduate of the General Theological Seminary. The brothers paid Spender an honorarium of $500 and issued the 623-page work, with thousands of lines of difficult Greek composition, for only $1. Spender found he had a liking for editorial work and went over to Appleton's to become their Anthon.

Schoolbooks on American history were an obvious lack. In 1840 the brothers had procured plates for a two-volume *History of the United States* by Salma Hale, a New Hampshire politician and one-time member of Congress. But it was more suitable in the *School District Library*, for which it had been purchased, than as a textbook, although it was also so listed. Sparks's *American Biography* too had little, if any, textbook use.

Except for the low level of business back in 1840, the brothers would have closed with Sparks for a second ten-volume series of American biographies, as indicated earlier. Sparks was willing to undertake the arduous task of selecting competent writers, paying the necessary honorariums, editing the manuscripts, and furnishing the stereotypes—all for $1,000 per volume. "I apply to no writers," he wrote the brothers, "but those in whom I have confidence . . . and they are not numerous. The pay is a small temptation to such men and I am often disappointed by those who promise to write. I am obliged in most cases, not only to indicate to them where the materials are to be found, but frequently to search out and furnish the materials." It was to this letter that the brothers had replied saying they would have to print ten thousand copies to get their money back, but they would be willing to experiment with one or three volumes. But Sparks was not interested in an experiment. He wanted another ten-volume series and pointed out that a new series should go well since the first one was now well established, although the original publishers, Hilliard, Gray & Co., could hardly have taken fewer pains to circulate it. But the business barometer on Cliff Street was then showing a decided low and the brothers regretfully declined. They hoped Sparks would come back to them sometime with another proposal.

It was too good a publishing idea to be pigeonholed for long. Three years later, in July, 1843, Sparks contracted with Little and Brown for the second series. When the brothers heard this news a few months later (the barometer now moving higher), they wondered how they could have been so stupid as to discourage Sparks earlier. The *Democratic Review* for February, 1844, carried two significant announcements. One, that the first issue of the new *Library of American Biography* by Sparks was in press in Boston; two, that Harper's *Cabinet Library of American Biography* was forthcoming—a new sixty-volume series, "the most complete and valuable collection of the kind ever published." Failing to find confirmation of such a series, or plans for it, one suspects that the brothers went no further than to order wood for the cabinet. Did they hope to frighten Boston into sending the new Sparks series down to start filling the cabinet up? The announcement sounds like publishing bravado in a time when advance announcements of books were often no more than trial balloons to test the bookselling weather.

Three years later (in 1847) Sparks did make another overture to Cliff Street, this time suggesting that the brothers bring out a new edition of his *Writings of Washington*. The *Writings* had first been published by the Hilliard firm in the thirties with the final volume out in 1837, ten years after Sparks had begun to assemble Washington's letters and papers. In doing research he had carted eight large boxes of manuscripts from Mount Vernon to Boston and picked up other papers elsewhere. Chief Justice Marshall was responsible for getting Washington's nephew, Bushrod Washington, to agree to Sparks's project. Their agreement called for a division of profits accruing from the work, 25 percent going to Washington and the same to Marshall or their estates. By 1837, Sparks was able to make a three-way split of more than $15,000 profit.

After first appearing in numbers, the Harper edition of twelve volumes, including Sparks's *Life of Washington*, began accumulating royalty at the rate of 25 cents a volume. The set of books was bound in sheepskin and in half calf as well as in cloth, and the retail price of the cloth edition had been lowered, in typical Cliff Street fashion, to $1.50 a copy, of $18 the set. The *American Literary Magazine* thought it was still a somewhat expensive work but "fairly within the ability of a considerable portion of the community to buy it."

Sparks has earned the continuing gratitude of scholars for collecting and collating the most important of Americana manuscripts, although they criticize him for having corrected Washington's spelling and grammar and for omitting passages without marking ellipses. Sparks's habit of using the editorial blue pencil during the years that he so competently edited the *North American Review* did serve him badly when he worked over Washington's papers. The strictures leveled against his editorial work by Lord Mahon and others in the early fifties helped, however, to sell the Harper edition. By that time the handsome and distinguished-looking Sparks had been named president of Harvard.

Another Harvard man, Richard Hildreth, had turned to writing American history—an ambition since his undergraduate days. His *History of the United States* came from Cliff Street in three volumes in June, July, and October, 1849, and carried the story of the country from the first settlement to the adoption of the Federal Constitution. The work appeared, as did Sparks's *Writings*, in three styles of binding; likewise the per-copy royalty was the same although the cloth edition sold for $2—fifty cents more per volume. The Hildreth contract was typical of many currently drafted; when they themselves paid for the stereotype plates, the brothers began royalty after one thousand copies had been sold. Royalties on the more expensive bindings were the same as on the cloth edition, still a customary publishing practice although leather editions of quality books are now the exception—then they were the rule. In 1851-52 Hildreth's second lot of three volumes was to come out, carrying the American story down to the end of Monroe's first term. The whole work ran to nearly four thousand pages. A revised edition was issued in 1854-55, with further printings steadily called for.

Unlike the cautious Sparks, who never contracted with a publisher for longer than a five-year period, Hildreth signed up for the life of the copyright. This twenty-eight-year period was also specified in the contract for his *Theory of Politics*. Writing this book for 1853 publication and making corrections for the revised edition of his *History* brought Hildreth often to Cliff Street. A warm friendship developed between him and the brothers. He was later to become a U.S. Consul in Trieste. He died in Florence, Italy, in 1865, and was buried in the Protestant cemetery near his friend Theodore Parker. A few years later the brothers engaged Hiram Powers, the American "autocrat sculptor of Florence," to carve a memorial for Hildreth's grave. The 1849 contract for the *History* outlived the four brothers and was renewed in 1877 by their sons and the son of Hildreth for the fourteen-year period then allowed for renewal of copyright.

Books such as Hildreth's *History*, however, never reach best-sellerdom. In *Golden Multitudes*, Mott tabulates American best sellers by decades, the estimated sales for such books being at least 1 percent of the population. Thus in the 1840's a book would have to sell 175,-000 copies to be called a best seller. During the closing years of the decade (1847-49), eight such best sellers were published. Five of these were Harper titles, *Home Influence*, *Jane Eyre*, *Wuthering Heights*, *Vanity Fair*, and *History of England*. The other three were Andersen's *Fairy Tales* (Wiley & Putnam) Dickens's *Dombey and Son* (various publishers), and Whittier's *Poems* (B. B. Mussey & Co.). Whittier stood bravely alone to represent native American authorship. Best sellers came from overseas.

CHAPTER XVI

Herman Melville, Novelist

1846–1853

IN *The House of Harper*, written in 1911, one looks in vain for a mention of the name of Herman Melville or of his book *Moby Dick*, now considered perhaps the greatest American novel ever published. Like his contemporaries, J. Henry Harper probably remembered *Moby Dick* as a rambling narrative with metaphysical overtones which had enjoyed only a modest success and thought of Melville as a kind of recluse and has-been who was long in debt to the House. He may have forgotten that shortly after Melville's death—twenty years earlier —he had, with Mrs. Melville's approval, disposed of the stereotype plates of the Harper editions of Melville's works. Their copyrights were expiring.

But the tide of opinion soon turned. Eight years later, in 1919, the centenary of Melville's birth, magazines published articles on Melville and his work was discussed. The rediscovery of Melville was soon to yield his first biography,* and in 1924 *Billy Budd* was published and a complete edition of his works was being printed in London. Men of

---

* *Herman Melville, Mariner and Mystic*, by Raymond M. Weaver (1921). Early in the twentieth century Frank Jewett Mather, Jr., had attempted to interest Houghton Mifflin & Co. in publishing a biography that he would write but the Boston publishers considered the necessary investment of $700 too risky.

letters were soon vying with each other to honor him, who in his later years was so little known that when the *New York Times* commented editorially on his death the writer called him "Henry Melville," although two other New York dailies got the name printed correctly in notices of his death and funeral. Some writers such as Van Wyck Brooks have assumed that *Moby Dick* was never reprinted because the plates were destroyed in the Harper fire two years after the book's publication, thus explaining why the story of the whale made so slight a stir of the literary waters during Melville's lifetime. However, the book appears to have been in print ever since its first issue, and scholarly opinion is swinging to the belief that the whale made only a small splash in the first place. Some of Melville's contemporaries continued to respect his genius, one of them being Thomas Low Nichols, who published his *Forty Years of American Life* in London in 1874. He claimed to be one of the first to have read the manuscript of Melville's first book, *Typee*, and to recognize its worth, calling Melville "a simplehearted, enthusiastic man of genius, who wrote with the consciousness of an impelling force, and with great power and beauty."

Nevertheless, those who knew Melville best during his creative period were singularly unaware of his genius. Paradoxically, Duyckinck and his coterie of New York literati were then praying for a literary messiah; when he came bearing the name of Melville his own received him not. Hawthorne recognized the power of *Moby Dick*, but his and others' enthusiasm was chilled by the seeming triviality of *Pierre*, published nine months later. How could a man of genius write such a book? The answer now seems obvious. Melville knew that an inner "literary tormentor" forced him to write but he lacked self-criticism and wanted no one else's critical opinion. And he was angry with his critics, so that he struck back in *Pierre*. He was also driven for financial reasons to turn out books for advances on half-profits or royalty contracts, which he could easily obtain from the brothers or from Murray or Bentley in London.

Another reason why Melville was written off by many nineteenth-century readers was that he was harsh toward Christian missionaries, strictures that had troubled the conscience of John Wiley when he read the proofs of *Typee* forwarded from London by Putnam, who apparently thought that the book's sale would be helped by its racy frankness. Duyckinck, whose job it was to see the book through the press, appears to have taken a mediating position between the two publishing partners. He recognized that the new author had talent, but in sending an early copy to Hawthorne the best he could say for the book was to describe it as "lively and pleasant, not overphilosophical, perhaps." The Wiley & Putnam edition of *Typee* came out on March 17, 1846, about three weeks after John Murray's first issue of the novel in London, where it was given the more sober title of a travel book, *Narrative of a Four Months' Residence among the Natives of a Valley of the Marquesas.*

As a travel book, the success of any narrative depends largely on its authenticity. Who was this Herman Melville? Despite Melville's claim in the preface that he had written "the unvarnished truth," Murray was as troubled about verification as the Harpers had been. Faced with skeptical reviews, Murray asked for some sort of documentary evidence. Duyckinck pressed Melville for help. He was caught between Murray's desire for something more substantial than lack of varnish and Wiley's plea that further printings soften Melville's downgrading of missionaries.

On June 3, Melville wrote triumphally to Duyckinck, "What will the politely incredulous Mr. Duyckinck now say to the true Toby's having turned up in Buffalo, and written a letter to the *Commercial Advertiser* of that Place, vouching for the truth of all that part of the narrative, where he is made to figure.—Give ear then, oh ye of little faith—especially thou man of the Evangelist [Toby was replying to a skeptical review in the *New York Evangelist*] and hear what Toby has to say for himself."

Melville was naturally delighted by the reappearance of his companion in adventure, Richard Tobias Greene, and proceeded at once to write a short sequel to *Typee* based on Toby's further experiences. In England, the sequel appeared first as a pamphlet and was later incorporated into the book itself. Wiley & Putnam included it in their second edition; there was ample room for the new material, for Wiley had stood firm and the revised edition was really an expurgated and shorter one. The new *Typee* appeared in the fall of 1846, and Melville collected an advance of $150—almost twice the earnings of the first edition. All was well for the moment, but abroad the doubters persisted— was there really any such person as Herman Melville?

Melville had been working for some time on his second book, *Omoo*. On the day after Thanksgiving he arrived in New York with the completed manuscript, left it with Wiley & Putnam, and went to Boston for a ten-day visit with the family of Judge Lemuel Shaw. He had dedicated *Typee* to Judge Shaw, whose daughter Elizabeth was a good friend of his sister Helen. And Elizabeth Shaw, Melville had decided, was a very attractive young lady whom he wanted to know better.

When he returned to New York on December 8, Melville found the manuscript of *Omoo* had been received with adverse criticisms, for it was much more severe on the missionaries than *Typee* had been. He meekly made revisions, but John Wiley decided that another Melville title was more than he wanted so passed the manuscript back to Melville, who retraced his steps to 82 Cliff Street.

How quickly a lost ball may be recovered was shown in Frederick Saunders's account of the Harper acceptance of *Omoo*.

"Melville came into my room at the Harper establishment with another manuscript and remarked, 'Saunders, I suppose there is no use of offering this to the house.'

" 'Wait a minute,' I said. 'Mr. [Fletcher] Harper is in his carriage now at the door about to start to Europe. I'll ask him.' I hurried out of the building without waiting to put on my hat and came to him just in time.

" 'What is it?' said he. 'Oh, another manuscript from Herman Melville. He is offering it to us. What do you say?'

" 'Take it at once!' said Mr. Harper, jumping into his carriage and driving off."

A week before Christmas the first of Melville's Harper contracts was signed. He would receive an advance of $400 on his one-half share of the profits and retain English rights.

The loss of his brother Gansevoort left Melville without an agent to handle his literary affairs in England; on December 30 he wrote to John Brodhead of the American ministry in London, asking him to act in his behalf for the sale of *Omoo*. Proofs were promised on a steamer leaving February 1—apparently the brothers had lost no time getting the new book on press. Brodhead received the proofs February 20 and took them at once to John Murray III, who said the new book lacked the novelty of *Typee* but was "full of talent and interest." He offered Melville £150, two-thirds of it by note eight months after the publication date. Melville sorely needed ready cash, however, and finally settled for £144 3s. 4d.; he drew £140 on March 31 and gave the odd sum to Brodhead for expenses.

On April 24, 1847, the *Literary World* printed a portion of *Omoo*, good advance publicity for the book itself, which was officially published from Cliff Street on May 1. There was still enough doubt about Melville's veracity to require a plea for credence in the preface: "A strict adherence to facts has, of course, been scrupulously observed."

With over $1,000 pocketed as advances on *Omoo* and earnings on *Typee* accumulating nicely, Melville was in better shape financially. The publicity he was receiving as a writer was bringing invitations to lecture on the South Seas, with additional income. And there was a bit more for an occasional contribution to the *Literary World*. Just as his financial and literary prospects improved, he began angling for a position as a government clerk in the Treasury Department in Washington, an overture that was unsuccessful. Melville's desire for complete financial security was doubtless inspired by his intention to marry Elizabeth Shaw. Judge Shaw, who had long known the Melville family and its pecuniary problems, might well have been dismayed at the prospect of his daughter's future with a man who was not only a Melville but an author to boot. Nonetheless, a wedding date was set for August 4, 1847, and Melville's future continued to brighten.

In early July, during the Boston social festivities in honor of the wedding, Melville met Richard Henry Dana, Jr., whom he already greatly admired. Back in New York on the 11th, he was induced by Cornelius Mathews to write a series of satires on Zachary Taylor ("Authentic Anecdotes of Old Zack") for Mathews's short-lived humor magazine, *Yankee Doodle*. On July 19 he received $150 from Wiley & Putnam, and just before the wedding his first statement came from Cliff Street. It revealed that four thousand copies of *Omoo* had been printed, with most of the edition sold in three months. This and other Harper semi-annual statements that Melville saved reveal how the brothers accounted to authors on half-profits books. For any six-month period they credited income from sales and charged the total cost to date of manufacturing books, including copies for review. Thus the first statement on *Omoo*, issued July 31, 1847, gave $1,499.40 as the total cost of manufacturing the 4,000-copy first edition. This amount was a charge against $2,936.98, the income from sales (1,841 paper and 1,766 cloth) less 5 percent deducted for guaranty, leaving a net profit of $1,437.58 to be divided. The statement also showed stock on hand: bound copies of each edition and folded sheets, totaling 268. Obviously a reprint was called for and the statement of February 1, 1848, was to show that a second edition of 1,500 copies had been printed, of which 500 were bound. Such regular statements enabled the author of a half-profits book to keep his own running record of manufacturing costs, including plates, and of total printings, sales, and net income.

Melville's first Harper statement also charged him with books purchased, including Webster's *Dictionary*, books of travel, and sea stories. That he was recharging his literary battery was revealed in the July 30 issue of the Lansingburgh *Gazette* (the home-town paper of the Melville family, near Albany), which announced that Herman Melville was at work on another book about the South Seas. Less the cost of these book purchases and the advance, the amount payable to Melville on July 31 was nearly $250. For a little while the sun was shining brightly on the young author, who was soon to cross the double threshold of matrimony and his twenty-eighth birthday.

His brother Allan, who was making a name for himself on Wall Street, was married on September 22 to the fashionable Miss Sophia Thurston. He and Herman decided to find a suitably large house in New York and there settle the entire Melville family—new brides and unwed sisters and, of course, their mother. This arrangement worked out surprisingly well for Herman; here he could have six wholly uninterrupted hours for writing each day, and he stuck quite rigidly to his new routine. Two months after the marriage, Judge Shaw gave his new son-in-law $2,000 to be used for the purchase of the house. Actually, he used only half that amount, and kept the rest as a nest egg, which remained untouched even during the times of great need that were to come.

The first signs of the lean times were beginning. John Murray wrote from England on December 3 that he had not yet made expenses on the first two books, so could not send a further payment. Melville still had $154.36 coming from Wiley & Putnam at the first of the year, and $102.63 a month later from the Harpers. Obviously he needed to finish his new book and turn it into cash. The book had turned out to be a romantic fantasy which he decided to call *Mardi*. During the spring of 1848, he wrote to Murray that proofs would be ready by the middle of July, and asked £150 for the first edition and half profits thereafter.

The terms were a bit extravagant, and Murray was apprehensive that Melville might be adding fuel to the smoldering fire of comment regarding books of questionable moral content. However, Murray was amenable to seeing the proofs, and Melville proceeded with his work on *Mardi*. On May 5, 1848, Elizabeth wrote her stepmother that the book was "done," and that the printer's copy she was making was in "fair progress." At that point, they expected to have the proofs en route to England before the end of June.

But Melville kept adding to the manuscript that was already "done"; his mind was hopping with the intense political situation, and he saw the possibility of imposing material from the real world onto his fantastic allegory. The French revolution was in full swing, and there were frequent reports that it was spreading across Europe. Troops were coming back from the Mexican War, among them Melville's cousin Guert Gansevoort, who had been a hero at Vera Cruz. In the eyes of many, Gansevoort's heroism was on the order of a redemption for his part in the *Somers* affair. Yet another member of the family was making news. Allan Melville, a staunch member of Tammany Hall, was a candidate for the New York Assembly, opposing a Whig and a Free-Soiler. All in all, the absurd chauvinism that Melville so detested was at fever pitch, and he intended to seize the opportunity for comment that this new book offered him.

The Harper agreement for *Mardi*, signed November 15, 1848, provided for a delay of four months from proof stage to publication to permit prior British publication. It also provided an advance of $500, which Melville badly needed, for his Cliff Street statement of August 1 had showed an indebtedness of $256.03 and that from Wiley & Putnam a few days later enclosed only $114.89. That autumn Melville gave John Wiley written notice that after sixty days he would take *Typee* out of his hands and requested a final accounting. He had decided, probably with the brothers' encouragement, that it could be better promoted to the trade jointly with *Omoo* and the forthcoming *Mardi*. Moreover, the transfer of the copyright to the brothers might also bring in some extra money (Melville was to be paid 15 cents for each copy sold—from a retail price of 87½ cents in muslin binding). But for some reason the transfer was not made until the following February, and the formal agreement was delayed until April 28, 1849.

Mardi was slow in appearing. The brothers apparently spent some uncertain weeks on the format before finally deciding to publish the book without illustrations and in the inexpensive style of *Omoo*. Melville finished reading proof on January 27, 1849, and wrote his preface, then set off for Boston, where Elizabeth was expecting their first child, Malcolm, who was born February 16. In his brother's absence, Allan forwarded the proofs to England early in February, and John Brodhead took them over to Murray.

Mardi did not overcome Murray's apprehensions. He had been criticized for publishing Melville, particularly by Sir Walter Farquhar, who had written to Lord Ashley saying that in the *Home and Colonial Library* Murray had promised that the works "*shall contain nothing offensive to morals or good taste . . .* he has entirely departed from it [his pledge] by the publication of *Typee* and *Omoo*." Such criticism was sure to be directed also against *Mardi*, a romance involving a young American sailor, Taji, who sought happiness in the islands of the West Pacific; while the novel purposed to teach the vanity of human craving, its metaphysical presuppositions were anything but Christian.

Murray's decision was obvious. He returned the proofs to Brodhead, who then approached Bentley, who accepted *Mardi* on March 3. Even though the book ran to over a thousand pages, Bentley got it manufactured in two weeks. He probably suspected that it would be seen by other, possibly piratical, eyes, and he didn't intend to be caught up short. His terms were not those Melville had hoped for—Bentley paid him two hundred guineas against his share of the profits—but *Mardi* had the distinction of being probably the first three-decker novel by an American to be published in England. Each volume sold for half a guinea, a fairly high price for a work of American origin. Sales at this price could hardly be extravagant, but Bentley apparently hoped he could realize a profit by selling out the first edition of a thousand copies.

In America Duyckinck was ready to assist the brothers against the expected attacks from critics. He began the campaign in December of 1848 by announcing *Mardi* in the gossip column of the *Literary World*, whose readers on February 10 also saw an advertisement for the book, declaring it was full of interest, dramatic, and "glowing." On March 26, 1849, Melville wrote to the brothers from Boston asking them to furnish Duyckinck with advance sheets of *Mardi*, "as ere this they must have been printed." He said he didn't want any of the chapters of the book printed in advance of book publication except in the *Literary World*. Three days later "Joe Brooklyn" (just beginning his publishing career) sent Volume I to Duyckinck with a covering letter saying that Volume II would follow shortly and that they would not publish "under a fortnight." The advance selection appeared on April 7, and the book was published the following week.

But nothing could save *Mardi* from its fate; it was not, to put it mildly, a success. The Boston *Post* found the two Harper volumes "not only tedious but unreadable." The English reviews were almost unanimously unfavorable. Melville himself was still halfheartedly optimistic, but deeply worried. Even Elizabeth was apparently unsure of the book; she wrote to her stepmother: "I suppose by this time you are deep in the fogs of *Mardi*—if the mist ever does clear away, I should like to know what it reveals to *you*." The brothers launched a valiant advertising campaign, finding somewhere in unfavorable reviews such limp but usable quotes as "the author is no common man" (from the *London Critic*). Even as the book was being published Melville had himself turned his back on *Mardi*: ". . . it seems so long now since I wrote it and my mood has so changed, that I dread to look into it and have purposely abstained from so doing since I thanked God it was off my hands."

In addition to his disappointment in his own book, Melville was saddened early in 1849 by the complete mental breakdown of his friend Charles Fenno Hoffman, who had been forced to retire from the *Literary World* the previous October. That autumn Hoffman was declared permanently insane and placed in an asylum in Harrisburg, where he spent the rest of his life. Melville wrote: "Poor Hoffman,—I remember the shock I had when I first saw the mention of his madness. —But he was just the man to go mad—imaginative, voluptuously inclined, poor, unemployed, in the race of life outdistanced by inferiors, unmarried—without a port or haven in the universe to make. His present misfortune—rather blessing—is but the sequel to a long experience of unwhole habits of thought.—This going mad of a friend or acquaintance comes home to every man who feels his soul in him,— which but few men do. For in all of us lodges the same fuel to light the same fire. And he who has never felt, momentarily, what madness is has but a mouthful of brains." Such speculations may have formed Melville's preoccupation with the "woe which is madness"—that key phrase to come later in both *Moby Dick* and *Pierre*.

Mardi had only one edition. And although Melville had talked the brothers into a new advance of $200 in April, 1849, he must have received it with the warning that his account was so heavily overdrawn that, even if *Mardi* should prove to be the success it was not, he could not expect further income from them without another manuscript in hand.

In any case, Melville knew that he had to begin work immediately on another book, for he had the added responsibilities of a wife and child, and *Mardi* had hurt his reputation. It must also have been obvious that the new book would have to be a return to the genre of *Typee* and *Omoo*, for in June he wrote to Bentley promising "A plain, straightforward, amusing narrative of personal experience . . . the son of a gentleman on his first voyage to sea as a sailor . . . no metaphysics, no conic-sections, nothing but cakes and ale."

The new work was to be shorter than *Typee*, and ready for publication in two or three months or less. As it happened, *Redburn* was ready for the press by the end of June, and the Harper contract was signed on July 2. Melville was to receive an immediate advance of $300, and the title changed from *My First Voyage* to *Redburn, His First Voyage* —but apparently that was the only change made, and the manuscript went right to press. The brothers were also bringing out their own edition of *Typee* (the copyright had been registered on May 25).

Bentley had lost money on *Mardi*, and was agitated by the recent copyright decision that no foreigner could hold copyright in Great

Britain. But he agreed to take on *Redburn* anyway, sight unseen, although he would pay only £100 advance. Melville had asked for a full third more, figuring that, because the book was longer than he had anticipated (it was now slightly longer than *Omoo*), it could be printed in two volumes and was therefore worth more to Bentley. However, Melville was in no position to decline an offer and accepted it on July 20, promising sheets in two or three weeks.

Bentley's payment turned out to be less than the amount of Melville's debt to the Harpers before he received their new advance. He set to work on another manuscript almost as soon as the agreements for *Redburn* were signed. He was writing at least three thousand words a day despite the interruptions of the proofs, along with Malcolm's teething, and the nearly insufferable heat. This was the summer of the cholera epidemic, and, with the death toll rising from one hundred to three hundred a day, everyone who could left town. But Melville stuck doggedly to his work. He would call the new book *White-Jacket* after the coat he had worn in the Navy as a symbol of his own individuality. *White-Jacket* turned out to be even longer than *Redburn* and was apparently finished by mid-August, with the brothers obtaining copyright on the 18th and proceeding at once to put the book in type. So they had both books in the works at the same time, being unable to release *Redburn* till November 14 after Bentley's issue was out in London.

Reviewers heralded this new book as Melville's return to sanity, and sales were good. The brothers were delighted both by his industry and by his return to his former subject matter. Melville had learned his lesson well, and though he was willing to play the part of the obedient child he privately thought *Redburn* "beggarly" and called it "a little nursery tale." *White-Jacket* was only slightly better in his eyes, and he never put either book in a class with his other works. "No reputation that is gratifying to me, can possibly be achieved by either of these books. They are two *jobs*, which I have done for money," he wrote Judge Shaw, adding, ". . . it is my earnest desire to write those sort of books which are said to 'fail'—pardon this egotism." He had, after all, turned the two novels out in a period of only four months.

Now Melville conceived the idea of taking proofs of *White-Jacket* to England, hoping to secure terms good enough to pay for his trip and leave him with a sizable profit as well. Under the circumstances, such a venture was hardly reasonable. His Cliff Street account that August showed an indebtedness of $1,332.29 after the advance on *Redburn*, and however effective his personal salesmanship it could hardly bail him out of his difficulties. It seems far more likely that the actual purpose of the journey was to collect material for future books. His fund of personal experiences—which had proved far more successful on the market than his imagination—was, he realized, running out. In any case, he set sail on the *Southampton* on October 11, with letters of introduction to several British luminaries. Among those he met in London was Joe Brooklyn, who sailed on the *Southampton*'s return voyage. Melville remarked in his journal that he thought the young Harper "a regular Yankee."

Negotiations with Bentley did not go as well as Melville had planned. He accepted a note at sixty days for £100 in payment for *Redburn*, but declined an offer of £200 for *White-Jacket* on the basis of a one-thousand-copy first edition. Hoping to do better, he tried four other publishers, but without success, for all were unwilling to risk *White-Jacket* without copyright protection. Melville once again swallowed his pride and returned to Bentley's office, accepting the £200 (Bentley was later to lose £100 on the publication) in the form of a note at six months, plus half profits on all editions after the first.

With *White-Jacket* finally issued in London, the Harpers brought out the American edition March 21, 1850. Again Duyckinck rallied to Melville's support. He ran a short excerpt from *White-Jacket* in his March 9th issue, gave it a two-page review on March 16, and printed a back-page Harper advertisement on March 23, two-thirds of which was devoted to the book—including quotes from the *Literary World* and four English periodicals. The first printing of four thousand sold quickly, and a second printing of a thousand copies was on press in mid-April.

Reviewers were, for the most part, enthusiastic, and *White-Jacket* was warmly received by legislators who needed support just now for their attempts to abolish flogging in the United States Navy. "To paint general life in the Navy," Melville had written, "I let nothing slip, however small." Dana, whose *Two Years Before the Mast* was undoubtedly useful to the author of *Redburn* and *White-Jacket*, was of course pleased with the propagandistic aspect of the book and apparently wrote Melville for the names of those responsible for such actions that he had observed. (Melville, in replying, hesitated to name them.)

There were a few dissenters, however; the *Democratic Review* thumped Melville soundly for having manufactured a book which was clearly designed to flatter the English market. The heroes of *Redburn* were all Englishmen, and the American chauvinists were plainly miffed. "London pays him better for his copyright than New York," they sneered, and the extravagant compliments to the English in his books "doubtless had their value with Bentley."

But Melville was soon hard at work on a book that was at last to give full scope to his genius. When he returned to the United States on February 1, 1850, he had in mind a novel about an American exile in England and Paris. He sat down to a rigid working schedule, with the journal he had kept during his voyage as a starting point. The idea was soon abandoned for on May 1 he wrote Dana that he was "half-way" on a book clearly dominated by whaling: "It will be a strange sort of book, though, I fear. Blubber is blubber, you know; tho' you may get oil out of it, the poetry runs as hard as sap from a frozen maple tree;— and to cook the thing up, one must needs throw in a little fancy, which from the nature of things, must be ungainly as the gambols of the whales themselves. . . . I mean to give the truth of the thing, spite of this."

Nearly two months later, on June 27, he was far enough along to be able to write Bentley offering *The Whale,* the complete manuscript to be ready in the late fall. "The book is a romance of adventure founded upon certain wild legends in the Southern Sperm Whale Fisheries, and illustrated by the author's own personal experience, of two years and more, as a harpooner."

It is altogether unlikely that Melville was ever a harpooner; still, he had ample sources available, and he did not hesitate to use them. Back in 1839 Gaylord Clark had printed a piece by Reynolds entitled "Mocha Dick, or the White Whale of the Pacific," a story that intrigued readers of *The Knickerbocker* less then than it does Melville scholars today. Melville had read not only this tale but also Reynolds's *Voyage of the United States Frigate Potomac,* a copy of which he had ordered in 1847 from Cliff Street.

Another Harper author who contributed to the background of *Moby Dick* was Henry Theodore Cheever, a theology student who set sail on a whaling ship around Cape Horn to Hawaii in 1840. His book *The Whale and His Captors* was published in 1849. Cheever wrote frequently for the magazines and gave the brothers his manuscripts for *The Island World of the Pacific, Life in the Sandwich Islands,* and a memoir of the shipmaster Captain Obadiah Congar, all of which appeared in 1851. Still another of Melville's many sources, as noted earlier, was J. Ross Browne's *Etchings of a Whaling Cruise,* the Harper book which had influenced George Putnam to publish *Typee.*

Melville was taking a chance with *Moby Dick.* The complete failure of *Mardi* had made it quite clear that "metaphysics" and "conic-sections" must be avoided if he intended to maintain his current popularity as a "cakes and ale" author. Early in 1850 such success seemed assured: *Redburn* had sold over four thousand copies, according to the Harper royalty statement in February, and two months later the first edition of four thousand copies of *White-Jacket* was exhausted, with a reprint of one thousand under way. Still, Melville had to be careful, and his advance description of *The Whale* to Bentley was strictly in terms of the tried and true formula: adventure in the South Seas, backed up by personal experience.

In late July of 1850, Melville's spirits were so good that he began plans for a house party in the Berkshire Mountains at the old Melville home, which was due to be sold in the fall. In this area near Pittsfield, Massachusetts, there were plenty of literary luminaries summering, including Oliver Wendell Holmes, Nathaniel Hawthorne, and the publisher James Fields. Duyckinck and Cornelius Mathews could be persuaded to come up from New York, and Joel T. Headley (a best-selling hack) would put in a brief appearance. The date was set for the first week in August, and the guest list expanded to include Mrs. Morewood, the jolly and indefatigable neighbor whose husband was to buy the Melville house, and Harry Sedgwick, the youngest and still unpublished member of the book-writing Sedgwicks.

On the third day of the party, the group had climbed nearly to the top of Monument Mountain when they were beset by a cloudburst. They found shelter under a cliff, and Holmes passed around a silver mug filled with champagne. At the summit, Melville climbed out on an overhanging rock which resembled a bowsprit and began to pull on the imaginary rigging. Holmes protested that he had vertigo; Hawthorne searched for that great carbuncle that was the subject of an earlier story of his. Mathews held forth, declaiming from a copy of William Cullen Bryant's poems that he had brought along for just that purpose. A small literary discussion was started, but did not develop fully until the group had gone to Fields's house for dinner.

Mathews, the hotheaded member of the New York clique, engaged in a rather violent argument with Holmes on the current expression of American bumptiousness known to the newspapers as "Young America." Melville finally came to Mathews's defense against the claims of English superiority, disgusted as he was with the Young America idea, both in politics and literature. He must have given a good deal of thought to the matter, for his feelings were clear in a review he wrote for the *Literary World* entitled "Hawthorne and his Old Mosses."

Duyckinck returned home from Pittsfield with a first-draft copy in his pocket. Holmes was not to be placated. Nine days later he wrote the Yale Phi Beta Kappa poem, *Astreae*, a withering blow to the New York crowd, including the couplet on the Harpers' teaching scholars how to spell.

Melville's disenchantment with New York had been slowly growing, and on September 14 he bought the house adjoining the old Melville home. The purchase price was $6,500; to meet it, he borrowed $3,000 from Judge Shaw, adding the $2,000 from the house in New York and a note for $1,500 in anticipation of royalties. But the whale book was far from finished that fall as Melville had hoped. It was not even ready in April, 1851, when he wrote to Fletcher asking for more money. Fletcher had to say No. They were making, he replied, "an extensive and expensive addition to our establishement: one which will demand all our resources." The real reason was enclosed with the letter: a statement of Melville's earnings showed a debit balance on his account of nearly $700. The implication was clear: the whale book must go to press as soon as possible. And in order to pay for the house in full—without using all he had obtained from his father-in-law—Melville had to borrow $2,050 at 9 percent interest.

On June 14, he turned up in New York with his new manuscript almost ready. But the construction work on Pearl Street, with new buildings backing up to the Cliff Street buildings, plus publication demands of *Harper's New Monthly Magazine,* had caused the printers to fall behind schedule. Also New York was too hot for good work, and Melville left town with the whale manuscript only half through the press.

Five weeks later he wrote to Bentley, who had agreed to pay £150 for the English rights, that the tail of the manuscript was in press, and the printer's copy would come in about two to three weeks. Duyckinck was a little tardy when he wrote his wife from the Berkshires on August 7, 1851: "By the way, tell Henry [Panton] that Harpers are to publish Melville's whale book. I have said a great deal for Redfield [J. S. Redfield, Poe's publisher] but it appears to have been concluded." Actually a formal agreement with the brothers had not yet been reached, but the book was in proofs by September 10, when they were sent off to Bentley under the title *The Whale.*

The Harper contract signed two days later stipulated that the publishers would pay for the plates and divide profits with the author. This time there was no advance. The agreement, like all the Melville contracts, was made for seven years; if, after that term, Melville wished to hold the rights to the book, he could do so by buying the plates at half cost less reasonable deductions for "wear and tear."

As soon as proofs were ready, someone in the "Literary Department" was asked to select a portion that could be printed in the October, 1851, issue of the *New Monthly Magazine*. The excerpt chosen was the exciting account of the chase of the whale. It was entitled "The Town-Ho's Story," and carried a footnote reading, "From 'The Whale.' The title of a new work by Mr. Melville, in the press at Harper and Brothers and now publishing in London by Mr. Bentley." Sometime after the *Magazine* went to press, the book's title was changed to *Moby-Dick; or the Whale,* and Melville made some corrections and added thirty-five passages not incorporated in Bentley's edition of *The Whale,* which was issued on October 18. (Originally hyphenated, the title has for many years been designated by two separate words.)

Moby Dick was published from Cliff Street on November 14, exactly two years after *Redburn.* It was given the lead position in the "Literary Notices" department of the December *Magazine,* the review running to a column and a half and praising both book and author: ". . . in point of richness and variety of incident, originality of conception and splendor of description [the book] surpasses any of the former productions of this highly successful author."

A few months earlier, "this highly successful author" had figured up earnings from his books. On April 29, he had grossed $3,775.05 from his English and $3,591.21 from his American contracts. After he knew the cost of Harper plates of *Moby Dick* and the size of the first printing, but before he received the February, 1852, Cliff Street statement, he added his receipts from Bentley on *The Whale.* The Bentley payment looked better on Melville's paper than it did on the books of Bentley, who was ruefully to note two years later that of his first printing of 500 copies 217 remained unsold.

The brothers decided to risk a 3,000-copy first printing of *Moby Dick* but the paper ordered was on the short side, permitting a run of 2,915 copies only. They designed a highly readable page, using a nine-point type with two point leading. The type page was 20 by 30 picas, thus permitting ample margins on the page, which was 5 by 7⅜ inches, full trim. By today's standards, however, the book's bulk (including colored end papers) of 1½ inches makes it somewhat cumbersome. The whiteness and opacity of the paper after more than one hundred years show the high percentage of rag used. Current economies in book production hardly guarantee such posterity for any unrecognized classic being issued today. Judging from known copies, six colors of muslin were used in binding: brown, black, red, plum, blue, and green. Title and author lines were stamped in gold leaf near the top of the spine, as was the publisher's imprint near the bottom. Also in gold at the top of the spine were three rules and a simple ornament of dots and inverted carets, a design that was repeated in reverse at the bottom. On the front cover "Harper and Brothers   New-York" was blind stamped within a sailor's life preserver, a stamping that is reproduced on the front cover of this volume. (See also illustration 17.)

The title page was designed with "Moby-Dick; or, The Whale" at the top, followed by the author's name and the titles of his five earlier works. The publisher's imprint included in smaller type at the bottom: "London: Richard Bentley" (prestige for Melville and good business relations for Harper's). Also centered at the bottom was the date, 1851. The title page was backed up with the copyright notice and facing it the printed dedication which Melville wrote out for the friend and fellow craftsman who best understood his inner compulsion and conflict: "In Token of my admiration for his genius, this book Is Inscribed to Nathaniel Hawthorne."*

The table of contents—set in double column—occupied two pages, and the next, the half-title, was backed up by a note headed "Etymology." "Etymology" was repeated on the facing page (ix) giving definitions of the whale and the spelling of the word in thirteen languages, beginning with the "Erromangoan." The following thirteen pages of front matter were headed "Extracts," giving quotations on the whale, both real and figurative, from the Bible, through Shakespeare, Bunyan, and Milton down to J. Ross Browne. The back matter contained a one-page epilogue, set in italics, and six pages of advertising, one page each on *White-Jacket*, *Omoo*, *Mardi*, *Typee*, and *Redburn*, and the last one divided between *Harper's New Monthly Magazine* and three new Harper books.

The English reviews were not, on the whole, encouraging. American reaction varied from the great enthusiasm of the *New Monthly* to total disfavor, with the Duyckinks' review in *Literary World* perhaps the most surprising. Evert Duyckinck strongly objected to Melville's challenging "the most sacred associations of life," and his brother

---

* A copy of the 1855 Harper edition autographed by Hawthorne was once spotted by John Drinkwater in a New York bookstore. He purchased it for "a few dollars" and later told Dr. A. S. W. Rosenbach, the famous book collector, of his find. "I wanted this copy as much as I had ever wanted any other book, and there was nothing for me to do but tell him so," Dr. Rosenbach recalled later. "I offered him twenty times what he paid for it and to my surprise and delight he generously let me have it."

George found the whaling details tedious. Melville might have anticipated the outrage: "I have written a wicked book," he wrote to Hawthorne, "and feel spotless as the lamb." The *Democratic Review* leveled yet another blow, speaking of Melville's imposing upon his readers his "immeasurable vanity."

"Call me Ishmael," the opening phrase in *Moby Dick,* is Melville's description of himself, a spiritual outcast and lonely wanderer over the earth. The story of Ahab in pursuit of the whale gave Melville a further opportunity to raise his own metaphysical questions and voice his criticism of conventional morality. Vernon L. Parrington writes, "His [Melville's] life—even more than Emerson's—laid upon America was a yardstick to measure the shortcomings of a professed civilization. . . . He outran Thoreau in contempt for current material ideals."

Even though the Harper edition of *Moby Dick* sold 1,535 copies in less than two weeks, Melville's finances were still in grave jeopardy. A Cliff Street statement of November 25 showed his account still overdrawn by $422.82, a sum which had to be paid off before he would receive any returns from the American edition of *Moby Dick.*

Desperate again, Melville set diligently to work on the curious novel that would be *Pierre: or the Ambiguities.* What he intended with the book was an examination in depth of what Hawthorne had termed "the truth of the human heart," something far more profound than the pursuit of the whale. "So, now, let us add Moby Dick to our blessing, and step from that," he wrote to Hawthorne. "Leviathan is not the biggest fish;—I have heard of Krakens."

The manuscript changed shape constantly and eventually resolved itself into an exploration of mysteries: love, morality, and knowledge. In his biography of Melville, Leon Howard calls *Pierre* a "deliberately ambiguous novel." It also became the vehicle for Melville's sarcastic attack on Young America, as well as a book that scandalized its Victorian readers with implications of incest that were all but spelled out on the pages. These two aspects of *Pierre* were connected; Melville surely knew that the priggish Duyckinck, who had objected to his earlier handling of such matters, would be thoroughly appalled by *Pierre.* It was on February 14, 1852, that Melville gave his brother Allan instructions for the Harper contract and canceled his subscription to the *Literary World.*

Melville had left himself no choice but to plunge to the end. But the mysteries he had proposed escaped him, and the conclusion of *Pierre* is a melodramatic hodge-podge of nearly meaningless violence. Bentley had lost money on all of the other books and refused to accept Melville's terms for *Pierre*. Melville went ahead and sent the proofs on April 16, trying to assure Bentley that *Pierre* had "unquestionable novelty, as regards my former ones,—treating of utterly new scenes and characters;—and, as I believe, very much more calculated for popularity than anything you have yet published of mine—being a regular romance, with a mysterious plot to it, and stirring passions at work, and withal, representing a new and elevated aspect of American life." He went on to say that perhaps *Pierre* should appear "anonymously, or under an assumed name" and finished off with the desperate suggestion "that on the new field of production upon which I embark in the present work, you and I shall hereafter participate in many not unprofitable business adventures."

Here one wonders if Melville's cheerful description of himself a few months earlier as "slightly insane" was not partially true. The book described in the letter bore no resemblance to the proofs enclosed, and it seems almost impossible that Melville could really have expected it to be his most popular work. Yet the fact of the matter is that *Pierre* rather closely followed the pattern of Madame de Staël's *Corinne*, a book Bentley had published and Melville had read with curiosity; it is altogether possible that Melville earnestly thought he was sending Bentley a book sure to find the publisher's favor. But Bentley saw no hope at all for *Pierre*—his costly experiment with his American author had come to an end. This was a great disappointment to Melville, who had to date received over half his literary income in England through advances.

The Harpers, however, were still game. Their latest statement showed that 471 additional copies of *Moby Dick* had been sold,* in addition to some copies of the earlier books, with the result that Melville's debt to them was reduced to less than $150. They advanced $500 for *Pierre*, which was to be published on a royalty basis of 20 cents a copy ($1 retail). After 1,190 copies were sold, there would be a sale to liquidate the costs of stereotypes and of review copies. This contract, as well as the earlier ones, was signed "Harper & Brothers" in John's handwriting, but William Demarest, not his brother Gerherdus, gave the attesting signature. The publishing imprint of the brothers' London agent, Sampson Low, were secured for the British edition, which would appear in November.

The American edition, dedicated to Greylock Mountain, came out on August 6, 1852, and was received with outrage and indignation. As

---

* There were still first edition copies late in 1852 to ship to Henry M. Whitney in Honolulu, who ordered four copies of each of the six Melville titles.

Melville might have expected, Duyckinck was livid: "The combined power of New England transcendentalism and Spanish Jesuitical casuistry could not have more completely befogged nature and truth, than this confounded Pierre has done. . . . The most immoral *moral* of the story, if it has any moral at all, seems to be the impracticability of virtue; a leering demoniacal spectre of an idea which seems to be peering at us through the dim obscure of this dark book, and mocking us with this dismal falsehood." The *Southern Literary Messenger* thought *Pierre* deserved to be "unbought on the shelves of the bookseller," as indeed it was; only 238 copies were purchased during the eight months after publication—an average of less than two sales for each of the 150 review copies sent. Other critics inclined to the explanation that "Herman Melville has gone 'clean daft.'"

Melville's mood was made clear in the postscript of a letter to Hawthorne: "If you find any *sand* in this letter, regard it as so many sands of my life, which ran out as I was writing it." He later received his statement from the brothers. *Pierre* had paid off only 10 percent of the advance, and despite $300 worth of sales from previous books Melville was still in their debt in the amount of $298.71. In the meantime, in the spring of 1853, Melville had begun work on a New England story which Hawthorne had encouraged him to write, but something went wrong and the work was abandoned around April.

Elizabeth was expecting their third child in May, and under the circumstances it was decided by the family that an appointment to a foreign consulship would be extremely beneficial. An elaborate campaign was launched, and letters of recommendation and inquiry were sent off in all directions. The answer finally came back that the only possibility was "one of the less lucrative consulates in Italy, say Rome." Such an appointment would not pay its own expenses, and so the project was dropped.

There was, however, one other avenue of income open to Melville: the magazines. He added to his bank account (which still contained the $1,000 he'd saved from Judge Shaw's first loan and the $500 advance on *Pierre*) another $500, of which no part came from books. "Bartleby the Scrivener," whose constant "I would prefer not to" probably echoed Melville's own sentiments, appeared in two installments in the November and December, 1853, *Putnam's*, and "Cock-a-Doodle-Doo!" in the December *Harper's*. Melville also remained on good terms with Bentley, who invited him to contribute to his *Miscellany*.

In the spring of 1853, Melville called on the brothers to show them the manuscript of the "Agatha" story which he had discussed with

Hawthorne. Did Harper's discourage him from publishing it? Such an inference might be made from the first sentence of a letter he wrote them on November 24: "In addition to the work which I took to New York last Spring, but which I was prevented from printing at that time, I have now in hand, and pretty well on towards completion, another book—300 pages, say—partly of nautical adventure, and partly—or, rather, chiefly, of Tortoise Hunting Adventure. It will be ready for press some time in the coming January. Meanwhile, it would be convenient to have advanced to me upon it $300.—My acct: with you, at present, can not be very far from square."

On receipt of this letter, Fletcher asked William Demarest for a record of the sales of Melville's books (see illustrations 16 and 18), and agreed to the advance, which Melville received three days before the Harper fire. But the manuscript of *Tortoises and Tortoise-Hunting*, to be ready in January, was never delivered. Melville evidently assumed that with the Harper establishment in ruins no new publications would be undertaken in January. It was not until February 20 that he finally wrote to express his concern that the manuscript, "owing to a variety of causes," was not submitted on the promised date. He assured the brothers that they would in no way "lose by the delay," and said he would come down to New York in several weeks' time to explain everything.

The real explanation, however, seemed to come from *Putnam's*, which published in its March issue the first of a Melville series called "The Encantadas," undoubtedly based on the work he had been preparing for the brothers. They were sorely piqued. This was the last straw. Unlike his English publishers, they had stuck by Melville through good days and bad, stoically absorbing losses on *Mardi* and *Pierre*. That Melville should turn about face during their own days of misfortune and hand over to a competitor the manuscript for which they had paid an advance was a bitter pill to swallow. Melville did not have to return the advance, but it would be twelve long years before the brothers published his *Battle-Pieces*, a book of Civil War poems, some of which had appeared in *Harper's Magazine*.

This book chalked up still another loss on the Harper ledgers, further proof that Melville's days as a productive author were over. Late in 1866 he took a job as deputy inspector of customs in New York and his monthly salary from the customhouse was to keep him and his family in funds for nineteen years. An apathetic reading public bought but few of his books although all eight of his Harper titles were regularly catalogued through 1890. In 1889 Melville was to give his publishers permission to print Chapter LXI from *Moby Dick* in their new *Harper Fifth Reader;* the title of the selection was changed from "Stubb Kills a Whale" to "Whale Fishing in the Indian Ocean." The last known Harper letter to Melville, dated September 25, 1889, accompanied a complimentary copy of the *Reader*, "published today."

Melville died on September 28, 1891, leaving his final draft of *Billy Budd* unpublished. On December 14 Mrs. Melville wrote to J. Henry Harper agreeing that the plates to *Typee* should be delivered to her home on East Twenty-sixth Street and that "as fast as the other volumes respectively appear, the plates thereof may be severally melted." Copyrights were expiring after forty-two years and the books were being reprinted by the United States Book Company. "I have already expressed to you my regret," Elizabeth Melville wrote, "that your house was not to bring out the volumes, and that the old imprint was not to be upon them."

CHAPTER XVII

The New Monthly Magazine

1850–1853

Henry W. Longfellow is the first author known to have received an invitation to submit an article to *Harper's New Monthly Magazine*. On October 1, 1849, Gerherdus Demarest wrote Longfellow requesting that five hundred copies of his *Poems* be forwarded to New York as the Cliff Street supply was running low. He then added, "We are about establishing a monthly Miscellany. . . . If you would be inclined to furnish any suggestions, or supply any article, prose or poetical for its pages, we will be glad to receive them. The first number will not be put in train 'till Nov. 1st."

This casual note seems to have been written more to share Cliff Street pride over a new publishing venture than to solicit a contribution. Otherwise Longfellow would surely have been offered payment rather than told that the magazine would retail for 25 cents a copy; he would have been assured that his name would honor the first issue rather than notified that this number would contain 160 pages, royal-octavo size.

However, the Demarest letter does show that by October, 1849, the Cliff Street engine was being fired to start pulling the new magazine. With luck it would start in the New Year with Volume I, Number 1.

Impressed by the public response to the 25-cent "numbers" of many works issued prior to book publication, the brothers had also noted the success of other "miscellanies," such as Bentley's in London and Littell's in Boston. It was but a short step from the publication of numbers to the monthly serialization of reprints. With "Current Events," "Literary Notices," and "Fashions" added, they would have "a tender to our business," as Fletcher was to remark later.

The decision to issue the *Magazine* in royal-octavo size (6 by 9) was a natural one, as was the decision to print the text in two columns. It was the size of Alison's *Europe* and other popular paperback serials, generally in two columns, a size that could be economically printed and bound. On the other hand, it was larger than the full-measure page of *The Knickerbocker* and seemed to be favored by the public over the three-column, quarto size (9 by 12) of Duyckinck's *Literary World*. But the original and logical plan to print 160 pages (five 32's) was abandoned, perhaps for editorial reasons, and the first issue ran only to 144 pages, setting a pattern for years to come.

The first number was not "put in train" till the late spring of 1850, with publication in June. Seventy-five hundred copies were printed, a quantity that was to skyrocket to 50,000 in six months. "The design of the Publishers in issuing this work," they said in "A Word at the Start," "is to place within the reach of the great mass of the American people the unbounded treasures of the Periodical Literature of the present day." They were anticipating by seventy-two years a public response that was to bring a similar success to DeWitt and Lila Acheson Wallace when they launched the *Reader's Digest*. As for Longfellow, while the brothers did not print an original contribution from him in that first number, they did include an abridgment of an article from the *Dublin University Magazine*, headed "Longfellow," which praised his poetry and told of the romance that had led to his second marriage. They also paid tribute to Prescott, printing a three-fourth-page engraving by Lossing of a bust of the historian and a 750-word account of his literary career. Similar treatment was given to the historians Alison and Macaulay, and the three engravings were the only illustrations printed in the June issue.* Excepting those in a section devoted to women's fashions. This section, generally three pages and a concession to the popularity of *Godey's Lady's Book*, was placed discreetly at the

---

* While the first issue was being read that June, Prescott was meeting Macaulay and Alison for the first time in London, where Prescott was enjoying a triumphal month of tours, receptions, dinners, and balls; he met leading personages of the social and political life of London and was presented to Queen Victoria. He also met Thackeray and other literati, and John Murray III gave him a big party.

end of the "book." But to hook the reader the lines of the engraver were cast in the early pages. Thus the August number carried a half-page engraving of Zachary Taylor, after a daguerreotype by Brady, along with a six-page biographical article on the President, who had died July 9. The November issue luxuriated in thirteen engravings by Lossing, including an ingeniously drawn capital letter *I* that depicted a broken cannon, but these blocks were at hand, with Lossing's *Pictorial Field-Book of the Revolution* already being issued in numbers. In January, 1851, the *New Monthly* began regularly to reprint two or three pages from *Punch*, always spotted liberally with cartoons. As circulation mounted, profits were plowed back into expensive engravings.

At the start the pressing editorial consideration was quality of text matter. The success of the first and subsequent issues depended on expert selection from "unbounded treasures" of what American readers would probably like most. The market was there—of that fact there was no doubt. The avidity of Americans for reading matter had been stimulated by the mammoth weeklies a decade earlier and nourished—beyond what Cliff Street enterprise could do through the book trade—in small towns and rural districts by colporteurs and by subscription selling, as illustrated by what Henry Howe was doing in Ohio. The brothers could also use agents to sell the *New Monthly* and also obtain subscriptions by mail. There was competition with other magazines, to be sure, but that would be met by presenting from one-third to one-half more reading matter, in better style and at a cheaper rate than any other monthly could offer. Also they had a prestige of name known wherever books were read. But the success of their new venture would depend upon their ability to give Americans the best of the desired English authors and an increasing amount of native writing of merit. Americans were still dependent on European culture, but they were a patriotic people, proud of their own culture in the East and South. And they were thrilled with the beauty of their plantations and forests, their prairies, rivers, and mountains. They were excited about their frontier country—now extending to the Pacific Ocean. They were eager to read what depicted and interpreted their America, but most native writers were more enamored of this literary ideal than competent to articulate it.

After the success of the *New Monthly* was assured, the Harper compositors liked to tell of the excitement in those weeks when the first number was shaping up. Fletcher brought copy to the composing room, made up the "dummy," cut copy to fit, or added lines to fill out columns, often working until late at night to make that first deadline. It was taken for granted that Fletcher would be managing editor, with Henry J. Raymond as the obvious "reader" to lean on for editorial direction. Just as they had relied for more than twenty years on readers' reports on books and manuscripts, so for the new *New Monthly* they would use competent literary advice, as essential to the editorial room as upper-case letters to the composing room.

Raymond had enjoyed his previous association with the brothers and was willing to undertake this new editorial responsibility. But his was the perennial problem of finding enough time. In addition to his *Courier and Enquirer* job, he had been doing an increasing amount of lecturing—particularly on politics—for which he had developed considerable flair. Indeed, this political activity led him in 1849—he was then in his thirtieth year—to campaign successfully for a seat in the New York Assembly. It may be that it was his absence that winter in Albany which contributed to the delay in launching the *New Monthly*. From the beginning Raymond wrote the "Monthly Record of Current Events," which occupied twelve pages in the first number, and was to remain an important feature of the magazine for years. In the December, 1850, issue, which was also the beginning of the second volume, the "Monthly Record" was about equally concerned with American and European events, not solely political events but also cultural concerns. In those first two volumes, the "Monthly Record" averaged about ten pages and then began to taper off to five and six pages, one reason being no doubt that Raymond, having established the *New York Daily Times* on September 18, 1851, had somewhat less time for his chores on the *Magazine*.

Another reason for reducing current coverage was the introduction of three new departments, one of which, the "Editor's Drawer," was mainly humor—a feature that was immediately popular with readers. The "Editor's Drawer" was named for the drawer in Fletcher's desk into which he tossed clippings or notations of amusing anecdotes and oddities. Clark of *The Knickerbocker* was asked to screen these items and add from his own file for the monthly assortments.

One of the most felicitous features of *The Knickerbocker* inspired a second department called "Editor's Table." Here Tayler Lewis, professor of Greek, Oriental Languages, and Bible at Union College, wrote regularly, beginning with the seventeenth number, on social, political, and philosophical subjects. When Fletcher asked Lewis to sit at this table, he was making an obvious choice, for Lewis had for ten years or more been turning out three or four articles a year in the *Biblical*

Repository, the New York *Observer*, the *Whig Review*, and the *Literary World*. In 1845, he had published *Platonic Philosophy, or Plato against the Atheists*, a Harper book that still may be read with interest by Grecians.

The third department introduced in the November, 1851, issue was destined to be the longest-lived of any. It was called the "Editor's Easy Chair" and its first occupant was Donald G. Mitchell (Ik. Marvel), whose book *Fresh Gleanings* had first shown his competence as a writer.

Dating from the first issue was a section of book reviews, forty in the sixth number and averaging nearly twenty in the first seven volumes. If book reviews were a part of the "tender" for Harper business, it was more a tender for others, for about 60 percent of the reviews covered works of other publishers. Most of the reviews were written by George Ripley.

Ripley had come to New York in 1847 after the failure of his Brook Farm experiment, a colony in West Roxbury, near Boston, which was an outgrowth of New England transcendentalism, although Emerson was not affiliated with it. Prescott, Ticknor, and their circle dubbed this effort to set up a rural utopia a "Hospital for Incapables," but no word was more unfair to the Unitarian Ripley than "incapable." Although his noble experiment was a failure, he did spend twenty years earning enough money to pay off the farm's indebtedness. Shortly after reaching New York, Ripley began reading manuscripts for the brothers, and in 1849 Horace Greeley made him literary editor of the New York *Tribune*, for years his chief source of income. To the shabby boarding house in Brooklyn where he and his wife (she was Sophia Dana Ripley, a cousin of Richard H. Dana, Jr.) lived in one room he carried not only Harper manuscripts to report on but also new books to write about under "Literary Notices." Of all the brothers, Wesley was the one with whom Ripley formed the closest ties, with whom he could share shop talk about books and ideas. Later he was to say of Wesley that "his conversation never failed to be pleasant and instructive, in harmony with his candid and affectionate bearing, and enlivened with quiet humor. . . ."

With Raymond, Clark, Lewis, Mitchell, and Ripley in his stable of regular contributors and advisors, and with 144 pages instead of the customary 80 or 96 of his competitors, Fletcher knew that he could give American readers a literary journey worth their money. Furthermore, the Cliff Street genius at publicity was making sure that all the important newspapers and magazines across the land regularly received advance copies and publicity releases. And advertising. Duyckinck ignored the new Harper venture in the editorial columns of the *Literary World*, but by the mid-June issue, he and his subscribers were reading the customary Harper back-cover advertisement. It carried one of the first commendations of *Harper's Magazine* ever reprinted, a blurb from the Auburn (New York) *Daily Advertiser:* "The Harpers have commenced the publication of a Monthly Magazine which bids fair to eclipse, in point of interest, anything in the periodical line that has yet appeared in this country."* Those forbidding and prophetic words made unhappy reading for Duyckinck, who only a few years earlier had written off Fletcher as "a kind of curly pated fellow," the least of the brothers.

In fact, Duyckinck had now to sit in two very uncomfortable chairs, both sent over to his office at 157 Broadway along with that first complimentary copy of the June issue. The chair he now used for business was too tight for comfort, reminding him that his best source of advertising revenue was also his strongest competitor for subscribers. The chair he now used for editorial work was too big even for his ample seat. He was not as able a journalist as Raymond nor as good a literary critic as Ripley. Furthermore the editorial chair forced him into such a position that he could not write what many of his literary clique were saying, that the new Cliff Street venture was just another slap at native American authors—the vaunted *New Monthly* was in the last analysis an assortment of clippings from *Household Words* and other British magazines, pieces from Dickens, and the start of a new Charles Lever novel. But Duyckinck could say nothing. He had only to look critically through that same June 15th issue that carried the big advertisement of his new rival to see that of his own seventeen pages of text, nine and one-half pages were filled with extracts from English periodicals.

With nearly every issue requiring a larger printing than the last one, the *New Monthly* was stepping on the toes of a lot of editors. According to the U.S. Census for 1850, there were 2,526 periodicals being issued, of which 254 were daily newspapers and 569 were journals designated "Literary and Miscellaneous." Specifically, there were 100

---

* Probably the first review of *Harper's New Monthly Magazine* was carried by the *New York Journal of Commerce,* which said in part, "Its plan and design are eminently commendable. That they will be ably and faithfully executed, the character of the publishers, and the ample facilities at their command abundantly guarantee. We have looked through the June number and read a portion of its contents with much gratification." (See illustration 19 for a typical Harper full-page advertisement in the *Literary World*.)

monthlies with a total circulation of nearly 9 million copies. All of these monthlies were being hurt. *"Harpers* is a good foreign magazine, but it is not *Graham's* by a long run . . . the veriest worshipper of the dust of Europe will tire of its dead level," George R. Graham wrote in March, 1851. Graham had made a significant contribution to American letters in ten years but he had only two more to go. The *American (Whig) Review* had earlier made a really savage attack: "The absence of an international copyright law cuts off British writers in America, and, *vice versa*, cuts off American writers from all profits in Great Britain. Hence a large publishing house like that of the Harpers, wealthy, influential, and anti-American in feeling as concerns literary development and encouragement may easily swell their enormous gains by pampering British writers. . . ."

Such words would not have been printed by the non-controversialist Duyckinck. However, what he wrote in October, 1852, was damning words of faint praise: "This magazine [*Harper's*], just entering its second hundred thousand shows no little tact and enterprise on the part of its publishers. Their outlay is liberal, and generally in the right direction." Faced with loss of subscribers to *Harper's* and loss of publishers' book advertising to the new *Norton's Literary Gazette and Publishers' Circular*, Duyckinck was seeing his bimonthly through its last difficult year. A disastrous fire was the crowning blow and the last issue came out in the summer of 1853. The last Harper page advertisement had appeared in the May 14th issue, with Fletcher purring over a saucer of rich cream, "The unparalleled and unexpected success (118,000 a month) has compelled the publishers to resort to extraordinary means for printing the work with the requisite rapidity."

Rufus Wilmot Griswold was out to give Fletcher competition from the start. He arranged with Messrs Stringer & Townsend of New York to publish the *International Monthly Magazine*, which he edited.* His knowledge of American writers and his affable and exuberant manner made him a formidable opponent. Even so Griswold was willing to hoist other literary flags along with his native banner, being shrewd enough to know that American readers persisted in their wish to read what their British cousins wrote, and that they especially wanted to read what Dickens was currently publishing in England.

Fifteen years later, *The American Literary Gazette and Publishers' Circular* was to publish a story of Griswold's abortive effort to obtain first proofs of Dickens's *Bleak House*. He authorized one of the pub-

* The periodical was actually launched July 1, 1850, as a weekly.

lishers of the *International Monthly Magazine* who was going abroad to offer Dickens $2,000 for advance sheets of his next novel. A "sensational paragraph" presented this news in the New York *Evening Post*.

The watchful Harpers sent out on the next steamer a messenger [Fletcher himself?] who went directly to Mr. Dickens and found him ready for any reasonable offer. "The Post" with Dr. Griswold's paragraph being shown him, he at once decided to hold the Yankees to the terms therein set forth, and agreed to furnish Harper & Brothers with advance sheets of the next novel which was "Bleak House." The messenger of "The International" had made the very great blunder of going to Mr. Dickens' publisher instead of to Mr. Dickens himself, was told that Mr. Dickens was busied about private theatricals which would probably absorb his attention for an indefinite period, and that no new novel was in contemplation. In fact, it is very probable that on account of the bargain with Harpers, "Bleak House" was written before it otherwise would have been.

This anecdote is at least partially apocryphal since the Harper *Priority List* listing payments for first proofs gives £360 ($1,728) as the sum paid for advance sheets of *Bleak House*. Serialization was begun in the April, 1852, issue of the *Magazine*. It was also published in numbers and complete in two volumes on September 21, 1853. That same April of 1852 saw the publication of the last issue of Griswold's *International*, with subscribers being notified that it was merging with *Harper's*, where it was hoped the best features of the *International* would be preserved. *Harper's* itself did not deign to mention the merger. If there was cheering on Cliff Street over another strike-out, with Griswold retired to the bench, it was not for the public to hear.

Even from the beginning some short pieces were reprinted in the *Magazine* without indicating English sources. By the end of the first year only a few sources were being listed, a drop from twenty-one in June to five in February. Soon attributions to *Household Words*, *Blackwood's*, etc., were dropped entirely, owing perhaps to criticisms, such as Graham's, that the *New Monthly* was anti-American. But the leading British authors continued to be named: Dickens, Howitt, Bulwer-Lytton, Southey, Mitford, De Quincey, Martineau, Carlyle, Thackeray. Especially Dickens, with many short pieces and *Christmas Stories*, which later were issued in book form, as was *Bleak House*.

English serials marched through the issues of the magazine as regularly as Orion across the winter skies. Charles Lever's *Maurice Tiernay*, which was the first *Harper's Magazine* serial, ran through nineteen numbers, and then came out in book form in February, 1852, the fourth Harper book by the Irish novelist, with fifteen more to come. The early record for length of serialization goes to Bulwer-Lytton. *My Novel; or, Varieties in English Life* extended through twenty-nine issues. Apparently the brothers no longer believed as they professed to believe in 1836 (when they issued *Rienzi* in one volume) that readers were vexed to wait long to know how an absorbing story turned out. They paid £75 for early proofs, a surprisingly low figure in view of the 1835 contract specifying £50 per volume.

The first November issue carried a selection from Charles Kingsley's book *Alton Locke*, which was published simultaneously. Both this book and *Yeast*, a year later, reflected the young author's interest in Christian socialism. The brothers were to publish more of Kingsley but missed out on *Water Babies* and his other books for children. The April, 1851, issue included two pieces from *London Labor and the London Poor* by Henry Mayhew, also being published in numbers prior to the appearance of Volume I in August. Mayhew's was the first attempt to describe the seamy side of London life from the point of view of practical philanthropy; his work was not to be completed till 1864, but the brothers carried it no further than Volume II. The 1853 catalogue lists four other books which Mayhew wrote in collaboration with his brother, Horace. One of them, *The Magic of Kindness* (1849), is important today because of the illustrations by Cruikshank.

The early 1851 issues ran two pieces from Agnes Strickland's *Lives of the Queens of Scotland* at the time Volume I was published. Seven further volumes appeared during the decade. Miss Strickland devoted the fifties to writing about the Scottish queens as she had devoted the forties to twelve volumes on the English queens, published in America by Lea & Blanchard, but later—in abridged form—by the brothers. There were also pieces by Harriet Martineau, well known to American women, remembered for her visit to America in the 1830's, for her deafness, and for her strong abolitionist feelings. Her articles caught the eyes of educational theorists, for she argued that freedom and rationality, not command and obedience, should be the basis of a child's education.

From a literary point of view, Mary Russell Mitford was the most important woman writer whose name appears in the early volumes of the *Magazine*. Miss Mitford moved easily among the literati of England, especially as a friend of Elizabeth Barrett Browning. Her articles included "Haunts of Genius" and "Personal Sketches and Reminiscences," the latter taken from *Recollections of a Literary Life; or,*

Books, Places, and People, which the brothers had just published—a 570-page book in cloth for $1. First proofs had been purchased for £15.

Opening pages of most of the early issues were devoted to selections from the works of English writers, all illustrated with engravings. Thus Fletcher was able to kill two literary birds with one editorial stone. Illustrations in the opening pages tempted the reader's interest, and the engravings were at hand and paid for since they had been used in books. Thus two poems by Goldsmith, "The Deserted Village" and "The Traveler," utilized available engravings and catered to the current appeal of poetry, as did Thomson's "Spring" and "Summer." The latter was the lead piece in the June, 1851, issue, beginning Volume III. Except for Gray's "Elegy" and one Scottish poem, it was the last of foreign works to lead off an issue. Thereafter readers opened the *Magazine* to the work of native American writers. Criticisms of Cliff Street Anglomania had hit home. In fact, they had begun the April and May, 1851, issues with American pieces, one of them a panegyric of Washington Irving, presumably written by Ripley. "With the exception of Mr. Paulding," he eulogized, "none of our eminent living authors have been so long before the public." For nearly fifty years Irving has been the acknowledged king of American literature and "the monarch that knew not Joseph has not yet ascended the throne." Yet Irving was not peculiarly a "national writer . . . he betrays none of the prejudices of national pride. . . . Even the English, who are slow to recognize a melody in their own language when spoken by a transatlantic tongue, have vied with his countrymen in rendering homage to his genius." This opening piece on the American master of prose was followed by one on William Cullen Bryant, the American poet whose works were said to merit shelf space along with Milton and Wordsworth. Each article carried engraved likenesses of the men by Lossing—Bryant's face without the flowing beard—and engravings of Sunnyside on the Hudson and Bryant's residence at Roslyn, Long Island.

Lossing also furnished articles as well as engravings for four other leaders, one a splendid piece entitled "Arlington House," written after he had spent several days as a guest of George Washington Parke Custis. The Custis house was filled with mementoes of Washington, many of which Lossing sketched as the seventy-two-year-old Custis related anecdotes of the Father of his Country who had adopted him as his own son. (Examples of Lossing's engravings are given in illustrations 20 and 26.)

The left bank of the Potomac had been given the lead position earlier in "A Sketch of Washington City" by Anne C. Lynch, so competently written that it makes interesting reading today. Miss Lynch felt compelled to begin with a comment on national vanity and national pride, expressed in the typical mid-century self-consciousness of Americans who must always compare their culture with the European. While she used her maiden name for her writing, she was also famous under her married name, Botta, for the literary salon in her New York home, the first important one in American letters, where Poe, Greeley, Ripley, and Margaret Fuller were frequent guests.

Lossing and his partner Barritt made the engravings for Miss Lynch's article and for three by T. Addison Richards, a member of the Hudson River school of artists. Richards's pieces on Lake George and the Susquehanna carried ten illustrations engraved from either paintings or drawings. "The Landscape of the South" was a lead article embellished by twelve engravings made from Richards's original work, featuring mountain and water scenes in Virginia, the Carolinas, and Georgia. That particular issue (May, 1853) carried forty-three additional illustrations. This pictorial wealth was financially possible after the *Magazine* had entered its second hundred thousand. Mott says that such extensive use of illustration was theretofore unknown in magazines.

Some of Lossing's magazine material was taken or adapted from his *Pictorial Field-Book of the Revolution*, which had been issued in thirty numbers, the last one appearing December 24, 1852. It made a two-volume work with 1,100 engravings in its more than 1,500 pages, and was bound in both muslin and half calf. Demarest assumed that the two volumes were issued just before Christmas, but this can scarcely be true because the 1853 book catalogue which leads off with this work was printed in late March or early April and leaves blank spaces where prices would normally be indicated.* The April issue of the *Magazine* announced the "completion of Lossing's *Pictorial Field-Book of the Revolution* in two large octavo-volumes"—but not the usual designation "Published by Harper and Brothers." For some reason book publication was delayed. Seven years later Lossing answered a correspondent who had asked where to procure a copy of the first edition, "I wish I could direct you where to find one on sale. But I cannot. The entire edition, unsold, was consumed by the fire that laid Harpers' establishment in ruins in 1853." Was publication held up pending an

* The April 9 issue of the *Literary World* announced the receipt of the 1853 catalogue, "The variety of the books it enumerates, as is well known, is so great, it may be preserved for reference as containing a very complete record of useful books in the English language."

agreement on terms? There is no record of a contract until June 17, 1856, when the brothers bought the work, lock, stock, and barrel for $14,303.76.

According to Derby, *The Pictorial Field-Book of the Revolution* was conceived in 1848 by the accidental meeting of Lossing with an old Revolutionary soldier. As Lossing was riding between Greenwich and Stamford, Connecticut, he noticed a partially concealed flight of rough, irregular steps near the roadside. He turned to an elderly gentleman standing nearby and asked the history of the rocky stairs. "Why, there is where General Putnam came down when chased by British troopers, and escaped. I saw the performance." Impressed by the old soldier's anecdote, Lossing immediately made a sketch of the locality and before he slept that night had resolved to visit battlefields of the Revolution and produce a book of text and pictures. In pursuit of his project he traveled nine thousand miles, much of the distance by horseback. Derby quotes a letter Washington Irving wrote Lossing on January 4, 1852, saying that he had the *Field-Book* (in numbers) constantly beside him for perusal and reference. "While I have been delighted by the freshness, freedom and spirit of your narrative and the graphic effect of your descriptions, I have been gratified at finding how scrupulously attentive you have been to accuracy as to facts, which is so essential in writings of an historical nature."

During its first three and a half years, the *Magazine* carried many uncredited articles obviously written by American authors. Why uncredited? Perhaps because they were written by staff members, perhaps because non-identification of source would help take the curse off the use of selections from English periodicals or books that were likewise printed without credit as to source. Such failure to give credit led Fletcher in 1853 to an embarrassing encounter with the nine-month-old *Putnam's Magazine*.

The September issue carried a two-page piece entitled "Uncle Bernard's Story," clipped from the British periodical *Eliza Cook's Journal*, but without acknowledgment. Unfortunately it had first been published in the June *Putnam's* over the name of the Rev. Dr. Bethune. Fletcher was in Europe at the time and had not got around to reading the June *Putnam's* until the storm broke. Both the *Post* and the *Tribune* ran editorials calling Harper's attention to the correct source and castigating the brothers for stealing "literary material which was the legal property of Mr. Putnam." Raymond of the *Times* came to his own and the *Magazine*'s defense on the following day. "We observe that the *Evening Post* has called Mr. Putnam's attention to the circumstances, published the law concerning violation of copyright, and urged a damage suit against the wealthy Harpers," he wrote. After detailing the circumstances of the inadvertent mistake, he reminded the *Post* that if it thought that the Harpers "would have designedly used Mr. Putnam's property" it was as ignorant of them as of the "civilities of common life." He blasted his morning rival, the *Tribune*, with a double negative: "Such a suggestion [legal action] could come from no source where malignity is not habitually allowed to overrule every consideration of justice and common sense."

The next day the *Post* said editorially that it had not been indignant with Harper's but "prodigiously jocose" and admitted that it may have "inadvertently" excerpted criticisms from foreign papers without credit. This apology was accepted the following day by Raymond, who wiped victorious hands on editorial pants and concluded that there were no grounds for further controversy. Fletcher wrote Putnam how sorry he was and blushed a second time when a western editor, hearing of the fracas second hand, congratulated *Putnam's* editorially for having outsmarted *Harper's* by being the first to copy "that article" from *Eliza Cook's Journal*. When the "Contents" to Volume VII was compiled, "Uncle Bernard's Story" went unlisted. But the sentimental story may even so be found by leafing through the pages. It is hardly worth the search.

A year later *Littell's Living Age* copied Longfellow's poem "The Two Angels" from *Bentley's Miscellany*, which had likewise lifted it without credit from *Putnam's*. Mr. Littell admitted that he had been asleep, asked Mr. Putnam to kiss and forgive, then fired a missile toward Britain: "This meanness of sundry English magazines in appropriating *as original in their own pages* the best of American periodicals, has been practiced too long with impunity . . . but though the American journals copy so largely from abroad, it is not a *common* sin . . . for them to *disguise* the origin of the goods they take. . . ."

The sport of spotting wrong credits made all editors more wary and the practice of excerpting each other's articles gradually waned. Fletcher soon was clipping little from British papers and Duyckinck noted in the *Literary World* that *Harper's* for February, 1853, had a piece by Abbott on Napoleon, a story of "Crusoe-Life" by J. Ross Browne, "also much other original American matter."

J. Ross Browne, whose *Etchings of a Whaling Cruise* had not only made him money but also ambitious, wrote to the brothers on March 12, 1851, "I contemplate leaving this city [New York] in a few days on a tour through Europe and Egypt, and would be pleased to furnish you with one letter a month for publication in Harper's mag., averaging two or three printed pages. My terms are ten dollars a letter—the postage at your expense." The brothers agreed, with the stipulation that either party could cancel out on three months' notice. The issues for December, 1851, and February, 1852, carried articles attributed to Browne, each of about three pages. Other pieces, unattributed, could easily be from his pen. In January, 1853, he contributed "Journey of the Frangi," which was credited to his forthcoming book, *Crusade in the East* (published in April). Beginning in February he had three pieces in consecutive issues of the *Magazine*, entitled "Crusoe-Life," telling of his adventures on the South Pacific island of Juan Fernandez. This latter-day Crusoe wrote in all nearly forty-four pages for the *Magazine*, and if "two or three printed pages" equaled $10, or about $4 a page, he did not do badly. The new *Putnam's Magazine*, launched that January with a bid to American authors, was promising $3 a page.

The passion for anonymity was still alive in the fifties and several splendid articles, obviously by competent "native" writers, go unnamed as to authorship. "Three Weeks in Cuba" in the December, 1852, issue could get acceptance in the *Magazine* if it were written today. The author was identified as "an artist," but he was certainly politically perceptive. (There were rumors rife in 1852, apparently, that the United States might invade Cuba.) Seven months later the traveling artist was writing engagingly about a trip to the Minnesota Territory. He wrote so well that it would be gratifying to know who he was.

The work of one or more staff writers, authors of many fairly short pieces of the encyclopedic sort, also went unacknowledged. These writers likewise made condensations of book matter. Such a man was Alfred H. Guernsey. According to J. Henry Harper, Guernsey "possessed the exceptional ability to make a readable article of eight or twelve pages out of a two-volume biographical or historical work." What he was then paid for his work is not known, but in 1863 for a special job he earned $40 per week. He could do a lot better than that today in Pleasantville, New York. Guernsey did see his name in the issue of December, 1852, however, where he was identified as the author of "Australia and its Gold." Three months earlier he had seen a first copy of a book he had translated from the German. It was entitled *Anna Hammer* and became Number 173 in the *Library of Select Novels*. Guernsey had been a favorite pupil of Professor Edward Robinson, who had hoped that Guernsey would join the Union Seminary faculty and eventually succeed to his chair, but his bright graduate student was typical of many who turned aside from careers in the classroom or pulpit to the more anonymous ones of journalism or publishing. In 1856, when Raymond resigned to give his full time to the *New York Times,* Fletcher named Dr. Guernsey, as he was famil- iarly called, managing editor of the *Magazine.*

In the early fifties a young man who was to have a more significant editorial association with the brothers than either Guernsey or Ray- mond first called at Cliff Street. His name was George William Curtis. He called not to ask for a job but to get a book published. Fresh from a trip abroad, he was unabashedly confident of himself and his manu- script, called *Nile Notes of a Howadji.* He was told to speak to John, who was standing before his desk. Busy with his accounts, John went on working as Curtis spoke with the eagerness of a first author about the importance of his travel book. Finally with a sly look and disin- genuous smile John said, "This manuscript may be the finest book that was ever written; perhaps you and I think so, but you must remember that to a merchant the commodity in which he deals is also merchan- dise." It was published in March, 1851, and its first printing of 2,500 copies sold out in six months. Bentley bought first proofs for $25 and translated the Arabic word in the title to "Traveler." Hawthorne read it and wrote Curtis, "I see now that you are forever an author," and Ripley said, "We foresee that a brilliant career in letters is opened to the author," when he reviewed it in the current issue of the *Magazine.*

Both Hawthorne and Ripley had known Curtis at Brook Farm, where he spent a year and a half. "I was there during the golden age," he said later. "I was young & saw none of the cracks and heard none of the creaking." At the end of his preface to *Blithedale Romance,* Haw- thorne wrote, "Even the brilliant Howadji might find as rich a theme in his youthful reminiscences of BROOK FARM, and a more novel one— close at hand as it lies,—than those which he has since made so distant a pilgrimage to seek, in Syria, and along the current of the Nile." (May, 1852.) From Brook Farm Curtis went to Concord, where he "saw a little of Emerson, a good deal of Hawthorne, a little of Henry Thoreau—at whose house-raising I assisted,—and a little of Ellery Channing."

The *Magazine's* review of *Nile Notes* did not mention Curtis by name, but a year later, in May, 1852, when *The Howadji in Syria* was reviewed and an excerpt printed, the author was given as George W. Curtis—the first appearance of his name in the magazine with which he was to be associated for many years. In 1853 he joined with Mitchell in writing the "Easy Chair," and beginning in 1859 and continuing until his death in 1892 he would call the Chair his own. His first and un-credited "contribution" to the *Magazine*, however, was made up of selections from a chapter of *Nile Notes* in the March, 1851, issue. The sensuous quality of much of this text, which was selected by Ray-mond, shocked many readers, including Curtis's father. In his biog-raphy of Curtis, Edward Cary devotes a chapter to "The Howadji Books." ". . . there remains, in the soft rich light of these old volumes, a portrait of the young Curtis, of a noble youth, delighting in life, in its novelty, its richness, and its opportunities, not unmindful of its duties or of its tragedies, of its infinite incitements and its relentless limita-tions, but keenly sensitive to its beauty. . . ." Biographer Cary con-sidered Curtis's picturesqueness of impression and rhythmic style the most noteworthy qualities of these books, qualities that were to con-tribute to the later success of Curtis as an orator.

The Howadji books were followed in August, 1852, by *Lotus-Eating*, a delightful book for summer reading made up of pieces he had written the previous summer for the *Tribune*, describing eastern vaca-tion places and pastimes. *Lotus-Eating*, illustrated with woodcuts made from sketches by the artist, J. F. Kensett, a close friend of his, was given the lead review in the August *Magazine*.

In that same issue Curtis began a series of eight stories. As none of them was credited to him by name, the series was probably unknown to his biographer. All were written in the first person, and all were pleasantly satirical pieces about a sophisticated young man's romantic adventures in such American watering places as Newport, Saratoga, and Cape May, and of his amusing experiences with aristocracy in Paris, Monaco, and New York. The first, identified only by its title, "All Baggage at the Risk of the Owner," told of the author's rejection by Lulu, a lovely Southern girl, who in turn had been snubbed by haughty New York belles, also summering at Saratoga. The second story came out in the December issue, a playful piece based on the authorship of the August story, and was entitled "Who Wrote It!" At the start "Dear Reader" is informed that the author's name is Smythe ("I spell it usually with a *y* and two *t*'s") and that Mr. Harper had agreed to print the "All Baggage" story on the condition that it be anonymous. " 'For,' he said, 'Mr. Smythe, our Magazine has a certain character to sustain, which I should be sorry to have compromised by the knowledge that you wrote it.' Mr. Harper has a firm mercantile way of doing business. . . ." Whereupon Curtis, alias J. Smythe, Jr., goes to Cape May, where various people including some society girls from Baltimore are buzzing about the slightly scandalous *Harper* story.

What clever fellow had written it? Could it be Ik. Marvel or the Howadji? A man whose only knowledge of books and authors came from what he read in the *Literary World* discovered the author to be Smytthe indeed. Whereupon, the secret out, the cautious Mr. Harper, when he compiled the contents to Volume VI, could give J. Smytthe, Jr., credit for "Who Wrote It!" and his later stories. It was an amusing bit of literary hide-and-seek and gave Curtis an opportunity to get in some digs at the pretentiousness of the socially elite. If we are to believe that in "Who Wrote It!" Curtis was not altogether spoofing, the *Magazine* was referred to as "Harper," and its pages were at least in part uncut.

Curtis was certainly quoting Fletcher correctly when he said that the *Magazine* had "a certain character to maintain." For that reason Fletcher did not need to cover the brothers John and Jacob Abbott with a white blanket of anonymity. As typically American as Sunday schools and horse carriages and Republican politics, they were authors whose style and subject matter were as impeccable as the best drawing-room conversation. And they turned out book and *Magazine* linage as fast as the Cliff Street compositors could set it up.

On November 4, 1851, Jacob signed an agreement whereby he would receive $5 per page "for writing and making up" an article for the *Magazine* plus his expense incurred in traveling, purchase of books "or otherwise," up to $1 per page. He would be paid as soon as his article was in type and any book to be made out of articles would pay a 10 percent royalty. On April 17, 1852, Abbott could bargain for a better deal. He had been given the lead position in the first four issues for 1852 and for the May issue coming up. Obviously he was worth more. Anyway he wanted to write a series of articles on the Holy Land and that would require money for travel. His new rate was $10 a page. *Memoirs of the Holy Land* began in the August issue.* That first installment and six to follow were opening articles. Of the forty-two issues making up the first seven volumes, Jacob Abbott led off in fourteen and John Abbott in four. Eighteen out of forty-two says something for the drawing power of the Abbott name.

* The Abbott series was advertised on the back cover of the July issue as "illustrated by maps, sketches of scenery and personal incident, and the finest series of Pictorial Embellishments ever given in any magazine in any part of the world. Each article will be complete in itself, and special pains will be taken to render the series beyond all comparison the most valuable and attractive of the kind ever published. Not less than FIVE HUNDRED DOLLARS will be expended upon the literary and artistic preparation. . . ." Such "preparation" was costing a total of more than $24,000 a year, the brothers told Henry Carey a few months later, and it was a direct charge against income from sales since no advertising was carried.

That name had first become known through the extraordinarily popular Jacob Abbott juveniles, the "Rollo," "Jonas," and "Lucy" books. (Verplanck did not care for either the early Abbott books or the "Peter Parley" output of Goodrich. "Dismal trash all of them!" he had written in 1836 in his introduction to the *Fairy Book*.) While the brothers did not take over these series, they did buy rights from William Pierce of Boston to Abbott's *Young Christian* and issued an "improved and enlarged" edition in October, 1851. The November issue of the *Magazine* dutifully gave review space, noting that this book (and *The Corner Stone* and *The Way to Do Good*, to be reissued early in '52) had enjoyed an extensive circulation "not only in our own country, but in England, Scotland, Ireland, France, Germany, Holland, India, and at various missionary stations throughout the world." By 1860 *Young Christian* had sold 200,000 copies. Another series, *Marco Paul's Voyages and Travels*, was taken over in June, 1850, by contract with J. H. Carter of Boston. It specified six volumes, including *At the Springfield Armory*, which was the subject of Jacob Abbott's lead article in the July, 1852, *Magazine*.

The three preceding issues had featured his *Rodolphus, A Franconia Story*. The material came out in book form just before Christmas, 1852, and was reviewed by Ripley as "clothing moral truth in winning costume." It was sixth in Abbott's "Franconia Stories"; the tenth and last was to come two years later. Abbott's two articles on Benjamin Franklin, sumptuously illustrated with engravings, were to be at hand when he wrote *Franklin, the Apprentice Boy* in 1855, a book which became Number 11 in his famous *Harpers' Story-books*, a series of 160-page juveniles that were to be issued one a month for three years, ending in October, 1857.

His brother, John Abbott, contributed significantly to the *Magazine* in a long, controversial, highly eulogistic, and popular series, *The History of Napoleon Bonaparte*. It began in September, 1851, was the leading article for four issues, and continued with only an occasional break through Volumes III to X inclusive. On June 15, 1855, it was to be published in book form—two volumes of nearly 1,300 pages, containing engravings that had brightened the *Magazine* pages for nearly five years. By contracts dated February 12 and March 19, 1852, the brothers agreed to pay Abbott $100 an article and to advance him $1,000 to finance a trip to England and France "to dispose of the copyright and electrotypes of the engravings of his Life of Napoleon for as much as he can . . . the electrotypes to be furnished at the cost of Harper & Brothers."

In August, 1853, Abbott signed a receipt for $150 for one install-ment of *Napoleon*, indicating that he was sharing more in the success of the *Magazine* in general and his serial in particular. That month he wrote Jacob in reference to a "noble article" in the *New York Times* defending him against the accusations of Bishop Alonzo Potter, the Harpers' friend in the early years of the *School District Library*. "I am at a great advantage over my assailants. I am *absolutely certain* that the views I present are *demonstrable,* and I can speak through a journal which has 125,000 subscribers. With such forces I ought to bear any assault." In that same vein he wrote the brothers a month later, "You have placed in my hands a magnificent engine of influence and so long as you are not frightened I shall not abate one single iota of what seems to me to be the truth."

During this time John Abbott was also turning out books for Cliff Street publication. In addition to one or more histories he prepared revised editions of his popular *The Mother at Home* and *The Child at Home,* both also "take-overs," which by 1860 had together piled up a sales total of 197,000 copies. The high regard the brothers Harper had for the brothers Abbott is indicated by the fact that the fifty Abbott letters they saved comprise far and away the largest collection of letters of any two authors of their time that have come down to the present day.

The Abbott name also distinguished American magazine publishing in the latter part of the century. Jacob was born in 1803 (three years before Fletcher) and was his brother's senior by two years. Both the Abbotts were graduated from Bowdoin College (John being a class-mate of Hawthorne and Longfellow) and both were ordained in the Congregational ministry. Jacob's literary and pastoral mantles were inherited by his son, Lyman Abbott, who was to be Henry Ward Beecher's associate editor of the *Christian Union* and editor-in-chief after Beecher left and the paper was renamed *The Outlook.* Lyman Abbott was also to succeed Beecher in the pulpit of the Plymouth Congregational Church, Brooklyn, and to publish three books with the Harper imprint, books that his father was to live long enough to ad-mire.

When Raymond came up to bat for the brothers in the *New York Times* editorials, he must have recognized that his readers were aware that his comments were naturally prejudiced in favor of the Harpers. That he could give many hours of each week to reading for the *Maga-zine* while he was guiding the *Times* to its early and sustained eminence as a daily newspaper is evidence of his ability to work efficiently and to write rapidly. Once he sent a note to Fletcher from Albany to say that the English magazines of the month were "exceedingly lean" and that current numbers of *Household Words* had not been sent to him. He forwarded excerpts from a new English work, *The Household of Sir Thomas More,* and said, "I fear we shall lack *first rate* matter this month." Raymond also had an alert eye for books that could be undertaken by the brothers. Early in 1853, he wrote to introduce Stephen Tracy, M.D., of Windsor, Vermont, who wanted to submit a manuscript and was "recommended by the president of Vermont University." Raymond called Tracy "a gentleman of character & position." That word "character," Raymond knew, was the brothers' key word, as it was his own. Four months later, Dr. Tracy's book was published under the title *The Mother and Her Offspring.* The importance of character was also being emphasized by Curtis in his Easy Chair pieces. The November, 1853, issue, which closed the seventh volume, carried his essay on Indian summer, in which he wrote poetically of Nature and ironically of people, hoping wistfully for "sympathy, toleration, and heroism which are the best fruits that the woods grow, and the sea tosses up. . . ."

A few days before the consuming fire of December 10, someone, probably Fletcher, wrote the "Advertisement" that faced the contents page of Volume VII. He hoped the contents as well as the list of illustrations would evidence that quality had kept pace with quantity. Electrotyping had been substituted for stereotyping, thus insuring that the last run of any one issue would be as perfect as the first run. Public approval had supported their articles on American scenery and American history. The best articles, whether of American or European origin, would continue to be selected. Then came both the brothers' answer and their challenge to critics who had charged them with an English bias; they were presenting a larger proportion of original matter than heretofore because they were able to procure better articles from American than from European sources. The closing paragraph read: "The Publishers again renew their thanks to the Press and to the Public for the unexampled favor which has been accorded to their efforts; and repeat their assurances that nothing shall be wanting on their part to secure the continuance and increase of that favor, which has enabled them to commence the Eighth Volume of their Magazine with an edition of One Hundred and Thirty-five thousand Copies."

That edition was printed, but it was destined never to be published.

CHAPTER XVIII

Harper Books in the Early Fifties

1850–1853

PUBLISHERS' REPRESENTATIVES have traveled millions of miles to call on the American book trade since 1852, when Charles B. Norton packed a bag of books and made the first sales trip on record. His two-month circuit of nearly four thousand miles took him as far south as New Orleans and enabled him to call on dealers in more than a dozen cities. He took subscriptions for his new trade periodical, *Norton's Literary Gazette and Publishers' Circular*, in which he also reported his trip. He took orders for books he was publishing, including *Poole's New Index to Periodical Literature* and *Guild's Librarians' and Book-Buyers' Manual*. He left New York in late January, traveling on the new Erie Railroad to Elmira, New York, his first stop.

Bookmen have a pleasant way of reading important new books of other publishers and gossiping about them with the trade. Such non-competitive book talk spills over into the broad stream of public interest and nicely helps the book business. So Norton had put a competitor's book in his bag. It had been published the previous May and was entitled *Harper's New York and Erie Rail-road Guide Book*. It promised to furnish "the traveler on the New York and Erie Rail-road with that kind of information which everyone passing over a new route

desires to have in his possession." Even though it was embellished with
136 delightful wood engravings by Lossing and Barritt, it was not the
kind of American literature that Duyckinck and his circle prayed for.
But it was a lot of fun—and inexpensive. Because the Erie people had
paid for one-half the cost of the engravings ($1,512.67), the brothers
had been able to price the book at 50 cents in paper and 62½ cents in
cloth. (See illustration 26.)

Good as the book was, it did not say what the crew and passengers
should do when the noble and smoke-belching locomotive got stuck in
January snowdrifts, but they finally dug through them and made
Elmira. After calling on the trade there, Norton continued by rail to
Rochester (six bookstores) and to Buffalo (seven bookstores). Be-
tween these cities the Iron Horse was again stalled in snowdrifts, and
Norton spent fourteen hours on the rails instead of the normal three.
Train service not then extending westward beyond Dunkirk, New
York, Norton continued by stagecoach to Cleveland (seven book-
stores) and to Columbus and Cincinnati, where he arrived on February 11, the trip across Ohio taking four days. Norton reported that the
Cincinnati book trade ranked next to Boston in importance and value,
saying that H. W. Derby & Co., in which the brothers owned a part
interest, had "without exception, the best arranged and largest bookstore in the United States," and that the Mercantile Library could boast
of twelve thousand volumes. From Cincinnati, Norton proceeded to
Louisville, where a population of forty-four thousand was served by
twelve bookstores, most of them small. At Louisville, Norton boarded
a river steamer and on February 19 arrived in New Orleans (five bookstores). His next stops were Mobile and Montgomery, Alabama (five
and two bookstores respectively), followed by Columbus (three) and
Macon, Georgia, where there were several stores with "well-selected
stocks of books, in many cases of a higher character than will be found
in towns of the same size at the North." This comment was sheer home-
town pride, for Norton had once lived in Macon; he tarried there for a
brief holiday before taking a train to Savannah, which was "adorned
with the verdant garment of Spring." Here he called on three bookstores before going on by steamer to Charleston, South Carolina, arriving on March 10. He did not mention William Gilmore Simms or his
books but reported calls on ten bookstores; neither did he tell of his trip
from Charleston to Philadelphia, but he was there in time to attend the
Spring Trade Sales.

Norton's trip not only makes him the patron saint of all bookmen
who type up itineraries for forthcoming sales' trips, but his *Literary*

Gazette makes him the founding father of the *Publishers' Weekly*, the bible of the book trade today. After at least two abortive efforts in the thirties and forties to establish such a journal, the one started by Norton in May, 1851, has continued by direct line and various names down to the present. The brothers apparently watched Norton's monthly with some suspicion at first, thinking that it might turn, like Langley's, into a house organ, but, after nearly two years, they began advertising regularly. They started with a bang, taking the back page in the March, 1853, issue to advertise school and college textbooks.

D. B. Cooke was one of the Cincinnati booksellers that Norton called on. That summer in company with George Derby, his partner's brother, Cooke took a vacation trip along the Great Lakes, where the two men had leisure to share their ambitions for the future. Derby, who ran a bookstore in Buffalo, had just shipped $5,000 worth of stock around Cape Horn and was full of talk about the new store in the Derby chain to be started in San Francisco. Cooke was not willing to go that far West but was attracted to Chicago, where he decided to end his vacation trip. "After carefully looking over the ground and studying the geographical location," he wrote, "I determined on locating myself in the 'Garden City,' which then seemed anything but a garden, with its streets almost impassable for the great depths of mud, and its unsightly rows of wooden shanties." Four years later, Marshall Field was to go to Chicago to start a business career which was to profoundly influence the merchandising of goods—and of books.

One reason for the expansion of the book trade westward was the "cheap postage law" which had gone into effect on June 30, 1851. Books could now be sent by mail throughout the country at a beginning rate of one cent per ounce for the first 500 miles, and stepping up a cent an ounce on each succeeding 1,000 miles to five cents an ounce for distances greater than 3,500 miles.* By 1854, the law was liberalized to permit books weighing four pounds or less to be sent by mail, prepaid, at one cent an ounce to any point within the United States under 3,000 miles. These laws were a great stimulus to the book trade.

Canadian sales were also becoming more important because of Dominion tariff revisions in 1849 and 1850, whereby American books could be imported duty free, excepting British copyrighted books which carried a 12½ percent duty. Prior to that time, few American books were imported, but by 1852 American publishers were furnish-

---

* This law did not go far enough according to "B.B." who wrote a 2½-page article for the November, 1951, issue of the *Magazine*. He argued for truly "cheap postage" legislation, urging seven reforms, including a uniform letter rate of two cents prepaid and free delivery of letter mail within large towns and cities.

ing the one million English-speaking Canadians with most of the new books purchased—more than $200,000 worth in 1851. The book trade in Canada, according to *Norton's Literary Gazette*, consisted of from sixty to seventy individuals, mostly young men who sold chiefly on commission for American houses.

Writing in *Recollections of a Lifetime* (1856), author-publisher S. G. "Peter Parley" Goodrich estimated that American publishers had invested $12,500,000 in the production of books in 1850, five times their 1820 outlay. Nearly one-half of the 1850 total was spent in manufacturing schoolbooks. Goodrich commented that in the forties schoolbooks ceased being published in brown paper covers; by the fifties they were being bound in good and durable muslin binding; the paper was better and there was much greater use of engravings. According to Goodrich, the following amounts were being spent to produce books by categories in specified years (the dollar figures indicate thousands):

	1820	1830	1840	1850
School books	$ 750	$1,100	$2,000	$ 5,500
Classical books	250	350	550	1,000
Theological books	150	250	300	500
Law books	200	300	400	700
Medical books	150	200	250	400
All others	1,000	1,300	2,000	4,400
	$2,500	$3,500	$5,500	$12,500
Percentage of original American works	30%	40%	55%	70%

The Harper output of schoolbooks by 1850 contributed significantly to the $5.5-million figure, as well as to the growing percentage of American works. In his 1853 pamphlet on international copyright, Henry Carey said that the number of Harper books used in the higher schools was "exceedingly great." He reported the sale of Anthon's *Classical Dictionary* had reached thirty thousand copies and that the yearly sale of Anthon's classical series was not less than fifty thousand copies. By 1853 this series had grown to thirty-one titles, seven being added after 1850. There was also one revision (*Tacitus*) listed in the 1853 catalogue and three new books were announced as in press. But according to Demarest's *Catalogue*, these three were never published, unless by different titles. Anthon was nearing the end of his vast productivity and could afford to rest from his labors. The "Anthon series" was still important when the Harper schoolbook business was sold in 1890 to the newly formed American Book Company. An apparent lack in the Anthon series, despite the 1846 work of Zumpt *cum* Schmitz *cum* Anthon, was a Latin grammar. This was supplied in 1852 by Dr. Gessner Harrison, professor of ancient languages in the University of Virginia.

Also to compete with Anthon's *Greek Grammar* (1838) was the 1851 publication of Buttmann's work with the same title. It ran to nearly twice the number of pages and sold for more than twice as much. It was translated from the eighteenth German edition by Dr. Edward Robinson, professor of Biblical literature in Union Theological Seminary, where the chair of Biblical theology still perpetuates his name. In 1850, Robinson had given the brothers the rights to his new and revised edition of *A Greek and English Lexicon of the New Testament,* the most important work of Robinson, who headed Duyckinck's list of American scholars in terms of honors received both at home and abroad. Robinson's Harper contract for the *Lexicon* called for an equal division of profits based on net receipts of 30 percent of the retail price. This 30 percent covered discounts to the trade and "guaranty of sales, advertising, insurance and all other incidental expenses and charges." By 1866 the brothers were to ask Robinson's estate that this discount be increased to 40 percent. It was acceded to by Robinson's son, who wrote on his mother's behalf that she wished "to treat with you with the same fairness that you have always treated us." In 1885 the Robinson heirs were to receive $400 for their share of the value of the plates.

Anthon's annual profits on his classics series were probably exceeded in 1853 by Loomis's earnings on his mathematical series. His recent books, including an elementary *Algebra* and a *Geometry and Calculus,* were being widely adopted and thirteen more titles were still to come in his Harper *Mathematical Series.* In 1860 he was to return to Yale, his alma mater, to teach, and at his death in 1889 Yale received his bequest of $300,000, the largest single donation the college had received up to that time. Much of his fortune had accumulated from the February and August Harper checks he regularly received, amounting to 10 percent of what thousands of school and college students were paying for his mathematical textbooks.

Several science books were issued in the early fifties. Alonzo Gray, whose *Elements of Chemistry,* published in Andover, Massachusetts, was in its fortieth printing, gave the brothers his *Elements of Natural Philosophy* and *Elements of Geology;* he had as collaborator on the latter book Professor C. B. Adams of Amherst. Before plates were made, the brothers had 250 copies of the former title and 150 of the latter printed from type and delivered free to the authors—apparently for early distribution to obtain text adoptions. In addition, complimentary copies were sent from Cliff Street to interested teachers. The *Geology* came out in January, 1853. It contained 370 pages and 218 engravings and sold for 75 cents. These facts, plus a 10 percent royalty, must have necessitated a first printing of no less than 10,000 copies. The following year the authors accepted a royalty of 4 cents a copy on 2,000 copies in order to make possible a sale to the school libraries of the state of Ohio.

An 1850 book was published especially for school use in Michigan. Entitled *Popular Education,* it was written by Ira Mayhew, Superintendent of Public Instruction in the state, and published by resolution of the Legislature. That same year the brothers issued *The English Language, in its Elements and Forms* by William Chauncey Fowler, who had taught rhetoric both at Middlebury and Amherst colleges. The brothers considered the book a bit risky, so delayed royalty till after 1,500 copies of the 792-page book were sold. But, despite its price of $1.75, Fowler's *English Language* proved so popular in schools and colleges that a year after publication they asked Fowler to make a revision "in the course of a few years" on a straight 10 percent royalty. He not only did so but made a redaction later for use in common schools. At least one of Fowler's titles was still in print forty years later.

Fowler had married a daughter of Noah Webster, as had Chauncey Goodrich, and both men had been caught up in the unhappy family situation that followed Webster's death, with rival claimants for editorial prestige and profits. Fowler had edited the 1845 university edition of Webster, which in 1854 the brothers contracted to take over; Goodrich himself must also have been impressed by what the Cliff Street operation was doing, for the revision of the abridged edition, which he edited, was available early in 1851.* Late that year Goodrich contracted for a 955-page book entitled *Select British Eloquence.* It was advertised as containing the best speeches of the most famous

---

* Demarest does not give a date for the revised edition of Webster's Abridged Dictionary in the royal-octavo size. However, the *Magazine* for February, 1851, devoted a column review to this Harper volume "of more than *thirteen hundred* pages . . . on excellent paper, with a clear type, and in stout binding, for about three dollars." (Later catalogued at $3.50.) The university edition was never issued by the Harpers and sometime between June, 1855, and October, 1856—dates of two extant catalogues—publication of the Harper abridged edition was discontinued, with the G. & C. Merriam Company controlling this as well as the unabridged edition.

orators of Great Britain for the last two centuries and contained biographical sketches and critical and explanatory notes.

This contract was one of the last to carry the witnessing signature of Gerherdus Demarest. Shortly afterward he moved with his wife and child to Cincinnati, where his Harper training helped him as publisher and editor of two publications of the Universalist Church, *The Star of the West* and *The Young Christian.* In 1856 he became a partner of H. W. Derby & Co., Fletcher, Jr., remaining as a "special partner." Gerherdus's move West may have been influenced by J. A. James, whom he had known on Cliff Street, where the young Mr. James learned to make stereotype plates. In 1831 he and his brother, U. P. James, went to Cincinnati and by 1854 their publishing and bookselling business was so extensive that it was sometimes called "the Harpers of the West." It has continued to the present day. Gerherdus became a minister of the Universalist Church, married his daughter into the James family, and returned to the East, where his successful ministry earned him an honorary doctorate from St. Lawrence University. He died in Manchester, New Hampshire, in 1909, at the age of ninety-two.

Another textbook was the 1851 publication *The Philosophy of Mathematics,* translated by Professor William M. Gillespie of Union College from *Le Cours de Philosophie Positive* by Auguste Comte. It may be the first translation into English of the work of the great French positivist philosopher. It was *avant-garde* publishing, not everywhere popular as was the *Morse Geography,* for example. Here was a book the brothers could hardly keep in stock. On August 23, 1853, Horace Mann wrote to the brothers to make sure he could have books for the opening of the preparatory school of Antioch College, Yellow Springs, Ohio. "We are expecting the school to be a large one," he wrote, satisfied that his newly established college was off to a good start.

Of the many books of nonfiction issued from Cliff Street in the early fifties, perhaps the one with greatest interest today as Americana was *Louisiana; its Colonial History and Romance* by Charles Gayarré. The author was a member of one of the state's oldest families, was active in politics, and is credited with being the father of the state library. Gayarré was also a competent historian, made careful use of source material, and wrote in a warm, flowing, sometimes poetical style. His life spanned most of the nineteenth century.

Gayarré had lived but half his years when, in 1852, far to the north, death took another and greater statesman, a man even more skilled in the use of words. Daniel Webster died on October 24 at his home in

Marshfield, Massachusetts. "The national heart throbbed with the pulsations of the telegraph which carried the news of his last moments through the land," Duyckinck wrote, saying that no death of a citizen, since those of Washington and Hamilton, had so moved the country. Always alert to the importance of a timely book, the brothers arranged with Webster's one-time secretary, Charles Lanman, to publish *The Private Life of Daniel Webster*. It was given top priority in the pressroom and copies were being shipped to the trade on December 4. The December issue of the *Magazine* contained excerpts from the Lanman book in a nine-page article on Webster, illustrated with six engravings of which three were likenesses of the great statesman made from daguerreotypes in Mr. Lanman's possession.

The big book for Christmas sales the preceding year had been Mrs. Sarah Hale's *Woman's Record*, comprising biographical sketches of distinguished ladies from Eve down to the present, with selections from the writings of those who were authors. The 950-page book contained 200 portraits, most of them engraved by Lossing. It had a lead position in the 1853 catalogue. A portion of Mrs. Hale's book was first printed in the *Magazine*, as were two pieces entitled "A Leaf from a Traveller's Notebook," by Maunsell B. Field. Field had been valedictorian of his class of 1841 at Yale, had traveled abroad and had lived for a while in Paris, where he was a member of the U.S. legation. He called at Cliff Street one Saturday afternoon, presumably in the autumn of 1852, and left a note regarding a translation from the French of *Three Tales* by the Countess D'Arbouville which he had completed. On the note John penciled some figures totaling $449, probably Field's compensation. The book was published the following April.

In February, 1852, Field had introduced the brothers to John R. Brodhead, who had given publishing aid to Melville in London. At that time Brodhead was with the American embassy, but he had been in England earlier, authorized by Governor Seward through an enabling act of the State Legislature, to collect original historical documents relating to the State of New York. He gathered source material also in Holland and France. "The ship on which he returned [in 1844] was more richly freighted with new materials for American history than any other that ever crossed the Atlantic," according to the historian George Bancroft. Brodhead collated the documents and supervised their publication in ten quarto volumes at the expense of the State of New York.

In 1852 Brodhead was ready to publish Volume I in his own projected *History of the State of New York.* Late in the morning of Monday, February 16, he and Maunsell Field talked at some length with the Mayor, who then turned them over to John and Wesley to work out the terms of a contract.

The agreement which Maunsell Field, trained as a lawyer, then drafted has publishing interest for several reasons, one being the clear implication that the brothers were now giving the trade a discount of 33⅓ percent. The royalty rate, according to Field, was "ten percent upon the catalog price, which Mr. John Harper explains to be about an equivalent of fifteen percent upon the actual sales price." Two, the brothers were now considering plates as a capital investment, apart from the value of a copyright, Maunsell Field writing, "The copyright to remain to Mr. Brodhead and the plates of course to be counted as capital." Third, it confirms the fact that as the brothers were moving from half-profits to royalty contracts, they were holding on to the principle that on expensive books the payment of royalty should be delayed till one-half the cost of plates had been covered by sales. In the Brodhead contract, royalty was not to be paid till after four hundred copies had been sold. The retail price was $3; thus $120, the equivalent in royalty, would be one-half plate cost, a figure which checks with other known costs of an octavo work of approximately eight hundred pages. Volume I of Brodhead's *History of the State of New York* covered the years 1609-64. Volume II did not get published till 1871 and a projected third volume was never to be printed.

Among general nonfiction books of this period, the number of travel books was comparatively small. Perhaps the best seller of the lot was *Parisian Sights and French Principles, seen through American Spectacles,* by James J. Jarves of Boston, who had traveled widely, lived abroad for several years, and had already achieved some fame as an author. Excerpts from *Parisian Sights* appeared in the *Magazine* for November, 1852, a month after book publication. It sold well enough to justify a sequel three years later—with more to come.

But in the early fifties the most interesting contribution from Paris to America was not a book but a woman. Mlle. Henriette Desportes.

At No. 10 Gramercy Park Miss Henrietta Haines conducted a finishing school for the daughters of some of New York's best families— the Dutch Van Horns, Brevoorts, Schuylers, and De Peysters, the English De Lanceys, Jays, and Wards, the Huguenot Lorillards, Jumels, and Delavans. To No. 10 in September, 1849, Mlle. Desportes came to teach French and drawing. She had left France under the shadow of tragedy—the innocent victim and also the *cause célèbre* in the widely publicized Praslin murder case that had shaken Paris in the summer of 1848. The Duc de Praslin had murdered the jealous duchess because she refused to give a letter of recommendation to Mlle. Desportes, whom she had dismissed in the belief that, during seven years of service, the young Protestant governess had gradually alienated the affection of her husband and children. When the laxity of the police permitted the imprisoned Duc de Praslin to commit suicide, the enraged populace was further aroused against the nobility, the aging Louis Philippe was exiled, and the writer Lamartine elevated briefly into the spotlight of French politics.

The associations that so frequently bring publishers into relation with personalities and historic events brought the Mayor still closer in 1851 when Mlle. Desportes's fiancé, the Rev. Henry M. Field (brother of Cyrus, but unrelated to Maunsell), went to Cliff Street with the manuscript of his new book, which was duly accepted for publication. During Field's two years abroad, he had not only met his future wife but furthered his research into the Irish rebellion of 1798. In March, two months before their wedding, Henry Field and his French fiancée saw a first copy of *The Irish Confederates*. (They had already seen a three-page excerpt in that month's issue of the *Magazine*.) To a publisher, a first copy of a new book is as routine an event as the birth of a child is to an obstetrician. But to an author, his first book is hardly less important an issue than that of his first child. As they admired the binding—rich gold leaf on lustrous black muslin—opened the book to the title page—"Henry M. Field" in handsome capital letters—and leafed through the 369 pages, they were thinking that except for wealthy brother Cyrus the book might not have been a reality in their hands. The brothers had told Henry that his manuscript had been recommended by their readers, but, since he was unknown as an author and his subject one of limited interest, they could not undertake the book unless he paid for the cost of plates. However, they would pay a straight 15 percent royalty and that might be a better arrangement than the customary 10 percent royalty after 1,000 copies, if they paid for the plates confident of a book's sales potential. But Henry had no extra funds to draw upon, his income for nearly a year having come as "pulpit supply" while he was completing the book. And he faced the expense of a wedding. So Cyrus Field signed a five-year contract for the book and gave the brothers his check for $264.71 to cover the cost of plates. On July 25, 1887, Cyrus Field was to agree that the contract could be terminated, the plates returned to him, and the remaining seventy copies jobbed without royalty payment. By that time Cyrus

Field had invested in the bigger projects of the transatlantic cable and the New York Elevated Railroad, and Henry was known as a Scribner author. The cautious brothers had not lost money but they had lost Henry Field. After Henriette's death in 1875, he spent two years in travel and the two books he wrote on his return went through twenty editions.

The brothers could well have rationalized such loss of an author by saying that they were doing quite well with religious books and no publisher is shrewd enough always to vote for the winning literary candidate. They had some mighty good ones catalogued, including the Rev. Dr. Barnes. With his *Notes* on Revelation out in 1852 and his series completed, Barnes could eventually boast of sales of nearly one-half of a million and earnings of $75,000. But his fame and fortune had been bought at the price of his eyesight. His near blindness now kept him away from his cherished study and he bought a home outside Philadelphia where he could read the notes that nature had written. These notes were not copyrighted, kept no sales totals, and paid no royalty either to man or his estate.

Barnes was often at Union Seminary in New York to lecture and to attend meetings of the Board of Directors. He may have influenced Dr. Edward Robinson to go to Cliff Street as well as two other members of that faculty. Professor H. W. Pierson gave the brothers an *American Missionary Memorial* with biographical and historical sketches. A not dissimilar book was a *History of the American Bible Society* by Dr. W. P. Strickland, published a few years earlier; the brothers would have issued it for reasons of prestige and pride—the society was only one year older than their own establishment. Professor Thomas H. Skinner of Union also gave them a translation from the French which he and his wife had made of Vinet's *Pastoral Theology*.

Other religious books included a book on scriptural prophecy by Professor Samuel H. Turner of the General Theological Seminary, and two books by Dr. Nicholas Murray, *Decline of Popery and its Causes* and *Romanism at Home*, both reflecting the zeal of the convert who must constantly seek to find reasons to justify a new faith and criticize an old one. Murray was on a first-name basis with Wesley and Fletcher, with whom he lived as a young man, but not with the elder brothers. For James and John he retained through his years the habit of respectful address he first used while in their employ. None of Murray's books would be read today. His chief claim to fame is his grandson, Nicholas Murray Butler, for forty-three years the president of Columbia University.

Finally there were two volumes of the posthumous works of President Stephen Olin of Wesleyan—sermons, addresses, and essays—and, a year later, two volumes of his life and letters. These works were prepared for the press by Dr. McClintock and other friends. Neither they nor the publishers expected much return for their labors. Both authors and publishers take occasional satisfaction in undertaking books that serve mainly to memorialize their friends. Olin was such a friend and he was described by Duyckinck as a man both large in stature and large in his influence with his students.

Among nonfiction reprints being issued, Leigh Hunt's *Autobiography* ranked high on the brothers' list for spring, 1850. They paid £15 for first proofs and placed a retail price of $1.50 on the two volumes. They had published his *Men, Women, and Books* three years earlier but not his poetical works. Samuel Taylor Coleridge was the more famous poet but not a member of Leigh Hunt's famous "circle." Coleridge's poetry as well as his prose works came out in seven volumes in 1853. The metaphyiscal bent of Coleridge drew clergymen to his work and Professor W. G. T. Shedd of Auburn Theological Seminary edited the Harper edition. Shedd later taught theology at Union Seminary and was known as a "high" Calvinist, one of the great theologians of the time. The edition of Coleridge followed by a few months a four-volume *Life and Works of Robert Burns* by Robert Chambers, the Scottish author and publisher, who had worked long and laboriously to obtain new biographical material, some of which came from the late poet's sister, Mrs. Begg, to whom Chambers turned over all profits from the work.

Good as Bishop Thirlwall's *History of Greece* was, it was being outsold in England by George Grote's more popular and extensive work. Learning early of the success of Grote's first volume, the brothers at once announced it and by November, 1853, they had published nine volumes. The final volume, Number XII, came out three years later, by which time Grote had given Americans six thousand pages of reading matter on Greece. Another work on an ancient civilization, A. H. Layard's *Popular Account of Discoveries at Nineveh*, was also opening up archeology as an important field for books. This work was followed a year later, in 1853, by Layard's *Discoveries among the Ruins of Nineveh and Babylon*. Not only did Layard (later Sir Austen) discover the location of Nineveh, but he also sent back archeological specimens to England, artifacts that comprise the greater part of the splendid collection of Assyrian antiquities now housed in the British Museum. He also succeeded in producing two of the best-written travel books in the English language.

Along with those of Coleridge, Burns, and Grote, two other multi-volume English works came out in this period, David Hume's *History of England*, advertised as a new edition based on the author's latest corrections and improvements, and that old favorite Gibbon's *Decline and Fall*, this time edited by Dean Milman of St. Paul's Cathedral. Both works ran to six volumes and were published at intervals between March and September, 1850. Their dates of publication indicate, as confirmed elsewhere, that for the most part books were grouped for Cliff Street publication at approximately two-week intervals, with Friday the most usual day of publication.

Another history, published with great expectations, turned out to be a failure—Archibald Alison's continuation of his *History of Europe*. Mindful of the success of the first four volumes, covering the years 1789-1815, the brothers planned to issue the new work also in numbers. But the demand for the first number was so slight, according to Demarest, that they quickly drew in their sails and imported sheets. The first two volumes, published in January and May, 1853, and the two to come later were not successful because they attempted to record recent history without adequate materials and reflected Alison's partisan political bias—an unbending Tory dealing with revolutionary movements. In 1851 Alison had been named rector of Glasgow University and in the following year honored with a baronetcy.

In January, 1851, the brothers paid £25 for *Rule and Misrule of the English in America* by Thomas Chandler Haliburton. Haliburton was then living in England although his family roots were in New England and he had spent most of his life in Canada, part of that time as a Nova Scotia judge. In 1836 he had published *Sam Slick of Onion County, Conn.*, with more Sam Slick stories the following year, all written in that Yankee dialect and characterization that were to identify an American type whose industry and inventiveness contrasted with a "blue-nose" intolerance. Artemus Ward called Haliburton the founder of the American school of humor. Sam Slick, a peddler, was a good likeness to Major Downing, the creation of Seba Smith. Even as late as 1847 the *Literary World* was speculating that Haliburton's claims to Major Downing were better than Smith's. However, Haliburton's *Rule and Misrule* was concerned with something more serious than Yankee humor.

Two further general works from England merit attention, one because of its contents and the other because of its sales. Every century brings its small quota of the "universal man," that man of genius whose mental and spiritual attainments cause him to tower above his fellows. Such a one was Alexander von Humboldt, and his seminal work was translated from the German and issued at intervals under the title *Cosmos*. The fourth volume was issued from Cliff Street in June, 1852, with a concluding one to come in 1859, the year of von Humboldt's death. For its day, this 1,650-page work was an intellectual tour de force, attempting to unify the philosophical ideals of the eighteenth century with the scientific precepts of the nineteenth. And the big seller of them all, published in 1851, was Edward Creasy's *The Fifteen Decisive Battles of the World*. The book of 364 pages began with Marathon and ended with Waterloo. The size of the first and subsequent Harper editions are not known, but Bentley risked only five hundred copies to start with, since the chapters had first appeared in his *Miscellany*. According to Bentley's biographer the book went back to press forty times and in one ten-year period showed profits of more than one thousand pounds. Presumably Harper's did as well or better. The *Harper Creasy* was printed in new and enlarged editions in 1908 and 1918, the later edition adding nine subsequent battles, including that of the Marne.

Most of the fiction published during this four-year period was English. While *Moby Dick* would make any publisher's list of American fiction significant for any period, it stands as a Harper mountain peak among tiny foothills. Three other "native" titles merit attention, one of them because of its author association. William C. Prime, younger brother of Samuel Irenaeus Prime, published *The Old House by the River*, the first of his seven Harper titles. William Prime was a lawyer, a part owner of the New York *Journal of Commerce*, a position that not only brought him considerable wealth but also enabled him to travel widely and indulge his hobbies of fishing and collecting coins, porcelains, and tapestries. He later wrote books on his hobbies, each of which Fletcher saw through the press. He also was to write the official biography of S. F. B. Morse, which, for some reason, Fletcher did not handle; otherwise the triune relationship of the brothers Morse, Prime, and Harper would have gone full circle. William Prime once remarked to Joe Brooklyn that he regretted he had no sons so that his cherished friendship with the brothers could be passed on to the coming generation.

On July 1, 1853—just two weeks after Prime's novel—the brothers issued *Home Pictures* by Mary Andrews Denison, already an established novelist. Her husband, C. W. Denison, was a contributor to *The Knickerbocker*. That same year a distant relative in Ohio, William S. Denison, pledged $10,000 to the struggling Granville Literary and Theological Institution; in gratitude for so munificent a sum, the trustees changed the name to Denison University, even though the cash itself was not paid over till after a series of bitter lawsuits. Mary Denison's husband was less parsimonious. In signing the Harper contract for *Home Pictures*, he agreed to use some of the 10 percent royalty to pay for one-half the expense of "editorial or complimentary copies." Apparently he asked for an unusually large distribution of review copies; anyway, the book got off to a good enough start to stay in print for thirty years, by which time Mary had published another Harper novel.

Uncle Tom's Cabin was published by John P. Jewett on March 20, 1852. Exactly five months later, on August 20, the brothers issued a novel by Mary Evelina Hunter, wife of R. M. T. Hunter, U.S. Senator from Virginia (later to become Secretary of the Confederacy), and a niece by marriage to the famous jurist Henry St. George Tucker. Her book was entitled *The Clifford Family; or, a Tale of the Old Dominion*. The manuscript had been submitted, reported on favorably by one or more readers, and provisionally accepted before the end of 1851. After several exchanges of letters, she accepted the brothers' proposed terms of January 5, 1852. Several interesting questions emerge. Why did they hold off publication till late August, since they were ordinarily publishing books two or three months after a manuscript was at hand and contracted for? Was publication delayed because everyone was talking about Mrs. Stowe's book? If they did have a chance to publish *Uncle Tom's Cabin* through Catharine Beecher's urging, as implied earlier, did their negotiations with Mrs. Hunter obviously rule out undertaking Mrs. Stowe's so different picture of southern life? If both novels were considered simultaneously, did they reason that they could not risk offending the Tucker family, for whom they had already published, as well as other southern authors? Could they afford to risk offending their southern trade? Because they were opposed to advance serialization of American fiction, did they rule out asking Mrs. Stowe for book rights when they first noticed her name as author of an extended serial in *The National Era?* Jewett, a small Boston publisher, was not too worried about the opinions of southern booksellers or advance serialization of a copyrighted novel, but with some reluctance he signed with Mrs. Stowe to publish her book. At the end of the first seven months he had sold more than 200,000 copies of *Uncle Tom's Cabin*. More than a million copies were sold in England that year, nearly all of them pirated.

However, the brothers saw no objection to the advance serialization of English fiction. After first being offered to readers of the *Magazine*,

Thackeray's *Pendennis* was published in 1851 in two volumes, priced at $1 per volume in cloth binding. According to Mott's estimate of best sellers, it was to enjoy a sale of at least 225,000 copies. It sold better than *The History of Henry Esmond, Esq.*, which Thackeray considered his best novel to date; it was issued in November, 1852, perfectly timed for Thackeray's arrival in America for his first lecture tour. On November 27, Thackeray wrote the brothers: "In reply to your proposal of yesterday, I shall be happy to part with my interest in the United States in my forthcoming volume, *Lectures on the Humorous Writers of the Last Century*, to be published simultaneously with the London Edition. The sum of One Thousand Dollars offered by you to be paid to my order, on my sending to you the last sheets of the English edition of the work."[*]

The Easy Chair, probably written by George W. Curtis, commented on Thackeray's visit by saying, "He convinced us of his intellectual integrity; he showed us how impossible it is for him to see the world and describe it other than he does. He does not profess cynicism, nor satirize society with malice [recalling Dickens]; there is no man more humble, none more simple; his interests are human and concrete, not abstract." The *New York Times* also compared Thackeray with Dickens in reviewing *Henry Esmond*, saying that the one was the measure of the other, with Thackeray being strong precisely where Dickens was weakest—in the delineation of human character.

Another magazine-heralded author was Eliot Warburton, whose 1851 novel, *Darien, or the Merchant Prince*, cost them £25 for first proofs. This fictional account of William Paterson told the engrossing story of the founder of the Bank of England, who, having amassed a fortune, sold the people of Scotland in 1685 on his scheme for a settlement on the Isthmus of Darien. How this grandiose Caribbean venture failed was told so well that the Atlantic and Pacific Junction Company sent Warburton from England to Darien (also famous because of the sonnet by Keats) to explore the isthmus and negotiate a treaty with the Indians. But Warburton's mission was also doomed to fail. He and nearly all his fellow passengers perished when the outgoing steamship *Amazon* burned at sea.

In addition to books of fiction from England that were issued after first being introduced to readers of the *Magazine*, four important titles came out without serving this "tender to the business." Three of them

---

[*] That same day Thackeray wrote Putnam declining his "very generous" offer, saying that he was accepting the one made by the Harpers "who have published my larger books and have paid my London publisher for my last work. . . . I think it best that I should accept their liberal proposal."

were "firsts"—books that would give their authors Harper identification with the trade, even as Bulwer and James, for many book years to come. Chief of these was Wilkie Collins, whose *Antonia* was published in 1850, the brothers paying £15 for early proofs. Having established their rights to his books in America, they were in 1858 to make a five-year agreement with Collins to pay a royalty of 5 percent on his books, and later to give £750 for each of his more popular titles, *Man and Wife* and *Moonstone*. Then there was Mrs. Margaret Oliphant, whose Harper debut came in 1851 with *Caleb Field*, followed by *Katie Stewart* in 1852 and twenty-three more through 1878. Finally there was Dinah Maria Mulock (D. L. Mulock). By 1878 she would have thirty Harper novels to her credit. Her first one came out in 1853. Entitled *A Hero and Other Tales*, it was issued in a new edition in 1859, the year that the brothers published her most famous work, *John Halifax, Gentleman*. Another classic book of fiction was Elizabeth Gaskell's *Cranford*, published from Cliff Street on August 5, 1853. For more than a century it was to appear in many editions on several publishers' lists. But Appleton's, not Harper's, was to publish Mrs. Gaskell's *Life of Charlotte Brontë*.

Every time a successful English reprint began to put American dollars into the pockets of papermakers, cloth manufacturers, type founders, stereotypers, engravers, printers, binders, publishers, and booksellers, someone was sure to speak up for the poor English authors' lack of dollars. Others, like Henry Carey, whose economic treatises were receiving respectful attention, argued that words and ideas were the common property of mankind. They were like flowers in a garden which a clever man such as Dickens could make into a lovely bouquet. It was his right to pick them, arrange them attractively, and possibly show them for a while at some profit to himself; but soon the gardener should ask to have the bouquet returned so that any who wished might enjoy it without charge, the artist being given full credit. Abraham Hart, Carey's former colleague, carried the fight against international copyright for the publishing fraternity. In fact, the Philadelphia publishers, rather than those in New York or Boston, were credited (or blamed) with having been the chief influence against legislation to protect the rights of English authors. The brothers were torn between their belief that authors deserved compensation (here they would have disagreed with Carey's parable of the gardener) and their business concerns. As book manufacturers they believed, as did all others in the graphic arts industry, that American copyrights of foreigners' works would flood the market with imports, including books by American authors, throwing people out of work and otherwise depressing the industry.

And to a certain extent they were right, although it took more than a hundred years to prove them so. Today, despite international copyright, books of English origin currently are reprinted as American paperbacks and flow back into the markets controlled by British publishers, while books of American origin, and English books for which American publishers have rights in the United States, are sold in vast quantities here. The blame is not chargeable to the cooperating publishers but to wholesalers who "buy round" and "sell round," claiming that in handling thousands of titles they cannot take time to check on the prescribed market of each one. It is also chargeable to individuals and institutions who want to get the most for their money—even as their great-grandparents did—and while they give lip service to international copyright they do not hesitate to ignore the rights of authors and publishers by importing the English edition for reasons of price and prestige. British and American publishers are attempting to meet the problem by simultaneous publication and by setting similar retail prices, but the problem of "buying round" will probably not be solved in America until our copyright law is fitted with some sharp teeth. Without such dentures in legislation, publishers will become increasingly shy about overseas cooperative endeavors. There will be a decrease in the exchange of works of new authors and in sharing translation costs of important foreign-language works, and a consequent shortage in the exchange of ideas—the humanistic ideal which is the bedrock of all publication of quality books.

The tightrope the brothers walked is well illustrated by an exchange of letters in 1852 with President Millard Fillmore. On August 9, Fillmore wrote to the brothers to ask their opinion about a possible copyright treaty with England. They took two weeks to compose a reply. Their letter (see Appendix 6) deserves a high place in that literature of diplomatic exchange which says nothing with great courtesy and aplomb.

But Abraham Hart did not hesitate to speak his mind. The following year (the treaty still hanging fire), he challenged Putnam to debate the matter with him at the Spring Trade Sales. Hart's superior ability as a public speaker not only won his audience but also forced Putnam to write out his arguments in the columns of *Norton's Literary Gazette*, thus saving them for posterity. Putnam first tried to show that American book manufacturers had not suffered because of imports from

England and that an international copyright law or a reciprocal treaty would, in fact, protect American printers. This latter point—the most critical issue—he tried to establish with a free-trade argument, based largely on the increasing output of original American works as compared to English reprints—a 300 percent increase in nineteen years, according to Putnam. American authors would also benefit financially for 850 of their works had been reprinted in England during the last ten years, often with little or no profit to them. However, he did not think that the lack of international copyright was throttling American genius, "the plaintive cry of some small authorlings [Cornelius Mathews?] that their genius was obscured . . . by the influx of uncopyrighted foreign books."* Furthermore, Putnam wanted English authors paid for their copyrights, meaning royalties, apparently, since he did not mention the increasing amounts being paid for "first proofs." His final argument tried to show that American readers would not have to pay more for English reprints—the most controversial issue—if copyright protection was forthcoming.

That Putnam was sincere in his beliefs was unquestioned. Authors applauded him, but most publishers and booksellers considered him an impractical idealist. The property rights of English and American authors to their works when sold abroad had not been established either by public conscience or by law. Even their domestic rights—and consequent compensation, which was thought to be sufficient—were limited in time. Their literary creations were not "properties" to be held, like real or chattel properties, in perpetuity; eventually their "bouquets" were handed back to the gardener, to enter the public domain. Hardly anyone believed that English reprints would continue to sell at low prices if international copyright was effected by a law or treaty. Americans loved competition and a reprint fight among publishers was fun to watch and kept the price of good books down. And maybe a law or treaty *would* put a lot of people out of work.

---

* After attending an international copyright meeting in London, Charlotte Brontë wrote on July 8, 1851, ". . . The argument brought forward about the damage accruing to American national literature from the present piratical system, is a good and sound argument, but I am afraid the publishers—honest men—are not mentally prepared to give such reasoning due weight."

CHAPTER XIX

The Harper Homes and Office

1850–1853

By 1852 ALL the brothers except Wesley had moved into sumptuous new houses that were to be their homes for their remaining
years. James was the first to move, one reason being that the house at
40 Rose Street was filled with sad memories. Eighteen months after his
mother's death, there had been another funeral. His wife, Maria, died
on March 4, 1847, "in great peace and with a strong hope for immortality." By late 1848 James had remarried, taking for his second wife
Augusta Thorne, related to Anne Thorne, who had been Maria's favorite shipboard acquaintance in 1835. James and Augusta moved into a
new house at No. 4 Gramercy Park (see illustration 21), one of the several three- and four-story houses being built around a hollow square
which gave residents a private park. Other houses were going up
nearby, northward along a new street called Lexington Avenue
and on nearby East Twenty-first Street, where diarist Strong was
building a $31,000 house for his bride, Miss Ellen Ruggles. Cyrus
Field, recently come into great wealth, also lived nearby. When James
moved to 4 Gramercy Park, he took with him the two wrought-iron
lampposts, emblematic of his office of mayor. They stand there today,
and match the original wrought-iron porticoes which have also been

kept, as have the ornamental ceiling and Corinthian pilasters in the main drawing room. For many years a full-length portrait of Thurlow Weed, testimony of a long friendship, hung in the dining room. Once the Mayor asked that an inventory be taken of Harper books in his library. The checked catalogue showed surprisingly few. Either he rarely took books home from the office or copies were borrowed by friends and relatives but not returned, since a man's conscience is often insensitive to the value of a borrowed book.

Fletcher moved in 1851 to 14 West Twenty-second Street, almost across the street from S. F. B. Morse. The street not only gave the sobriquet "22nd Street" to his son Joe, but also named the Monday dinners that Fletcher gave regularly to authors and associates. John's house was No. 234 Fifth Avenue, the property being purchased in July, 1852. He subsequently bought lots 5 through 11 West Twenty-seventh Street to provide a garden and the more essential carriage house and stables. Of all the brothers, John was the one who most enjoyed carriage rides. He was often to drive up Harlem Lane, where he occasionally had a brush with Commodore Vanderbilt and with Robert Bonner, prominent journalist and turfman. But he had only to walk a block to dine at Delmonico's or five blocks down to Madison Square for the 1859 opening of the Fifth Avenue Hotel, for fifty years the city's leading hostelry.

While Wesley did not get involved in this mid-century house hunting of his brothers, he did build a house for his newly married daughter Elizabeth. He had it built of stone from Dr. Chalmers's Scotland (stone that had been used as ships' ballast) on a Brooklyn Heights lot adjacent to his own, formerly his rose garden. Elizabeth was married to Dr. Dillon S. Landon on December 5, 1849. She was a year older than Joe Brooklyn, whom Melville had met in London. Joe got back in time for the wedding and continued to work beside his father on Cliff Street. He had gone through Anthon's Grammar School and had been graduated from Columbia in the class of '48, of which he was valedictorian. His 1852 marriage to Abigail Sleeper, daughter of Jacob Sleeper of Boston, was one of the best matches, to date, of the second generation. Abigail's father was then worth $250,000, made in the clothing business, a fortune that was multiplied many times over by shrewd real-estate investments. Like the brothers, Jacob Sleeper was a devout Methodist; he was a long-time trustee of Wesleyan and a founder of Boston University.

Fletcher, Jr., had also married into a family with good Methodist—and Harper—connections. His December, 1850, wedding to Margaret

Durbin made a Harper-in-law out of her author-father, John P. Durbin. When young Fletcher got Dr. Durbin's "yes" for his daughter's hand in marriage, there may have been a joking prod—the kind that authors like to make—about now expecting more promotion for his two books of travel, published in 1844 and '45. Dr. Durbin had been president of Dickinson College and took a leading part in the 1844 debate which resulted in the division of the Methodist Church, North and South. At the time of his marriage, Fletcher, Jr., was beginning his climb up the Cliff Street ladder after learning his way around the factory. Shortly after Henry J. Raymond started the *New York Daily Times* in 1851, Fletcher, Sr., bought a block of stock, and for a while the *Times* (the word "Daily" soon dropped) was published by Raymond, Harper & Co., with Fletcher, Jr., helping out there at the same time Raymond was being paid regularly for acting as managing editor of the *Magazine*.

Two other second-generation Harpers were married in 1853. (See Genealogical Chart, Appendix 8.) These were John's two sons. The elder, John W. Harper, was married on March 24 to Hannah Amelia Harper, Wesley's second daughter. This marriage of the cousins was a great day for the whole family. John W. Harper was to be the head of the House during the financially dark years of the 1890's. It is significant perhaps that he succeeded to leadership on the retirement of J. W. Harper, Joe Brooklyn, who was both his cousin and his brother-in-law. John's younger brother, Abner, had followed his cousin Joe 22nd Street by going to Europe for culture and romance. His father gave him $500 for spending money and a leather-bound journal in which dutifully to record his travel notes. Abner did the usual sightseeing in the British Isles (Edinburgh was his favorite city) and on the Continent. Fleas in Florence interested him more than Botticelli's paintings, but by that time he had seen enough of the old masters. He too fell in love—with petite and pretty Caroline ("Carrie") Sackett, an American girl who was touring Europe with her parents. They were married two years later. Abner too had started in the family business, his special responsibility to be that of the textbook department.

Philip, the Mayor's son, had been the first to marry, and by 1853 his son James was six years old. That year marked the third birthday of J. Henry Harper, the son of Joe 22nd Street. James and J. Henry Harper were to be the first members of the third generation to become partners. And, as the four brothers counted their blessings of sons and grandsons, they could believe that the business they had given so many of their years to would surely go on after their time.

Not only that, but the second generation of Harpers was bringing

new excitement and enthusiasm to the firm. "We must confess a pleasant surprise at the eloquent speaking abilities of the young Messrs
Harper," the New York *Evening Mirror* commented on December 26,
1851, when reporting a Christmas Day "Festival of the Harpers'
'Guard.' " Preceded by a band, twenty-eight Harper employees, armed
with muskets, wearing plumed hats and uniformly dressed in black
trousers and frock coats trimmed with gold lace, marched from Cliff
Street to each of the uptown houses of the three brothers, where guests
had assembled. Thence the whole party went by omnibus to the birth-
place of the brothers at Newtown, Long Island, "scattering music and
Merry Christmas profusely on the way." After several hours of
competitive target shooting, the company went to Wheeler's Newtown Hotel for a sumptuous temperance dinner. There were many
toasts proposed and speeches made in which the young Harpers extolled and described the honors which literature confers on all who
serve it, and there were many letters read, including congratulatory
notes from General Morris, Hiram Fuller, Anthon, and Lossing. Then
the best marksmen of the "Guard" were awarded prizes valued at
$600, including gold watches and silver goblets, gold pens and pencils,
a diamond ring, and an autographed, morocco-bound copy of Verplanck's *Shakespeare*. "Altogether," Duyckinck commented in the *Literary World*, "a very sparkling rivulet pouring into the full stream of
the Christmas festivities."

This spirit of liveliness and fun was a new phenomenon on Cliff
Street, where business had always carried the restricting adjective of
"serious," even though flavored by the Mayor's jokes and Fletcher's
witticisms. In school and college, the young Harpers had learned to
take as a matter of course a prestige of name that their fathers as young
men had not known. They approached their business responsibilities in
the fifties with a more confident and relaxed spirit than their fathers
could possibly have had in the twenties. When they once met the
somewhat intoxicated Poe on the street, the encounter resulted in a jolly
good story, not a moral judgment.* Practical jokes and horseplay did
not have to be put aside with hat and coat on entering the counting

---

* In *The House of Harper*, J. Henry Harper wrote: "I recall an anecdote which
John Kendrick Bangs related to me in regard to Poe. He told me that late one evening
on their way home from a club dinner, his father, Francis N. Bangs, the brilliant lawyer, who was for years our legal adviser and friend, and my cousin, 'Joe Brooklyn,' saw
a man clinging to a lamp-post. His hat had rolled into the street, and Francis Bangs
politely picked it up and handed it to the limp gentleman, who thanked him profusely,
and said that they might probably like to know the name of the man indebted to them
for so much courtesy, and he then solemnly introduced himself as Mr. Edgar Allan
Poe. Bangs replied that it was curious coincidence, as his name was Tay and his
friend's Toe. Poe immediately observed that they were well met, for together they
made a potato, and, bowing very low, continued his uncertain perambulations."

room. In fact, his old top hat furnished Joe Brooklyn with a property that would have done credit to a vaudeville actor. Should a particularly pompous visitor call, he would surely be invited to sit down while a chair bearing the hat was surreptitiously placed behind him. The feel and sound of the squelching hat invariably brought a jack-in-the-box response which was a joy to see. And profuse apologies which Joe would generously wave aside, saying it was an old hat anyway.

How his Uncle James treated one such visitor made a story that got told so often it has survived in various versions. Once he had to entertain an out-of-town clergyman who had called with no object but to satisfy his curiosity and to be able to tell the folks back home of his visit with the famous Harper brothers. After many questions about the business, the visitor remarked, "You say that your brother John sees to the accounts, that your brother Wesley looks after the correspondence, and that your brother Fletcher receives authors and supervises the publication of new books and the *Monthly*, but you, Mr. Mayor, I have never been able to discover what you do."

"Oh, they leave me an enormous amount of work; I have more to do than all of them put together."

"Indeed! That is very curious. Allow me to ask what it is."

"I'll tell you," James replied in a whisper, "but you must never tell a soul. I entertain the bores."

One of the Mayor's responsibilities was to represent the firm at the New York and Philadelphia Trade Sales. "James Harper was the life and soul of these meetings," according to a contemporary who wrote in "Representative Booksellers," "Every man knew him; when his tall, erect form was seen entering the room, every eye was turned from the catalog; and when the Harper list was reached, [as] he went to the auctioneer's desk, everyone knew that something good was coming. Some joke or anecdote was sure to put life into the dullest bidding. Every one felt that he was not merely desirous to make business brisk, but that he had something lively to say, which must come out." (See illustration 27.)

One of the most interesting descriptions of such book auctions was published in the Boston *Transcript* after the editor, possibly Epes Sargent, had attended the fifty-seventh Trade Sale in New York in March, 1853. He wrote:

Twice a year the "Trade" from all parts of the Union come together in Philadelphia and New York to buy and to be bought. All the new books, all the old books, all the literature that can be gathered together, centre in one spot for the space of ten or twelve days. It is a curious thing to watch day after day the operations going on in the big hall of the auctioneer. Opposite the "Park" and vis à vis with the Astor House, are the extensive sale rooms of Bangs & Co. Let us step up for half an hour, as we did last week during the book sales. High above all the busy, bustling crowds, stands, with his head uncovered and in his best clothes, Mr. Merwin, the partner of the great house, who usually "sells." Five or six hundred gentlemen of the trade sit before him in arm chairs, with their huge octavo catalogues spread out like maps of the great literary voyage they are about to undertake during the year.

"Gentlemen," begins the elevated selling partner, "it is half-past eight o'clock, and we are to sell this morning the excellent books published by the Messrs. Harpers, a well known house of this city. I shall not enlarge on the fame and literary ability of this establishment, but proceed at once to introduce to you His Honor, the former Mayor of this metropolis." The Honorable James, neatly clad in sombre black, with spectacles on nose, then rises with great solemnity, and bows three times very profoundly to all present, at which all present immediately burst into three violent roars of laughter and stamp prodigiously. This proceeding throws the honorable gentleman himself into a bland and appreciating smile, and he makes a brief speech expressive of the thanks of himself and "brethren" for the "kindness always evinced toward a humble house like theirs, which is endeavoring to get an honest living." The auctioneer grows impatient, as compliments of this nature increase, and he knocks vigorously on the stand before him, and the fun begins. Toward the middle of the day the buyers get tired, and some falls [sic] into naps. Pretty soon, announced in a loud voice by Mr. Harper, "Webster's Dictionary" is put up. Now all ears are open. A price is fixed upon, and "give in your names," is the cry. This is always one of the most ludicrous items in the business to a stranger's ears. Some of the booksellers, not wishing to have the whole assembled "Trade" know what books they are buying, give in fancy names representing their own, and known only to the auctioneers. "Give in your names," chimes in the seller, and a list, somewhat after this fashion, is cried in various voices, in every key, from the deep bass of the western merchant to the shrill or nasal shout of the member from Maine or Connecticut: Mussey, 20; West, 10; Sampson, 20; O.K., 10; Detroit, 10; Vermont, 5; Buffalo, 20; W., 10; L., 20; G., 50; Ticknor, 20; Jewett, 20; Burnham, 10; O. W., 10; Blind, 5; and so on to the end of the list. The last name called is spoken quietly by a blind bookseller from the West, who always sits in front of the auctioneer, and is seen constantly to rise and feel the size and binding of the book offered. He makes up his mind in a moment after he has handled the volume, and at once sinks into his seat again and waits for the next book.

There are generally six or seven auctioneers employed during the day, as it would be impossible for one man to hold out from 8 in the morning to 11 at night. Now and then, an amateur seller, from the ranks of the trade, comes forward, and offers his services for an hour or two. One of the most popular of this class is Mr. Hart, of the formerly celebrated house of Carey & Hart, in Philadelphia. This gentleman has a sharp, ringing tone, and his words rattle out as clear as a bell. He is very rapid and judicious, always knowing all the rules of the business, and just where to be firm and unalterable in his decisions.

At half-past 12, a daily luncheon is served in the same building with the sales room, and at the gratuitous board oftentimes may be seen the popular authors mingle with their publishers. We have often seen Fenimore Cooper in former days earnestly talking amid the din of dinner. Cooper had an eye to business, and did not fail to express his disapprobation aloud if his novels were bringing less than the usual prices.

As each list is offered for sale, the publisher stands by the side of the auctioneer and puts in a word of encouragement now and then, tending to make his brethren pay good prices for his publications. His phrases run thus: "Bid sharp!" "They'll all go this time!" "Quick, or you'll lose them!" "Wide awake, gentlemen; get all the bargains," etc.

It is a pleasant thing to see the trade thus meeting together once a year, shaking hands and exchanging toasts after a separation of twelve months. Good fellowship is always a good thing in any business, and as much of that commodity exists among the *book* trade as among any other class of merchants in the country.

Because of its mid-century pre-eminence in the world of books, the Cliff Street establishment was often referred to in magazines and newspapers, with estimates of sales and dollar volumes varying considerably. One of the most dependable reports appeared in the *Literary World* (London) of January 5, 1850, reprinted in *Littell's Living Age*, the original article carrying the initials "F. S." (Frederick Saunders). It claimed that the three largest publishers in the world were Chambers of Edinburgh, Brockhaus of Leipzig, and Harper of New York, with "Messrs Harper & Brothers . . . the most important, as to the numerical extent of their operations, of any in the world." While acknowledging Harper's lead in the size of their operation, the Saunders article argued that Longmans of London was the world's "largest publishers" in view of capital invested in copyrights. "Still the Harpers pay by far the largest premiums for the priority of new English works, and to some of their popular American authors they have been enabled to give munificent sums." Prescott, Stephens, Barnes, Anthon, Morse, and Andrews were named along with the approximate earnings of each. Saying that the Harpers were possessed of unrivaled resources and facilities, the article described their operations in detail:

Within their own establishment, all the details and machinery of publishing are carried on, with the exception of paper making and type founding. Their extensive range of buildings, equal to six or seven five story houses, they divide into the several departments of composing rooms, stereotype foundry, press rooms, warehouses, bindery, &c. Nineteen double medium power presses, besides Napier presses, are constantly throwing off printed sheets, to the extent of some 70 reams per diem; while in the bindery 50 barrels of flour are required for making paste every year, as well as 1,200 dozen sheepskins, 750 pieces of muslin of 40 square yards each, and sixty tons of pasteboard. Over 40,000 lbs. of metal are used per annum for casting stereotype plates, of which their vaults contain about $300,000 worth; they also have about 70,000 lbs. of various fonts of type in their composing rooms. Even the cuttings from the edges of the books, in the process of binding, amount to 18 tons of shavings per annum, which are sold to the paper-makers. Their annual sales have been estimated in round numbers at 2,000,000 volumes, including pamphlets. There are attached to this establishment usually from 300 to 350 employees, in the various departments of the business, among that number about 100 being females, who fold and sew the sheets of books.

By 1853 the annual total of volumes issued, including numbers of the *Monthly*, had risen to more than four and a half million, with the Cliff Street presses turning out an average of twenty-five volumes a minute, ten hours a day, six days a week. The brothers' annual income from sales was estimated by the *New York Times* that year at $2 million.

Another account, in 1853, revealed a remarkable expansion of the Harper operation in the nearly four years following the Saunders article. Dr. Davis W. Clark, of Cincinnati, visited the brothers with notebook in hand to gather information for an inspirational article for *The Ladies' Repository*, a monthly magazine that had been started several years earlier to shield Methodist womanhood from the distractions of *Godey's Lady's Book*. According to Dr. Clark, there were now 30 power presses; the paper used per day averaged 100 reams and the annual expenditure for paper was $160,000; flour for paste was up to 70 barrels; the value of stereotype plates had risen to nearly $400,000; the number of employees was 500 and the annual payroll more than $200,000. In 1853, one hundred and eighty young women were employed in the bindery, 10 of them for laying gold leaf on expensive bindings; one of the "young women" had been with the firm for twenty-three years.*

While American writers were often in the Harper office, authors from abroad came less frequently. One such author was brought by a

---

* While his statistics of book sales and authors' earnings seem exaggerated, Clark was a good reporter and his description of the Mayor, who probably showed him around the establishment, is typical. He first saw James in the middle of the counting room surrounded by an animated group that often laughed heartily over his exchanges. He looked younger than his age (fifty-eight), was "tall and commanding," and completely at ease with others. He was "facetious, possessing a keen perception of the ludicrous,

competitor, and the story of the visit was told by George Haven Putnam in the *Memoir* he wrote in 1912 of his father, George P. Putnam. The author that the senior Putnam brought to Cliff Street was Miss Fredrika Bremer, who arrived in New York from Sweden in 1849 for an extended visit. Mr. Putnam helped to arrange speaking engagements for Miss Bremer and planned to issue editions of *The Home* and *The Neighbors*, her most popular novels, on a royalty basis. As the story was told, Mr. Putnam was seeing the books through the press when he read in *Harper's Magazine* that the brothers were soon to publish cheaper editions. Whereupon he took Miss Bremer to Cliff Street, where they were

very courteously received by Mr. Fletcher Harper, who was the most active of the four, and was given an opportunity of examining the printing-office and the other details of the establishment which was at that time the most important of its class in the country. She was then taken to her carriage and my father returned for a last word with Mr. Harper. "Do you not think, Mr. Harper," said my father, "bearing in mind that the little lady has come over here trusting to American hospitality and to American good faith, that it might be in order for you to withdraw your announcement of those competing volumes?" Mr. Harper's reply was in substance that courtesy was courtesy and business was business. The competing editions came onto the market within a few weeks.

George Haven Putnam had probably heard this anecdote from his father, who died in 1872. Had he attempted to verify his father's story, he would have discovered that no announcement of the Harper editions could have been made in *Harper's New Monthly Magazine* since it was not started till the following year, and that the Bremer novels were not new, as he supposed. Since 1843 they had been selling at 25 cents each in the *Library of Select Novels*. Fletcher could hardly withdraw the novels in print for six years, simply because a competitor wished to be generous toward a visiting author.

Furthermore, Fletcher exercised his "rights" to Miss Bremer's

---

an inexhaustible fund of anecdote, and a ready use of quaint and striking illustrations . . . [a] man of large business capacity, one that deeply reads human nature to good purpose, [whose] profound philosophy of life and the fund of general knowledge with which his mind is enriched, has been gathered more from large experience and observation than from books." John, according to Clark, had about the same physical dimensions as his older brother, "what he lacks in longitude is amply compensated in latitude—a robust, hearty man; countenance grave almost to severity; yet as from the corner of his eye he glances now and then upon the central group, it sparkles as from the impulse of an unexpressed emotion, and a playful smile [lights up] his features." Clark described Wesley as "active, keen-eyed, middle-sized. . . . His step is light, his motions rapid. Nothing escapes the glances of his eye. He moves like a man who has work to do."

Homes in the New World, the book she wrote on her return to Sweden following her American visit. He paid £100 for the privilege. *Homes in the New World* was translated by Mrs. Howitt, not altogether to Miss Bremer's satisfaction, and was given a lead review in the *Magazine* the month of publication. The news of differences between author and translator was revealed by Norton in the *Literary Gazette.* He was also saying, "Here everybody *reads* and everybody travels." Therefore publishers were issuing books for people "to read on the rails." But Miss Bremer probably did not find travel on American trains conducive to reading. "After the first two hours," she wrote, "there is an end of all pleasure of traveling, and one sinks into a suffering and stupid state." Crowded coaches, smoke, cinders, and dust, however, did not keep the little "potato-nosed" Swedish novelist from making interesting travel notes on people and places for her book, which came out in two volumes, totaling 1,300 pages.

G. P. R. James also called at the Harper establishment several times during his residence in America. For several years, beginning in 1850, he served as British Consul, first in Massachusetts and later at Richmond, Virginia. The most famous visitor from overseas was William Makepeace Thackeray. Shortly after arriving for his first American visit, Thackeray came by to pay his respects and to collect some dollars. Thackeray was surprised to hear from the Mayor that novelist James was the most popular author in America. But with *Henry Esmond,* published just three days later, Thackeray had produced three novels whose total American sale would soon be four times that of Britain and outdistance the whole voluminous output of the now-forgotten James. During Thackeray's call, the Mayor's little daughter Julia was brought into the counting room to see where her father spent his time when he was not at home. Thackeray bowed low over Julia's tiny hand and delighted the Mayor by saying, "So this is a pirate's daughter, is it?"

When Thackeray called on the brothers, they took considerable pride in showing him around their new premises. Earlier that year they had finally closed the door of 82 Cliff Street that for more than a quarter of a century had been synonymous with their publishing enterprise. By February, two new buildings, 329 and 331 Pearl Street, were ready for occupancy, the street floors fitted up with a reception room where the brothers now had their desks and with enlarged counting and sales rooms. The low-ceilinged and somewhat dingy quarters on Cliff Street were now piled high with stacks of books. The new airy and spacious quarters on Pearl Street also had floor space for desks of "the young Messrs Harper," as they finished their apprenticeships in the composing rooms, pressrooms, and bindery. The new buildings were firmly constructed to carry the new heavy presses—thirty of them now in use—that were throwing off sheets of the *Magazine* and of books, sometimes by night as well as by day. The buildings were described in the *Literary World* as "plain, strong, suitable, unambitious."* The two new buildings, as well as the ones erected in 1844 and 1851 (the latter referred to by Fletcher in his letter to Melville), had openings into the rear of the Cliff Street buildings so that the entire space between these two streets—180 feet in depth—was used for the processes of book manufacture and book storage. The book "depository" was portioned off into numbered "avenues" and named "alleys." Thus it is known that by the end of 1853 five buildings, one unfinished, stood on lots 327 to 335 Pearl Street.

After January, 1852, the 82 Cliff Street address ceased being used in advertising. Soon the new Pearl Street address was being used on the cover of the new *Monthly*, in advertisements, and on stationery and invoices. Franklin Square was also fancied as an address, and an extant letter to Thurlow Weed, drafted by James in June, 1852, was headed "Franklin Square," presaging an address that was to be used by the House from 1855 to 1923. (See illustration 25.) Even so, the old Cliff Street address was the remembered address. After the move Dr. John Wakefield Francis referred to Cliff Street in a speech before the New York Typographical Society when he referred to the brothers' first book production in 1817. *Seneca's Morals* was an acorn that "has become the pride of the forest—the Cliff Street Tree, whose roots and branches now ramify over the land."

Opposite the new entrance on Pearl Street was the well-known Walton house, built in 1754 as a country seat by William Walton, who wanted a home out of the city and could afford to import bricks from Holland for its construction. This grand old mansion with its pre-revolutionary associations now stood insecurely against the northward tide of business and industry. It was particularly vulnerable to the hazards of fire.

---

* Duyckinck also wrote, "Messrs Harper & Bros. book establishment, so often described, commented on, and pointed at in its hugeness as the surprising perfection of system governing hundreds of enterprises with all their masses of materials and means, through all their details, to completion and success, now growing apace with its own requirements, has recently added in the new buildings in Franklin Square in Pearl Street and the rearrangements of the whole parts, fresh cause for wondering and imagining."

CHAPTER XX

The Last of 82 Cliff Street

1853

THE GREAT HARPER FIRE occurred on Saturday, December 10, 1853. According to the New York *Tribune*, it was the most alarming that had occurred in New York City since 1835, when buildings covering thirteen acres in Lower Manhattan were destroyed at a property loss of $18 million. The fire broke out about 1 P.M. in what was known as the camphine room, to which the rollers used to spread ink over the printing plates were brought to be cleaned. Because of its highly inflammable nature, the camphine was not taken from this room, and the walls, ceiling, and floor were lined with zinc. Paradoxically, the fire originated in the excessive caution of a plumber, who needed to extinguish a small roll of burning paper he had used to light a lamp. Deciding not to stamp out the small flame on the floor for fear of fire, he tossed it into what he assumed to be a pan of water. But it was a pan of camphine instead, and in a moment the room was ablaze, with rivulets of flaming camphine breaking through the walls to ignite combustible materials stored nearby.

The cry "Fire! Fire!" soon reached the counting room, where the brothers were at their desks. "The camphine room on fire?" asked John Harper incredulously. "Then we are lost. Save the hands."

"What part of the property shall we try to save?" someone asked.

"Never mind the property, save the lives!"

John took $3,000 from his desk and sent it by a boy to a nearby bank. He ran upstairs to the pressroom, where he truly saw the futility of trying to save anything there. Others in the counting room gathered valuable papers at hand and put them in a large iron chest which was dragged to the street. A boy who had come from Appleton's with a large order for books was forced to leave his $80 purchase behind him when the clerk who was tying up the parcel rushed out carrying his knife but leaving the heavy cord uncut. Joe Brooklyn said later that his Uncle James came to him to ask his aid in finding his rubbers; it was damp outside and he didn't want to go without them. Believing that all employees were safe, the brothers left the flaming buildings.

However, on the fourth floor a panic had spread among women working at stitching and folding machines. According to the *Times*, many lives were saved by the presence of mind and courage of Captain Rosenquest, foreman of the bindery, who corralled employees and forced them to take safe exits. Some escaped by ladders run up by firemen. Even so, a young woman flung herself from a window. Her fall was broken by a man who was himself unhurt, although she suffered a fractured leg, the only serious accident of the afternoon. Fortunately, many employees were away from the building during the dinner hour.

A city counselor who was standing beside Fletcher attempted to commiserate with him over the loss being sustained. Fletcher replied that, great as the tragedy was, it could be overcome, but the recent loss by death of his grandson Freddy was irreparable. About two o'clock John looked at his watch, remarked that it was past dinnertime, and, turning to his brothers, said, "You had better come to my house after supper so that we can talk things over." An officer made a way for them through the crowds, but the curious—an estimated fifty thousand—stayed on to watch the display.

About 2:30 P.M. the walls of the Pearl Street buildings crashed in, carrying more fire to the avenues and alleys of books in what for so many years had been the Cliff Street counting room. Thirsting for air, the flames burst through windows and doors. Through the door numbered 82 Cliff Street. Moments later the Cliff Street walls fell in.

Short dispatches giving news of the Harper fire were telegraphed that afternoon to daily papers across the nation. The New York press covered the fire fully and all accounts spoke of the great crowd of spectators drawn by the size of the fire and its literary associations. One reporter quoted a bystander who "professed to be able to tell when poetry went sparkling skyward, when romances cast a lurid glare around or when smoke as of Tophet came from the tomes of orthodox divinity."

The best description of the fire was written not by a reporter but by diarist George Templeton Strong, an avid "fire bug":

Great fire today. Saw the smoke swelling out in great masses against the clear sky at two o'clock, and put out for the scene. The "devouring element" was occupied with Harpers' premises (Cliff Street through Pearl) and the Walton House (I believe) on the opposite side of Pearl. Very fierce and obstinate, and more than commonly dramatic and splendid was the conflagration. From the corner of Peck Slip and Pearl Street you looked up a little ascent to Franklin Square, crowded and busy, with three or four great double-banked engines rising above the crowd and working slowly. Fire on both sides, sometimes arching the street, more generally kept down by columns of water that *stood*, like bars, penetrating the smoke and ruin. Walls thundering down at intervals, each fall followed by a rush upwards of tawny, ropy, blinding smoke and a rain of powdered mortar. Across Pearl Street there stood in beautiful contrast with the lurid masses of flame and smoke, an arch of rainbow, brightening and fading as the northwest wind fell, formed on the spray of the engines. . . .

Not only did crowds of people rush to watch the fiery spectacle on Saturday but more thousands also came on Sunday to view the smoldering ruins and to exclaim over the further tragic loss of the ancient Walton house. An enterprising newsboy hawked "Souvenir of the great Harper fire" and filled his pockets with pennies in exchange for half-burned pages of the *Magazine*.

Saturday night the brothers added up their losses. Their approximate totals were published in the *New York Times* on Monday (see page 356).

In addition to property saved, they had cash in the banks and accounts receivable totaling more, presumably, than accounts payable. They would receive insurance payments from several companies, totaling approximately $200,000. Even though, according to the *Times*, they had done everything possible to minimize fire hazards, insurance rates were high because of intercommunicating buildings and large stocks of combustible materials. High rates had discouraged the brothers from carrying more insurance and had discouraged Adams from carrying any at all on his share of Bible sheets and bound stock.

Having figured their net losses, the brothers faced the question of their future. Would they continue in publishing? They had lost only those plates of books that were on press. All other plates were secure in fire-proof, subterranean vaults, and with those they could begin again. However, the plates could be auctioned off and other assets liquidated.

Value of Property before the Fire

Binding Establishment, estimated to be worth about	$	60,000
Thirty-four Adams Presses, valued at		75,000
Nine Hydraulic Presses		15,000
Materials in the composing room		15,000
Stereotype foundry and Electrotype apparatus		5,000
Printed Sheets of the Pictorial Bible, half of which was owned by J. G. Adams		30,000
Steam Engine and boiler		5,000
Stock of books and printed sheets, estimated in the inventory to be worth not far from		800,000
Wood-cuts, estimated at		50,000
Ten buildings, worth probably		150,000
Stereotype plates, valued at		400,000
Total value of property		$1,605,000

Value of Property Saved

Stereotype plates	$400,000	
Wood-cuts	40,000	
Books, papers, and miscellaneous	10,000	450,000
Value of Property Lost		$1,115,000

While their losses were great, there was still enough left to provide amply for each of them for the rest of their years. They had worked hard. Why not call it quits?

Again John was to speak the authoritative word. "Our business is too valuable to be given up or to pass into other hands," he counseled his brothers. "We have all of us sons. They have helped us and will soon be able to take our places. We will carry on the business, and show the boys we are not 'old fogies' yet."

Actually the decision to begin again may have been made before nightfall, because Raymond was asked to come to 234 Fifth Avenue for the after-supper conference. The most pressing problem was the January issue of the *Magazine*, on press that Saturday with no proofs or manuscripts salvaged. Decisions were quickly made. Raymond should immediately telegraph contributors to forward replacement copy. Henry Marsh, foreman of the composing room, should order type at once and see what use could be made of the brick building at 79 and 81 Cliff Street, which fortunately had survived the fire.

As soon as the ruins had cooled sufficiently that entry could be made to the vaults, plates should be recovered and dispatched to other printers. What titles should be given precedence for reprinting? Since they would begin immediately to plan a new building, should they not order printing presses at once? It took months for Adams to fill orders. Yes, a telegram should be dispatched, asking for twenty presses. (Fortunately it arrived in Boston a few hours in advance of other orders sent by mail, thus saving the brothers three months of valuable time.) And before the evening conference broke up they had drafted an advertisement to appear in the Monday morning papers. The public should know that they would stay in business and that they appreciated the help of the fire and police departments and others in rescuing employees and saving portions of their property from destruction.

The decision not to give way to discouragement and self-pity but to carry on brought forth unexpected resources of energy. To paraphrase Shakespeare, they were men who, enraged by their loss, were "thrice themselves." The immediate involvement in the multitude of new problems gave a positive outlet to emotional feelings and fostered a new excitement. "This has been more like an evening of social festivity than a consultation over a great calamity," Raymond remarked as he bade the brothers goodnight.

George W. Curtis responded to Raymond's telegram, "Copy destroyed. Send fresh copy immediately," by writing from Chicago, where he was lecturing, to Fletcher saying he enclosed new Easy Chair matter and that the brothers were showing how American enterprise could recover without a visible scar. Lossing wrote to George Ripley, "To see men in the decline of their life, beginning anew to establish a mighty business . . . unawed by the great calamity, and even scarcely depressed in spirits beneath its crushing weight, was to me a moral spectacle of great and newfound interest. . . . In this great misfortune is involved the greatest triumph of their career."

John Abbott reacted to the telegram by taking the next train to New York. On Thursday he had written to Fletcher from his home in Brunswick, Maine, to suggest subjects for Doepler, the engraver, to work on. Knowing that this letter was lost, he wrote again on Monday from his customary New York address, "I know not what to say except to express my fraternal sympathy and affection, and to give you the assurance that my time and energies are entirely at your disposal, if I can do anything to assist you, in the vast accumulation of your cares." Abbott also offered to have them withhold further payments, above what he needed for bare living expenses, till they could recover. Prescott wrote that in their next remittance they should deduct the copyright payment on sheets and bound stock of his histories that were destroyed. James wrote from Norfolk, Virginia, "I cannot but feel as I have always declared, that you have uniformly treated me with kindness and liberality and that you have been eminently gentlemanly and fair in our mutual dealings." Probably the greatest solace the brothers received was contained in such letters of sympathy that came from authors.

Cyrus Field called on the Mayor on Sunday to offer a loan of $10,000,* and before nightfall on Monday more than $100,000 had been offered by sympathizers, most of them unknown to the brothers personally. Employees asked that payment of wages be deferred or reduced temporarily if such courses would enable them to refinance the business. All such offers, according to J. Henry Harper, were refused although deeply appreciated as tokens of sympathy and affection.

Financial losses could be—and were—recovered, but literary losses were permanent. Gone forever were holographs of famous authors, such as Melville, Thackeray's handwritten manuscript of his lecture "Charity and Humor," and all records of book disposals. Thus the brothers were not to be able to give any sales statistics to the author of the famous Boston *Post* series of articles "Who Reads an American Book?" to appear in the fall and winter of 1859. For his article on the Harper establishment, the author, "Nor'wester," had to depend largely on his visit with the brothers and the January, 1854, issue of the *Magazine*, which gave a historical sketch of the firm.

This three-page piece, "A Word of Apology," written by Raymond, was given the lead position in the *Magazine*, its 135,000 edition ready on January 10. The "book" ran to its usual length of 144 pages but there were no illustrations. Words can be quickly spun off and put into type; engravings take longer. Of special interest is Raymond's summary statement of the number of titles that the brothers had then in print:

	Works	Volumes	Original	Reprints
History and Biography	329	585	158	171
Travel and Adventure	130	187	73	57
Theology and Religion	120	167	68	52
Educational	156	165	124	32
Art, Science, Medicine	96	110	46	50
Dictionaries and Gazetteers	28	34	23	5
General Literature	690	780	230	460
Total	1549	2028	722	827

Since this table appears in what was written largely as a historical statement, some commentators have taken it as a total record, but it

---

* Field's offer was not altogether altruistic. He was head of one of the country's leading wholesale paper houses, and the brothers may well have been a good customer or a potentially important one.

seems clear from the context that Raymond meant the table, as in fact he says, to give the approximate "number of works on hand." Also interesting is Raymond's statement that a new electrotyping department* had recently been set up to supply copper plates for all engravings and most "valuable books."

It is not clear whether Raymond's table of books in print included new works just published and those on press at the time of the fire. During the prior ten days four new books had been dispatched to dealers to fill advance orders. Among them was *Liberia, or Mr. Peyton's Experiments* by Mrs. Hale, a fact, however, which she did not comment on when she sent a letter of condolence. Neither did James refer in his letter to *Lectures on Modern Civilization*, which Demarest believed to be on press at the time of the fire. Among the new books thus destroyed he does list John Easton Cooke's *Leather Stocking and Silk, a Story of Virginia*, saying that the whole edition was destroyed. It was reset, printed, and published in July, 1854, its first issue being its second printing. The book was widely read and picked up by Tauchnitz for a cheap European reprint.

Another book was off press, a few copies disposed of, and the plates returned to the vault just before the fire broke out. It was *The United States Grinnell Expedition in Search of Sir John Franklin* by Dr. Elisha Kent Kane, a Naval officer. The *Times* story of December 12 assumed that plates of the Kane book and all bound stock were destroyed except one advance copy that had been presented to Henry Grinnell, a New York merchant and philanthropist who had helped to finance Kane's Arctic expedition; stock was being held back till a larger supply could be produced. However, Demarest says that a few copies had been "issued." This book was given priority and the plates sent out to another manufacturer. In this case also the second printing was really the first issue and came out on March 9. George W. Curtis was responsible for getting Dr. Kane's book for the brothers and told later of attending a small dinner at the Century Association, arranged during Thackeray's first visit in order that Thackeray might meet Kane and hear the story of his recent Arctic adventures. According to J. Henry Harper, "The tale and the telling were equally delightful, and as the

* While Raymond gives July, 1853, as the date for establishing an electrotyping department, the brothers had been making electrotypes prior to that time. In their supplementary agreement with John S. C. Abbott of March 19, 1852, they agreed to supply electrotypes at cost for use abroad. The process of electrotyping consisted of taking a wax mold from the type page and immersing it in a solution of copper through which an electric current, activated by batteries, carried the copper to the wax mold. After about twelve hours, the mold with its thin coating of copper was removed from the bath, the wax removed, and the copper shell affixed to a metal base.

brave little man paused in speaking Thackeray arose from his chair to his full height and gravely asked the giver of the feast whether Dr. Kane would probably permit him to kneel down and kiss his boots. Kane himself was as much surprised as any one of the guests, and laughed as gaily at the droll homage of the Englishman."

One of the most tragic losses—certainly for the author—was Professor Henry Drisler's *English-Greek Lexicon* based on the work of C. D. Yonge. Drisler had kept neither a copy of his manuscript nor a copy of the proofs. All were destroyed. It took Drisler eighteen years to redo his work. Anthon's successor as Jay Professor of Greek at Columbia University, Drisler collaborated with Anthon on some of his books but did not seek authorship for himself. But he gave much to the brothers in the way of counsel and friendship. In their partnership agreements of 1860 and 1869, among the six men authorized to arbitrate possible disputes Drisler and Demarest were the only ones named in each. The qualities of integrity and wisdom which recommended Drisler to the brothers were also to impress the trustees of Columbia when he was named dean and later acting president.* His son, Henry Drisler, Jr., was to have an even closer Harper connection—that of a long-time employee—William Demarest's successor.

Other new books on press that fatal December day included illustrated works containing the poems of James Beattie and of William Collins, eighteenth-century poets. The plates had probably been imported, for the works were never issued. Scott's two-volume *History of Scotland* was being reprinted with a consequent loss of plates. Likewise Stephens's *Yucatan* was on press in order to have more stock available for Christmas sales. Although the plates were lost, the work was reset, and according to Stephens's biographer it was reissued every two years thereafter "until, during the Civil War, *Yucatan* was buried under a mountain of grapeshot." Stephens had died in New York in 1852, passing into a coma on the very day that a ship bearing his name was launched—the flagship of the Panama Mail Steamship Company. Although the newspapers published lavish obituaries, he was not long remembered. He was buried in New York's Marble Cemetery in the wrong tomb and in an unmarked grave.

On the day of the fire J. C. Derby was in the counting room negotiating for the lease of a few stereotype plates. (Some of our knowledge of what happened that day is because of his call.) He told the brothers he had disposed of his interest in the Auburn, New York,

---

* The first book published by Columbia University Press, in June, 1894, was *Classical Essays in Honor of Henry Drisler*. Not inappropriately, the present warehouse of the Columbia University Press in Irvington-on-Hudson stands, at least in part, on property once owned by Fletcher Harper, where his summer home was located.

store and had come to New York to set himself up in the publishing business. He probably asked if he could buy some plates; if so, the answer was No, but he could lease a few. On December 17 the brothers had a contract drawn up with Derby giving him reprint rights, though not excluding Harper editions, of eight titles. (See page 391.) Derby promised to give six-month notes dated February 1, 1854, on agreed quantities, with specified royalty payments, and to repeat the same on each of the two following years. Since most of the titles were royalty free, the brothers could count on nearly $5,000. They would also be doing a favor for their friend Derby, who now had the beginnings of a back list, that essential to a successful publishing business. They also had no objection to Derby's asking Ripley to advise him on manuscripts. In 1856, Derby was to obtain ten further titles from the brothers, including all of the novels of Charlotte Brontë, of which in 1859 Derby said 100,000 copies had been sold.

Ready cash was also obtained by selling Mrs. Sigourney the plates for her four books, totaling over $1,000. However, the proposal apparently originated with her, since they wrote on January 25 agreeing that it would be to her pecuniary interest to get her books reissued elsewhere more quickly than they could promise. They appreciated her "consolatory and encouraging remarks," and regretted any separation of "business and friendly" relations. She was to come back to them with a new book—years later.

The plates of Herman Melville's books were not lost in the December holocaust, for apparently none were then being reprinted. Neither was Verplanck's *Shakespeare* destroyed at that time, even though later commentators were correct in saying that the plates were lost in a fire that destroyed Harper books. There was a second fire, although only a few Harper titles were involved. Shortly after the first of the year, forty-two presses in New York, Philadelphia, Boston, Cambridge, and Andover, Massachusetts, were occupied with Harper reprints. One of the New York printers was housed on Spruce Street. To add fiery insult to Harper injury this building and four adjacent ones went up in smoke on March 5. While the Harper loss of plates and paper was less than $6,000 (out of a total loss to printers and publishers of $125,000), it did include some of the plates of Verplanck's *Shakespeare* and sounded the tolling bell for that work.

School and college texts were the first works reissued, and by the end of January Anthon's works and the large lexicons were off press. These were followed by "standard works," such as Prescott's histories, with reprints of novels—including Thackeray's—coming last. For each book reissued new stamping dies had to be made, all brass stamps having been kept in the bindery. New works were also being manufactured and the *New York Times* commented that the effects of the fire would scarcely be appreciable to the public. Early in February the brothers procured office space in a new iron building at 82 Beekman Street. Here the counting room was crowded with clerks finishing off old business carried over from Cliff Street and accounting for the new. By late March they could give the Mayor titles and quantities of books that he could offer at the Spring Trade Sale in New York. More than 100,000 volumes were sold and the Mayor promised their "usual full assortment" at the Fall Sale.

In the meantime John had been busy with plans for their new building. He was all for moving uptown, accepting an offer to swap the Franklin Square property for an entire block on Broadway facing Madison Square. But his more conservative brothers prevailed against him. They would stay where they were on Franklin Square. They contracted with John B. Corlies as architect-builder. "You must make this new building fireproof," was John's first instruction to Mr. Corlies.

The new structure was not only to be fireproof but also to have the distinction of being the first of such size to make structural use of flanged beams of wrought iron, a product of the newly developed rolling mills. Peter Cooper, who had just begun manufacturing these beams at his mill in Trenton, New Jersey, was to watch them being put up on Franklin Square with mixed emotions: he was seeing a first use of flanged wrought-iron beams in a large commercial building, but by making them available to the brothers he was having to delay the erection of his own Scientific Institution (later Cooper Union) on Astor Place.

In the spring of 1855, the brothers published their first catalogue following the fire. More than one thousand new and old titles were listed. By summer the two new fireproof buildings were completed. They were five stories in height and covered a half-acre of ground. They were to house the Harper operation for nearly seventy years—beyond the years of the brothers and of the brothers' sons.

A motto worded by George W. Curtis was later cut in wood above the fireplace in the new counting room. It was a free translation of Plato's phrase

ΛΑΜΠΑΔΙΑ ΕΧΟΝΤΕΣ ΔΙΑΔΩΣΟΥΣΙΝ ΑΛΛΗΛΟΙΣ

It read, "My flame expires, but let true hands pass on an unextinguished torch from sire to son."

Bibliographical Notes

Resource material was made available by the courtesy of many librarians and directors of historical societies, to whom credit is given below. Gilbert A. Cam, executive assistant of the reference division of the New York Public Library, not only extended the privileges of the Frederick Lewis Allen Room but also contributed to my work in many other ways; in thanking him I am mindful of his own colleagues and those in other institutions. Similarly John S. Van E. Kohn of the Seven Gables Bookshop, New York, by searching out Harperiana for my use is chief among antiquarian bookmen who have contributed to this study. Several descendants of the four brothers have given generously of their time to answer questions and make family records available. In mentioning Clara McDonald Harper, historian of the family, I am also recognizing others, some of whom are mentioned below.

What follows makes no pretense to being a complete bibliographical listing of periodicals and books covering the subject matter of *The Brothers Harper*. I have read as extensively as time and necessity seemed to warrant, my concern being the primary one of studying material relative to my subject. Perhaps some of the sources I have used will be helpful to others as I have been helped by sources listed by such writers as David Kaser, W. S. Tryon, William Charvat, and James J. Barnes. A scholarly bibliography of works relating to American publishing in the first half of the nineteenth century is yet to be compiled; of necessity it must include British sources as well since in the early decades American publishers were largely dependent on English authors and publishers.

I have made use of the original Harper records that escaped the 1853 fire. These records are minimal and include some correspondence now in the Pierpont Morgan Library or in the process of transference; originals of some contracts; Volume I of a series of bound ledgers into which contracts were copied; a volume, "Priority List," containing amounts paid for advance sheets of English reprints; several volumes of business papers, memoranda, and clippings—although these relate to years following 1853. The most important reference work held by the House is Demarest's *Catalogue,* listing Harper titles from 1817 on. While it contains some inaccuracies and omits some titles, the *Catalogue* is on the whole dependable and stands as a monument of Demarest's devotion to the four brothers.

For biographical data on authors I have depended upon the books listed herein by chapters and three invaluable sources: *The Dictionary of American Biography, The Dictionary of National Biography,* and *The Encyclopaedia Britannica,* eleventh edition. *Cyclopedia of American Literature* by Evert A. and George L. Duyckinck (1855), despite the strictures of Dr. Griswold, seems to me to be an important contemporary estimate of authors and their works. I have made frequent use of Volume II, and unless otherwise noted quotations from Duyckinck are from the *Cyclopedia.*

My chief sources on American history are *Empire for Liberty, The Genesis and Growth of the United States of America,* Volume I, by Dumas Malone and Basil Rauch, and *Main Currents in American Thought,* Volume II, *The Romantic Revolution in America, 1800-1860* by Vernon Louis Parrington. The diaries of Philip Hone and George Templeton Strong, the former edited by Allan Nevins and the latter by Allan Nevins and Milton Halsey Thomas, were helpful not only as quoted but also to give background material, for example Hone's description of his New Year's calling, January 1, 1840. Other sources on the history of America or of New York City are listed according to chapter.

For one who studies book publishing there is no choice but to wade through the periodicals that carry news about books, authors, and publishers. For the period covered by this book the important ones, as indicated by frequency of their mention in the text, are the *American Monthly, The Knickerbocker,* the *New Yorker,* the *Southern Literary Messenger, The United States Literary Advertiser and Publishers' Circular,* the *Literary World,* and *Norton's Literary Gazette and Publishers' Circular* (first issued as *Norton's Literary Advertiser*). The historical records on the Harper firm contained in the Adolph Growoll Collection, *American Book Trade History,* by the R. R. Bowker Company, New York, have been of special value. The *Trade Sales Catalogs,* of which the New York Public Library and the American Antiquarian Society hold many issues, are extremely important records of books published in America, a source overlooked in "Guide to Resources" (on book publishing) in the valuable bibliographical volume in the series edited by Robert E. Spiller, *et al., Literary History of the United States.* Also important to my study are *Literary Publishing in America, 1790-1850* by William Charvat, *The Book in America* by Hellmut Lehmann-Haupt, O. A. Roorbach's *Bibliotheca Americana* (1852), *Bibliographical Guide to American Literature* (1859) compiled by Nicolaus Trübner, and the more recent works of Lyle H. Wright, *American Fiction, 1774-1850,* and Jacob Blanck's *Bibliography of American Literature.* I have also made much use of *The House of Harper,* by J. Henry Harper, but more often have gone to the generally unacknowledged sources that he drew upon.

In an effort to keep footnotes to a minimum I have indicated sources in the text itself, with further references listed according to chapters below. Here I have included some material that might have footnoted the text and have also credited historical societies and libraries to whom I am indebted for permissions to quote. For specialists who may want to pursue further studies of material I have used, I am placing fully annotated copies of *The Brothers Harper* in the Pierpont Morgan Library, 29 East Thirty-sixth Street, New York, and in the library of the R. R. Bowker Company, 1180 Avenue of the Americas, New York.

I: Messrs. J. & J. Harper, Printers

The best account of the early years of the Harpers was written by R. R. Bowker in the *Publishers' Trade List Annual, 1877*. Other sources are the obituary accounts of each of the brothers in the New York newspapers, especially the *Times* and the *Tribune*, and in *Harper's Weekly*, accounts in the latter written by George W. Curtis; also the *Southern Literary Messenger*, November, 1843; *The Ladies' Repository*, November, 1853, and its successor, *National Repository*, September, 1877; *The American Publishers' Circular*, November 1 and 17, 1855; *The American Literary Gazette*, October 15, 1868; *Publishers' Weekly*, June 2, 1877; *The American Bookseller*, June 1, 1885, and *Harper Brothers, Publishers: A Brief Historical Sketch* by G. W. Barker and other papers in the Growoll Collection. Three autobiographies of publishers contain Harper anecdotal and background material, listed in order of contribution: *Fifty Years Among Authors, Books and Publishers*, by J. C. Derby; *Memoirs*, by Thurlow Weed (also his letter to the New York *Tribune*, June 22, 1876); *Recollections of a Life Time*, Volume II, by Samuel G. Goodrich. Information on the New York book trade in the early part of the century is contained in *Norton's Literary Gazette*, April 1 and 15, 1854; on the Carey firm in *Messrs Carey & Lea of Philadelphia*, by David Kaser, in the Carey *Account Books*, American Antiquarian Society, and in the Carey *Letter Books*, the Historical Society of Pennsylvania, by whose permission the Harper letters to Carey are quoted. Also helpful for background material are two books by James D. McCabe, *Great Fortunes* (pp. 367-379) and *Annals of American Book-Selling*, by Henry Walcott Boynton.

II: From Printers to Publishers

Several literary magazines of the 1820's were read for early reviews of Harper books and notes about Cliff Street publishing activity, all except the first-named being comparatively short-lived: *Port Folio* (Philadelphia), *United States Literary Gazette* (New York), *The Critic* (New York), and *The Virginia Evangelical and Literary Magazine* (Richmond). Dated issues of the following periodicals gave specific information: the *Literary Advertiser*, May 1, 1825; the *Southern Literary Messenger*, September, 1839; *Harper's New Monthly Magazine*, January, 1854; *Norton's Literary Gazette*, April 15, 1854; *Harper's Weekly*, April 17, 1869; *Publishers' Weekly*, March 11 and June 2, 1877; the *Publishers' Trade List Annual, 1877*. Pertinent books are *Recollections of a Life Time, ibid.*; *Literary Publishing in America, 1790-1850, ibid.*; *The House of Harper, ibid.*; *Mathew Carey*, by Earl L. Bradsher; and *Bookbinding in America*, by Joseph Rogers.

The Harper boast of editorial acumen was printed in the back matter of

The History of Modern Europe, the third volume of which carried title page recognition of booksellers. Volume I of this work, printed earlier in the year, contained the names of only two out-of-town dealers, those from Albany. During the few months' interval between the publication of Volumes I and III, title page prestige had also lined up dealers in Philadelphia, Boston, Hartford, and Baltimore, as well as four additional New York booksellers. The Boston firm of Carter & Hendee had been organized the year before and was later to be known as the Old Corner Book Store. (See p. 22.)

III: Stereotypes and Series

Periodicals referred to include *Littell's Living Age*, October 21, 1854, *American Publishers' Circular*, July 15, 1863, and *Harper's Weekly*, July 15, 1863. A secondary source for quotations from reviews of Harper books, sometimes relied upon, are advertisements of new publications carried in the back matter of books such as Thatcher's *Indian Biography*. Books consulted include a history of the house of John Murray entitled *A Publisher and His Friends* by Samuel Smiles; *Life of Irving*, Vol. II, by S. T. Williams; *Messrs Carey & Lea of Philadelphia, ibid.; Parnassus Corner, a Life of James T. Fields, etc.* by W. S. Tryon; *William Gilmore Simms* by William P. Trent; *Fifty Years Among Authors, Books and Publishers, ibid.; Bookbinding in America, ibid.; Literary Publishing in America, 1790-1850, ibid.; Marginalia*, by Edgar A. Poe; *Recollections of a Life Time*, Vol. II, *ibid.; American Fiction, ibid.* I have made use of Vol. III of the *Diary of William Dunlap*, 1766-1839, published by The New-York Historical Society and have checked the extracts against the Dunlap diary manuscript, by courtesy of Yale University Library. This diary is also the source of Cooper's letter to Dunlap regarding the Harper proofs.

IV: The Beginning of Harper & Brothers

Periodicals supplying data for this chapter are the *Southern Literary Messenger*, September, 1839; the *Trade Circular Annual*, 1871; the New York *Tribune*, May 30, 1877; *Publisher's Weekly*, June 2, 1877; *Harper's Weekly*, May 8, 1875, and June 16, 1877; and the *Publishers' Trade List Annual*, 1877. The letters of John Sargent are owned by The Houghton Library, Harvard University by whose permission a quotation is given. Information regarding Paulding-Harper relations are contained in an article on Paulding's literary income by Ralph M. Aderman in the *Bulletin of the New York Public Library*, March, 1960, and from *James Kirke Paulding: Versatile American* by Amos L. Herold. The New-York Historical Society holds manuscript material of Gulian Verplanck, an excerpt from which is quoted by their permission. I have also drawn upon *The Essential New Yorker, Gulian Crommelin Verplanck*, by Robert W. July; *William Hickling Prescott*, by Rollo Ogden; *Golden Multitudes*, by Frank Luther Mott; and *American Fiction, ibid.*

V: Competition for English Reprints

The main sources drawn upon are *Theodore Bliss, Publisher and Bookseller* (1911), edited by Arthur A. Bliss; the *Literary Inquirer* (several issues); the *American Monthly*, November, 1835; *Booksellers' Advertiser and Monthly Register*, Vols. I and III; the New York *American*, April 3, 1837; *Norton's Literary Gazette*, April 1, 1854; *American Publishers' Circular*, September 19, 1855, and September 19, 1857; the London *Athenaeum,* October 18, 1862; *American Literary Gazette,* May 15, 1867; the *American Bookseller,* July 1, 1885; and *Fifty Years Among Authors, Books and Publishers, ibid.,* in which the exciting contest over *Rienzi* is related. Quotations from the Carey & Lea *Letter Books* are by permission of the Historical Society of Pennsylvania; from the letter by Edward L. Bulwer, by permission of the Rare Book Room, Boston Public Library; from "The Early History of International Copyright" (manuscript) by Frederick Saunders, containing the account of his early conflict with the Harpers, by permission of the New York Public Library. Dr. David Kaser kindly loaned me microfilms of the *Letter Books.*

VI: Launching American Authors

In addition to periodicals quoted in the text, the following dated issues of periodicals contributed material: *Bulletin of the New York Public Library,* March, 1960; *The Knickerbocker,* April, 1835; the *American Monthly,* December, 1835; the *Southern Literary Messenger,* April, 1839; and the *Publishers' Trade List Annual, 1877.* Books consulted include *The House of Harper, ibid.; The World of Washington Irving* by Van Wyck Brooks (for the comment on Dunlap); *Herman Melville* by Leon Howard; *William Gilmore Simms, ibid.; Passages from the Correspondence of Rufus Wilmot Griswold,* edited by William M. Griswold; *Recollections of a Life Time, ibid.; A Biography of William Cullen Bryant* by Parke Godwin; *The Southern Literary Messenger* by Benjamin B. Minor and *Life and Letters of Catherine M. Sedgwick* by Mary E. Dewey. While Morris's name does not appear as editor of *Atlantic Club Book,* nor is he thus identified by Demarest, he is so credited in Foley's *American Authors 1795-1895.* The Bryant-Stone encounter is taken from *Memorial History of the City of New York,* Wilson edition, Vol. IV. A slightly different account, more favorable to Bryant, is given in *New York Dissected,* by Walt Whitman, edited by Emory Holloway and Ralph Adamari.

The description of Miss Sedgwick is from Poe's *The Literati* (1846), as are several later characterizations of American authors. Bryant's remarks at the Crystal Palace banquet were reported in the *New York Times,* April 6, 1855. Quotations from letters to Longfellow by Clark and the Harpers are by permission of the Houghton Library, Harvard University; from the Lothian-Harper correspondence by permission of the Pierpont Morgan Library; from the Harper letter to Edgar Allan Poe by courtesy of the Trustees of the Boston Public Library. Miss Helen Leale Harper, Jr., of Pelham, N.Y., kindly consented to the use of the letter of Maria Arcularius Harper.

VII: Depression Years

The account of the booksellers' dinner is based upon *Old New York, or Reminiscences of the Last 60 Years,* by Dr. John Wakefield Francis, and (primarily) on the New York *American,* April 3, 1837. Bennett's sarcastic dig at the committee is given in *Charles Fenno Hoffman,* by H. F. Barnes. The amusing book by Asa Greene, *A Glance at New York,* was published by the author. The *New Yorker* gave the statistics regarding circulation of periodicals on July 8, 1837. "The House of Harper shall not go to the wall" anecdote is given in the New York *Despatch* of March 27, 1869. The correspondence of Theodore Sedgwick Fay here *et seq.* is from his *Statement* (see Chapter XIII). William

Gowans's reminiscence of James Harper is related in *The House of Harper;* an account of Gowans appears in *Old Booksellers of New York* by William Loring Andrews. The letter of Simms agreeing to the sale of his copyright is in the Harper files and the Ingraham letters to Fletcher are in the Harper collection of the Pierpont Morgan Library and are quoted by permission. The sources for the John L. Stephens introduction to the Cliff Street publishers are *Mayan Explorer* by Victor W. Von Hagen; "The Late John L. Stephens" by Dr. F. L. Hawkes in *Putnam's Magazine,* January, 1853; and *Forty Years of American Life* by Thomas Low Nichols. Mr. Bryant's reference to Wesley was made in his Appendix to *Life and Letters of Catherine M. Sedgwick* by Mary E. Dewey. Miss Martineau's experience with British publishers is related in her *Autobiography.* The Harper letter to Longfellow is quoted by permission of the Houghton Library, Harvard University.

VIII: The End of the Decade

The Herbert-Mackenzie-Harper encounter is related by Luke M. White in *William Herbert and the American Publishing Scene 1831-1858.* Sumner's letter to Judge Story is given in *Memoir and Letters of Charles Sumner,* Vol. I, by Edward L. Pierce. In 1876 D. B. Cooke wrote a series of articles of reminiscence for the *Publishers' Weekly* from which the account of his trip to Ohio is taken. In that periodical a year later Peter Carter recalled his early reading of the *S.D.L. The Knickerbocker* told how rapidly the Fisk book sold, about the Gilman competition with Sedgwick, and spoke of *Letters to Mothers* as virtually a new work. Quotations from Governor Seward's messages to the New York State Legislature are from *Messages From the Governors, Vol. III,* (1823-1842), edited by Charles Z. Lincoln. The account of Fletcher's trip to Albany follows almost verbatim Derby's splendid narrative in *Fifty Years,* etc. Weed recalled Spencer's characterization of Fletcher in a letter to the New York *Tribune,* dated June 22, 1876. (*The House of Harper* reprints a letter from the brothers to Weed acknowledging the compliment of being called "Brothers Cheeryble," from beneficent characters in Dickens's *Nicholas Nickleby.*)

That the *S.D.L.* was known in all parts of the nation is reported in an undated article by G. W. Barker in the Growoll papers; commendations of school officials were printed in Harper catalogues. The popularity of Mosheim's work among Yale students is reported in *Yale and the Ministry* by Roland H. Bainton. The phrase about Harper's harping on Halleck's poetic string is from the *Southern Literary Messenger,* which periodical also preserves the story of the Paulding-Willis controversy. The Perry Miller quotation about anonymity is from *The Raven and the Whale,* which also speaks of Poe's dependency on Reynolds. Other sources on Poe's publication *Pym* are *Edgar Allan Poe,* by Edgar Wagenknecht, and *Literary History of the United States, ibid.* Information about Bentley's payments to Bulwer are contained in Royal A. Gettmann's recent and informative study of the Bentley papers, *A Victorian Publisher.* Richard Bentley began his career as a British publisher in 1829 and was active for nearly forty years. His interest in American books and authors was paralleled a century later by Hamish Hamilton, who began publishing in 1931, after several years as Harper's London representative.

The account of early efforts to establish international copyright is based largely on a study of contemporary periodicals, chiefly the *New York Review* and the *Southern Literary Messenger,* and on Perry Miller's comments in *The Raven and the Whale.* Putnam's observation of the treatment of American books pirated in England is from *American Facts* (1847), and Van Wyck Brooks's prejudiced generalization is from *The World of Washington Irving.* Hoffman rather than his co-editor, Herbert, is credited with the quotation from the *American Monthly* (1835) about Harper's liberality to young American writers, since he would be the more interested in native output. The December, 1829, issue of that periodical carried the initials "K. K." to the article, "The Profession of Authorship," admitting to scarcely any "professed."

The *Southern Literary Messenger* carried John Quincy Adams's recommendations for a library in its January, 1839, issue and in September printed the splendid piece on the Harpers, giving earnings of several Harper authors, statistics of the firm, and a description of Joseph Harper. Except for limitations of space it would be reprinted in full. The article was, in fact, a New York letter, signed "Probus," veiling the initials "P.B." That the author was Park Benjamin is stated in *The Contributors and Contributions of the Southern Literary Messenger (1834-1864),* by David K. Jackson. Under the cloak of his pseudonym Benjamin could write enthusiastically of his brother-in-law, John L. Motley, and admit that his own manuscript of poems was being favorably considered for Cliff Street publication.

IX: Before the Mast with Dana

"The Publishing History of Richard Henry Dana's *Two Years Before the Mast,*" by Robert F. Metzdorf, in the *Harvard Library Bulletin,* Autumn, 1953, is a scholarly and informative essay. It deserves a wider reading than its original publication permitted, and is marred only by a failure to present the publishing milieu in which Dana's book was issued. My chapter attempts to supply this lack. Mr. Metzdorf also edited *Richard Henry Dana, Jr., an Autobiographical Sketch* (1815-1842), in which Dana devoted a few paragraphs to his memory of the Harper arrangements. Quotations from this autobiographical sketch and from the Harper-Dana correspondence are by courtesy of Mr. Metzdorf and the Massachusetts Historical Society, which houses the Dana letters. One such, written to Dana by a relative, refers to "those Harpies" who had bought his work for little, a now mute testimony to the intensity of feeling which the Harper contract evoked. The reference of Dana, Sr., to the limited merchandising ability of Boston publishers is contained in a letter he wrote to Bryant on July 9, 1839.

Epes Sargent's report on the poverty of New York publishers was quoted in a letter that Longfellow wrote to George Greene, January 2, 1840, as given in *Young Longfellow* by Laurance Thompson, and his testimony to help he received from James Harper is contained in a letter he wrote to the firm following the Mayor's death, now in the possession of Helen Leale Harper, Jr. Lossing's eulogy of James Harper appears in his *History of New York City,* Vol. II. The quotations from the Jared Sparks letters are by permission of the Houghton Library, Harvard University. Bryant's authorship of the long review of the Dana book in the *Democratic Review* is verified by his letter to Dana, Sr., in the Craigie House papers (Cambridge, Mass.) according to W. C. Bryant, II, to whom I am indebted for help regarding references to his great-uncle appearing in this book.

That the brothers had received many letters urging Anthon to prepare a *Greek Reader* was told by *The Knickerbocker*. Information about the Renwick family is given in Allan Nevins's edition of Hone's *Diary*. Barnes's declination of an offer to contribute to an "Annual," contained in a letter held by the Historical Society of Pennsylvania, is quoted by their permission, and the description of him is from *The Union Theological Seminary, Historical and Biographical Sketches of Its First Fifty Years*, by George L. Prentiss. The title of the Irving biography is *The Life of Washington Irving* by S. T. Williams. Sam Ward's letter to Longfellow is quoted by permission of the Houghton Library, Harvard University. The letter Fletcher wrote the *Athenaeum* (London) appeared in its issue for October 18, 1862, and George Bentley's rationalization of his purchase of the Reeves book is given in *A Victorian Publisher, ibid.*

X: Publishing on Narrow Margins

The letter of Fletcher to Griswold is quoted by courtesy of the Trustees, Boston Public Library. Griswold's movements from city to city and paper to paper are related by Joy Bayless in *Rufus Wilmot Griswold;* she also quotes Holmes's cryptic comment on Griswold. Henry James recalls his early memory of Griswold in his book *William Wetmore Story, Sculptor and Man of Letters.* For this reference I am indebted to Perry Miller, who regretted that he did not know of it earlier to use in *The Raven and the Whale.* Greeley's and Cooper's letters to Griswold are given in *Passages,* the compilation of Griswold's correspondence and miscellania by his son, William, who could barely have remembered his father. *Passages* gives a fascinating picture of the literary world of mid-century America. The letters from Buckingham to the brothers and the Wadsworth-Harper correspondence are now in the Harper collection of the Pierpont Morgan Library.

The most complete collection of issues of the *United States Literary Advertiser and Publishers' Circular* is in the Harvard Library, and a reading of this periodical throws much light on American publishing in this dark period, as, for example, Harper announcements of books in press and their tardy publication, and Appleton's importing business. The encomium to Dr. Reese was probably publicized widely; it appears in the back matter of *Physiology* (1844) by Magendie, translated by Revere. The chief source for the account of Bishop Hughes's attack on the New York Public School Society is *Church and State in the United States,* Vols. I and II, by Anson Phelps Stokes, who also quotes the Barnes letter to Beecher. In his letter to the *Tribune, ibid.,* Weed tells of bringing Wadsworth to Cliff Street. The Van Wyck Brooks tribute to Longstreet is from *The World of Washington Irving;* the Ward-Longfellow correspondence is from *Uncle Sam Ward and His Circle,* by Maude Howe Elliott. The material on Dickens's arrival in America and visit to New York is based upon accounts in *Charles Dickens in America* by W. Glyde Wilkins and in *The Raven and the Whale, ibid.*

XI: Fighting the Mammoth Weeklies

The Southern Literary Messenger is one of the best sources for publishing history during the period of June, 1842, through 1844, partially because at the beginning editor Maury, who loved to buy books cheap, was for high tariffs and *against* international copyright. He was succeeded by editor Minor, who in

1844 published a series of letters by Simms which is one of the best presentations of the time *for* international copyright. Simms also gives (March, 1844) the best explanation of the brothers' stand during this period (see p. 157). The chronology of editors and publishers of the mammoth newspapers is given somewhat by Frank Luther Mott in *Golden Multitudes,* but awaits clarification in a forthcoming work by Roger Butterfield. I am indebted to both these writers and to Griswold's *Passages* for my efforts to depict the rise and fall of this literary phenomenon of the weeklies.

The Sparks letter to Putnam is quoted in *George Palmer Putnam, a Memoir* by George Haven Putnam. The total earnings of Adams are given in *The House of Harper* and his engraving work is described in an article in the *American Antiquarian Association Review,* Vol. I, and another by R. R. Bowker in *Harper's Magazine,* July, 1887. The date, 1840, for the installation of the six-roller press in Cliff Street comes from *The Publishers' Trade List Annual, 1877.*

Gould's protest against Harper's orthography is from his letter in the Duyckinck "Papers" of the New York Public Library, by whose permission it is quoted, as are passages from Duyckinck's "Diary," appearing here *et seq.* Henry Carey's estimate of the sales of the abridged *Dictionary* are from *Letters on International Copyright* (1853); The Harper disposal of "over 100,000 copies" is taken from the *Ladies' Repository,* November, 1853. Maria Brooks wrote to Griswold saying that Harpers had rejected her novel; her letter appears in *Passages.* Langley announced his forthcoming book, *Rambles in Yucatan* in his *Literary Advertiser.* English readers' response to Stephens's books is given in *Mayan Explorer* and the *Literary Advertiser.* The Boston bookseller, unidentified save for initials, wrote to the *Publishers' Weekly* in 1877, following Fletcher's death. Cooke's articles had appeared the preceding year. The best account of the Derbys is given in "The Derby Brothers, 19th Century Bookmen," by Walter Sutton, in *The University of Rochester Bulletin* (1848), and in the same author's *The Western Book Trade: Cincinnati as a Ninteeenth Century Publishing Center,* which book also gives the "James and Sue, Forever" advertisement.

Prescott's letters are quoted by permission of the Massachusetts Historical Society. The best study of Prescott has been made by C. Harvey Gardiner in a presently unpublished biography and in his *Prescott and His Publishers.* The Ticknor comment on Prescott was obtained by Duyckinck for his *Cyclopedia.* Thoreau's failure to get a Cliff Street job is related in a letter to his mother, quoted in *Thoreau,* by Henry Seidel Canby. Catharine Beecher's efforts on behalf of her sister's novel are related in Derby's autobiography. The *Melville Log,* Vol. I, tells of *Family Library* volumes being placed aboard the *United States,* and the quotation about the treatment of natives in the South Sea Islands is from *Herman Melville* by Leon Howard.

XII: His Honor, the Mayor of New York

To The New-York Historical Society I am indebted for permission to quote from the papers of Mayor James Harper, including the letters of Thomas McElrath, General Scott, and others to the Mayor, his letters to the American Republican party and to R. L. Schiefflin, and the short acceptance speech. The Mayor's letter to the New York *Sun* and the lost dog anecdote are from *The House of Harper,* and knowledge of the Mayor's performance of an early-morning marriage is from papers held by Helen Leale Harper, Jr. The Mayor's election-night remarks to his neighbors are related in the *American Bookseller,* June 15, 1885.

New York City's lack of cleanliness is reflected in the quotation from *A Glance at New York, ibid.;* its feelings toward abolitionists in *The Old Merchants of New York* by Walter Barrett and *Memorial History of the City of New York, ibid.* (sources also for general background); and its lack of ecumenical relations in *Church and State in the United States, ibid.,* in *Life of Archbishop Hughes* by John R. G. Hassard, and other publications mentioned in the text. A description of Rose Street is given in a pamphlet by Thomas Picton, *Rose Street, Its Past, Present, and Future.*

Sources of the Maria Monk story are given for the most part in the text. Many puzzling questions remain: Did the brothers print other books for Howe & Bates? Who was "P. Gordon," who took out the copyright and received some of the royalties? Can the U.S. Circuit Court records be located? Efforts to date have been unsuccessful and the records might further clarify printing, publishing, and authorship problems.

For providing photostats of pertinent Madison letters that relate to Harper negotiations for original publication of certain works of President Madison I am greatly indebted to William T. Hutchinson, senior editor of the *Papers of James Madison,* which the University of Chicago Press is publishing. In addition to this major source, I have found *James Madison,* Vol. VI, by Irving Brant, helpful, and in a lesser degree the biographies of Dolley Madison by Katherine Anthony and Elizabeth Lippincott Dean. For permission to quote excerpts from letters I am grateful to the following: The Library of Congress for Mrs. Madison's letter of November 15, 1836, and for the letter of November 12, 1838, written by Andrew Stevenson to Todd regarding Bentley's proofs. Knowledge that the Harpers were promising publication is revealed in a diary entry of John Quincy Adams; in Mrs. Madison's letter of June 15, 1838, to Charles J. Ingersoll (holograph owned by R. Sturgis Ingersoll, Philadelphia); and in her letter to Richard D. Cutts of April 20, 1840 (owned by Mr. and Mrs. George B. Cutts, Brookline, Mass.). The Paulding letter to Mrs. Madison, dated January 4, 1844, is of the Frederick B. McGuire—Madison Catalog, February 26, 1917.

Professor Thomas O. Mabbott gave me valued assistance on Poe matters. The exchange of letters between Poe and Anthon is given in full in *The House of Harper* and the Saunders account is from his manuscript autobiography quoted by permission of the New York Public Library. The source of my discussion of New York periodical publication in 1844-45 is largely *The Raven and the Whale, ibid.* The three stories illustrating the Mayor's humor are from the *Publishers' Trade List Annual, 1877.* The "Colonel Jones of Nebraska" visit may not have occurred during the Harper mayoralty. In 1849 the brothers published *Oregon and California* (see p. 255) with a splendid two-color, tipped-in map of the western part of the nation showing the extensive Territory of Nebraska; this map may have given James the inspiration for his cognomen.

The Simms blurb on Verplanck's Shakespeare was quoted in the Harper 1847 catalogue. The Choate-Wainwright-Potts controversy was detailed by Duyckinck and in the *Southern Literary Messenger,* November, 1844. That Fletcher, Jr., sailed "before the mast" is told in the *American Bookseller,* June 1, 1885.

XIII: Mr. Fay Issues a Statement

The obvious source for this discussion and what has preceded (see Index) is the *Statement* issued by Fay in Berlin in mid-July, 1845. Unless the copy catalogued in the New York Public Library can be located, there is only one known to exist, fortunately preserved in the Library of Congress. No copies of the first 36-page pamphlet are known; it is, however, incorporated in the larger and later *Statement*. I first learned of the existence of the pamphlet in reading C. Harvey Gardiner's *Prescott and His Publishers*. "A blistering denunciation of the house of Harper published that same year [1845] by Theodore Sedgwick Fay was a matter of common knowledge," Mr. Gardiner wrote. But hardly of common knowledge now! What strained author-publisher relations lay behind this published *Statement?* Thus Mr. Gardiner's book led to an absorbing study of an overlooked page of literary history. It also provided me with a detailed analysis (perhaps one-third of 312 pages of text) of the Prescott-Harper association. Thus I am greatly indebted to Mr. Gardiner, as well as to the Massachusetts Historical Society and to the Huntington Library, for permission to quote from the Prescott correspondence. The quotations from letters of Prescott to Everett are taken from *The Correspondence of William Hickling Prescott, 1837-1847*, edited by Roger Wolcott.

XIV: Big-Name Authors

According to *Parnassus Corner*, by W. S. Tryon, James Fields was to be paid $800 a year as specified in a partnership agreement drawn in 1843; he may have been earning more by 1846. *Littell's Living Age*, February 9, 1850, gives the Harper expenditures for advertising. (This amount was increased sizably after the new *Monthly* was launched.) The Beach letter is quoted by permission of the Pierpont Morgan Library. D. B. Cooke, *op. cit.*, gives interesting comment on leading publishers of the period, and is my authority for saying that the Harpers had an interest in the Derby store. The 1847 Harper catalogue imprinted for Zieber is in the Historical Society of Pennsylvania; a similar 1848 catalogue is in the American Antiquarian Society. The Longfellow correspondence is by courtesy of Houghton Library, Harvard University. Ticknor's 1847 arrangement with Longfellow is detailed in *The Cost Books of Ticknor and Fields* by W. S. Tryon and William Charvat, and discussed in Tryon's *Parnassus Corner*. The Harper letter to Hoffman is quoted in *Charles Fenno Hoffman, ibid*. The Griswold correspondence with Hoffman and Harper's and the letter of William Allen are quoted by courtesy of the Trustees, Boston Public Library, and Hoffman's letter regarding O'Callaghan's manuscript by that of the Historical Society of Pennsylvania. Griswold's *Passages*, Miss Bayless's biography and Demarest's *Catalogue* are sources for the abortive *Dictionary*. The brothers kept three copies of the Griswold contract; the Boston Public Library has Griswold's copy.

The "Americanism" controversy is detailed in *The Raven and the Whale*; Perry Miller gives Simms's view of Duyckinck and Duyckinck's view of the importance of a magazine. Saunders's manuscript autobiography, quoted by permission, is the source for Harper's declination of *Typee*. Emerson's letters are from Volumes III, IV, and V of *Letters of Ralph Waldo Emerson*, edited by Ralph L. Rusk, and Fletcher's "Dear Judge" letter is quoted by permission

of the Houghton Library. The failure of Ik. Marvel's *Battle Summer* is also re-
vealed in a series of forty-three articles, *The Bookmakers*, which began in the
New York *Evening Post*, November 4, 1874. "Los Gringos" was translated
"Greenhorn" by Duyckinck, *Cyclopedia*, Vol. II.

The sale of the *Illuminated Bible* was given in the *American Publishers' Circu-
lar*, August, 1858. The sales of Prescott's books are detailed in *Prescott and His
Publishers, ibid.*, as is the correspondence giving business conditions on Cliff
Street. In *The Western Book Trade* Walter Sutton devotes a chapter to Henry
Howe, the reading of which led to my discovery of Howe's Harper book that
adds something to our knowledge of the role of new books at trade auctions.
According to Demarest a sixth edition of Liddell and Scott was published in
1865. This may well have been the "pirated" edition that aroused the Dean's ire.

XV: Books from Overseas and Textbooks

Basic to the early pages of this chapter are two letters given in full in *The
House of Harper*, one from Wainwright to Fletcher dated December 31, 1846,
and one from Fletcher to his brothers dated London, July 3, 1847. Wainwright
speaks of a "tour abroad," hoping that Fletcher's wife would benefit therefrom,
and implies that travel on the Continent would precede a visit to England. It
seems unlikely that Fletcher would have returned to New York for a short
period before again going to London. While his letter to his brothers does not
mention Jane, he asks to be remembered to "father and mother Lyon," which
he hardly would have done if he were writing to Jane in New York. Clara
McDonald Harper remembers the story of her great-grandmother's lace cap.
John's trip abroad is mentioned in the *Publishers' Weekly*, May 1, 1875, a part of
the Growoll Collection, which is also the source of what I have written about
Fletcher's son Joe. Mrs. Howitt tells of the early publication of translations of
the Bremer novels in her *Autobiography*, Vol. II. Charlotte Brontë's letter was
written September 4, 1848, to her friend Mary Taylor and is quoted in *The
Brontës; Life and Letters*, Vol. I, edited by Clement Shorter. Boston's dis-
like of *Wuthering Heights* is told in *Parnassus Corner, ibid*. I am indebted to
Messrs. Longmans, Green and Company of London for information about
publication date and early editions of Macaulay's *History*. *The American*
publishers of Macaulay are given by Roorbach, and the Harper letter to their
best-selling author is given in *The Life and Letters of Lord Macaulay*, Vol. II,
by G. Otto Trevelyan. Jacob Abbott has a chapter, "Marbling," in *The Harper
Establishment* (1855), a book recently reissued by the Shoestring Press, Hamden,
Connecticut.

The Harper-Liddell anecdote was related to me by the late Charles Burton
Gulick, who taught Greek at Harvard from 1895 to 1937. Dr. Gulick credited
the story to his predecessor, Professor John William White. Confirmation of
"Joe Brooklyn's" visit is given in a letter he wrote to Evert Duyckinck on
December 26, 1877. After saying that he had just returned from abroad, he wrote,
"My chief object in going to England was to see Dean Liddell in regard to a
Greek Dictionary—and I was gone about two months." Another letter from
J. W. Harper, Jr., in reference to this Oxford visit is in the files of Messrs John
Murray, London.

The following have kindly given permission to quote from letters in their
possession: The Massachusetts Historical Society, for Fletcher's letter to

Prescott; the New York Public Library for his letter to Webster from Webster Collection; the Houghton Library, Harvard University, for the letters from Sparks dated December 30, 1839, and January 13, 1840. *The Life and Writings of Jared Sparks*, Vol. II, by Herbert B. Adams, gives $15,384.63 as the amount Sparks divided three ways. The source for the sales is the Boston *Post* series "Who Buys an American Book?" The letter Abraham Lincoln wrote to the Abbott Brothers is from *The House of Harper, ibid.*

The friendship between Fletcher and John McClintock is indicated by a letter McClintock wrote on July 9, 1849, while on a vacation trip: "Pray write a line at once. You are the only man in New York, I think, that misses me—Certainly you are the only one for whom I cherish a strong personal affection." (Quoted by permission of the University Library, Emory University.)

XVI: Herman Melville, Novelist

My chief sources for this chapter, in addition to Harper records, are *Herman Melville* by Leon Howard, the *Melville Log* (2 vols.) by Jay Leyda, *The Raven and the Whale, ibid.*, and the collection of Melville papers in the Houghton Library, to which I am indebted for permission to quote. The Saunders autobiographical material in the New York Public Library is also used by permission, as are the quotations from Melville's letter of April 5, 1849, to Duyckinck speaking of his change of mood regarding *Mardi* and his letter regarding Hoffman. *Main Currents in American Thought*, Vol. II, *ibid.*, from which an excerpt is quoted, contains an excellent short introduction to Melville. The Pierpont Morgan Library has kindly consented to the reproduction of Melville's letter to Harper's, with its appended note of sales in Demarest's handwriting.

The British criticisms of Melville are detailed in *At John Murray's* by George Pastor, and the Rosenbach quotation is from the biography of him written by Edwin Wolf II, in collaboration with John F. Fleming.

The extant copies of first editions of *Moby Dick* that have been examined to determine colors of cloth used include those in the New York Public Library, Princeton University Library, and the University of Virginia Library.

XVII: The New Monthly Magazine

The Demarest letter to Longfellow in the Houghton Library is quoted by permission. Fletcher's "tender to our business" comment is from an article by editor Henry Mills Alden in the sesquicentennial issue of *Harper's Magazine*, May, 1900. Prescott's London experiences are told in *Prescott and His Publishers, ibid.* Ripley's characterization of Wesley is from *Fifty Years Among Authors, Books and Publishers, ibid.* The U.S. Census for 1850 is inadequate in reporting on periodicals according to Frank Luther Mott in *American Magazines*, Vol. II, from which the *Graham's* and *American Whig Review* criticisms of *Harper's* is taken; the Census report as given in *Norton's Literary Gazette*, February 15, 1855, is used here. The Goodrich characterization of Griswold is from *Recollections*, Vol. II, *ibid.* The Griswold-Harper competition for Dickens's *Bleak House* is taken from *The American Literary Gazette, etc.* of May 1, 1867, which gives *The Nation* as its source.

Lossing's statement that the first edition of this *Field-Book* was never issued is from a letter to Oscar H. Harpel and is quoted by permission of The New-

York Historical Society. Sources for the turmoil aroused by "Uncle Bernard's Story" are from the *New York Times*, September 6 and 8, 1853, and *Memoir* by George Haven Putnam, which book also refers to Mr. Littell's careless use of his scissors. Littell apologized in his issue of August 5, 1854. *Memoir* is also the source for amounts paid to authors in early issues of *Putnam's*. *The House of Harper* gives an appreciative account of Guernsey, and the amount paid Guernsey (for *Harper's Pictorial History of the Rebellion*) is from Harper's "Contract Book," Vol. I.

Curtis told of his reception by John Harper in *Harper's Weekly*, May 8, 1875. Other sources on Curtis are *George William Curtis* by Edward Cary, and the Duyckinck Papers in the New York Public Library, quoted by permission. By courtesy of the Pierpont Morgan Library the Raymond and Abbott letters are quoted.

XVIII: Harper Books in the Early Fifties

Norton's sale trip is reported in *Norton's Literary Gazette*, issues of March 15, 1852, *et seq*. Cooke writes of his vacation trip in the *Publishers' Weekly, op. cit*. Derby tells in his autobiography of his brother George's San Francisco venture, as does Walter Sutton in *The Western Book Trade: Cincinnati as a Nineteenth Century Publishing Center*. The latter volume also gives information on Gerherdus Demarest, as does *The Universalist Leader*, October, 1909. Both the *American Register and Magazine*, Vol. V, and *Norton's Literary Gazette*, October 2, 1854, tell of lowered postage rates for books. The Goodrich table on book production, often referred to, appears in Vol. II of his *Recollections*. The letter of Horace Mann to the brothers is by permission of the Pierpont Morgan Library. Sources on Brodhead's search for documents of American history are *Scribner's Magazine* (Vol. XIII) and Duyckinck's *Cyclopedia* (Vol. II).

The account of Mlle. Desportes is based on Rachel Field's engrossing story of her great-aunt in *All This and Heaven Too*. I give the estimated total sales and royalty earnings on Barnes's *Notes* with some temerity. *Norton's Literary Gazette*, June 1852, Carey's *Letters* on international copyright (1853), Dr. Clark's article in the *Ladies' Repository*, the Boston *Post's* series (1859), and *The Publishers' Trade List Annual, 1877*, give estimates of sales from 300,000 to 450,000 and income to Barnes from "more than $30,000" to $75,000. My decision to take the top figures is based on Dr. Clark's statement that the annual profit on *Notes* was $25,000, by which he probably meant total earnings of author and publisher. Thus if Barnes earned $12,500 in 1852, the year his series was completed and probably its biggest year, 100,000 copies were sold.

William C. Prime's testimony to his friendship with the brothers is given in Derby's autobiography. The naming of Denison University is given in *Granville, the Story of an Ohio Village*, by William C. Utter. Thackeray's letter to Harper's is from *The House of Harper* and his letter to Putnam is from *The Letters and Private Papers of William Makepeace Thackeray*, Vol. III, edited by Gordon N. Ray. Carey's parable of the gardener appears in his pamphlet (above), and Putnam's letter in reply to Hart appears in *Norton's* issue of April 15, 1853. Charlotte Brontë's comment on the well-meaning publishers is quoted by Elizabeth Gaskell in *Life of Charlotte Brontë*, Vol. II.

XIX: The Harper Homes and Office

The early Harper association with Raymond on the *Times* is told by Elmer Davis in *The History of the New York Times*. The journal Abner Harper kept on his trip abroad is owned by Mrs. Arvid Eaton Taube of Katonah, New York. My version of the Mayor's entertaining the bores follows that given by Derby in his autobiography. In his history of the House, J. Henry Harper relates the anecdote of Joe Brooklyn's top hat. The comment on the Mayor's appearance at the Trade Sales is from "Representative Booksellers" in the Growoll Collection, and the Boston *Transcript*'s reporting of the 1853 Trade Sale in New York is from *Norton's Literary Gazette*, April 15, 1853. The Harper 1853 output is taken from the *New York Times* for December 12, 1853, and their sales volume is from G. P. Putnam's speech of September 27, 1855, at the Crystal Palace dinner of publishers in honor of booksellers and authors. The article on the brothers was written by Dr. Clark for the August, 1853, issue of the *Ladies' Repository*. The story of Thackeray's call on the Mayor is credited by J. Henry Harper to *Thackeray in the United States* by James Grant Wilson. Duyckinck reported on the new Harper buildings in the *Literary World* of March 20, 1852. Further information on this building expansion and use of floor space is given in the *Ladies' Repository*, August, 1853, and the *New York Times*, December 12, 1853. The "pride of the forest" remark of Dr. Francis is from the *Literary World*, January 24, 1852.

XX: The Last of 82 Cliff Street

The story of the Harper fire is based largely on the *New York Times* of December 12, 1853; *The House of Harper, ibid.*; Derby's autobiography; the *American Bookseller*, June 1 and 15, 1885; and *The Diary of George Templeton Strong*, Vol. II. The authoritative word of John is given in *Harper's Weekly*, May 8, 1875, and Curtis quoted Raymond's telegram in the *Weekly* of April 17, 1869. The Shakespearean reference is to *King Henry IV, Part II*, act I, scene 1. Lossing's letter to Ripley, J. P. R. James's letter to the brothers, and Cyrus Field's offer are from *The House of Harper*, as is the Kane-Curtis anecdote. The John Abbott letter is quoted by permission of the Pierpont Morgan Library. The comment on Stephens is taken from *Mayan Explorer*. The Brontë sales are from the Boston *Post* series "Who Reads an American Book?" The order of reissues of titles and the second Harper fire are given in *Norton's Literary Gazette* for January 1 and March 15, 1854. The temporary location of Harper's offices is given in *Harper's Weekly*, April 17, 1869. Norton's periodical also described the new Franklin Square catalogue on May 15, 1855. The Harper motto is from Plato's *Republic*, section 328a, line 4. A more literal translation would be, "Will they, having torches, pass them on to each other?", or "Holding torches, they will pass them on one to another." Professor William P. Kent, of the University of Utah, noted the use of the vignette on title pages of Whewell's books and discovered a summary of its design and use in *William Whewell, an Account of his Writings* (2 vols., 1876) by Isaac Todhunter. (*See Harper Books and Authors*, Vol. X, No. 2.) The adoption of the Whewell vignette as a colophon by 1847 may have been inspired by the apprenticeships of the second generation of Harpers'—Philip, by 1847, surely, with Fletcher, Jr., and Joe Brooklyn following shortly thereafter.

NOTES ON ILLUSTRATIONS

Illustration

1. The Mathew Brady photograph of the brothers is here reproduced by courtesy of the Library of Congress, which kindly made a new print from the original plate for use in this book. This photograph is dated 1863 by James D. Horan in *Mathew Brady, Historian with a Camera*, on the evidence of Brady's "Register" (New York Public Library), with the entry "Harper Brothers" after the date February 14, 1863. However, an earlier dating seems justified. Fletcher appears much younger here than in the 1862 portrait by Charles Loring Elliott, owned by Mrs. Fletcher Harper (IV) of the Plains, Virginia, an engraving of which appeared in the July, 1879, issue of *Harper's Magazine*. Furthermore, the clothing depicted by Brady, especially collars and cravats, would indicate a near mid-century date according to *The Cut of Men's Clothes, 1600-1900*, by Norah Waugh.

4. The advertisements from the New York *Commercial Advertiser* are reproduced by courtesy of the New York Public Library.

5-8 The portrait of James Harper hangs in City Hall, New York, and is reproduced by courtesy of the Art Commission of the City of New York and the Honorable Robert F. Wagner, Mayor, City of New York. The bust of Benjamin Franklin was painted in the background to indicate the inspiration of the Mayor's career as a printer and publisher. The portrait of John Harper is owned by Mrs. Charles A. Silliman, Wilmington, Delaware; that of J. Wesley Harper, by Mrs. John W. Frost, New York City; and that of Fletcher Harper, by Mr. Harry E. Wells, Birmingham, Alabama; each of whom has graciously consented to its reproduction in this book. I am also indebted to the Frick Art Reference Library for assistance in identifying the artists who painted the portraits.

9. The first edition of *Two Years Before the Mast* is reproduced by courtesy of the Parke-Bernet Galleries, Inc.

11. The cover of the Bulwer letter to Harper's is reproduced by courtesy of the Boston Public Library.

14-15 Several Harper catalogues issued during and prior to 1853 are held by the House. Others are held by libraries including the American Antiquarian Society and the New York Public Library; by courtesy of the latter the two catalogue title pages are reproduced.

16-18 The Melville letter to Harper's and the Fletcher Harper–Demarest memorandum are reproduced by courtesy of the Pierpont Morgan Library, and the New York Public Library made available a photograph of one of their first-edition copies of *Moby Dick*.

19. The Harper full-page advertisement in the *Literary World* is by courtesy of the New York Public Library.

20. The engraving of the Custis-Lee mansion by Lossing was taken from the September, 1853, issue of *Harper's New Monthly Magazine*. The grave of President John F. Kennedy is now located just below this mansion, then known as Arlington House.

21. The present-day photograph of the Gramercy Park house of Mayor Harper is used by the kind permission of the Museum of the City of New York.

26-27 The New York Public Library kindly allows reproductions of the title page to *The New York and Erie Rail-road Guide Book* and the engraving of the New York Trade Sales from *Frank Leslie's Illustrated Newspaper* of April 5, 1856. The article in *Leslie's* carrying this illustration said in part, "It is something to see all the publishers together, for they are the men whose united labors circulate the mental wealth of the country, who take the ideas of the authors, and stamp upon them the form that facilitates their currency, and to a very great extent give the great public its idea of their value." The Trade Sales engraving was reproduced in the *Literary Collector* of November, 1902, which is my authority for identifying individuals.

Appendices

---

1. HARPER'S FAMILY LIBRARY

Year by year, as it increased in size, the *Family Library* was sold at the Trade Sales and elsewhere in quantities at specified prices. Thus the Trade Sale catalogues show that in the fall of 1839 eighty-four volumes were available at $36.95, and in the fall of 1840, one hundred and five volumes at $46.40. Books were cloth bound and also available then in a "handsome case with lock and key" for $47.05; for $52.50 the set of books could be bought in half-morocco binding with marbled edges. At the completion of the series single copies retailed for forty-five cents and the set of books for $80.00.

Titles marked with an asterisk were listed as important titles in the series when *Harper's Weekly* published an obituary article on James Harper in its issue of April 17, 1869.

* 1-3. Milman's History of the Jews.
4, 5. Lockhart's Life of Napoleon.
* 6. Southey's Life of Lord Nelson.
7. Williams's Life of Alexander the Great.
8. Natural History of Insects. Vol. I.
* 9. Galt's Life of Lord Byron.
10. Bush's Life of Mohammed.
* 11. Scott's Letters on Demonology and Witchcraft.
12, 13. Gleig's History of the Bible.
14. Leslie's Discovery in the Polar Seas.
15. Croly's Life of George IV.
16. Jameson's Discovery and Adventure in Africa.

* 17-19. Cunningham's Lives of celebrated Painters. Vols. I.-III.
20. James's History of Chivalry and the Crusades.
21, 22. Bell's Life of Mary Queen of Scots.
23. Russell's View of Ancient and Modern Egypt.
24. Fletcher's History of Poland.
25. Smith's Festivals, Games, and Amusements.
* 26. Brewster's Life of Sir Isaac Newton.
27. Russell's History of Palestine.
28. Memes's Memoirs of the Empress Josephine.

29. Court and Camp of Napoleon Bonaparte.
30. Lives and Voyages of Drake, Cavendish, and Dampier.
31. Pitcairn's Island and the Mutiny of the Ship Bounty.
32. Turner's Sacred History of the World. Vol. I.
* 33, 34. Mrs. Jameson's Lives of celebrated Female Sovereigns.
* 35, 36. Lander's Travels in Africa.
37. Abercrombie's Essay on the Intellectual Powers.
38-40. St. John's Lives of celebrated Travelers.
41, 42. Dover's Life of Frederick the Great.
43, 44. Smedley's Sketches from Venetian History.
45, 46. Thatcher's Lives of the Indians.
47-49. Murray's British India.
50. Brewster's Letters on Natural Magic.
51, 52. Taylor's History of Ireland.
53. Tytler's Discovery in North America.
54. Humboldt's Travels.
55, 56. Euler's Natural Philosophy.
57. Mudie's Guide to the Observation of Nature.
58. Abercrombie's Philosophy of the Moral Feelings.
59. Dick's Improvement of Society.
60. James's History of Charlemagne.
61. Russell's Nubia and Abyssinia.
62, 63. Russell's Life of Oliver Cromwell.
64. Montgomery's Lectures on Literature, Poetry, &c.
65. Barrow's Life of Peter the Great.
66, 67. Cunningham's celebrated Painters. Vols. IV. and V.
68, 69. Crichton's History of Arabia.
70. Fraser's Historical and Descriptive
71. Combe's Principles of Physiology. World. Vol. II.
73. Russell's History of the Barbary States.
Account of Persia.
72. Turner's Sacred History of the
74. Natural History of Insects. Vol. II.

75, 76. Paulding's Life of Washington.
77. Ticknor's Philosophy of Living.
78. Higgins's Physical Condition of the Earth.
79. Sforzosi's History of Italy.
80, 81. Davis's China and the Chinese.
82. Circumnavigation of the Globe.
83. Dick's Celestial Scenery.
84. Turner's Sacred History of the World. Vol. III.
85. Griscom's Animal Mechanism and Physiology.
86-91. Tytler's Universal History.
92, 93. Life and Writings of Franklin.
94, 95. Pursuit of Knowledge under Difficulties.
96, 97. Paley's Natural Theology.
98. Rennie's Natural History of Birds.
99. Dick's Sidereal Heavens.
100. Upham on Imperfect and Disordered Mental Action.
101, 102. Murray's Historical Account of British America.
103. Lossing's History of the Fine Arts.
104. Rennie's Natural History of Quadrupeds.
105. Life and Travels of Mungo Park.
106. Dana's Two Years before the Mast.
107, 108. Parry's Three Voyages.
109, 110. Life of Dr. Johnson, with Selections from his Writings.
111. Bryant's Selections from American Poets.
112, 113. Halleck's Selections from British Poets.
114-118. Keightley's History of England.
119, 120. Hale's United States.
121, 122. Irving's Life and Writings of Oliver Goldsmith.
123, 124. Lives of Distinguished Men of Modern Times.
125. Renwick's Life of De Witt Clinton.
126, 127. Mackenzie's Life of O. H. Perry.
128. Head's Life of Bruce.
129. Renwick's Life of John Jay and Alexander Hamilton.
130. Brewster's Lives of Galileo,

Tycho Brahe, and Kepler.
131. History of Iceland, Greenland, and the Faroe Islands.
132. Siebold's Japan and the Japanese.
133. Dwight's History of Connecticut.
134, 135. Bucke's Ruins of Ancient Cities.
136, 137. History of Denmark, Sweden, and Norway.
138. Camp on Democracy.
139. Lanman's History of Michigan.
140. Fenelon's Lives of the Ancient Philosophers.
141, 142. Segur's History of Napoleon's Expedition to Russia.
143, 144. Henry's Epitome of the History of Philosophy.
145. Bucke's Beauties, Harmonies, and Sublimities of Nature.
146. Lieber's Essays on Property and Labor.
147. White's Natural History of Selborne.
148. Wrangell's Expedition to Siberia.
149, 150. Hazen's Popular Technology.
151-153. Spalding's History of Italy and the Italian Islands.
154, 155. Lewis and Clarke's Travels.
156. Smith's History of Education.
157. Fraser's History of Mesopotamia and Assyria.
158. Russell's History of Polynesia.
159. Davenport's Perilous Adventures.
160. Duer's Constitutional Jurisprudence of the United States.

161-163. Belknap's American Biography.
164. Natural History of the Elephant.
165. Potter's Hand-book for Readers and Students.
166. Mrs. A. J. Graves's Woman in America.
167, 168. Stone's Border Wars of the Revolution.
169. Vegetable Substances used for the Food of Man.
170. Michelet's Elements of Modern History.
171. Bacon's Essays, and Locke on the Understanding.
172. Voyages round the World.
173. Murray's Travels of Marco Polo.
174, 175. Sargent's American Adventure by Land and Sea.
176. Bunner's History of Louisiana.
177. Florian's Moors in Spain.
178. Lee's Elements of Geology.
179. Brougham's Pleasures and Advantages of Science.
180. Moseley's Illustrations of Mechanics.
181, 182. Selections from the Spectator.
183. Potter's Political Economy.
184. Maury's Principles of Eloquence.
185. Robertson's History of America. Abridged.
186. Robertson's History of Charles V. Abridged.
187. Ferguson's History of the Roman Republics. Abridged.

2. *HARPER'S SCHOOL DISTRICT LIBRARY*

The initial price of each volume was thirty-eight cents, with the exception of six volumes, and of each series, $19. These prices were maintained in Harper catalogues for many years. From 1846 on the catalogues described titles at length in appropriate sections.

First Series

1, 2. Paulding's Life of Washington.
3. Miss Sedgwick's The Poor Rich Man and the Rich Poor Man.
4, 5. The Swiss Family Robinson.
6, 7. Natural History of Insects.
8. Mrs. Hofland's The Son of a Genius.
9-11. Miss Eliza Robin's Tales from American History.
12. Thatcher's Tales of the American Revolution.
13, 14. Lockhart's Life of Napoleon.
15. Combe's Principles of Physiology.
16, 17. Thatcher's Indian Traits.
18. Jameson's Discovery and Adventure in Africa.
19. Uncle Philip's American Forest.
20. Mudie's Guide to the Observation of Nature.
21. Perils of the Sea.
22. Abercrombie's Essay on the Intellectual Powers.
23. Montgomery's Lectures on Literature, Poetry, &c.
24. Dick's Celestial Scenery.
25. Russell's History of Palestine.
26. James's Chivalry and the Crusades.
27. Brewster's Life of Sir Issac Newton.
28. Miss Sedgwick's Live and Let Live.
29, 30. Davis's China and the Chinese.
31. Circumnavigation of the Globe.
32. Williams's Life of Alexander the Great.
33, 34. Euler's Natural Philosophy.
35. Barrow's Life of Peter the Great.
36, 37. Russell's Life of Oliver Cromwell.
38. Dick's Improvement of Society.
39. Higgins's Physical Condition of the Earth.
40. Abercrombie's Philosophy of the Moral Feelings.
41, 42. Mrs. Jameson's Lives of celebrated Female Sovereigns.
43. Uncle Philip's Conversations about the History of Virginia.
44. Mrs. Hughs's The Ornaments Discovered.
45. Uncle Philip's Natural History.

46, 47. Uncle Philip's Whale Fishery and the Polar Seas.
48. Lives and Voyages of Drake, Cavendish, and Dampier.
49, 50. Dunlap's History of New York.

Second Series

51, 52. Life and Writings of Franklin.
53, 54. Buel's Farmer's Instructor.
55, 56. Pursuit of Knowledge under Difficulties.
57. Griscom's Animal Mechanism and Physiology.
58. Natural History of the Elephant.
59. Vegetable Substances used for the Food of Man.
60-65. Tytler's Universal History.
66. Moseley's Illustrations of Mechanics.
67. Leslie's Discovery in the Polar Seas.
68, 69. Paley's Natural Theology.
70-79. Sparks's American Biography.
80. Humboldt's Travels.
81. Goldsmith's History of Greece.
82. Rennie's Natural History of Birds.
83. Familiar Illustrations of Natural Philosophy.
84, 85. Selections from the Spectator.
86. Lee's Elements of Geology.
87. Goldsmith's History of Greece. Abridged.
88. Armstrong's Treatise on Agriculture.
89. Rennie's Natural History of Quadrupeds.
90. Chaptal's Agricultural Chemistry.
91. Dwight's Signers of the Declaration of Independence.
92-95. Plutarch's Lives.
(The last six volumes of this series were priced at 76 cents each.)

Third Series

96, 97. Hale's History of the United States.
98. Brewster's Letters on Natural Magic.
99. Renwick's Practical Mechanics.
100, 101. Parry's Three Voyages to the North Pole.
102-106. Keightley's England.

107, 108. Mackenzie's Life of Commodore O. H. Perry.

109, 110. Irving's Life and Writings of Oliver Goldsmith.

111, 112. Murray's Historical Account of British America.

113. Upham on Imperfect and Disordered Mental Action.

114. Bryant's Selections from American Poets.

115, 116. Halleck's Selections from British Poets.

117. Florian's Moors in Spain.

118, 119. Lives of Distinguished Men of Modern Times.

120. Nott's Counsels to the Young.

121. Head's Life and Travels of Bruce.

122, 123. Life of Dr. Johnson, with Selections from his Writings.

124. Potter's Political Economy.

125. Life and Travels of Mungo Park.

126. Brougham's Pleasures and Advantages of Science.

127. Dana's Two Years before the Mast.

128. Uncle Philip's History of the Lost Colony of Greenland.

129, 130. Gaylord and Tucker's American Husbandry.

131, 132. Uncle Philip's History of Massachusetts.

133, 134. Uncle Philip's History of New Hampshire.

135. Dick's Sidereal Heavens.

136. Renwick's First Principles of Chemistry.

137. Russell's Barbary States.

138. The Family Instructor.

139. Dwight's History of Connecticut.

140. Miss Sedgwick's Stories for Young Persons.

141-143. Crowe's History of France.

144, 145. Scott's History of Scotland.

Fourth Series

146-148. Belknap's American Biography.

149. Siebold's Japan and the Japanese.

150, 151. Segur's History of Napoleon's Expedition to Russia.

152. Brewster's Lives of Galileo, Tycho Brahe, and Kepler.

153, 154. Sargent's American Adventure by Land and Sea.

155. History of Iceland, Greenland, and the Faroe Islands.

156. Fenelon's Ancient Philosophers.

157. Lossing's History of the Fine Arts.

158. Davenport's Perilous Adventures.

159. Lanman's History of Michigan.

160, 161. Bucke's Ruins of Ancient Cities.

162. Lieber's Essays on Property and Labor.

163. Bucke's Beauties, Harmonies, and Sublimities of Nature.

164, 165. History of Denmark, Sweden, and Norway.

166. White's Natural History of Selborne.

167. Wrangell's Expedition to Siberia.

168, 169. Thatcher's Lives of the Indians.

170. Bacon's Essays, and Locke on the Understanding.

171, 172. Lander's Travels in Africa.

173. Memes's Memoirs of the Empress Josephine.

174, 175. Henry's Epitome of the History of Philosophy.

176. James's History of Charlemagne.

177, 178. Hazen's Popular Technology.

179. Scott's Letters on Demonology and Witchcraft.

180. Bunner's History of Louisiana.

181. Court and Camp of Bonaparte.

182. Fletcher's History of Poland.

183. Maury's Principles of Eloquence.

184. Mrs. Graves's Woman in America.

185. Russell's Nubia and Abyssynia.

186. Barrow's Pitcairn's Island and the Mutiny of the Bounty.

187. Fraser's Historical and Descriptive Account of Persia.

188. Cooper's Xenophon's Expedition of Cyrus.

189. Sismondi's Italian Republics.

190. History of Switzerland.

191-195. Dunham's History of Spain and Portugal.

278. Frost's Beauties of English History.
279. Miss M'Intosh's The Cousins.
280. Frost's Beauties of French History.
281. Isabel; or, the Trials of the Heart.
282. History of the American Revolution.
283. Blake's Juvenile Companion.
284. Parental Instruction.
285, 286. Bell's Life of Mary Queen of Scots.
287. Mrs. Dana's Young Sailor.
288. Alden's Elizabeth Benton.
289. Hutton's Book of Nature laid Open.
290. Salkeld's Grecian and Roman Antiquities.
291. Sketches of the Lives of Distinquished Females.
292. Ticknor's Philosophy of Living.
293. Keeping House and Housekeeping.
294. Voyages round the World.
295. Southey's Life of Nelson.

3. *THE BEACH BIOGRAPHY OF THE HARPERS*

This fourth edition of the Beach pamphlet was entitled *Wealth and Pedigree* instead of the usual designation *Wealth and Biography*. It was published in May, 1842.

Harper Brothers — — — — — — — — — — — — — 200,000

These are the *four* remarkable men, who of a highly respectable English family that anciently settled upon Long Island, have risen by their enterprise and industry from *journeymen printers* to become the most celebrated publishers in America, and among the names that will go down to posterity with the *Galignanis* and *Murrays,* and *Constables* of Europe. The Harpers have done more practically for the encouragement not only of domestic authors but for the diffusion of the literature and science of other countries than all the universities, colleges, academies and schools of the Union put together. Nor have their profits, though large, been proportionate to their truly patriotic and noble exertions. New York may be proud of the birth-right of these men, and that she has produced these great operators, these high-priests of Minerva, who have erected here a holy temple, as it were, in the midst of money-changers and shopkeepers, to keep alive the undying fires of intellect, to guard and trim the lamp where genius may kindle its illuminating torch and learning diffuse abroad its milder beams. Without them or some such as shall follow in their footsteps, darkness would come over the land. But for these humble printers who have appreciated the spirit of the times, and saw and felt the necessity of acting in keeping with the accelerated movement of thought and of industry which steam-power has given to this age, our people in the dissemination of that most useful and potent of all influences, mental power and the knowledge which it produces, would have been a century behind the rapid and advanced progress they have made. It was to compete with them that the free press of our country was stimulated to endeavors and prodigious results, which have astonished the world. The lightning-like rapidity with which the choicest coinings of the brain in foreign lands, are almost immediately made the common property and universally circulating cheap commodity of our own people, threaten in time to make the book-business, if not periodical literature also, a *dead letter* and destructive pursuit to those who embark in it. For it would seem that every production that hereafter emanates from the closet of the author must seek this every-day channel of the penny press, to reach the public market. To the universal taste for reading whatever is worthy to be perused, and which the Harper cheap press gave the first great impulse to, are we then to ascribe indirectly the immense diffusion which is now immediately given by the penny press in our country, to whatever reaches us from abroad, fresh almost and at the moment that it is wrought from the mind of its author. Once thus gratified with what, from the extreme cheapness of penny publications may be deemed the almost gratuitous offerings to our countrymen, of the cream and marrow of foreign literature, it is not to be imagined after the practical workings of this operation as exemplified recently in the national reception of Boz, and the familiarity of every one that can read, with all the writings of such shining luminaries as he and Bulwer, and others, that our people will ever surrender so dear a privilege, however wrong it may be fact, when the subject of international copy-right is fairly canvassed. The Harpers, be it added to this peroration, are *exemplars* also in private life and as moral and religious men, being all of them, we believe, members of the Methodist Church and of many Temperance and charitable societies. So much for a brotherhood of New York born printers, to show what mechanic industry can accomplish.

4. *LETTER TO THE* ANTIQUARIAN BOOKMAN

Letter to the *Antiquarian Bookman*, June 22, 1959, regarding the Harper book that was printed but never published.

Missing Volume of Constitutional Writings, by James Madison

It seems incredible that a volume of writings on the Constitution by its principal author and expounder, James Madison, could have been set in type and then disappear so completely that today it is difficult to find definite proof that such a volume was printed but never published by Harper's under a contract with Dolley Madison.

Failing in an effort to have her husband's writings published commercially after his death, Mrs. Madison sold the most valuable portion, the Notes on the Debates of the Federal Convention of 1787 and certain related papers, to Congress in 1837. These were published in three volumes in the District of Columbia by Langtree & O'Sullivan in 1840, and other editions of the same material were printed in at least two different places within three years. While these volumes were being published, Mrs. Madison attempted to have a fourth volume of later writings on the Constitution brought out commercially. In 1838 or 1839 she sent the volume in manuscript form and perhaps even in Madison's hand, to Harper's of New York. Sometime between then and 1842, Harper's set type for the volume, printed page proofs, and perhaps even manufactured some volumes of the completed book. On her return to Washington after a visit to New York in 1842, Mrs. Madison left page proofs in Philadelphia to be corrected by her old friends Edward Coles and Richard Rush. Under a new contract with Harper's, signed in September 1844 by Mrs. Madison through her son, Payne Todd, the firm made further efforts to publish the volume. At the same time, Mrs. Madison renewed her attempts to sell the remaining Madison Papers to Congress. Perhaps these efforts helped stall the publication of the Constitutional volume by Harper's. In any event, Congress did not purchase the remainder of the Madison Papers until 1848, and Harper's did not proceed with publication. After the 1844 negotiations, the type, page proofs, and any volumes that might have been printed disappeared from view. In 1858, William C. Rives, Madison's biographer, surmised that the "printed copy" produced by Harper's was in the hands of James C. McGuire who used it as a basis for his 1853 publication *Selections from the Private Correspondence of James Madison*. If McGuire was indeed in possession of the mysterious "printed copy," he no doubt obtained it from Dolley Madison's son, Payne Todd, along with the thousands of Madison Manuscripts he acquired from that same source. No mention is made of such a printed volume in the great McGuire Sale of Madison material by Henkels in December 1892. (Catalogue 694).

The location of any part of the material printed by Harper's would be a discovery of the utmost importance to bibliophiles and scholars alike. The editors of the Madison Papers would be deeply grateful for any information about the mysterious Constitutional volume of Madison's writings printed by Harper's. Please address: THE PAPERS OF JAMES MADISON, 1126 East Fifty-Ninth Street, Chicago 37, Illinois.

5. FAY'S STATEMENT OF ACCOUNT

Statement of Account

Issued to Theodore Sedgwick Fay, October 4, 1844

Fay Debit Account

1836	April 23	To cash	$500.00	
		Interest to Oct. 4, 1844	295.66	$ 795.66
	May 14	His note this day unpaid	$150.00	
		Interest to Oct. 4, 1844	88.08	238.08

May 16	To cash		$500.00	
	Interest to Oct. 4, 1844		293.42	793.42
				$1,827.16

Fay Credit Account

1841	June 8	One-half profits on *Norman Leslie* [stereotyped]	$510.53	
		Interest to Oct. 4, 1844	277.26	
1841	June 8	One-half profits on *The Countess Ida*	519.50	
		Interest to Oct. 4, 1844	120.81	
1844	Oct. 4	Further profits on *The Countess Ida* 28.47		
		Profits on *Hoboken*	61.44	1,518.01

Balance due Harper & Brothers, General Account $ 309.15

Judgment docketed 1/7/39	$1,776.74
Interest still due as of 1/18/40	87.23
	$1,863.97
General Morris payment 6/27/40	415.37
Balance due 6/27/40	$1,448.60
Interest due to 10/27/44	439.40
	$1,888.00
Amount claimed on General Account	309.15
Total due	$2,197.15

6. *PRESIDENT FILLMORE-HARPER LETTERS*

WASHINGTON *August* 9, 1852.

MESSRS. HARPER & BROTHERS:

GENTLEMEN,—It has become my duty to consider the propriety of negotiating an international copyright treaty with England, and knowing you must have given some attention to the subject, I shall be happy to have your views, and also to receive from you any arguments you may have in your possession, pro or con, affecting the subject.

I am your obedient servant,

MILLARD FILLMORE.

The firm answered as follows:

August 23, 1852.

DEAR SIR,—We have carefully considered the subject of an *International Copyright* to which our attention was called by your letter of the 9th inst. The great importance of such an arrangement, as that which is proposed to make by treaty with Great Britain, becomes more and more manifest the more the subject is considered. But although our experience and observation have led us to form opinions more or less definite upon it, we have concluded, in consequence of our close relations with all the parties to be affected by it—with the authors of England and this country on the one hand, by whom its enactment is mainly sought, and with the industrial interests of the reading public of the United States on the other, by whom its operation would be largely felt,—to abstain from taking any steps to influence the action of our Government in regard to it. Feeling entirely confident, that, under your Administration, nothing of such marked and far-reaching consequence to the best interests of the country will be done without the most full and impartial inquiry into its direct and remote results upon all the parties to be affected by it, we are quite content to submit our own interests and opinions to whatever action the good of the country may induce you to take.

To His Excellency,
   MILLARD FILLMORE, *President United States,*
      WASHINGTON, D. C.

7. WORKS LEASED TO J. C. DERBY

Works leased to J. C. Derby on December 17, 1853, with royalties specified and yearly printings guaranteed for three years beginning February 1, 1854

Title	Retail price	Royalty	Edition	Total rec'd
Complete Works of Hannah More (2 vols.)	2.75	30 cents	1,000	$ 300
Stephens' *Egypt*	1.75	20 "	2,000	400
Life of *Franklin*	.90	12½ "	2,000	250
Thatcher's *Boston Tea Party*	.625	4 "	2,000	80
Webster's *Encyclopedia of Domestic Economy*	3.00	20 "	2,000	400
Howe's *Eminent Mechanics*	.75	7½ "	2,000	150
Bunyan's *Pilgrim's Progress*	.75	5 "	2,000	100
Layard's *Nineveh*	.75	6 "	3,000	180
				$1,860

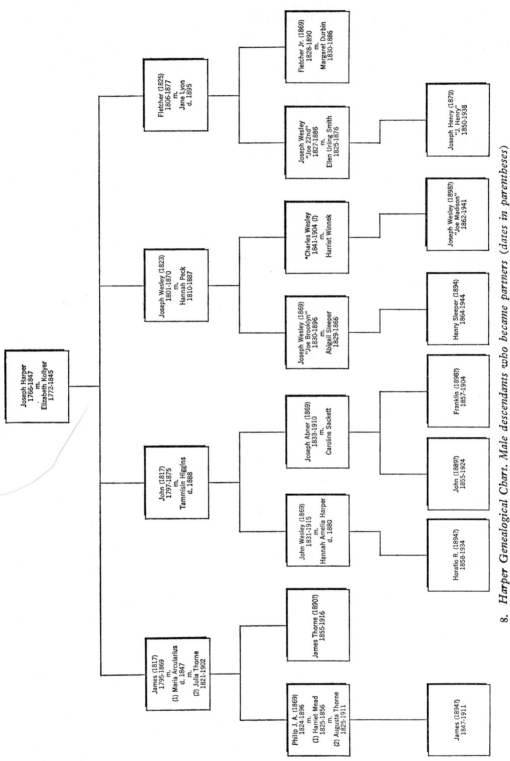

8. *Harper Genealogical Chart. Male descendants who became partners (dates in parentheses) or members of the firm after Harper & Brothers became a stock company in 1896. Female*

9. HARPER-BULWER CORRESPONDENCE

The Harper letters to E. L. Bulwer, considerately brought to my attention by Professor James J. Barnes, of Wabash College, as this book goes to press, are held by the Hertfordshire County Record Office, Hertford, England, and the following quotations are made by courtesy of Mr. Peter Walne, County Archivist, and with the kind permission of Lady Hermione Cobbold, heir of Lord Lytton. The letters extend from 1830 to 1867 with the bulk of them covering the decade 1830-39. Most of them relate to payments made by the Harpers to Bulwer for first proofs and reveal their anxiety because proofs were often received after rival publishers had obtained bound copies of the English edition. This circumstance led to their request that Bulwer should forward manuscript sheets of the closing sections of the books as well. The early letters also reveal Harper concern that Bulwer's novels were being criticized by reviewers on moral grounds. On February 24, 1832, they promised to send by the next packet "a quantity of newspapers containing the unbought opinions of the press in the United States," of the recently published *Eugene Aram*.

The letters also reflect Harper opinion of the reading habits of Americans. "We are too busy in this country to be great readers of poetry," they wrote on August 31, 1830. However, they would pay for proof sheets of any book of poems that he sent, "at least enough to pay you for the trouble, and as much more as the profits accruing from it would allow. The amount of the remittance will depend on its sale. Were the work to take like 'Don Juan' the sum would be something handsome. We are certain that our facilities for bringing a work before the public & for selling are greater than any other establishment in America."

On January 15, 1835, the Harpers wrote a long apologia for their competence as publishers. It was apparently written in response to a letter from Bulwer saying that he had received offers from other American publishers and requesting the Harpers to increase their regular payment of £100 for a new novel to £150, or £50 per volume. Their reply was marked "Strictly Confidential." After acknowledging that they had profited from his writings and that his popularity in America made him a highly desirable author, they went on to say that his popularity was due in part to their own exertions and "to keep it undiminished requires no small share of labor, management and expense," particularly with the periodical press. "Our influence with editors, throughout the Union, is very great . . . and is not kept up without constant attention and outlay." They boasted that they had not only succeeded in obtaining favorable notices for his novels, but had also prevented unfavorable ones from being printed. Many magazines were hostile to his novels, being opposed to fiction in general. "Without our intervention, your works would have been and still be attacked . . . with bitterness and pertinacity; we have succeeded almost universally in keeping them silent, at least, in many instances, we have elicited . . . notices which did service, either by actual commendation, or by such remarks as . . . were of a nature to excite interest and curiosity." They urged him to ask any intelligent American, visiting in England, for confirmation of the fact that the Harper name on the title page of a book secured favorable criticism and seldom failed "to mitigate the severity even of those censors who do not acknowledge our influence." Explaining that they did not mean to detract from Bulwer's splendid talents and vast popularity, the brothers thought he should keep in mind what they had done and "should look with little favor upon the offers of others who would step in, after the road is cleared, and reap the advantage which we have assisted in procuring."

The letter pointed out that the popularity Bulwer enjoyed in America, partially because of Harper's "judicious management and effort," was, in fact, a reason for their hesitancy in meeting his request for more money. It encouraged piracy. They were forwarding a copy of *Pompeii* that had been printed on them at less than half the price of the Harper edition. But even so, if Bulwer still should insist on his terms they would capitulate. "We pretend to liberality in our transactions with authors and men of talent," they said, "and having acquired the character, it is our disposition to maintain it." Then they added a long postscript saying that if he should arrange to sell early proofs of later books to some other American publisher they would be constrained to continue making them available in their uniform, stereotyped editions because of assurances given "both publicly and privately, to our customers in all parts of the United States. . . . Add to this the fact that the booksellers who have hitherto been supplied by us, would give our edition the preference." This dependency of booksellers on their output, plus their facilities for getting a complete novel before the public within twenty-four hours after obtaining a copy, would really discourage other responsible American firms from trying to outbid them for his forthcoming works. "We have always made it a rule not to pursue any course that must prove injurious to another publisher, unless driven to it by aggression, but in this case we should have no alternative."

To this letter Bulwer reacted strongly. On February 19, he wrote that he could not allow that his popularity was dependent on the publisher in America rather than on the public, and they had done him no service, on his side of the Atlantic, by preventing American bigots from attacking him. Furthermore he construed their postscript as a threat of retaliation if he should contract with another publisher. The brothers wrote back on April 7 to clear the air and to send a contract to meet his terms. They admitted that the assaults of bigots could do Bulwer no harm personally, but such attacks did make a vast difference to their publishing income and added to their risks. Further, they did not mean to imply that Bulwer's reputation in America depended upon the publisher and not the public—such an assumption would be "egregious folly" on their part; they simply wanted him to know how "rapidly and extensively" they had placed his books before the public and aided in getting the backing of the press. They enclosed a 183-word contract, the basis of which was the payment of £50 per volume of each work to be written by Bulwer thereafter, he to ensure Harper's early possession of such works.

The Harper letters to Bulwer throw new light on their early conflict with

Frederick Saunders. They saw a direct threat to their proprietary interest in Bulwer by the establishment of a New York branch office of Saunders and Oatley, to which firm Bulwer had gone after Bentley had declined to publish a political pamphlet. They eventually sold 90,000 copies of this and, beginning with *Rienzi*, became Bulwer's book publisher in England. On September 12, 1836, Harper's wrote to Bulwer, "You are probably aware that your publishers in London have established a branch House in this city. Its agent [Frederick Saunders] has claimed it as his right, and has announced it as his intention, to republish exclusively in this country works published by the House in London. We can recognize no such right. But we are threatened by Mr. Saunders, in case we do not respect his claims (which we shall certainly feel ourselves under no obligation to do)—that among other works he shall reprint upon us your 'Athens'—we expect him to do so." Since Harper's was paying Bulwer £150 for advance proofs (£50 per volume), they urged him to forward "the work in the manner and time specified." The propriety of their course they said could further be shown by an advertisement "from the pen of Mr. Saunders" which they enclosed.

The *Rienzi* competition was a bitter pill for the brothers to swallow. They had paid £150 for early proofs. In an undated letter, probably May, 1836, they wrote Bulwer, "Rienzi has been well received in this country and has sold extensively. The irregularity in the arrival of the packets, we are sorry to inform you, put Messers Cary & Hart, of Philadelphia, in possession of a perfect copy of the work before we received the whole of the copy sent to us by you. They printed the whole work at less than *two shillings* Sterling. We did the same so that nothing was made by publishing it." Nevertheless payment for Harper "rights" was made personally to Bulwer by James who was in London early that summer. Obviously something more than early proofs was needed as insurance, as they wrote again on September 12, 1836. "When we entered into our agreement [with you] we presumed that the last sheets of the *Manuscript* would be copied and forwarded to us before they were delivered to the printer in London, as has been done in some previous cases—and this, as may be seen in the case of 'Rienzi,' is the only possible way in which the earliest copy can be received by us."

When James was in London that July he nearly upset the Bulwer apple cart by declining to take a volume of Bulwer's plays, saying that the price proposed was too high in view of the limited sales for plays. However, his younger brothers, not daring to risk losing so important an author, overruled James as shown by their letter of September 12. "We regret that our brother declined taking the volume of *Plays*. Had the copy been sent to us without consulting him, we should have included them in our agreement. As it is, as far as the 'Plays' are concerned, we shall be under the necessity of completing up our plates and appearing in the market after, instead of before our neighbors."

The impact of the 1837 panic is also revealed in the Harper letters. They were unable to send £150 for *Athens*. On May 25 they wrote, "Nearly all our bankers have failed. . . . We were treating with one of our large Houses for a bill —but before the sailing of the packet the House failed. We cannot remit the specie, as the banks have suspended specie payments." In fact, they resorted to a bit of international financing to pay Bulwer that summer. In July they received a statement from Henry T. Hall, of Calcutta, their agent in India, showing that he owed them $536.13 for three cases of books received from New York. They arranged to have this sum forwarded to a London banking firm which in turn paid it to Bulwer. Except for this correspondence, we would not have known that by the 1830's Harper's were energetically developing an export business.

That Obadiah Rich continued to act as Harper's London agent at least through 1842 is indicated by two references to his receiving proofs from Bulwer and paying Bulwer directly for them. The impact of the competition with the mammoth weeklies is given dramatic evidence on January 31, 1843, when the brothers wrote Bulwer that they had printed 42,500 copies of his new novel, *The Last of the Barons,* with their edition out "some twelve or fifteen hours before our competitors." Their price of 12½ cents was higher than rival editions and they prophesied, "In the first fortnight there will be at least *one hundred thousand copies of the work sold.*" (Their italics.)

INDEX